20 $\frac{00}{0}$

REPRESENTATIONS

The MIT Press / Bradford Books

Edward C. T. Walker, Editor. *Explorations in THE BIOLOGY OF LANGUAGE.* 1979. The M.I.T. Work Group in the Biology of Language: Noam Chomsky, Salvador Luria, *et alia.*

Daniel C. Dennett. *BRAINSTORMS: Philosophical Essays on the Mind and Psychology.* 1979.

Charles E. Marks. *COMMISSUROTOMY, CONSCIOUSNESS AND UNITY OF MIND.* 1980.

John Haugeland. *MIND DESIGN.* 1981.

Fred I. Dretske. *KNOWLEDGE AND THE FLOW OF IN-FORMATION.* 1981.

Jerry A. Fodor. *REPRESENTATIONS: Philosophical Essays on the Foundations of Cognitive Science.* 1981.

Representations

Philosophical Essays on the Foundations of Cognitive Science

Jerry A. Fodor

A Bradford Book

The MIT Press
Cambridge, Massachusetts

Library of Congress Catalog Number 81-24313
MIT ISBN 0-262-06079-5
Printed in the United States of America

Library of Congress Cataloging in Publication Data appear on the last printed page of this book.

For my mother and daughter; for Zenon and Linda; and for the crew of the INSOLVENT

Acknowledgments

I wish to thank the following publishers and journals for their kind permission to reprint papers appearing in this volume: *The American Philosophical Quarterly* for the use of "Operationalism and ordinary language," 1965, Vol. 2, No. 4; *The Journal of Philosophy* for the use of "The appeal to tacit knowledge in psychological explanation," 1968, Vol. 65, No. 20; *The Philosophical Review* for the use of "What psychological states are not," 1972, Vol. 81, No. 2; Lawrence Erlbaum Associates, Inc. for the use of "Three cheers for propositional attitudes," which is republished, with extensive revisions, from Cooper and Walker (1979) *Sentence Processing;* D. Reidel Publishing Company for the use of "Special sciences," which is reprinted from *Synthese,* 1974, Vol. 28, pp. 77–115; The University of Minnesota Press for the use of "Computation and reduction," which is reprinted from Minnesota Studies in the Philosophy of Science, *Perception and Cognition,* Vol. 9, 1978, W. Savage (ed.); *The Monist* for the use of "Propositional Attitudes", 1978, Vol. 61, No. 4; *Cognition* for the use of "Tom Swift and his procedural grandmother", 1978, Vol. 6; and *The Behavioral and Brain Sciences* for the use of "Methodological solipsism considered as a research strategy in cognitive psychology", 1980, Vol. 3, No. 1. I am also indebted to Professors Ned Block and Charles Chihara for their permission to use articles that we wrote together.

The introductory essay and chapter 10 were supported by a research grant from the National Science Foundation and by a sabbatical leave from M.I.T.. I should like to express my gratitude to both institutions.

Contents

Introduction: Something on the State of the Art   *1*

Part I. Functionalism and Realism

1. (with Charles Chihara) Operationalism and Ordinary
   Language   *35*
2. The Appeal to Tacit Knowledge in Psychological Explanations   *63*
3. (with Ned Block) What Psychological States Are Not   *79*
4. Three Cheers for Propositional Attitudes   *100*

Part II. Reduction and Unity of Science

5. Special Sciences   *127*
6. Computation and Reduction   *146*

Part III. Intensionality and Mental Representation

7. Propositional Attitudes   *177*
8. Tom Swift and His Procedural Grandmother   *204*
9. Methodological Solipsism Considered as a Research Strategy in
   Cognitive Psychology   *225*

Part IV. Nativism

10. The Present Status of the Innateness Controversy   *257*

Notes   *317*

References   *335*

Index   *341*

I do feel a distance between myself and those people. I can be lively at times, and they like it in moderation. But I'm not, at least in the areas they respect, a properly serious person. . . .

—J.I.M. Stewart

REPRESENTATIONS

Introduction
Something on the State of the Art

Here are some essays. I think of them as much of a kind with
false starts, verbal slips, sawings off of limbs that one is sitting on,
and other comic inadvertences: as projects, that is to say, which
didn't turn out in quite the ways they were intended to. For they
were, most of them, written as occasional pieces: where I thought
there was an itch, I scratched. But, taken together, and viewed in
the retrospect of two decades of my own and other people's work,
what they propose looks a lot like a theory of mind.

The theory of mind it looks a lot like is Descartes', blending, as
it does, elements of mentalism and nativism. But much of Descartes' ontological and epistemological baggage has gone overboard,
and what is left has recognizable affinities with the Empiricist tradition too. Even the psychological speculations of John Stuart Mill
emerge, in the final pages of these papers, as containing much that
is commendable; along with ideas cribbed from David Hartley,
John Locke, David Hume, William James and, at one point, just a
soupçon of Heidegger.

In the general case, I dislike introductions; what they convey,
when not superfluous, is usually premature. But it is a mildly interesting story how what started as little more than a sense that all
was not well with the logical behaviorists should have eventuated
in the present orgy of philosophical eclecticism. And, while I hope
the reader will find the digressions fun to browse in, some signposts
to the main line of the argument in these papers may not be out of
place. What I think holds the bits together is the interweaving of

three ideas: functionalism, intensionality, and mental representation. This introduction is about the ways in which those threads connect.

A census of the main problems in the philosophy of mind as they presented themselves in, say, the early 1960's would reveal quite a different population from the one with which philosophers are now primarily concerned. To begin with, the central preoccupations of the discipline were then largely ontological. It is not quite accurate to characterize inquiry as having been directed to the question: 'What are mental states and processes?'; philosophers of physicalist persuasion (i.e., adherents of the central-state identity theory; see below) took it that the nature of the mental was an empirical issue, hence not one for philosophers to solve. But it was widely held that philosophers ought to provide a survey of the conceptually coherent options, and that there are, in fact, fewer of these than might be supposed. It was, in particular, the rejection of Cartesian dualism and the consequent need to work out a philosophically acceptable version of materialistic monism that provided the main preoccupation of philosophers of mind at the beginning of the period these essays subtend.

The stumbling block for a dualist is the problem of mind/body interaction. If you think, as Descartes did, that minds are immaterial substances, you ought to be worried (as Descartes was) about how there can be mental causes of behavioral effects. Cynicism might suggest that the question how an immaterial substance could contribute to the etiology of physical events is not, after all, much more obscure than the question how material substances could interact causally with one another. But there is this difference: whereas we can produce lots of untendentious examples of the latter kind of interaction, there are no untendentious examples of the former kind. Physical causation we will have to live with; but non-physical causation might be an artifact of the immaterialist construal of the claim that there are minds.

Viewed this way, the issue is one of ontological parsimony. A Cartesian dualist is going to hold that there are species of causal relations over and above physical interactions. He is therefore in need of an argument why mind/body causation should not itself be viewed as an instance of physical interaction. Most philosophers now agree that no such argument has successfully been made. Even philosophers like Ryle, whose preferred style of anti-Cartesian argument was so very often epistemological, insisted on the force of such considerations: "there was from the beginning felt to be a major theoretical difficulty in explaining how minds can influence and be influenced by bodies. How can a mental process, such as willing, cause spatial movements like movements of the tongue? How can a physical change in the optic nerve have among its effects a mind's perception of a flash of light?" (1949, p. 19).

It is precisely the advantage of materialistic monism that it provides for the subsumption of mind/body interaction as a special case of physical interaction, thereby making problems like the ones that Ryle mentions go away. By the early 1960s, it was becoming clear that there are two quite different strategies for performing this reduction, one corresponding to the program of *logical behaviorism* and the other corresponding to the program of the *central state identity theory*. And it was also becoming clear that each of these strategies has its problems.

The essence of one kind of logical behaviorism is the idea that every truth-valuable ascription of a mental state or process to an organism is semantically equivalent to the ascription of a certain sort of dispositional property to that organism. (A different, but related, version of the doctrine is discussed in Chapter 1.) In particular, in the interesting cases, mental ascriptions were supposed to be semantically equivalent to ascriptions of *behavioral dispositions*. A behavioral disposition is one that an organism has if and only if (iff) it satisfies a certain indefinite (possibly infinite) set of *behavioral hypotheticals* which constitute the *analysis* of the disposition. A behavioral hypothetical is a (possibly counterfactual) statement whose antecedent is couched solely in terms of *stimulus parameters* and whose consequent is couched solely in terms of *response parameters*. Heaven only knows what stimulus and response parameters were supposed to be; but it was an Article of Faith that these notions could, in principle, be made clear. Perhaps stimulus and response parameters are species of physical parameters (parameters that would be acknowledged by an ideally completed physical theory), though not all logical behaviorists would have accepted that identification. In any event, precisely because the ontological impulse of behaviorism was reductionistic, success depended on the possibility of expressing stimulus and response parameters in a vocabulary which contained no mental terms.

What is attractive about logical behaviorism is that the proposed identification of mental properties with dispositional ones provides for a sort of construal of statements that attribute behavioral effects to mental causes—a construal that is, moreover, conformable to the requirements of materialistic monism. Roughly, mental causation is the manifestation of a behavioral disposition; it's what you get when an organism has such a disposition and the antecedent of a behavioral hypothetical that belongs to the analysis of the disposition happens to be true. It is, no doubt, a travesty to say that for a logical behaviorist "Smith is thirsty" means "if there were water around, Smith would drink it" and "Smith drank because he was thirsty" means "if there were water around Smith would drink it; and there was water around." But it is a travesty that comes close enough for our present purposes. It allows us to see how logical behaviorists proposed to assimilate worrisome etiologies that invoke mental causes to relatively untendentious etiologies like "it broke because it was fragile; it bent because it was pliable," etc.

So, logical behaviorism provides a construal of mental causation, and the glaring question is whether the construal it provides is adequately robust to do the jobs that need doing. In the long run this is the question whether the identification of mental properties with behavioral dispositions yields a notion of mental causation that is rich enough to reconstruct the etiologies propounded by our best psychological theories: the ones that achieve simplicity, explanatory power, and predictive success. However, we needn't wait for the long run, since there are plenty of cases of *pre*-theoretically plausible etiologies for which plausible behavioristic construals are not forthcoming, and these, surely, are straws in the wind.

Here is a quick way of making the point. Suppose "John took aspirin because he had a headache" is true iff conjunction *C* holds:

> *C:* John was disposed to produce headache behaviors and being disposed to produce headache behaviors involves satisfying the hypothetical *if there are aspirin around, one takes some*, and there were aspirin around.

So, *C* gives us a construal of "John took aspirin because he had a headache." But consider that we are also in want of a construal of statements like "John was disposed to produce headache behaviors because he had a headache." Such statements *also* invoke mental causes and, pre-theoretically at least, we have no reason to doubt that many of them are true. Yet in these cases it seems unlikely that the putative mental causes can be traded for dispositions; or if they can, the line of analysis we've been pursuing doesn't show us how to do it. We cannot, for example, translate "John had a headache" as "John had a disposition to produce headache behaviors" in these cases, since, patently, "John was disposed to produce headache behaviors because he had a headache" doesn't mean the same as "John was disposed to produce headache behaviors because he had a disposition to produce headache behaviors." Yet, "John had a headache" surely means the same in "John took aspirin because he had a headache" and in "John was disposed to produce headache behaviors because he had a headache," so if the behavioristic analysis is wrong for the second case, it must also be wrong for the first.

This is, no doubt, a relatively technical kind of difficulty, but it points in the direction of what is now widely viewed as a hopeless problem for logical behaviorism. Mental causes typically have their overt effects *in virtue of their interactions with one another,* and behaviorism provides no satisfactory analysis of statements that articulate such interactions. Statements that attribute behavioral dispositions to mental causes are of this species, but they are far from exhausting the kind. Consider that having a headache is sufficient to cause a disposition to take aspirin only if it is accompanied by a battery of other mental states: the desire to be rid of the headache; the belief that aspirin exists; the belief that taking aspirin leads to a reduction of headache; the belief that its side effects are not worse than headaches are; the belief that it is not grossly immoral to take aspirin when one has a headache; and so on. Moreover, such beliefs and utilities must be, as it were, *operative;* not only must one *have* them, but some of them must come into play as causal agents contributing to the production of the behavioral effect.

The consequences of this observation are twofold. First, it seems highly unlikely that mental causes can be identified with *behavioral* dispositions, since the antecedents of many putatively behavioral

hypotheticals turn out to contain mentalistic vocabulary ineliminably. But, moreover, we shall have to find analyses for etiologies
in which interactions among mental states involve possibly quite
long and elaborate causal chains; and here we have a fertile source
of counterexamples to the generality of *any* kind of dispositional
construal of mental ascriptions, behavioral or otherwise. "It
occurred to John to move his knight, but then he noticed that that
would leave his king in trouble, and since he wanted to avoid
check, he thought on balance that he'd better temporize and push
a pawn. When, however, he had considered for a while which pawn
to push, it all began to look boring and hopeless, and he thought:
'Oh, bother it,' and decided to resign. (Overt behavior finally ensues.)" Surely, the mental life is often like that; such cases occur
everywhere where mental *processes* are at issue, and it is, perhaps,
the basic problem with behaviorism that it can't reconstruct the
notion *mental process*. But these cases seem to be most glaringly the
norm in reasoning and problem solving, so it's not surprising that,
among psychologists, it has been the cognition theorists who have
led the recent antibehaviorist campaign. It seems perfectly obvious
that what's needed to construe cognitive processes is precisely what
behaviorists proposed to do without: causal sequences of mental
episodes and a "mental mechanics" to articulate the generalizations
that such sequences instantiate. The problem was—and remains—to
accommodate these methodological requirements within the ontological framework of materialism.

Which is why the physicalist reading of materialistic monism
seemed so very attractive an alternative to the behavioristic version. Suppose we assume that mental particulars (events, states,
processes, dispositions, etc.) are identical with physical particulars,
and also that the property of being in a certain mental state (such
as having a headache or believing that it will rain) is identical with
the property of being in a certain physical (e.g. neural) state. Then
we have a guaranty that our notion of mental causation will be
as robust as our notion of physical causation, the former having
turned out to be a special case of the latter. In particular, we will
have no difficulty in making sense of the claim that behavioral
effects may sometimes be the consequence of elaborate chains of
mental causes; or, indeed, that mental causes may interact elaborately *without* eventuating in behavioral effects. If mental processes

are, in fact, physical processes, they must enjoy whatever ontological autonomy physical processes are conceded. More than that
we surely should not ask for.

This is bracing stuff from the point of view of the psychologist.
Endorsing the central state identity theory is tantamount to
accepting a Realist interpretation of explanations in which appeal
to mental causes figure: If mental particulars are physical particulars, then the singular terms in (true) psychological theories denote. Indeed, they denote precisely the same sorts of things that
the singular terms in (true) physical theories do. Moreover, since
physicalism is not a semantic thesis, it is immune to many of the
kinds of arguments that make trouble for behaviorists. It is, for
example, uninteresting from the physicalist's point of view that
"John has a headache" doesn't mean the same as "John is in such
and such a brain state." The physicalist's claim is not that such
sentences are synonymous—that the second provides a linguistically or epistemologically adequate construal of the first—but only
that they are rendered true (or false) by the same states of affairs.

I remarked that the identity theory can be held either as a
doctrine about mental *particulars* (John's current headache, Bill's
fear of cats) or as a doctrine about the nature of mental *properties*
(universals like having a pain or being afraid of animals.) These
two variants—known as "token physicalism" and "type physicalism" respectively—differ in both strength and plausibility. For,
while the former claims only that all the mental particulars that
there happen to be are neurological, the latter makes that claim
about all the mental particulars that there *could* be. Token physicalism is thus compatible with the logical—perhaps even the nomological—possibility of unincarnate bearers of mental properties (e.g.
angels) and of bearers of mental properties that are incarnate but
not in flesh (e.g. machines). Whereas, type physicalism does not recognize such possibilities, since, if the property of having a pain is the
same property as that of being in a certain neural state, nothing
can have the former property that does not have the latter.

Type physicalism is, on balance, not a plausible doctrine about
the nature of mental properties—not even if token physicalism is
a plausible doctrine about the nature of mental particulars; not
even if token physicalism is a *true* doctrine about the nature of
mental particulars. The argument against type physicalism is often

made in a way that does it less than justice: "Why shouldn't (e.g.) silicon-based Martians suffer pains? And why shouldn't machines have beliefs? But if it is conceivable that mental properties should have such bearers, then it cannot be that mental properties *are* neural properties, however much the two may prove to be *de facto* coextensive. And neither can it be that they are *physical* properties if what you mean by a physical property is one that can be expressed by a projectible predicate in (say) an ideally completed physics. What silicon-based Martians and IBM machines and you and I are likely to have in common by way of the physical constitution of our nervous systems simply isn't worth discussing." (For discussion, see Chapter 5.)

But that's really not the point. The real point is that, if we want a science of mental phenomena at all, we are required to so identify mental properties that the kinds they subsume are natural from the point of view of psychological theory construction. If, for example, we identify mental properties with neural properties, then we are in effect claiming that domains consisting of creatures with a certain sort of neural organization constitute natural kinds for the psychologist's purposes. (Compare: if we claim that the property of being a fish is the property of living in the water, then we are in effect claiming that a domain consisting of creatures that live in the water constitutes a natural kind for the purposes of the marine biologist. Either that or we are claiming that "is a fish" is not a projectible predicate in marine biology. The essays that follow are neutral on fish, but they do assume the projectibility of properties like those expressed by typical mental predicates.)

Now, there is a level of abstraction at which the generalizations of psychology are most naturally pitched and, as things appear to be turning out, that level of abstraction collapses across the differences between physically quite different kinds of systems. Given the sorts of things we need to say about having pains and believing Ps, it seems to be at best just accidental, and at worst just false, that pains and beliefs are proprietary to creatures like us; if we *wanted* to restrict the domains of our psychological theories to just us, we would have to do so by ad hoc conditions upon their generalizations. Whereas, what does seem to provide a natural domain for psychological theorizing, at least in cognitive psychology, is something like the set of (real and possible) information processing systems. The point being, of course, that there are possible—and, for all we know, real—information processing systems which share our psychology (instantiate its generalizations) but do not share our physical organization.

It would be hard to overemphasize this point, but I shall do my best: Philosophical theories about the nature of mental properties carry empirical commitments about the appropriate domains for psychological generalizations. It is therefore an argument against such a theory if it carves things up in ways that prohibit stating such psychological generalizations as there are to state. And it looks as though type physicalism does carve things up in the wrong ways, assuming that the sort of psychological theories that are now being developed are even close to being true.

This is a state of affairs which cries out for a *relational* treatment of mental properties, one which identifies them in ways that abstract from the physiology of their bearers. Indeed, there is a sense in which behaviorists had the right end of the stick in hand, despite the sorts of objections we reviewed above. Behaviorists, after all, *did* offer a relational construal of mental properties: to have a belief or a pain was to be disposed to exhibit a certain pattern of relations between the responses that one produces and the stimuli that one encounters. So there seemed, ten or fifteen years ago, to be a nasty dilemma facing the materialist program in the philosophy of mind: What central state physicalists seemed to have got right—contra behaviorists—was the ontological autonomy of mental particulars and, of a piece with this, the causal character of mind/body interactions. Whereas, what the behaviorists seemed to have got right—contra the identity theory—was the relational character of mental properties. Functionalism, grounded in the machine analogy, seemed to be able to get both right at once. It was in the cheerful light of that promised synthesis that the now dominant approaches to the philosophy of mind first began to emerge.

It's implicit in the preceding that there is a way of understanding the new functionalism that makes it simply an extension of the logical behaviorist's program. Having a belief (say) was still to be construed as having a relational property, except that, whereas behaviorists had permitted only references to stimuli and responses to appear essentially in specifications of the relata, functionalists allowed reference to *other mental states* as well. A functionalist could thus concede many platitudes that behaviorists are hard put even to construe—as, for example, that it is plausibly a necessary condition for having certain beliefs that one is disposed to draw certain inferences (no belief that P&Q without a disposition to infer that P and a disposition to infer that Q); that it is plausibly a necessary condition for performing certain acts that one be in certain states of mind (no prevariacation without the causal involvement of an intent to deceive); and so forth.

But, in fact, reading functionalism this way—as a liberated form of behaviorism—is more than mildly perverse; for *all* that functionalism and behaviorism have in common is the relational construal of mental properties. If one considers the ontological issues (to say nothing of the epistemological issues), striking differences between the doctrines emerge at once. Unlike behaviorism, functionalism is not a reductionist thesis; it does not envision—even in principle—the elimination of mentalistic concepts from the explanatory apparatus of psychological theories. In consequence, functionalism is compatible with a physicalist (hence Realist) account of mental particulars. It thus tolerates the ascription of causal roles to mental particulars and can take literally theories which represent mental particulars as interacting causally, with whatever degree of complexity, in the course of mental processes. That, as we have seen, was the primary advantage the central state identity theory enjoyed. So it is possible for a functionalist to hold (1) that mental kinds are typically relationally defined; and (2) that the relations that mental particulars exhibit, insofar as they constitute the domains of mental processes, are typically *causal* relations: to stimuli, to responses, and to one another. Of these claims, a logical behaviorist can endorse only the first with an absolutely clear conscience, and a type-physicalist only the second.

So functionalism appeared to capture the best features of the previously available alternatives to dualism while avoiding all the major embarrassments. Viewed from one perspective, it offered behaviorism without reductionism; viewed from another, it offered physicalism without parochialism. The idea that mental particulars are physical, the idea that mental kinds are relational, the idea that mental processes are causal, and the idea that there could, at least in logical principle, be nonbiological bearers of mental properties were all harmonized. And the *seriousness* of the psychologist's undertaking was vindicated by providing for a Realistic interpretation of his theoretical constructs. Bliss!

I remarked that the standard form of materialistic monism is now a functionalism *grounded in the machine analogy.* So far, however, the machines have been notable by their absence. Where, then, do the machines come in? This is a matter of some delicacy to which I propose that we now direct our attention. From this point forward we will no longer be practicing consensus philosophy.

The intuition that underlies functionalism is that what determines which kind a mental particular belongs to is its causal role in the mental life of the organism. Functional individuation is individuation in respect of aspects of causal role; for purposes of psychological theory construction, only its causes and effects are to count in determining which kind a mental particular belongs to. Now, maybe that helps, but it doesn't help much. For one thing, supposing that token physicalism is true, it's going to turn out that some (maybe all) of the causes and effects of any given mental particular will satisfy descriptions in neural (or anyhow physical) vocabulary. If, in the course of functional individuation, we are allowed to advert to causes and effects under those descriptions, the intended distinction between functionalism and type physicalism is going to be lost; the intention was precisely that physical specifications of mental particulars were *not* to satisfy the conditions upon functional individuation. Clearly, what's needed is a normal form—and, in particular, a canonical vocabulary—for functional individuation; one that restricts the kinds of descriptions under which you're allowed to specify causes and effects insofar as such specifications enter into the analysis of psychological kinds. That's one problem.

The second problem is harder to make explicit; it consists,

really, in a lurking suspicion that functional individuation—and thus functional explanation—is just too easy. Molière had a finger on it: *In virtue of what did the morphine put Jones to sleep? In virtue of one of its functional properties. In virtue of WHICH of its functional properties did the morphine put Jones to sleep? In virtue of its having dormative power. In what does having this dormative power consist? It consists in being the cause of a certain kind of effect; viz. in causing sleep.* Now, it is, of course, *true* that morphine has dormative power, and there are even imaginable circumstances where an etiology that adverts to the dormative power of morphine might be the illuminating one to offer (what with explanation being interest relative and all that.) But in the crucial cases, what one is asking when one asks how the morphine put Jones to sleep might just as well be asked by asking what makes morphine sleep-inducing. And if *that's* what you want to know, then Molière is right and the putative explanation is question-begging.

Still worse: the appearance of functional specification can be sustained even where we know—on independent grounds—that nothing could perform the function specified. Here, for example, is a theory of the (occasional) human capacity to provide true answers to questions posed: Inside everyone's head there is a universal question-answering device. The class of such devices is functionally specified as follows. A universal question-answerer is a function from questions onto their answers; given a question as input, it provides the answer as output. (Interacting variables account for our occasional lapses into fallibility, along the lines of the performance/competence distinction).

Now, this story doesn't even manage to be true-but-question-begging. It has got to be false, since there couldn't be anything that has the input/output characteristics that the universal question-answerer is alleged to have. "Is a device which takes each question onto its answer" doesn't, as it were, succeed in being a functional definition. Yet it *looks* like a functional definition; only inputs and outputs are appealed to, so nothing in the notion of functional definition as thus far elaborated rules this one out. Something appears to have gone wrong.

Intuitively, the problem is that we want to allow functional individuation only where there exists a mechanism that can carry out the function and only where we have at least some idea of what such a mechanism might be like. The mere possibility of specifying a causal role in, as it were, the abstract, does not guaranty the satisfaction of these conditions—hence the danger of the sorts of functional pseudo-explanations illustrated in the preceding couple of paragraphs. All this suggests, to return to cases, that the identification of psychological properties with functional properties runs risks that type physicalism is immune to. On the latter view, canonical descriptions of psychological processes are couched in neurological vocabulary, so you *can't* specify a psychological kind without specifying a mechanism. Functionalism purchases a certain autonomy for psychological explanation by relaxing this requirement; but, then, how is pseudo-explanation going to be avoided?

Here, at last, is where the machines come in. (Turing) machine functionalism (for exposition, see especially Putnam's classic paper "Minds and machines," 1960) provided a serious remedy for both of the problems we've been raising. To begin with, it supplied the required canonical form for functional definitions of psychological kinds. The idea was that the conceptual mechanisms exploited in such definitions were to be identical with those employed in specifying the program states of (a restricted class of) computers. Roughly, specifications of such states can advert to (a) inputs to the machine; (b) outputs of the machine; (c) any of a designated set of elementary machine operations; and (d) other program states of the machine. Inputs and outputs are themselves restricted to symbol strings. Since list a–d is exhaustive, the idea that mental states are essentially relational is captured by the computational version of functionalism. In particular, you may not, in the canonical specification of a machine state, make essential reference to the physical character of the computational device that is in that state. Machine functionalism thus succeeds in being incompatible with type physicalism, which, as we saw above, is a desideratum.

Moreover, it provided a way of coping with Molière's worry too. For if the relations in terms of which psychological kinds are functionally defined can be restricted to those in terms of which

Turing machine program states are specified, the mechanical realizability of the psychological theory which posits the kinds is thereby guaranteed. This is not particularly mysterious; it's simply that the inputs and outputs of Turing machines are extremely restricted, and their elementary operations are extremely trivial. Since Turing machines are, in this sense, very simple devices, it is a correspondingly simple problem to build mechanisms that can realize them. The moral is: a psychological explanation that can be formulated as a program for a Turing machine is ipso facto mechanically realizable even though, *qua* functional explanation, it is not a specification of a mechanism.

There are, of course, kinds of computational devices other than Turing machines, so there are ways of construing machine functionalism which permit a richer notion of psychological kind than the Turing machine version acknowledges. Indeed, there are reasons for supposing that the relativization to Turing machines is much too austere for a psychologist's purposes. See Chapter 3, and also the discussion of the coordinate notions of machine architecture and "cognitive penetrability" in Pylyshyn, (1980). In short, what Turing machine functionalism provides is just a *sufficient* condition for the mechanical realizability of a functional theory. What makes it an *interesting* sufficient condition, however, is that Turing machines can do all sorts of interesting things; in particular, they can simulate literally *all* formally specifiable symbol manipulations and—for reasons that will presently become clear—much recent theorizing in cognitive science has tended to view the mind as in important respects a symbol-manipulating device. Suppose that, through some significant range of cases, mental processes are functionally specified by reference to operations on some kind of symbol-like objects. Then we know, at very least, that there exists for each such mental process a corresponding Turing machine process, and that there exists for each such Turing machine process a mechanical realization. Where symbol manipulations are at issue, Turing machines seem to provide a sort of universal nexus between functional explanation on the one hand and mechanistic explanation on the other.

So there is a sense in which—as a number of commentators have remarked (see, for example, Chapter 2)—to provide a psychological theory in Turing-machine-normal-form is thereby to exorcise the homunculi; you get a guaranty that no process has been appealed to except such as some mechanism can perform. We cannot, for example, posit a "universal question-answerer" as a component of our cognitive theory unless we can specify a Turing machine that can answer every question. We cannot even advert to "letter-recognizers" as components of a theory of how one reads printed words unless we are prepared to provide—or at least to envision providing—specifications of a Turing machine (plus transducers) which will recognize letters.

Not, of course, that one literally has such a specification in hand for each functionally individuated component of each psychological theory that one is prepared to take seriously. In practice, the flow of argument usually goes in the opposite direction: it *must* be possible to specify the mechanics of a letter-recognizer because (a) we are, in fact, able to read words; (b) reading words is surely causally dependent on recognizing letters; and (c) whatever is actual is possible: psychological processes must be mechanically realizable. Here we infer from the—independently patent—existence of the psychological process to the possibility of its mechanical (e.g. Turing-mechanical) simulation, rather than going the other way around. Even so, the possibility-in-principle of Turing specification functions as a sort of Ideal of Pure Reason, determining what it would be like to know that you have explained everything that could possibly want explaining.

I want to reemphasize these points because, as we shall see presently, they have been rather widely misunderstood (in particular, they have become tangled in unedifying ways with questions about intensionality) and the misunderstanding has led theorists to claim more for TM-functionalism than the traffic will bear. A Turing machine is, in a certain sense, a universal symbol manipulator; and it is, in virtue of its extreme simplicity, trivially mechanically realizable. Certain kinds of question-begging functional explanations depend on postulating processes for which no mechanical realization is known, or for which none can be imagined, or—in the extreme case—for which none can exist. In cases where the processes under analysis involve symbol manipulations (as may be true for a range of mental processes), this sort of question begging often takes the form of explaining intelligent processes by postulating (other) intelligent processes of equal obscurity, with a consequent gain of no yardage overall. Ryle says: "The crucial objection to the intellectualist legend is this. The consideration of propositions is itself an operation the execution of which can be more or less intelligent, less or more stupid. But if, for any operation to be intelligently executed, a prior theoretical operation had first to be performed and performed intelligently, it would be a logical impossibility for anyone ever to break into the circle" (1949, p. 30). Now, against *this* sort of question begging, Turing machine functionalism is foolproof. For even though an operation on symbols may, in the relevant sense, involve the consideration of propositions (in particular, even though it may be the kind of operation on symbols which respects the meaning of the symbols), still if the operation is formally specifiable it is Turing-reducible; and if it is Turing-reducible, then we *know* it to be mechanically realizable; to be performable, that is to say, by systems that are "unintelligent" in any understanding of the term that could be pertinent in the present discussion. That's the sense —and it's the only sense—in which a functional theory in Turing-machine-normal-form is ipso facto proof against lapses to which less exigent kinds of functional explanations are prone.

So much for the origins of contemporary functionalism, its provenance and early promise. The question now arises: how much has it actually paid off? This question isn't easy to answer, since much of what is currently going on in the philosophy of mind—and, for that matter, in the cognitive sciences at large—is a sustained investigation of the scope and limits of this sort of functional psychological explanation. There are, however, a number of points that have become clear in recent discussions, and I propose now to consider some of them.

To begin with, we really need a division of the question. I've been running the discussion more or less indifferently on *having a pain* and *believing that P,* but the functionalist story is not in fact equally plausible in its application to qualitative phenomena and to propositional attitudes. It's not hard to see why this is so. Functionalism applies only to kinds whose defining properties are relational. And while it is arguable that what makes a belief— or other propositional attitude—the belief that it is is the pattern of (e.g. inferential) relations that it enters into, many philosophers (I am among them) find it hard to believe that it is *relational* properties that make a sensation a pain rather than an itch, or an after-image a green after-image rather than a red one. What convinces those of us who are convinced is the following (putative) fact: Though "qualia inversion" is conceptually possible (my experience might be just like yours in respect of its causes and effects, but what looks red to you might nevertheless look green to me), "propositional attitude inversion" is *not* a conceptual possibility. It makes no sense to speak of my belief being different from yours despite the identity of their inferential (etc.) roles. This asymmetry is—plausibly—attributable precisely to the relational character of beliefs; that the belief that P is one from which Q is inferable is, so the story goes, constitutive of its being the belief that P. From this root difference between propositional attitudes and qualitative states, all sorts of obscure but interesting consequences follow: for example, the fact that while one is prepared to live with the postulation of unconscious beliefs, the mind simply boggles at postulating much in the way of unconscious qualia; the fact that while we have at least first-order approximations to computational theories of propositional attitudes, we have no psychology of qualitative states at all. And so on.

There are only two ways out of this asymmetry that are popular in the functionalist literature. One is to deny the conceptual coherence of qualia inversion, and the other is to deny that there are mental states with qualitative content. Neither of these solutions strikes me as very plausible; arguments for the first typically rely upon verificationist principles which, I think, simply ought not to be conceded. (However, see Shoemaker, 1972, and Block, 1980). And the only argument for the second seems to be that if there are sensations, then functionalism is, to that extent, not going to work; which would be too sad for words. It seems to me, for what it's worth, that functionalism does not provide an adequate account of qualitative content; that, in fact, we have no adequate materialist account of qualitative content. Since I have nothing at all to add to this discussion—either here or in the papers that follow—I shall simply assume that the functionalist program applies at most to the analysis of propositional attitudes.

Here, however, the prospects seem less gloomy. For one thing, in the case of qualitative states our perplexity is so deep that we can't even say just what it is that we would like a theory to do: If, as the inversion arguments rather suggest, qualitative contents are in some sense ineffable, it would hardly seem reasonable to require a philosophy of qualia to eff them. Whereas, it does seem relatively clear what we want from a philosophical account of the propositional attitudes. At a minimum, we want to explain how it is that propositional attitudes have semantic properties, and we want an explanation of the opacity of propositional attitudes; all this within a framework sufficiently Realistic to tolerate the ascription of causal roles to beliefs and desires.

By saying that propositional attitudes have semantic properties, I mean to make the untendentious point that beliefs (for example) are the kinds of things that can be true and false, and that there is typically an answer to the question who or what a given belief is true or false of (who or what it is a belief about).[1] By saying that propositional attitude contexts are opaque (intensional), I mean to make the familiar point that such principles of inference as existential generalization and substitutivity of identicals apparently do not apply to formulae embedded to verbs of propositional attitude in the same ways that they apply to morphosyntactically comparable formulae occurring unembedded. You cannot, for example, validly infer from "John thinks that Santa's beard is fuzzy" to "There is someone whose beard John thinks is fuzzy" (though the corresponding inference from "Santa's beard is fuzzy" to "There is someone whose beard is fuzzy" is valid); and you cannot infer from "The Morning Star is thought to be fuzzy" and "The Morning Star is the Evening Star" to "The Evening Star is thought to be fuzzy" (though, the corresponding inference is valid for unembedded formulae of the form *the Morning Star is F*).

A philosophical theory of propositional attitudes must explain their semantic properties and their intensionality. But, of course, we want a *psychology* of propositional attitudes as well. There are, for example, lots of interesting generalizations to state about how the propositional attitudes that an organism has are affected by aspects of its experience, and its genetic endowment, and by the other propositional attitudes that it entertains. One of the goals of a (cognitive) psychology is to state these generalizations and, whenever possible, to systematize and explain them. Insofar as the psychologist succeeds in this enterprise, his results ipso facto constrain philosophical theory construction. For, trivially, propositional attitudes have whatever properties a true psychology ascribes to them. Since, for example, perception is a species of the fixation of belief, a philosophy of propositional attitudes that makes it clear how beliefs can have truth values but is incompatible with an adequate psychology of perception would be at best an intellectual curiosity and at worst a waste of time. I think, in fact, that many philosophical accounts of propositional attitudes have been a waste of time in just this sort of way. If, to continue the example, you tie having beliefs to talking a language in order to account for their truth-valuability, then you make a mystery of the fact that much of our perceptual psychology generalizes to infrahuman species. The micromoral is that you should not tie having beliefs to talking a language; theories that do so appear to be false on the evidence. The macromoral is precisely that the evidence bears: the philosophical analysis is constrained by the psychologist's results and, patently, vice versa.

We might just as well say: we want a theory of propositional attitudes that covers such facts about them as we know of—hence a theory that covers their semantic and intensional properties inter alia. The distinction between a philosophical and a psychological theory is heuristic: a quick way of indicating which kinds of constraints are operative in motivating a given move in theory construction. In any event, that is the spirit in which the essays in this book are written; philosophical and psychological considerations are appealed to indiscriminately. I wish I could learn to be less discriminating still, for I am morally certain that real progress will be made only by researchers with access to an armamentarium of argument styles that considerably transcends what any of the traditional disciplines offer. That, despite frequent lapses into mere carnival, is what is hopeful about the recent interest in developing a cognitive science.

Anyhow: there is a lot we want a theory of propositional

attitudes to do, and the present question is what, if anything, functionalism is supposed to contribute to the undertaking. I want to make two points, both of them negative.

1. Although functionalism tends, in general, to license Realistic readings of psychological ascriptions, you need *more* than functionalism to license Realism about propositional attitudes.
2. Recent suggestions to the contrary notwithstanding, neither functionalism nor the notion of Turing-machine-normal-form provides for a theory of intensionality. What (in my view) you need to account for in intensionality is the notion of mental representation.

I'll take these points in reverse order.

In a deservedly influential paper called "Intentional systems,"[2] Dennett has the following passage:

> Intentional theory is vacuous as psychology because it presupposes and hence does not explain rationality or intelligence. . . . Skinner is right in recognizing that Intentionality can be no *foundation* for psychology, and right to look for purely mechanistic regularities in the activities of his subjects. . . . In seeking knowledge of internal design, our most promising tactic is to take out intelligence loans, endow peripheral and internal events with content, and then look for mechanisms that will function appropriately with such "messages" so we can pay back the loans. This tactic is hardly untried. Research in artificial intelligence . . . proceeds by working from an intentionally characterized problem . . . to a design stance solution.   (1971, p. 89)

"Intentional systems" is discussed at length in Chapter 4, where exception is taken to Dennett's claim that psychological explanations, insofar as they advert to propositional attitudes in the etiologies they propound, can aspire to heuristic value but not to truth. In the passage just quoted, however, the underlying issue seems to be what you do or don't buy vis-à-vis a theory of intensionality by subscribing to the machine-functional account of the canonical form of psychological explanations. And here, I think, it is very easy to become confused.

Here is *a* reading of Dennett's text. (The text strikes me as in some respects obscure, and I do *not* guaranty that this reading is the one that Dennett had in mind. If it isn't and I have erred, apologies are hereby tendered. Dennett is a friend of mine.) (a) Intensional explanations (those which postulate such intensional states as beliefs and other propositional attitudes) need to be eliminated from serious psychological theorizing, at least in the long run. This is because (b) intensional explanation inherently involves question-begging appeals to unanalyzed intelligent processes. (c) The way to rid psychology of intensional idiom is to carry through the program of machine functionalism, viz. to show how the putative intelligent processes are reducible to micro-processes that are, in turn, mechanically realizable.

This reading takes it that Dennett is, in effect, *equating* "taking out intelligence loans" with "endowing . . . events with content." Looking at things that way, it would be easy to get the idea that, insofar as machine functionalism has a program for reducing intelligent processes to mechanical processes, it *also* has a program for eliminating intensional idiom from psychological explanations—indeed, that to do the former *would be* to do the latter. And, of course, to accept that view would be to understand machine functionalism as providing a very radical and comprehensive theory of intensionality indeed, one which, in effect, provides a reduction of intensional to mechanistic explanations. (Dennett is sometimes pretty explicit in looking at the relation between intensionality and "intelligence loans" this way. He says, for example: "Intentionality . . . serves as a reliable means of detecting exactly where a theory is *in the red* relative to the task of explaining intelligence; wherever a theory relies on a formulation bearing the logical marks of Intentionality, there a little man is concealed" (p. 96, emphasis Dennett's). Contrapositively, a theory from which all the little men have been exorcised—e.g. by reduction to Turing-normal-form—should ipso facto be one which dispenses with intensional ascription.)

But that is not a good way to look at things. On the contrary, the problem of eliminating question-begging appeals to intelligence from psychological explanations is quite different from the problem of eliminating intensional contexts. And whereas the kind of reduction of complex mental processes to elementary ones that TM (and other) versions of machine functionalism contemplates provides a sufficient condition for solving the first problem (see above), *it does not provide a solution for the second.*

The point is that machine operations—*including elementary machine operations*—are themselves characterized in ways that involve intensional idiom insofar as their specification is relevant to their role in psychological explanations. For intensionality— as opposed to intelligence—it's (as you might say) a dual-aspect theory all the way down, with intensional characterization specifying one of the aspects and mechanical characterization specifying the other. Because this is true from top to bottom, reduction of complex operations to their elementary components buys nothing vis à vis the elimination of intensionality.

In the case of machines, the intensionality enters in at least two places:

1. Machine operations are driven by instructions which have their effect in virtue of being encoded by the formulae that constitute the program of the machine: These formulae have their causal roles—to put it loosely—in virtue of their syntactic rather than their semantic properties (see Chapter 9), so there is no general guaranty that the machine will produce identical computations for distinct but coextensive instructions ("print zero" vs. "print Dostoyevsky's favorite number"). So long as we describe the machine the way the psychologist wants to do—viz. as *following instructions*—the idiom of the description is intensional. It makes utterly no difference in this respect whether the instructions we describe it as following are elementary or complex.

2. Typical machine operations are operations on symbols—on semantically interpreted objects. But machines operate on symbols in virtue of their formal (not their semantic) properties, and it is thus entirely possible that the machine should operate differently upon (e.g.) co-referring symbols. Indeed, this will generally be the case where the fact that the symbols co-refer isn't "known" to the machine. (And even where it *is* known, the pattern of computation which leads to the derivation of, e.g. "4 – 2 = 1 + 1" will normally be different from the pattern of computation which leads to the derivation of, e.g., "1 + 1 = 1 + 1.")

The point that underlies these considerations is that computers are symbol-driven symbol-manipulators: their programs are sets of semantically interpreted formulae and their typical operations consist in the transformation of sets of semantically interpreted formulae. Only because the first is true can we think of the machine's operations as *rule-governed* (*un*interpreted strings of formulae aren't *rules*), and only because the second is true can we think of the machine's operations as *eventuating in proofs* (sequences of strings of uninterpreted formulae aren't *proofs*). It is, in short, because they are in this sense *semantic* engines that descriptions of what computers do and how they do it are characteristically shot full of intensional idiom. Turing machine functionalism dispenses with appeals to intelligence without dispensing with this intensionality, viz. by providing a class of formalisms for which mechanical realizations are trivially available. But insofar as we view the operations of such machines as *computations* (a fortiori, insofar as we view such machines as psychological models), we are taking these very mechanical processes to be "endowed with content." So the moral is: either taking out "intelligence loans" isn't *inherent* in intensional ascription or, if it is, then mechanical reduction does not pay back the loans.

Moreover—and I think this is the really important point—the way that intensionality enters into specifications of unintelligent (viz. computational) operations is quite revealing from the philosophical point of view. As we've seen, what makes intensional descriptions pertinent in the case of the computer is not the complexity of its operations but the fact that its operations are defined over—and driven by—semantically interpreted objects. Whereas the theory of intelligence needs an account of *mechanisms,* the theory of intensionality needs an account of *symbols.* If, then, we propose to take the computer seriously as a model of the mind, the obvious suggestion is that we should think of the intensionality (and semanticity) of propositional attitudes as similarly derived. Here, then, is a major theme in the essays that follow: There are *two,* quite different, applications of the "computer metaphor" in cognitive theory: two quite different ways of understanding what the computer metaphor *is.* One is the idea of Turing reducibility of intelligent processes; the other (and, in my view, far more important) is the idea of mental processes as formal operations on symbols. The doctrine of these essays is precisely that the objects of propositional attitudes are symbols (specifically, mental representations) and that this fact accounts for their intensionality and semanticity. More of this in the immediate future.

We were considering the question what functionalism does and does not achieve vis-à-vis a theory of propositional attitudes, and I've argued that among its nonachievements is the elimination of intensional idiom from psychological explanation. The next point is one that such philosophers as Putnam (1978) and Stich (1980) have recently emphasized. Functionalism tends to vindicate Realistic construals of mentalistic etiologies; but it does not, per se, vindicate a Realistic reading of etiologies in which appeals to propositional attitudes figure.

The point is sufficiently clear: pretheoretical intuition says that beliefs are causes, and moreover that they are causes distinct from stimuli, responses, and dispositions. Functionalism subscribes to all that.[3] But pretheoretical intuition also says that beliefs are causes which have *contents,* and on this issue functionalism is neutral (as, indeed, it must be if—as I've been arguing—the program of functional analysis has no bearing on the issue of intensionality.)

It is, in particular, quite compatible with functionalism that behavioral processes should have mental causes, but that there should be no coherent construal of the idea that a belief has the effects that it does in virtue of being the belief that P rather than, say, the belief that not-P. Indeed, this is the *normal* situation for functional explanation in *non*-psychological contexts. Reference to a mousetrap may figure largely in your story about what happened to the mouse. And the property of being a mousetrap may be functionally (hence non-mechanistically) defined. But functional stories of that kind do not advert to mousetraps with propositional content; to mousetraps-that-P. Whereas, stories about the causal consequences of beliefs *do* advert to objects that have propositional content, at least according to our pretheoretical intuitions about beliefs. In short, it is perhaps true (and it is perhaps edifying in the context of discussions of behaviorism and physicalism) that mental properties are functionally defined. But even if functionalism is true and edifying, it is not a solution to the problem that makes cognitive psychology special among the sciences—viz. the (apparently ineliminable) adversion to etiologies in which objects that have propositional content figure as causal agents. On *this* topic, functionalism is neutral, hence uninformative.

It follows that we have—at least in principle—the option of adopting a functionalist account of psychological constructs but nevertheless refusing to "endow internal states with content." Psychological theories in canonical form would then look rather like machine tables, but they would provide no answer to such questions as "Which of these machine states is (or corresponds to, or simulates) the state of believing that P?" But though we could take this line (functionalism allows it), it would be Pickwickian— not to say vastly self-defeating—for us to do so. Philosophers who recommend this course have, it seems to be, rather lost track of the state of play.

Remember what urged functionalism in the first place. It was *not* the need to posit ontologically autonomous causes for behavioral effects; for those purposes, token physicalism will do quite adequately. Rather, we were driven to functionalism (hence to the autonomy of psychology) by the suspicion that there are empirical generalizations about mental states that can't be formulated in the vocabulary of neurological or physical theories; neurology and physics don't, we supposed, provide projectible kind-predicates that subtend the domains of these generalizations. But now if we think about what these generalizations are like, what's striking is that all of the candidates—literally *all* of them—are generalizations that apply to propositional attitudes in virtue of the content of the propositional attitudes. We don't need the clever examples from linguistics or psychology to make this point; commonsense psychological etiologies will do. So consider: seeing that a is F is a normal cause of believing that a is F; the intention that it should be the case that so and so is a normal cause of actions whose goal is to bring it about that so and so; statements that P are normally caused by beliefs that P; observations that many of the xs are F often contribute to the etiology of the belief that all the xs are F; the belief that a thing is red is a normal cause of the inference that the thing is colored; and so on and on. The point of such examples is not, of course, that any of them are likely to figure in a serious cognitive psychology. It's rather that our attempts at a serious cognitive psychology are founded in the hope that *this kind* of generalization can be systematized and made rigorous; it's precisely this kind of generalization that we abandoned type physicalism in hopes of preserving. And: YOU CAN'T SAVE THESE GENERALIZATIONS WITHOUT APPEALING TO THE NOTION OF THE CONTENT OF A MENTAL STATE, since, as previously remarked, these generalizations are precisely such as apply to mental states in virtue of their contents.

Here is where we've got to: what we need—and what functionalism tolerates but does not, per se, provide—is a theory of what it is for mental states to have propositional contents. Such a theory is propounded in the following essays (and in Fodor, 1975) under the rubric "The Representational Theory of Mind." It is, in fact, a Good Old Theory—one to which both Locke and Descartes (among many others) would certainly have subscribed. (It's among the cruder ironies of cognitive science that insofar as the Representational Theory of Mind is the content of the computer metaphor, the computer metaphor predates the computer by perhaps three hundred years. Much of cognitive science is philosophy rediscovered—and, I think, vindicated.)

This is the theory:

(a) Propositional attitude states are relational.
(b) Among the relata are mental representations (often called "Ideas" in the older literature).
(c) Mental representation are symbols: they have both formal and semantic properties.
(d) Mental representations have their causal roles in virtue of their formal properties.
(e) Propositional attitudes inherit their semantic properties from those of the mental representations that function as their objects.

There's quite a lot of discussion of these points in the essays that follow, especially Chapters 7 and 9, so I won't review them here. There is, however, one consideration that I do want to raise.

Some people who have read one or other of these papers have wanted to chastise me for inferring from the (now widely acknowledged) fact that propositional attitudes are representational to the existence of mental representations which function as (approximately) the objects of those states. Now, I *am* inclined to draw this inference, but not in a demonstrative tone of voice. The idea is, rather, that the postulation of mental representations provides for a theory of mental content, and that that theory is plausible on a number of independent grounds. To give some sense of the kinds of considerations involved, I'll suggest a couple of the arguments here.

To begin with, I'm impressed by the fact that—so far as I can tell—all psychologies that have taken the notion of mental content seriously (in effect, all nonbehaviorist psychologies) have been ontologically committed to mental representations: in particular they have sought to account for the causal and/or semantic properties of mental states by reference to features of the mental representations that are assumed to be entertained when one is in those states. (A simple and traditional example is the idea that the relation between a thought and what it is a thought about can be accounted for by assuming that Ideas are like pictures and *resemble* their referents.)

The ubiquity of this strategy seems to me to establish an impressive prima facie case that quantification over mental representations is the natural move for theory construction in cognitive psychology. The least it shows is that anyone who accepts the attribution of content to mental states but is *not* prepared to acknowledge mental representations is under an obligation to show either that all theories that are ontologically so committed are false (cf. the theory that thoughts are pictures) or that they are translatable into theories which reconstruct the notion of mental content *without* appealing to the mental representation construct.

I think that philosophers have seriously underestimated the difficulty of providing such translations (perhaps because they haven't very often tried to give them). Here is an example of a psychological explanation; one that is chosen not because it is spectacular and dramatic but precisely because it is simple and obvious and, for all that, apparently turns ineliminably upon the postulation of mental representations.

There is a well-known and very robust psycholinguistic phenomenon known as the "frequency effect." What it comes to is that if I flash a letter sequence on a screen and ask you to reply as rapidly as you can whether it constitutes a word you know,

then (for cases where the correct response is "yes") the speed of
your response will be proportional to the relative frequency with
which tokens of the word occur in corpora of your language:
relatively high frequency words (like "find") elicit faster responses
than relatively low frequency words (like "crib"). This phenomenon persists when boring variables (like word length, etc.) are
controlled for.

Now here is one story about the frequency effect.[4] There is,
in your head, a *mental lexicon:* a list of such of the words in
your language as you know. When you are asked whether a letter
string *is* a word you know, you search for the letter string in this
mental lexicon. If you find it, you say "yes"; if you fail to find
it, you say "no." And: the words in the mental lexicon are listed
in order of their frequency and they are searched in the order in
which they are listed. (It may have occurred to you that, assuming
that an ambiguous word is one that is listed *twice* in the mental
lexicon, then if the theory is true, response times in the experimental task ought to be controlled by the reading with the *higher*
frequency: an ambiguous word that is high frequency on one
construal and low frequency on the other—like "still'—ought to
elicit fast reaction times rather than slow ones. This prediction
has been tested and proves to be the case. (Forster, 1976.)

I'm not, at present, primarily interested in whether this story
is true, only in whether it can be told without attributing properties to (hence quantifying over) mental representations. I admit
to not seeing how. Notice, for example, that we can't get the force
of the explanation merely by attributing to the subject the belief
that (e.g.) "find" is a high frequency word and that "crib" is not.
For though it is doubtless true that subjects *have* such beliefs, it
isn't assumptions about the beliefs that the subject has, but
rather assumptions about the ways in which his mental representations are arranged and processed, that do the work in the theory.
You need the notion that recognizing a word involves being related in a certain way to a mental representation of the word in
order to make the story go. And that notion *is* an aspect of the
representational theory of the mind.

You aren't, of course, required to like this explanation of the
frequency effect. You are at liberty to discharge its ontological
commitments by showing that the explanation is false or by finding

some other explanation that is less prodigally committed. But what strikes me as simply *irresponsible*—though it is, alas, a standard philosophic practice—is to reject the mental representation construct without bothering *either* to disconfirm *or* to reconstruct the explanations it occurs in. And, to repeat, many of these explanations are a great deal more complicated—and cover a vastly richer and subtler range of experimental phenomena—than the tinker-toy example just discussed. Just for starters, try doing linguistics without recourse to mental representations.

I think the best kind of ontological argument is the kind I've just given: we need this construct to do our science. But many philosophers seem unwilling to accept that sort of argument when the construct is *mental representation* and the science is psychology. So I will give another kind of argument, a philosophically respectable one.

There is an infinite set of beliefs, just as there is an infinite set of sentences. It seems inescapable—and is, so far as I know, untendentious—that the semantic properties of some beliefs (call them the *complex* ones) are inherited under some sort of combinatorial operations from the semantic properties of other beliefs (call them the *simple* ones). Much of Chapter 10 is about the empirical motivations for (and consequences of) drawing the boundary between simple and complex mental structures at one point rather than another. But wherever you draw it, an important part of the theory of propositional attitudes will be about such questions as: "How are the semantic properties of the belief that John left and Mary wept inherited from the semantic properties of the belief that John left and the belief that Mary wept?

My point is that it makes a difference here whether we recognize only (as it were, nonrelational) states of believing to which propositional content is somehow ascribed and over which the apparatus for combinatorial inheritance of semantic properties must then be defined; or whether we are allowed to take beliefs as relations to mental representations and thus to define the combinatorial mechanisms over the latter. You can see *where* it makes a difference by considering, for example, disjunctive beliefs. The state of believing that PvQ is surely a complex state in the sense intended. Yet the state of believing that PvQ need not have the state of believing that P or the state of believing that Q among its constituents; so, on the nonrelational model, it's hard to see just where the semantic properties of the belief that PvQ are supposed to be inherited *from*.[5]

If, however, believing that PvQ is being related to a complex mental representation, there's no reason why the latter shouldn't inherit its semantic properties from constituent representations which *would* function as the objects of the belief that P and the belief that Q *were* one to entertain those beliefs. The postulation of mental representations provides for a theoretical domain distinct from the system of propositional attitude states per se, and it's no particular surprise that the constituency relation should work differently in the two domains. The model here is the relation between *asserting* and *uttering*. You can assert that PVQ without asserting that P or asserting that Q. But you can't utter "PVQ" without uttering "P" and uttering "Q." The constituency relation for utterances is based on the constituency relation for formulae, and it differs systematically from the constituency relation for assertions.

So, in the present case, the postulation of mental representations provides plausible structures for the principles of combinatorial inheritance of semantic properties to apply to, just as, in the case examined above, it provided plausible structures for the mental operations underlying word recognition to apply to. Once again, I see no natural way of doing the trick short of such postulation, and it would surely be absurd to hold that the demands of ontological parsimony must *always* outweigh those of explanatory adequacy.[6]

There have been three strands to this discussion, and I have been considerably exercised to pick them apart: the idea that mental states are functionally defined; the idea that, in order to specify the generalizations that mentalistic etiologies instantiate, we need to advert to the contents of mental states; and the idea that mental states are relations to mental representations, the latter being viewed as, inter alia, semantically interpreted objects. Much of what goes on in the essays that follow consists of trying to see how one or other of these ideas fits into a network of constraints and desiderata that ought to condition a theory of mind. Questions like the following are in the forefront: If there are mental representations, where—ontogenetically speaking—do they come from? If mental representations have both semantic and causal properties, how do the two connect? If we are going to take the notion of propositional content seriously, how will that affect what we say about the position of psychology among the other sciences? And so on.

What would we have achieved if we were able to answer such questions? Viewed one way, quite a lot: we would have at least the methodological outlines of a cognitive psychology; and that, surely, is more than we started with. But viewed another way, we would have done little more than to motivate a direction of analysis. If the present views can be sustained, then it is mental representations that have semantic properties in, one might say, the first instance; the semantic properties of propositional attitudes are inherited from those of mental representations and, presumably, the semantic properties of the formulae of natural languages are inherited from those of the propositional attitudes that they are used to express. What we need now is a semantic theory for mental representations; a theory of how mental representations represent. Such a theory I do not have; If I'd had one, I would have written quite a different sort of book. (Instead, I wrote Chapter 8, which is about what it's like to think you have one when you don't.)

So whatever else these papers are, they are certainly programmatic. The test of such a program is, ultimately, empirical fruitfulness, and about that we shall have to wait and see. In the meantime, at least there's this to say: the idea of mental representation has an enormously impressive provenance in the philosophical tradition; it opens a wide range of possibilities for psychological theory construction; and, at a minimum, we don't *know* that it's incapable of coherent explication. It's an *interesting* idea; maybe we ought to give it a run.

And maybe some of this stuff counts as philosophy after all. The form of a philosophical theory, often enough, is: *Let's try looking over here.*

I.
Functionalism and Realism

Chapter 1

Operationalism and Ordinary Language

(with Charles Chihara)

Introduction

This paper explores some lines of argument in Wittgenstein's post-*Tractatus* writings in order to indicate the relations between Wittgenstein's philosophical psychology on the one hand and his philosophy of language, his epistemology, and his doctrines about the nature of philosophical analysis on the other. We shall hold that the later writings of Wittgenstein express a coherent doctrine in which an operationalistic analysis of confirmation and language supports a philosophical psychology of a type we shall call "logical behaviorism."

We shall also maintain that there are good grounds for rejecting the philosophical theory implicit in Wittgenstein's later works. In particular we shall first argue that Wittgenstein's position leads to some implausible conclusions concerning the nature of language and psychology; second, we shall maintain that the arguments Wittgenstein provides are inconclusive; and third, we shall try to sketch an alternative position which avoids many of the difficulties implicit in Wittgenstein's philosophy. In exposing and rejecting the operationalism which forms the framework of Wittgenstein's later writings, we do not however, suppose that we have detracted in any way from the importance of the particular analyses of the particular philosophical problems which form their primary content.

I

Among the philosophical problems Wittgenstein attempted to dissolve is the "problem of other minds." One aspect of this hoary problem is the question "What justification, if any, can be given for the claim that one can tell, on the basis of someone's behavior, that he is in a certain mental state?" To this question, the sceptic answers: "No good justification at all." Among the major motivations of the later Wittgenstein's treatment of philosophical psychology is that of showing that this answer rests on a misconception and is *logically* incoherent.

Characteristically, philosophic sceptics have argued in the following way. It is assumed as a premiss that there are no logical or conceptual relations between propositions about mental states and propositions about behavior in virtue of which propositions asserting that a person behaves in a certain way provide support, grounds, or justification for ascribing the mental states to that person. From this, the sceptic deduces that he has no compelling reason for supposing that any person other than himself is ever truly said to feel pains, draw inferences, have motives, etc. For, while his first-hand knowledge of the occurrence of such mental events is of necessity limited to his own case, it is entailed by the premiss just cited that application of mental predicates to others must depend upon logically fallible inferences. Furthermore, attempts to base such inferences on analogies and correlations fall short of convincing justifications.

Various replies have been made to this argument which do not directly depend upon contesting the truth of the premiss. For example, it is sometimes claimed that, at least in some cases, no *inference* from behavior to mental states is at issue in psychological ascriptions. Thus we sometimes *see* that someone is in pain, and in these cases we cannot be properly said to *infer* that he is in pain. However, the sceptic might maintain against this argument that it begs the question. For the essential issue is whether anyone is *justified* in claiming to see that another is in pain. Now a physicist, looking at cloud-chamber tracks, may be justified in claiming to see that a charged particle has passed through the chamber. That is because in this case there is justification for the claim that certain sorts of tracks show the presence and motion of particles. The physicist can explain not only how he is able to detect particles, but also why the methods he uses are methods of detecting *parti-cles*. Correspondingly, the sceptic can argue that what is required in the case of another's pain is some justification for the claim that, by observing a person's behavior, one can *see* that he is in *pain*.

Wittgenstein's way of dealing with the sceptic is to attack his premiss by trying to show that there do exist conceptual relations between statements about behavior and statements about mental events, processes, and states. Hence, Wittgenstein argues that in many cases our knowledge of the mental states of some person rests upon something other than an observed empirical correlation or an analogical argument, viz. a conceptual or linguistic connection.

To hold that the sceptical premiss is false is *ipso facto* to commit oneself to some version of *logical behaviorism* where by "logical behaviorism" we mean the doctrine that there are logical or conceptual relations of the sort denied by the sceptical premiss.[1] Which form of logical behaviorism one holds depends on the nature of the logical connection one claims obtains. The strongest form maintains that statements about mental states are translatable into statements about behavior. Wittgenstein, we shall argue, adopts a weaker version.

II

It is well known that Wittgenstein thought that philosophical problems generally arise out of misrepresentations and misinterpretations of ordinary language. (*PI*, §§ 109, 122, 194).[2] Philosophy," he tells us, "is a fight against the fascination which forms of expression exert upon us" (*BB*, p. 27). Thus Wittgenstein repeatedly warns us against being misled by superficial similarities between certain forms of expression (*BB*, p. 16) and tells us that to avoid philosophical confusions, we must distinguish the "surface grammar" of sentences from their "depth grammar" (*PI*, §§ 11, 664). For example, though the grammar of the sentence "*A* has a gold tooth" seems to differ in no essential respect from that of "*A* has a sore tooth," the apparent similarity masks important conceptual differences (*BB*, pp. 49, 53; *PI*, §§ 288–293). Overlooking these differences leads philosophers to suppose that there is a problem about our knowledge of other minds. It is the task of the Wittgensteinian philosopher to dissolve the problem by obtaining a clear view of the workings of pain language in this and other cases.

The Wittgensteinian method of philosophical therapy involves taking a certain view of language and of meaning. Throughout the *Investigations*, Wittgenstein emphasizes that "the speaking of language is part of an activity" (*PI*, § 23) and that if we are to see the radically different roles superficially similar expressions play, we must keep in mind the countless kinds of language-using activities or "language games" in which we participate (*BB*, pp. 67–68).

It is clear that Wittgenstein thought that analyzing the meaning of a word involves exhibiting the role or use of the word in the various language games in which it occurs. He even suggests that we "think of words as instruments characterized by their use . . ." (*BB*, p. 67).

This notion of analysis leads rather naturally to an operationalistic view of the meaning of certain sorts of predicates. For in cases where it makes sense to say of a predicate that one has determined that it applies, one of the central language games that the fluent speaker has learned to play is that of making and reporting such determinations. Consider, for example, one of these language games that imparts meaning to such words as "length," e.g., that of reporting the dimensions of physical objects. To describe this game, one would have to include an account of the procedures involved in measuring lengths; indeed, mastering (at least some of) those procedures would be an essential part of learning this game. "The meaning of the word 'length' is learnt among other things, by learning what it is to determine length" (*PI*, p. 225). As Wittgenstein comments about an analogous case, "Here the teaching of language is not explanation, but training" (*PI*, § 5). For Wittgenstein, "To understand a sentence means to understand a language." "To understand a language means to be master of a technique" (*PI*, § 199).

In short, part of being competent in the language game played with "length" consists in the ability to arrive at the truth of such statements as "x is three feet long" by performing relevant operations with, e.g., rulers, range-finders, etc. A philosophic analysis of "length," insofar as it seeks to articulate the language game played with that word, must thus refer to the operations which determine the applicability of length predicates. Finally, insofar as

the meaning of the word is itself determined by the rules governing the language games in which it occurs, a reference to these
operations will be essential in characterizing the meaning of such
predicates as "three feet long." It is in this manner that we are led
to the view that the relevant operations for determining the
applicability of a predicate are conceptually connected with
the predicate.[3]

By parity of reasoning we can see that to analyze such words as
"pain," "motive," "dream," etc., will *inter alia* involve articulating
the operations or observations in terms of which we determine
that someone is in pain, or that he has such and such a motive, or
that he has dreamed, etc. (*PI*, p. 224). But clearly such determinations are ultimately made on the basis of the behavior of the individual to whom the predicates are applied (taking behavior in the
broad sense in which it includes verbal reports). Hence, for Wittgenstein, reference to the characteristic features of pain behavior
on the basis of which we determine that someone is in pain is essential to the philosophical analysis of the word "pain," just as
reference to the operations by which we determine the applicability of such predicates as "three feet long" is essential to the philosophical analysis of the word "length." In both cases the relations
are conceptual and the rule of language which articulates them is
in that sense a rule of logic.

III

But what, specifically, is this logical connection which, according to Wittgenstein, is supposed to obtain between pain behavior
and pain? Obviously, the connection is not that of simple entailment. It is evident that Wittgenstein did not think that some
proposition to the effect that a person is screaming, wincing,
groaning, or moaning could entail the proposition that the person
is in pain. We know that Wittgenstein used the term "criterion" to
mark this special connection, but we are in need of an explanation
of this term.

We have already remarked that one of the central ideas in Wittgenstein's philosophy is that of a "language game." Apparently
Wittgenstein was passing a field on which a football game was
being played when the idea occurred to him that "in language we
play *games* with *words*."[4] Since this analogy dominated so much

of the later Wittgenstein's philosophical thinking, perhaps it would be well to begin the intricate task of explicating Wittgenstein's notion of a criterion by considering some specific game.

Take basketball as an example. Since the object of the game is to score more points than one's opponents, there must be some way of telling if and when a team scores. Now there are various ways of telling that, say, a field goal has been scored. One might simply keep one's eyes on the scoreboard and wait for two points to be registered. Sometimes one realizes that a field goal has been scored on the basis of the reactions of the crowd. But these are, at best, indirect ways of telling, for if we use them we are relying on someone else: the score-keeper or other spectators. Obviously, not every way of telling is, in that sense, indirect; and anyone who is at all familiar with the game knows that, generally, one *sees* that a field goal has been scored in seeing the ball shot or tipped through the hoop. And if a philosopher asks, "Why does the fact that the ball went through the basket show that a field goal has been scored?" a natural reply would be, "That is what the rules of the game say; that is the way the game is played." The ball going through the basket satisfies a *criterion* for scoring a field goal.

Notice that though the relation between a criterion and that of which it is a criterion is a logical or conceptual one, the fact that the ball goes through the hoop does not entail that a field goal has been scored. First, the ball must be "in play" for it to be possible to score a field goal by tossing the ball through the basket. Second, even if the ball drops through the hoop when "in play," it need not follow that a field goal has been scored, for the rules of basketball do not cover all imaginable situations. Suppose, for example, that a player takes a long two-handed shot and that the ball suddenly reverses its direction, and after soaring and dipping through the air like a swallow in flight, gracefully drops through the player's own basket only to change into a bat, which immediately entangles itself in the net. What do the rules say about that?

An analogous situation would arise, in the case of a "language game," if what seemed to be a chair suddenly disappeared, reappeared, and, in general, behaved in a fantastic manner. Wittgenstein's comment on this type of situation is:

> Have you rules ready for such cases—rules saying whether one may use the word "chair" to include this kind of thing? But do

we miss them when we use the word "chair"; and are we to say
that we do not really attach any meaning to this word, because
we are not equipped with rules for every possible application of
it?   (*PI,* § 80)

For Wittgenstein, a sign "is in order—if, under normal circumstances it fulfils its purpose" (*PI,* § 87).

It is only in normal cases that the use of a word is clearly pre-
scribed; we know, are in no doubt, what to say in this or that
case. The more abnormal the case, the more doubtful it becomes what we are to say.   (*PI,* § 142)

Let us now try to make out Wittgenstein's distinction between
criterion and *symptom,* again utilizing the example of basketball.
Suppose that, while a game is in progress, a spectator leaves his
seat. Though he is unable to see the playing court, he might realize
that the home team had scored a field goal on the basis of a symptom—say, the distinctive roar of the crowd—which he had observed to be correlated with home-team field goals. This correlation,
according to Wittgenstein, would have to be established *via* criteria, say, by noting the sound of the cheering when the home team
shot the ball through the basket. Thus a symptom is "a phenomenon of which experience has taught us that it coincided, in
some way or other, with the phenomenon which is our defining
criterion" (*BB,* p. 25). Though both symptoms and criteria are
cited in answer to the question, "How do you know that so-and-so
is the case?" (*BB,* p. 24), symptoms, unlike criteria, are discovered
through experience or observation: that something is a symptom
is not given by the rules of the "language game" (not deducible
from the rules alone). However, to say of a statement that it expresses a symptom is to say something about the relation between
the statement and the rules, viz., that it is not derivable from them.
Hence, Wittgenstein once claimed that "whereas 'When it rains the
pavement gets wet' is not a grammatical statement at all, if we say
'The fact that the pavement is wet is a *symptom* that it has been
raining' this statement is 'a matter of grammar'."[5] Furthermore,
giving the criterion for (e.g.) another's having a toothache "is to
give a grammatical explanation about the word 'toothache' and, in
this sense, an explanation concerning the meaning of the word
'toothache'" (*BB,* p. 24). However, given that there is this important

difference between criteria and symptoms, the fact remains that
Wittgenstein considered both symptoms and criteria as "evidences"
(*BB*, p. 51).

Other salient features of criteria can be illuminated by exploiting our illustrative example. Consider Wittgenstein's claim that "in
different circumstances we apply different criteria for a person's
reading" (*PI*, § 164). It is clear that in different circumstances we
apply different criteria for a person's scoring a field goal. For example, the question whether a player scored a field goal may arise
even though the ball went nowhere near the basket: in a "goal-
tending" situation, the question will have to be decided on the
basis of whether the ball had started its descent before the defen-
sive player had deflected it. According to the rules it would be a
decisive reason for not awarding a field goal that the ball had not
reached its apogee when it was blocked.

One can now see that to claim that X is a criterion of Y is not
to claim that the presence, occurrence, existence, etc., of X is a
necessary condition of the applicability of 'Y', and it is not to
claim that the presence, occurrence, existence, etc., of X is a sufficient condition of Y, although if X is a criterion of Y, it may be
the case that X is a necessary or a sufficient condition of Y.

Again, consider the tendency of Wittgenstein, noted by Albrit-
ton,[6] to write as if X (a criterion of Y) just *is* Y or is what is called
'Y' in certain circumstances. We can understand a philosopher's
wanting to say that shooting the ball through the basket in the appropriate situation just *is* scoring a field goal or is what we call
"scoring a field goal."

Consider now the following passage from the *Investigations*
(§ 376) which suggests a kind of test for "non-criterionhood":

> When I say the ABC to myself, what is the criterion of my do-
> ing the same as someone else who silently repeats it to himself?
> It might be found that the same thing took place in my larynx
> and in his. (And similarly when we both think of the same
> thing, wish the same, and so on.) But then did we learn the use
> of the words: "to say such-and-such to oneself" by someone's
> pointing to a process in the larynx or the brain?

Obviously not. Hence, Wittgenstein suggests, something taking
place in the larynx cannot be the criterion. The rationale behind

this "test" seems to be this: For the teaching of a particular predicate 'Y' to be successful, the pupil must learn the rules for the use of 'Y' and hence must learn the criteria for 'Y' if there are such criteria. Thus if the teaching could be entirely successful without one learning that X is something on the basis of which one tells that 'Y' applies, X cannot be a criterion of Y. For example, since a person could be taught what "field goal" means without learning that one can generally tell that the home team has scored a field goal by noting the roar of the home crowd, the roar of the home crowd cannot be a criterion of field goals.

Finally, let us examine the principle, which Wittgenstein appears to maintain, that any change of criteria of X involves changing the concept of X. In the *Investigations*, Wittgenstein makes the puzzling claim:

> There is *one* thing of which one can say neither that it is one metre long, nor that it is not one metre long, and that is the standard metre in Paris.—But this is, of course, not to ascribe any extraordinary property to it, but only to mark its peculiar role in the language-game of measuring with a metre-rule.—Let us imagine samples of colour being preserved in Paris like the standard metre. We define: "Sepia" means the colour of the standard sepia which is there kept hermetically sealed. Then it will make no sense to say of this sample either that it is of this colour or that it is not.   (*PI*, § 50)

Wittgenstein evidently is maintaining not only that the senses of the predicates "x is one meter long" and "x is sepia" are given by the operations which determine the applicability of the respective predicates (the operations of comparing objects in certain ways with the respective standards),[7] but also that these operations cannot be performed on the standards themselves and hence neither standard can be said to be an instance of either the *predicate* for which it is a standard or of its negation. (Cf., "A thing cannot be at the same time the measure and the thing measured" [*RFM*, I, § 40, notes].)

Wittgenstein would undoubtedly allow that we might introduce a new language-game in which "meter" is defined in terms of the wave length of the spectral line of the element krypton of atomic weight 86.[8] In this language-game, where such highly accurate and complex measuring devices as the interferometer are required, the standard meter does not have any privileged position: it, too, can be measured and "represented." In this language-game, the standard meter is or is not a meter. But here, Wittgenstein would evidently distinguish two senses of the term "meter." Obviously what is a meter in one language-game need not be a meter in the other. Thus, Wittgenstein's view seems to be that by introducing a new criterion for something's being a meter long, we have introduced a new language-game, a new sense of the term "meter," and a new concept of meter. Such a position is indicated by Wittgenstein's comment:

> We can speak of measurements of time in which there is a different, and as we should say a greater, exactness than in the measurement of time by a pocketwatch; in which the words "to set the clock to the exact time" have a different, though related meaning. . . .   (*PI*, § 88)

Returning to our basketball analogy, suppose that the National Collegiate Athletic Association ruled that, henceforth, a player can score a field goal by pushing the ball *upward* through the basket. Obviously, this would involve changing the rules of basketball. And to some extent, by introducing this new criterion, the rules governing the use or "grammar" of the term "field goal" would be altered. To put it somewhat dramatically (in the Wittgensteinian style), a new *essence* of field goal would be created. (Cf. "The mathematician creates *essence*" [*RFM*, I, § 32].) For Wittgenstein, not only is it the case that the criteria we use "give our words their common meanings" (*BB*, p. 57) and that to explain the criteria we use is to explain the meanings of words (*BB*, p. 24), but also it is the case that to introduce a new criterion of Y is to define a new concept of Y.[9]

In summary, we can roughly and schematically characterize Wittgenstein's notion of criterion in the following way: X is a criterion of Y in situations of type S if the very meaning or definition of 'Y' (or, as Wittgenstein might have put it, if the "grammatical" rules for the use of 'Y')[10] justify the claim that one can recognize, see, detect, or determine the applicability of 'Y' on the basis of X in *normal* situations of type S. Hence, if the above relation obtains between X and Y, and if someone admits that X but denies

Y, the burden of proof is upon him to show that something is abnormal in the situation. In a normal situation, the problem of gathering evidence which justifies concluding Y from X simply does not arise.

IV

The following passage occurs in the *Blue Book* (p. 24):

> When we learnt the use of the phrase "so-and-so has toothache" we were pointed out certain kinds of behavior of those who were said to have toothache. As an instance of these kinds of behavior let us take holding your cheek. Suppose that by observation I found that in certain cases whenever these first criteria told me a person had toothache, a red patch appeared on the person's cheek. Supposing I now said to someone "I see A has toothache, he's got a red patch on his cheek." He may ask me "How do you know A has toothache when you see a red patch?" I would then point out that certain phenomena had always coincided with the appearance of the red patch.
>
> Now one may go on and ask: "How do you know that he has got toothache when he holds his cheek?" The answer to this might be, "I say, *he* has toothache when he holds his cheek because I hold my cheek when I have toothache." But what if we went on asking:—"And why do you suppose that toothache corresponds to his holding his cheek just because your toothache corresponds to your holding your cheek?" You will be at a loss to answer this question, and find that here we strike rock bottom, that is we have come down to conventions.

It would seem that, on Wittgenstein's view, empirical justification of the claim to see, recognize, or know that such and such is the case *on the basis of some observable feature or state of affairs* would have to rest upon inductions from observed correlations, so that, if a person claims that Y is the case on the grounds that X is the case, in answer to the question "Why does the fact that X show that Y?" he would have to cite either conventions or observed correlations linking X and Y. Thus Wittgenstein appears to be arguing that the possibility of ever inferring a person's toothache from his behavior requires the existence of a criterion of toothache that can sometimes be observed to obtain. A generalized form of this argument leads to the conclusion that "an 'inner process' stands in need of outward criteria" (*PI*, § 580).

As an illustration of Wittgenstein's reasoning, consider the following example: It appears to be the case that the measurement of the alcohol content of the blood affords a reasonably reliable index of intoxication. On the basis of this empirical information, we may sometimes justify the claim that X is intoxicated by showing that the alcohol content of his blood is higher than some specified percentage. But now consider the justification of the claim that blood-alcohol is in fact an index of intoxication. On Wittgenstein's view, the justification of *this* claim must rest ultimately upon correlating cases of intoxication with determinations of high blood-alcohol content. But the observations required for this correlation could be made only if there exist independent techniques for identifying each of the correlated items. In any particular case, these independent techniques may themselves be based upon further empirical correlations; we might justify the claim that the blood-alcohol content is high by appealing to some previously established correlation between the presence of blood-alcohol and some test result. But ultimately according to Wittgenstein, we must come upon identifying techniques based not upon further empirical correlations, but rather upon definitions or conventions which determine criteria for applying the relevant predicates. This is why Wittgenstein can say that a symptom is "a phenomenon of which experience has taught us that it coincided, in some way or other with the phenomenon which is our defining criterion" (*BB*, p. 25).

A similar argument has recently been given by Sidney Shoemaker, who writes:

> If we know psychological facts about other persons at all, we know them on the basis of their behavior (including, of course, their verbal behavior). Sometimes we make psychological statements about other persons on the basis of bodily or behavioral facts that are only contingently related to the psychological facts for which we accept them as evidence. But we do this only because we have discovered, or think we have discovered, empirical correlations between physical (bodily and behavioral) facts of a certain kind and psychological facts of a certain kind.

And if *all* relations between physical and psychological facts were contingent, it would be impossible for us to discover such correlations. . . . Unless some relationships between physical and psychological states are not contingent, and can be known prior to the discovery of empirical correlations, we cannot have even indirect inductive evidence for the truth of psychological statements about other persons, and cannot know such statements to be true or even probably true.[11]

Malcolm argues in a similar manner in *Dreaming*.[12]

Of course, Wittgenstein did not claim that all predicates presuppose criteria of applicability. For example, Wittgenstein probably did not think that we, in general, see, tell, determine, or know that something is red on the basis of either a criterion or a symptom. The relevant difference between ascriptions of "red" and third-person ascriptions of "pain" is that we generally see, recognize, determine, or know that another is in pain on the basis of something which is not the pain itself (as for example, behavior and circumstances) whereas, if it made any sense at all to say we generally see, recognize, etc., that an object is red on the basis of something, what could this something be other than just the object's redness? But Wittgenstein's use of the term "criterion" seems to preclude redness being a criterion of redness. If someone asks "How do you know or tell that an object is red?" it would not, in general, do to answer "By its redness." (Cf. Wittgenstein's comment "How do I know that this color is red?—It would be an answer to say: 'I have learnt English'" [*PI*, § 381].) Evidently, some color predicates and, more generally, what are sometimes called "sense datum" predicates (those that can be known to apply—as some philosophers put it—*immediately*), do not fall within the domain of arguments of the above type. But the predicates with which we assign "inner states" to another person are not of this sort. One recognizes that another is in a certain mental state, Y, on the basis of something, say, X. Now it is assumed that X must be either a criterion or symptom of Y. If X is a symptom, X must be known to be correlated with Y, and we may then inquire into the way in which this correlation was established. Again, X must have been observed to be correlated with a criterion of Y or with a symptom, X_1, of Y. On the second alternative, we

may inquire into the basis for holding that X_1 is a symptom of
Y. . . . Such a chain may go on for any distance you like, but it
cannot go on indefinitely. That is, at some point, we must come
to a criterion of Y. But once this conclusion has been accepted,
there appears to be no reasonable non-sceptical alternative to Wittgenstein's logical behaviorism, for if "inner" states require "outward" criteria, behavioral criteria are the only plausible candidates.

V

As a refutation of scepticism, the above argument certainly will
not do, for, at best, it supports Wittgenstein's position only on
the assumption that the sceptic is not right. That is, it demon-
strates that there must be criteria for psychological predicates by
assuming that such predicates are sometimes applied justifiably. A
sceptic who accepts the argument of Section IV could maintain his
position only by allowing that no one could have any idea of what
would show or even indicate that another is in pain, having a
dream, thinking, etc. In this section we shall show how Wittgenstein argues that that move would lead the sceptic to the absurd
conclusion that it must be impossible to teach the meaning of
these psychological predicates.
    "What would it be like if human beings showed no outward
signs of pain (did not groan, grimace, etc.)? Then it would be impossible to teach a child the use of the word 'toothache'" (PI,
§ 257). For just imagine trying to teach a child the meaning of the
term "toothache," say, on the supposition that there is absolutely
no way of telling whether the child—or anyone else for that matter
—is actually in pain. How would one go about it, if one had no
reason for believing that gross damage to the body causes pain or
that crying out, wincing, and the like indicate pain? ("How could
I even have come by the idea of another's experience if there is no
possibility of any evidence for it?" [BB, p. 46; cf. also BB, p. 48].)
    Again, what would show us that the child had grasped the
teaching? If anything would, the argument of Section IV requires
that there be a criterion of having succeeded in teaching the child.
(As Wittgenstein says of an analogous case, "If I speak of communicating a feeling to someone else, mustn't I in order to understand what I say know what I shall call the criterion of having
succeeded in communicating?" [BB, p. 185].) But the only

plausible criterion of this would be that the child applies the psychological predicates correctly (cf. *PI*, § 146); and since the sceptical position implies that there is no way of knowing if the child correctly applies such predicates, it would seem to follow that nothing could show or indicate that the child had learned what these terms mean.

We now have a basis for explicating the sense of "logical," which is involved in the claim that scepticism is a logically incoherent doctrine. What Wittgenstein holds is not that *"P and not-P"* are strictly deducible from the sceptic's position, but rather that the sceptic's view presupposes a deviation from the rules for the use of key terms. In particular, Wittgenstein holds that if the sceptic were right, the preconditions for teaching the meaning of the mental predicates of our ordinary language could not be satisfied.[13]

We now see too the point to the insistence that the sceptic's position must incorporate an extraordinary and misleading use of mental predicates. The sceptic's view is logically incompatible with the operation of the ordinary language rules for the application of these terms, and these rules determine their meanings. (Cf. "What *we* do is to bring words back from their metaphysical to their everyday usage" [*PI*, § 116].) As Wittgenstein diagnoses the sceptic's view, the sceptic does not have in mind any criteria of third person ascriptions when he denies that he can know if anyone else has pains (cf. *PI*, § 272). The sceptic tempts us to picture the situation as involving "a barrier which doesn't allow one person to come closer to another's experience than to the point of observing his behavior"; but, according to Wittgenstein, "on looking closer we find that we can't apply the picture" (*BB*, p. 56); no clear meaning can be attached to the sceptic's claim: no sense can even be given the hypothesis that other people feel "pains," as the sceptic uses the term "pain." ("For how can I even make the hypothesis if it transcends all possible experience?" [*BB*, p. 48].) And if the sceptic says, "But if I suppose that someone has a pain, then I am simply supposing that he has just the same as I have so often had." Wittgenstein can reply:

That gets us no further. It is as if I were to say: "You surely know what 'It is 5 o'clock here' means; so you also know what 'It's 5 o'clock on the sun' means. It means simply that it is just the same time there as it is here when it is 5 o'clock."—The explanation by means of *identity* does not work here. For I know well enough that one can call 5 o'clock here and 5 o'clock there "the same time," but what I do not know is in what cases one is to speak of its being the same time here and there.   (*PI,* § 350)

Thus, we can see how Wittgenstein supports his logical behaviorism: the argument in Section IV purports to show that the only plausible alternative to Wittgenstein's philosophical psychology is radical scepticism; and the argument in the present section rules out this alternative. For Wittgenstein, then, "the person of whom we say 'he has pains' is, by the rules of the game, the person who cries, contorts his face, etc." (*BB,* p. 68).

Undoubtedly, there is much that philosophers find comforting and attractive in Wittgenstein's philosophical psychology, but there are also difficulties in the doctrine which mar its attractiveness. To some of these difficulties, we shall now turn.

VI

In this section, we shall consider some consequences of applying the views just discussed to the analysis of dreaming, and we shall attempt to show that the conclusions to which these views lead are counter-intuitive.

According to Wittgenstein, we are to understand the concept of dreaming in terms of the language-game(s) in which "dream" plays a role and, in particular, in terms of the language-game of dream telling. For, to master the use of the word "dream" is precisely to learn what it is to find out that someone has dreamed, to tell what someone has dreamed, to report one's own dreams, and so on. Passages in the *Investigations* (e.g., *PI,* pp. 184, 222–223) indicate that for Wittgenstein a criterion of someone's having dreamed is the dream report. On this analysis, sceptical doubts about dreams arise when we fail to appreciate the logical bond between statements about dreams and statements about dream reports. The sceptic treats the dream report as, at best, an empirical correlate of the occurrence of a dream: a symptom that is, at any event, no more reliable than the memory of the subject who reports the dream. But, according to Wittgenstein, once we have understood the criterial relation between dream reporting and dreaming, we see that "the question whether the dreamer's memory deceives him when he reports the dream after waking cannot arise . . ." (*PI*, p. 222). (Compare: "Once we understand the rules for playing chess, the question whether a player has won when he has achieved checkmate cannot arise.")

The rules articulating the criteria for applying the word "dream" determine a logical relation between dreaming and reporting dreams. Moreover, the set of such rules fixes the language-game in which "dream" has its role and hence determines the meaning of the word.

It is important to notice that there are a number of *prima facie* objections to this analysis which, though perhaps not conclusive, supply grounds for questioning the doctrines which lead to it. Though we could perhaps learn to live with these objections were no other analyses available, when seen from the vantage point of an alternative theory they indicate deep troubles with Wittgenstein's views.

(1) Given that there exist no criteria for first person applications of many psychological predicates ("pain," "wish," or the like), it is unclear how the first person aspects of the game played with these predicates are to be described. Wittgenstein does not appear to present a coherent account of the behavior of predicates whose applicability is not determined by criteria. On the other hand, the attempt to characterize "I dreamt" as criterion-governed leads immediately to absurdities. Thus in Malcolm's *Dreaming* it is suggested that:

> If a man wakes up with the impression of having seen and done various things, and if it is known that he did not see and do those things, then it is known that he dreamt them. . . . When he says "I dreamt so and so" he implies, first, that it seemed to him on waking up as if the so and so had occurred and second, that the so and so did not occur.   (p. 66)

That this is an incredibly counter-intuitive analysis of our concept of dreaming hardly needs mentioning. We ask the reader to consider the following example: A person, from time to time, gets the strange feeling that, shortly before, he had seen and heard his father commanding him to come home. One morning he wakes with this feeling, knowing full well that his father is dead. Now we are asked by Malcolm to believe that the person *must have dreamt* that he saw and heard his father: supposedly, it would be logically absurd for the person to claim to have this feeling and deny that he had dreamt it!

(2) Wittgenstein's view appears to entail that no sense can be made of such statements as "Jones totally forgot the dream he had last night," since we seem to have no criteria for determining the truth of such a statement. (We have in mind the case in which Jones is totally unable to remember having dreamed and no behavioral manifestations of dreaming were exhibited.) It is sometimes denied that observations of what people ordinarily say are relevant to a description of ordinary language. But insofar as statements about what we would say are susceptible to empirical disconfirmation, the claim that we would feel hesitation about saying that someone completely forgot his dream appears to be just false.[14]

(3) The Wittgensteinian method of counting concepts is certainly not an intuitive one. Consider Malcolm's analysis of dreaming again. Malcolm realizes that sometimes, on the basis of a person's behavior during sleep, we say that he had a dream, even though he is unable to recall a dream upon awaking. But, in such cases, Malcolm claims, "our words . . . have no clear sense" (*Dreaming,* p. 62). On the other hand, Malcolm admits that there is a *sense* of the term "nightmare" where behavior during sleep is the criterion. However, a different concept of dreaming is supposedly involved in this case. An analogous situation is treated in the *Blue Book* (p. 63), where Wittgenstein writes:

> If a man tries to obey the order "Point to your eye," he may do many different things, and there are many different criteria which he will accept for having pointed to his eye. If these criteria, as they usually do, coincide, I may use them alternately and in different combinations to show me that I have touched my eye. If they don't coincide, I shall have to distinguish between different senses of the phrase "I touch my eye" or "I move my finger towards my eye."

Following this suggestion of Wittgenstein, Malcolm distinguishes not only different senses of the term "dream," but also different concepts of sleep—one based upon report, one based upon nonverbal behavior. But surely, this is an unnatural way of counting concepts. Compare Malcolm's two concepts of sleep with a case where it really does seem natural to say that a special concept of sleep has been employed, viz., where we say of a hibernating bear that it sleeps through the winter.

(4) As Malcolm points out, the language-game *now* played with "dream" seems to exhibit no criteria which would enable one to determine the precise duration of dreams. Hence, it would seem to follow (as Malcolm has noticed) that scientists who have attempted to answer such questions as, "How long do dreams last?" are involved in conceptual confusions rather than empirical determinations. For such questions cannot be answered without adopting criteria for ascribing the relevant properties to dreams. But since, on Wittgenstein's view, to adopt such new criteria for the use of a word is, to that extent, to change its meaning, it follows that the concept of "dream" that such researchers employ is not the ordinary concept and hence that the measurements they effect are not, strictly speaking, measurements of *dreams*.[15] The notion that adopting any test for dreaming which arrives at features of dreams not determinable from the dream report thereby alters the concept of a dream seems to run counter to our intuitions about the goals of psychological research. It is not immediately obvious that the psychologist who says he has found a method of measuring the duration of dreams *ipso facto* commits the fallacy of ambiguity.[16]

(5) Consider the fact that such measures as EEG, eye-movements and "dream-behavior" (murmuring, tossing, etc., during sleep) correlate reasonably reliably with one another and dream reports. The relation between, say, EEG and dream reports is clearly not criterial; no one holds that EEG is a criterion of dream reports. It would seem then that, on Wittgenstein's view, EEG provides us with, at best, a symptom of positive dream reports; and symptoms are supposedly discovered by observing co-occurrences. The difficulty, however, is that this makes it unclear how the expectation that such a correlation must obtain could have been a rational expectation even *before* the correlation was experimentally confirmed. One cannot have an inductive generalization over no observations; nor, in this case, was any higher level "covering law" used to infer the probability of a correlation between EEG and

dream reports. Given Wittgenstein's analysis of the concept of dreaming, not only do the researches of psychologists into the nature of dreams appear mysterious, but even these experimental predictions which proved to be *true* are made to seem irrational.

The difficulties we have mentioned are not peculiar to the Wittgensteinian analysis of dreams. Most of them have counterparts in the analyses of sensation, perception, intention, etc. Whether or not these difficulties can be obviated, in some way, noticing them provides a motive for re-examining the deeper doctrines upon which Wittgensteinian analyses of psychological terms are based.

VII

The Wittgensteinian argument of Section IV rests on the premiss that if we are justified in claiming that one can tell, recognize, see, or determine that 'Y' applies on the basis of the presence of X, then either X is a criterion of Y or observations have shown that X is correlated with Y. Wittgenstein does not present any justification for this premiss in his published writings. Evidently, some philosophers find it self-evident and hence in need of no justification. We, on the other hand, far from finding this premiss self-evident, believe it to be false. Consider: one standard instrument used in the detection of high-speed, charged particles is the Wilson cloud-chamber. According to present scientific theories, the formation of tiny, thin bands of fog on the glass surface of the instrument indicates the passage of charged particles through the chamber. It is obvious that the formation of these streaks is not a Wittgensteinian criterion of the presence and motion of these particles in the apparatus. That one can detect these charged particles and determine their paths by means of such devices is surely not, by any stretch of the imagination, a *conceptual* truth. C. T. R. Wilson did not learn what "path of a charged particle" means by having the cloud-chamber explained to him: he *discovered* the method, and the discovery was contingent upon recognizing the empirical fact that ions could act as centers of condensation in a supersaturated vapor. Hence, applying Wittgenstein's own test for non-criterionhood (see above), the formation of a cloud-chamber track cannot be a criterion of the presence and motion of charged particles.

It is equally clear that the basis for taking these streaks as indicators of the paths of the particles is not observed *correlations* between streaks and some criterion of motion of charged particles. (What criterion for determining the path of an electron could Wilson have used to establish such correlations?) Rather, scientists were able to give compelling explanations of the formation of the streaks on the hypothesis that high-velocity, charged particles were passing through the chamber; on this hypothesis, further predictions were made, tested, and confirmed; no other equally plausible explanation is available; and so forth.

Such cases suggest that Wittgenstein failed to consider all the possible types of answers to the question, "What is the justification for the claim that one can tell, recognize, or determine that Y applies on the basis of the presence of X?" For, where Y is the predicate "is the path of a high-velocity particle," X need not have the form of either a criterion or a correlate.

Wittgensteinians may be tempted to argue that cloud-chamber tracks really are criteria, or symptoms observed to be correlated with criteria, of the paths of charged particles. To obviate this type of counter, we wish to stress that the example just given is by no means idiosyncratic. The reader who is not satisfied with it will easily construct others from the history of science. What is at issue is the possibility of a type of justification which consists in neither the appeal to criteria nor the appeal to observed correlations. If the Wittgensteinian argument we have been considering is to be compelling, some grounds must be given for the exhaustiveness of these types of justification. This, it would seem, Wittgenstein has failed to do.

It is worth noticing that a plausible solution to the problem raised in VI. 5 can be given if we consider experiments with dreams and EEG to be analogous to the cloud-chamber case. That is, we can see how it could be the case that the correlation of EEG with dream reports was anticipated prior to observation. The dream report was taken by the experiments to be an indicator of a psychological event occurring prior to it. Given considerations about the relation of cortical to psychological events, and given also the theory of EEG, it was predicted that the EEG should provide an index of the occurrence of dreams. From the hypothesis that dream reports and EEG readings are both indices of the same psychological events, it could be deduced that they ought to be reliably correlated with one another, and this deduction in fact proved to be correct.

This situation is not at all unusual in the case of explanations based upon theoretical inferences to events underlying observable syndromes. As Meehl and Cronbach have pointed out, in such cases the validity of the "criterion" is often nearly as much at issue as the validity of the indices to be correlated with it.[17] The successful prediction of the correlation on the basis of the postulation of a common etiology is taken both as evidence for the existence of the cause and as indicating the validity of each of the correlates as an index of its presence.

In this kind of case, the justification of existential statements is thus identical neither with an appeal to criteria nor with an appeal to symptoms. Such justifications depend rather on appeals to the simplicity, plausibility, and predictive adequacy of an explanatory system as a whole, so that it is incorrect to say that relations between statements which are mediated by such explanations are either logical in Wittgenstein's sense or contingent in the sense in which this term suggests simple correlation.

It cannot be stressed too often that there exist patterns of justificatory argument which are not happily identified either with appeals to symptoms or with appeals to criteria, and which do not in any obvious way rest upon such appeals. In these arguments, existential claims about states, events, and processes, which are *not* directly observable are susceptible of justification despite the fact that no *logical* relation obtains between the predicates ascribing such states and predicates whose applicability *can* be directly observed. There is a temptation to hold that in such cases there *must* be a criterion, that there must be some set of possible observations which would settle *for sure* whether the theoretical predicate applies. But we succumb to this temptation at the price of postulating stipulative definitions and conceptual alterations which fail to correspond to anything we can discover in the course of empirical arguments. The counter-intuitive features of philosophic analyses based on the assumption that there must be criteria are thus not the consequences of a profound methodological insight, but rather a projection of an inadequate philosophical theory of justification.

VIII

It might be replied that the above examples do not constitute counter-instances to Wittgenstein's criterion-correlation premiss since Wittgenstein may have intended his principle to be applicable only in the case of ordinary language terms which, so it might seem, do not function within the framework of a theory. It is perhaps possible to have indicators that are neither criteria nor symptoms of such highly theoretical entities as electrons and positrons, but the terms used by ordinary people in everyday life are obviously(?) in a different category. (Notice that Wittgenstein considers "making scientific hypotheses and theories" a different "game" from such "language-games" as "describing an event" and "describing an immediate experience" [BB, pp. 67–68; Cf. PI, § 23].) Hence, Wittgenstein might argue, it is only in the case of ordinary language terms that the demand for criteria is necessary.

Once one perceives the presuppositions of Wittgenstein's demand for criteria, however, it becomes evident that alternatives to Wittgenstein's analyses of ordinary language mental terms should at least be explored. Perhaps, what we all learn in learning what such terms as "pain" and "dream" mean are not criterial connections which map these terms severally onto characteristic patterns of behavior. We may instead form complex conceptual connections which interrelate a wide variety of mental states. It is to such a conceptual system that we appeal when we attempt to explain someone's behavior by reference to his motives, intentions, beliefs, desires, or sensations. In other words, in learning the language, we develop a number of intricately interrelated "mental concepts" which we use in dealing with, coming to terms with, understanding, explaining, interpreting, etc., the behavior of other human beings (as well as our own). In the course of acquiring these mental concepts we develop a variety of beliefs involving them. Such beliefs result in a wide range of expectations about how people are likely to behave. Since only a portion of these beliefs are confirmed in the normal course, these beliefs and the conceptual systems which they articulate are both subject to correction and alteration as the consequence of our constant interaction with other people.

On this view, our success in accounting for the behavior on the basis of which mental predicates are applied might properly be thought of as supplying *evidence* for the existence of the mental processes we postulate. It does so by attesting to the adequacy of the conceptual system in terms of which the processes are understood. The behavior would be, in that sense, analogous to the cloud-chamber track on the basis of which we detect the presence and motion of charged particles. Correspondingly, the conceptual system is analogous to the physical *theory* in which the properties of these particles are formulated.

If something like this should be correct, it would be possible, at least in theory, to reconstruct and describe the conceptual system involved and then to obtain some confirmation that the putative system is in fact employed by English speakers. For example, confirmation might come *via* the usual methods of "reading off" the conceptual relations in the putative system and *matching them* against the linguistic intuitions of native speakers. Thus, given that a particular conceptual system is being employed, certain statements should strike native speakers as nonsensical, others should seem necessarily true, others should seem ambiguous, others empirically false, and so on, all of which would be testable.

To maintain that there are no criterial connections between pains and behavior does not commit us to holding that the fact that people often feel *pains* when they cry out is *just* a contingent fact (in the sense in which it is just a contingent fact that most of the books in my library are unread). The belief that other people feel pains is not gratuitous even on the view that there are no criteria of pains. On the contrary, it provides the only plausible explanation of facts I know about the way that they behave in and *vis à vis* the sorts of situations I find painful. These facts are, of course, enormously complex. The "pain syndrome" includes not only correlations between varieties of overt behaviors but also more subtle relations between pain and motivations, utilities, desires, and so on. Moreover, I confidently expect that there must exist reliable members of this syndrome other than the ones with which I am currently familiar. I am in need of an explanation of the reliability and fruitfulness of this syndrome, an explanation which reference to the occurrence of pains supplies. Here, as elsewhere, an "outer" syndrome stands in need of an inner process.

Thus it is at least conceivable that a non-Wittgensteinian account ought to be given of the way children learn the mental predicates. (It is, at any event, sufficient to notice that such an account *could* be given, that there exist alternatives to Wittgenstein's doctrine.) For example, if the concept of dreaming is *inter alia* that of an inner event which takes place during a definite stretch of "real" time, which causes such involuntary behavior as moaning and murmuring in one's sleep, tossing about, etc., and which is remembered when one correctly reports a dream, then there are a number of ways in which a child might be supposed to "get" this concept other than by learning criteria for the application of the word "dream." Perhaps it is true of many children that they learn what a dream is by being told that what they have just experienced was a dream. Perhaps it is also true of many children that, having grasped the notions of *imagining* and *sleep,* they learn what a dream is when they are told that dreaming is something like imagining in your sleep.

But does this imply that children learn what a dream is "from their own case?" If this is a logical rather than psychological question, the answer is "Not necessarily": a child who never dreamed, but who was very clever, might arrive at an understanding of what dreams are just on the basis of the sort of theoretical inference we have described above. For our notion of a dream is that of a mental event having various properties that are required in order to explain the characteristic features of the dream-behavior syndrome. For example, dreams occur during sleep, have duration, sometimes cause people who are sleeping to murmur or to toss, can be described in visual, auditory, or tactile terms, are sometimes remembered and sometimes not, are sometimes reported and sometimes not, sometimes prove frightening, sometimes are interrupted before they are finished, etc. But if these are the sorts of facts that characterize our concept of dream, then there seems to be nothing which would, in principle, prevent a child who never dreamed from arriving at this notion.

A similar story might be told about how such sensation terms as "pain" are learned and about the learning of such quasi-dispositionals as "having a motive." In each case, since the features that we in fact attribute to these states, processes, or dispositions are just those features we know they must have if they are to fulfill their role in explanations of behavior, etiology, personality, etc., it would seem that there is nothing about them the child could not in principle learn by employing the pattern of inference we have described above, and hence nothing that he could in principle learn *only* by an analogy to his own case.

Now it might be argued that the alternative to Wittgenstein's position we have been sketching is highly implausible. For, if children do have to acquire the complicated conceptual system our theory requires to understand and use mental predicates, surely they would have to be taught this system. And the teaching would surely have to be terribly involved and complex. But as a matter of fact, children do not require any such teaching at all, and hence we should conclude that our alternative to Wittgenstein's criterion view is untenable.

The force of this argument, however, can to some extent be dispelled if we consider the child's acquisition of, e.g., the grammar of a natural language. It is clear that, by some process we are only now beginning to understand, a child, on the basis of a relatively short "exposure" to utterances in his language, develops capacities for producing and understanding "novel" sentences (sentences which he has never previously heard or seen). The exercise of these capacities, so far as we can tell, "involve" the use of an intricate system of linguistic rules of very considerable generality and complexity.[18] That the child is not taught (in any ordinary sense) any such system of rules is undeniable. These capacities seem to develop naturally in the child in response to little more than contact with a relatively small number of sentences uttered in ordinary contexts in everyday life.[19] Granting for the moment that the apparent complexity of such systems of rules is not somehow an artifact of an unsatisfactory theory of language, the fact that the child develops these linguistic capacities shows that a corresponding "natural" development of a system of mental concepts may not, as a matter of brute fact, require the sort of explicit teaching a person needs to master, say, calculus or quantum physics.

IX

It is easily seen that this unabashedly nonbehavioristic view avoids each of the difficulties we raised regarding Wittgenstein's analyses of mental predicates. Thus the asymmetry between first and third person uses of "dream" discussed in Section VI need not arise since there need be no criteria for "X dreamed," *whatever* value X takes: we do not have the special problem of characterizing the meaning of "I dreamed" since "dream" in this context means just what it means in third person contexts, viz., "a series of thoughts, images, or emotions occurring during sleep." Again, it is now clear why people find such remarks as "Jones totally forgot what and that he dreamed last night" perfectly sensible. It is even clear how such assertions might be confirmed. Suppose, for example, that there exists a neurological state a such that there is a very high correlation between the presence of a and such dream behavior as tossing in one's sleep, crying out in one's sleep, reporting dreams, and so on. Suppose, too that there exists some neurological state β such that whenever β occurs, experiences that the subject has had just prior to β are forgotten. Suppose, finally, that sometimes we observe sequences, a, β, and that such sequences are not followed by dream reports though the occurrences of a are accompanied by other characteristic dream behaviors. It seems clear that the reasonable thing to say in such a case is that the subject has dreamed and forgotten his dream. And since we have postulated no criterion for dreaming, but only a syndrome of dream behaviors each related to some inner psychological event, we need have no fear that, in saying what it is reasonable to say, we have changed the meaning of "dream." We leave it to the reader to verify that the other objections we raised against the Wittgensteinian analysis of "dream" also fail to apply to the present doctrine.

Thus, once we have abandoned the arguments for a criterial connection between statements about behavior and statements about psychological states, the question remains open whether applications of ordinary language psychological terms on the basis of observations of behavior ought not themselves be treated as theoretical inferences to underlying mental occurrences. The question whether such statements as "He moaned because he was in pain" function to explain behavior by relating it to an assumed mental event cannot be settled simply by reference to ordinary linguistic usage. Answering this question requires broadly empirical investigations into the nature of thought and concept formation in normal human beings. What is at issue is the question of the role of theory construction and theoretical inference in thought and argument outside pure science. Psychological investigations indicate that much everyday conceptualization depends on the exploitation of theories and explanatory models in terms of which experience is integrated and understood.[20] Such pre-scientific theories, far from being mere functionless "pictures," play an essential role in determining the sorts of perceptual and inductive expectations we form and the kind of arguments and explanations we accept. It thus seems *possible* that the correct view of the functioning of ordinary language mental predicates would assimilate applying them to the sorts of processes of theoretical inference operative in scientific psychological explanation. If this is correct, the primary difference between ordinary and scientific uses of psychological predicates would be just that the processes of inference which are made explicit in the latter case remain implicit in the former.

We can now see what should be said in reply to Wittgenstein's argument that the possibility of teaching a language rests upon the existence of criteria. Perhaps teaching a word would be impossible if it could not sometimes be determined that the student has mastered the use of the word. But this does not entail that there need be *criteria* for "X learned the word *w*." All that is required is that we must sometimes have good reasons for saying that the word has been mastered; and this condition is satisfied when, for example, the simplest and most plausible explanation available of the verbal behavior of the student is that he has learned the use of the word.

Chapter 2

The Appeal to Tacit Knowledge in Psychological Explanations

> Remember thee!
> Ay, thou poor ghost, while memory holds a seat
> In this distracted globe.
>
> *Hamlet,* Act I, scene V

In this paper I want to defend "intellectualist" accounts of mental competences and to suggest that, in attributing tacit knowledge to organisms, intellectualist theories exploit a legitimate form of non-demonstrative inference: the inference from like effects to like causes. In passing, I shall have a few things to say about the distinction between knowing how and knowing that.

Here is the way we tie our shoes:

There is a little man who lives in one's head. The little man keeps a library. When one acts upon the intention to tie one's shoes, the little man fetches down a volume entitled *Tying One's Shoes.* The volume says such things as: "Take the left free end of the shoelace in the left hand. Cross the left free end of the shoelace over the right free end of the shoelace . . . ," etc.

When the little man reads the instruction 'take the left free end of the shoelace in the left hand', he pushes a button on a control panel. The button is marked 'take the left free end of a shoelace in the left hand'. When depressed, it activates a series of wheels, cogs, levers, and hydraulic mechanisms. As a causal consequence

This chapter was first presented in an APA symposium on Implicit Knowledge, December 28, 1968.

of the functioning of these mechanisms, one's left hand comes to seize the appropriate end of the shoelace. Similarly, *mutatis mutandis,* for the rest of the instructions.

The instructions end with the word 'end'. When the little man reads the word 'end', he returns the book of instructions to his library.

That is the way we tie our shoes.

What is wrong with this explanation?

In the first place, the details are surely incorrect. For example, the action of the arm and hand in tying a shoelace cannot literally be accounted for on mechanical and hydraulic principles. We shall presumably need chemical and electrical systems as well and, among these, feedback devices to mediate hand/eye coordinations. We are not, then, to take the foregoing account as proposing a serious theory of the physics of shoe tying.

Second, some of the behaviors we have supposed to be involved in shoe tying are of considerable complexity. It would seem, for example, that there can be no *single* button marked 'take the left free end of a shoelace in the left hand'. Seizing a shoelace involves the production of a complicated pattern of behavior having a characteristic unity and integrity of its own. A serious theory of the behavioral integrations involved in tying one's shoes must explicate this complexity.

There is, then, a problem about when we are to represent a given form of behavior as "complex" and what the theoretical consequences of such a representation might be. We shall return to this problem presently. Prima facie, however, grasping a shoelace should be considered complex behavior, because doing so involves the production of motions that also play a role in other actions.

We might thus consider expanding the population in one's head to include subordinate little men who superintend the execution of the "elementary" behaviors involved in complex sequences like grasping a shoelace. When the little man reads 'take the left free end of the shoelace in the left hand', we imagine him ringing up the shop foreman in charge of grasping shoelaces. The shop foreman goes about supervising that activity in a way that is, in essence, a microcosm of supervising tying one's shoe. Indeed the shop foreman might be imagined to superintend a detail of wage slaves, whose functions include: searching inputs for traces of shoelace, flexing and contracting fingers on the left hand, etc.

But these are matters of empirical detail. Psychologists too seek to carve nature at the joints: to assign to the operation of a single causal agent whatever aspects of behavior have a common etiology. So questions about how many little men there are and about what functions each little man superintends can be left to them. What this paper will be most concerned with is the philosophical opinion that there is something *methodologically* wrong with the sort of account I sketched.

It is alleged, for example, that this kind of explanation is viciously circular. And indeed there *would* be something wrong with an explanation that said, *"This* is the way we tie our shoes: we notify a little man in our head who does it for us." This account invites the question: "How does the little man do it?" but, *ex hypothesi*, provides no conceptual mechanisms for answering such questions.

But this sort of objection is irrelevant to the explanation I had envisaged. For my theory included a specification of instructions for tying one's shoes, and it was there that its explanatory power lay. In my story, appeals to the little man do not function as a way to avoid explaining how we tie our shoes. Rather the little man stands as a representative *pro tem* for psychological faculties which mediate the integration of shoe-tying behavior by applying information about how shoes are tied. I know of no correct psychological theory that offers a specification of these faculties. Assigning psychological functions to little men makes explicit our inability to provide an account of the mechanisms that mediate those functions.

We refine a psychological theory by replacing global little men by less global little men, each of whom has fewer unanalyzed behaviors to perform than did his predecessors. Though it may look as though proceeding in this way invites the proliferation of little men *ad infinitum,* this appearance is misleading.

A completed psychological theory must provide systems of instructions to account for the forms of behavior available to an organism, and it must do so in a way that makes reference to no unanalyzed psychological processes. One way of clarifying the latter requirement is the following. Assume that there exists a class of *elementary* instructions which the nervous system is specifically wired to execute. Each elementary instruction specifies an *elementary operation,* and an elementary operation is one which the normal nervous system can perform but of which it cannot perform a proper part. Intuitively speaking, the elementary operations are those which have no theoretically relevant internal structure. Now to say an operation is elementary is to say that certain kinds of "how"-questions cannot arise about it. In particular, we cannot ask for instructions for performing it by performing some further sequences of operations. (It makes sense to ask how to spell 'add' but not to ask how to spell 'n'.) So, given a list of elementary instructions for producing a type of behavior, we need no further instructions for carrying out the instructions on the list and no little men to supervise their execution. The nervous system carries out its complex operations in some way or other (i.e., by performing one or another sequence of elementary operations). But the nervous system performs elementary operations in no *way* at all: it simply performs them. If every operation of the nervous system is identical with some sequence of elementary operations, we get around proliferating little men by constraining a completed psychological theory to be written in sequences of elementary instructions (or, of course, in abbreviations of such sequences).

We have been suggesting that the distinction between the homunculus and the instructions whose performances he supervises is the distinction between what psychologists understand about the etiology of behavior and what they do not. The paradigmatic psychological theory is a list of instructions for producing behavior. A constraint upon the vocabulary in which the instructions are formulated is that its terms designate only operations that are elementary for the organism in question. The little man's how-to books are, then, written in this vocabulary. Since, *ex hypothesi,* the nervous system *just is* a device for performing elementary operations, the more we know about the little man's library, the less we need to know about the little man.

Or, to vary the image, every box name in a computer flow chart is the name of a problem. If the computer is to simulate behavior, every box name will be the name of a psychological problem. The problem is to specify a sequence of instructions which

(a) will convert the input to the box into the output from the box, and
(b) can be written in a way that mentions only operations that are elementary for the organism whose behavior we are trying to simulate.

The problem is solved (an optimal simulation is achieved) when instructions are formulated which satisfy both these conditions and which meet the usual methodological constraints upon theories: simplicity, conservatism, coherence with theories in related sciences, etc.

Philosophers who don't like the kind of psychological explanations I have been discussing have hoped to get mileage out of the distinction between "knowing how" and "knowing that." They hold that intellectualist explanations fudge the distinction between knowing how to do something and knowing how the thing is done. In particular, such explanations assume that in doing a thing one knows how to do, one employs the information that the thing can be done in such and such a way. In effect, intellectualist theories undertake to explain each bit of knowledge-how by postulating some corresponding bit of knowledge-that. Thus intellectualist theories appear to blur an important distinction.

Ryle, for example, says, "according to the (intellectualist) legend, whenever an agent does anything intelligently, his act is preceded and steered by another internal act of considering a regulative proposition appropriate to this practical problem" (1949, p. 31). But, he continues, this legend needs to be debunked. ". . . the general assertion that all intelligent performance requires to be prefaced by the consideration of appropriate propositions rings unplausibly, even when it is apologetically conceded that the required consideration is often very swift and may go quite unmarked by the agent . . . the intellectualist legend is false and . . . when we describe a performance as intelligent, this does not entail the double operation of considering and executing" (ibid., pp. 29–30).

The issue of consciousness lies athwart the issues about knowing how and knowing that. If the intellectualist says that in tying one's shoes, one rehearses shoe-tying instructions to oneself, then the intellectualist is wrong on a point of fact. Children perhaps give themselves instructions when they tie their shoes, and new sailors tie bowlines to the dictates of a small inner voice. But an adult tying his shoes normally has other things to think about. Indeed thinking about tying one's shoes may get in the way of doing it. "Thus the native hue of resolution is sicklied o'er with the pale cast of thought . . . ," etc.

Well, why doesn't the discussion end here? The intellectualist says we give ourselves instructions when we tie our shoes. But it is introspectively obvious that we normally do no such thing. Hence intellectualist accounts must be false.

One begins to see what is wrong with this argument when one notes that much of our behavior is responsive to internal and external stimuli we are unable to report. Psychologists are forever finding out surprising things about the etiology of our behavior, often by employing quite unsurprising methods of investigation.

For example: texture gradients, stereopsis, overlap, flow pattern, and other cues contribute to causally determining our visual estimates of depth. This is not a philosophical contention but a routine experimental finding. The significance of these sorts of variables can be demonstrated by untendentious employments of the method of differences. In a properly arranged experimental situation, any of these "cues" can make the difference between "seeing" depth and "seeing" a flat surface.

But, of course, no subject who is not himself sophisticated about psychology can *tell* you what cues determine his estimates of visual depth. It is a *discovery* that one responds to flow patterns in judging spatial relations, and there are, doubtless, many more such discoveries waiting to be made.

What is thus a matter of fact, and not of philosophy, is that the organism is unable to report a wide variety of its causal interactions with its environment. But it might well be argued that this fact does not demonstrate the methodological probity of intellectualist theories. For the intellectualist is required to say not just that there are causal interactions in which the organism is unconsciously involved, but also that there are unconscious processes of learning, storing, and applying rules which in some sense "go on" within the organism and contribute to the etiology of its behavior.

So, the anti-intellectualist argument could go like this: "Of course we are unconsciously affected by things like texture gradients, just as we are unconsciously affected by things like cosmic radiation. But intellectualists appeal to *unconscious mental operations;* and demonstrating unreportable causal agencies in perception provides no precedent for such an appeal."

The answer, surely, is this. If the story about the causal determination of depth estimates by texture gradients is true and if the central nervous system is the kind of organ most sensible people now think it is, then some of the things the central nervous system *does,* some of the physical transactions that take place in the central nervous system when we make estimates of depth, must satisfy such descriptions as 'monitoring texture gradients', 'processing information about texture gradients', 'computing derivatives of texture gradients', etc. For, on one hand, varying texture gradients does, in fact, cause concomitant variation in depth estimates, and, on the other, the central nervous system is the organ whose functioning mediates this causal relation. And it is a point of logic that the central nervous system *can* be the organ that mediates the causal relation between texture gradients and depth estimates only if its operations satisfy the sort of descriptions mentioned above, since whatever physical system mediates our perception of depth must, *ipso facto,* perform whatever operations are nomologically necessary and sufficient for depth perception. If, then, our perceptions of depth are mediated by the central nervous system and if depth estimates vary as a function of the first derivative of texture gradients, then among the operations of the central nervous system must be some which satisfy such descriptions as 'is computing the first derivative of texture gradient *t*'.

But perhaps this shows only that the notion of some physical system mediating causal relations like the one between texture gradients and depth perception is somehow confused. For how *could* some bioelectrical exchange in my nervous system satisfy a description like 'is processing information about texture gradients'? That is, how could an event which satisfies *that* sort of description also satisfy physiological descriptions like 'is the firing of a phase sequence of neurons'?

But this is an odd question. Suppose someone were to ask, "How *could* a contraction of the muscles of the heart count as the heart pumping the blood?" Well, we might explain, what the heart is doing when it contracts in that way is: forcing the blood through the arteries. Just so, what the nervous system is doing when it exhibits *that* pattern of firing is: computing the first derivative of a texture gradient. Of course this is not the sort of thing we find out just by looking at the heart (nervous system). To know this sort of thing is part of knowing how the circulatory (nervous) system works; hence it is to know something of what the heart (brain) does.

But doesn't the intellectualist account fudge the difference between knowing how and knowing that?

To begin with, there is not one but a family of distinctions that goes by that name.

There is, for example, the distinction between what we know how to do and what we know how to explain. The cases that come to mind here are skills, and the relevant gossip is that the best practitioner need not be the best teacher. (Analogously, many skills are best taught not by explanation but by example: golf, philosophy, etc.)

Again, there are cases where we know how to do X and can give an account of what we do when we do X, but where it seems clear that the ability to give the account is logically and psychologically independent of the abilities involved in X-ing. Thus if I think about it, I can tell you which fingers I put where when I type 'Afghanistan' or tie my shoes. So, I know how to do it, and I know that when I do it I do it *that* way. But what I do when I do it has, I imagine, very little or nothing to do with what I do when I explain how I do it. What suggests that this is so is that I don't have to think when I type 'Afghanistan' or tie my shoes, but I do have to think when I try to explain how I type 'Afghanistan' or tie my shoes. Many of the examples that come to mind here are habits, and the relevant gossip is that habits "run off automatically," are "smoother," "faster," "more unitary," etc., than corresponding unhabituated behaviors.

But this is too crude. For if tying my shoes is a habitual act, then typing 'Afghanistan' surely is not. I *learned* to tie my shoes, but I did not learn to type 'Afghanistan'. I have tied my shoes a thousand times before, but I cannot remember ever having typed 'Afghanistan' before. I am good at tying my shoes because I have practiced tying my shoes. But I am good at typing 'Afghanistan' because I have practiced typing things like 'the quick, sly fox jumped over the lazy brown dog'. There are, in short, many kinds of cases of knowing how, and being serious would involve distinguishing among them.

This much does seem clear: even where an agent knows how and is able to say how, there may be serious reasons for supposing that the logical and psychological relations between the two abilities are fortuitous. There is a real and important distinction between knowing how to do a thing and knowing how to explain how to do that thing. But *that* distinction is one that the intellectualist is perfectly able to honor. Dogs, cats, and preverbal children know how to do all sorts of things they can't explain how to do; the ability to give explanations is itself a skill—a special kind of knowing how, which presupposes general verbal facility at the very least. But what has this to do with the relation between knowing how and knowing *that*? And what is there here to distress an intellectualist?

Certain of the anti-intellectualist arguments fail to go through because they confuse knowing that with being able to explain how. Ryle argues that the humorist "knows how to make good jokes and how to detect bad ones, but he cannot tell us how to make good jokes and how to detect bad ones. . . . Efficient practice precedes the theory of it" (Ryle, 1949). From this Ryle infers that "some intelligent performances are not controlled by any anterior acknowledgment of the principles applied to them" (Ryle, 1949). But this conclusion does not follow unless an "acknowledgment" is taken to be some kind of an avowal. What follows is only that *if* intelligent performances are controlled by anterior acknowledgments of the principles applied in them, then it must be possible to "acknowledge" a principle (in whatever sense of acknowledging is relevant to the operation of that principle in controlling behavior), but to be unable to formulate the principle on demand. What, precisely, is the reason for believing that this is not possible?

If I know how to do X, it does not follow that I know how to explain how X is done. There is at least that much to the distinction between knowing how and knowing that. Are intellectualist accounts of having and exercising mental competences precluded by this consideration? There is another question with which this one must not be confused.

To ask whether the distinction between knowing how and knowing that vitiates intellectualist accounts of *mental competences* (such as the ability to play chess, type 'Afghanistan', or speak Latin) is *not* the same as asking whether the distinction between knowing how and knowing that vitiates putative intellectualist accounts of *mental traits* (like intelligence, stupidity, wit, sensibility, cupidity, judiciousness, and so on).

This distinction between mental traits and mental competences is important. If John can play chess, then there is a specific activity, chess playing, at which John is more or less good. Similarly for typing 'Afghanistan', speaking Latin, or any other mental competence that John may have. But if John is intelligent, there is no *specific* activity he need be good at, and if John is stupid, there is no specific activity he need be bad at. In this sense being intelligent is not a matter of *doing* something, and 'John is now being intelligent' is not a well-formed state description—unless it means "John is now doing something that it is intelligent of John to do."

Being able to play chess is being able to do a certain sort of thing; being intelligent is being able to do things in a certain way. That is why John can be good at playing chess or bad at speaking Latin but cannot be good at being intelligent or bad at being stupid. 'Being intelligent' and 'being stupid' do not name actions or types of actions; hence they do not name actions that can be performed well or badly.

Traits give rise to adverbs, competences to verbs: we exhibit our competences in our activities and our traits in our style. Thus one can type 'Afghanistan' dashingly, speak Latin amusingly, and play chess intelligently, but it won't go the other way 'round. There is no X that you can do chess-playingly, Latin-speakingly, or 'Afghanistan'-typingly. Things named by mental adverbs are categorically different from things named by mental verbs.

Now, according to Ryle, "the crucial objection to the intellectualist legend is this. The consideration of propositions is itself

an operation, the execution of which can be more or less intelligent, less or more stupid. But if, for any operation to be intelligently executed, a prior theoretical operation had first to be
performed and performed intelligently, it would be a logical
impossibility for anyone ever to break into the circle" (Ryle,
1949).

This is, I think, perfectly correct. The little man, as we might
say, has in his library pamphlets entitled *Tying One's Shoes,
Speaking Latin,* and *Typing 'Afghanistan',* but no pamphlet
entitled *Being Intelligent* or *Speaking Latin Fluently* or *Typing
'Afghanistan' with Panache.* There are no titles corresponding to
mental adverbials because the mental adverbials refer not to acts
the little man is required to execute, but rather to the manner or
quality of his performance qua executive. To put it another way,
the pamphlet the little man consults on how to speak Latin will
be the same pamphlet he consults on how to speak Latin well.
This had better be true on threat of a version of Ryle's regress: if
instructions for speaking Latin are distinct from instructions for
speaking Latin well, then these latter must, in turn, be distinct
from instructions for speaking ((Latin well) well) and so on *ad
infinitum.* Again: 'speaking Latin well' is not the name of an activity distinct from that of speaking Latin. We learn to speak Latin
well by practicing speaking Latin *tout court.* The man who is
speaking Latin and the man who is speaking Latin well are doing
the same thing, though the second man is doing it better.

In short, the intellectualist legend is not about the mental adverbials but about mental competence terms, and a vicious circle
would indeed be generated if we attempted to apply the intellectualist model for having and exercising mental *competences* to
the explanation of having or exhibiting mental *traits.* But there
is nothing in the intellectualist position that commits the holder
of it to any such error. Intellectualism is a theory about the role
that mental processes play in the production of behavior—but
having a trait is not a matter of producing behavior.

Someone may know how to X and not know how to answer
such questions as "how does one X?" But the intellectualist account of X-ing says that, whenever you X, the little man in your
head has access to and employs a manual on X-ing; and surely,

whatever is his is yours. So, again, how are intellectualist theories to be squared with the distinction between knowing how and knowing that?

The problem can be put in the following way. Intellectualists want to argue that cases of X-ing involve employing rules the explication of which is tantamount to a specification of how to X. However, they want to deny that anyone who employs such rules *ipso facto* knows the answer to the question "How does one X?"

What, then, *are* we to say is the epistemic relation an agent necessarily bears to rules he regularly employs in the integration of behavior? There is a classical intellectualist suggestion: if an agent regularly employs rules in the integration of behavior, then if the agent is unable to report these rules, then it is necessarily true that the agent has *tacit* knowledge of them.

So far, of course, this is just a way of talking. The serious questions are: what, if anything, would make it reasonable to decide to talk this way, and, if we decide to talk this way, what kinds of evidence should we take to be relevant to assessing claims that some organism tacitly knows some proposition? The following remarks are intended to be pertinent to both these questions.

Although an organism can know how to X without knowing the answer to the question "How does one X?," it cannot know how to X unless there *is* an answer to the question "How does one X?" Now, one kind of requirement it would be rational to place upon a psychological theory is this: for every behavior an organism knows how to perform, a psychological theory of that organism must supply an answer to the question "How does one produce behaviors of that kind?"

Not every way of formulating a psychological theory does, in fact, permit it to meet this requirement. For example, a psychological theory might be formulated as a set of laws that relate the behavior of an organism to its inputs or to its neurological states or to both. Such a theory might, in principle, correctly predict each occurrence of a certain type of behavior, thus explaining the occurrences by subsuming them under general laws. Yet this kind of theory would not, in any obvious sense, provide answers to the question "How does one produce behaviors of that type?," and hence would fail to satisfy the condition we have stipulated.

I think these considerations underlie one of the more funda-mental methodological worries in contemporary psychology. Psychologists in the tradition of American behaviorism, who have taken the nomological-deductive model of scientific explana-tions as self-evidently appropriate for the formalization of psy-chological theories, have had a gnawing hunch that the kinds of questions about behavior they seek to answer are not the kinds of questions that concern theorists interested in the machine simula-tion of behavior. Now if what we have been saying is correct, this may be literally true. For a psychological model in the form of a machine program for simulating the behavior of an organism ipso facto provides, for each type of behavior in the repertoire of that organism, a putative answer to the question "How does one pro-duce behaviors of that type?," the form of the answer being a set of specific instructions for producing the behavior by performing a set of machine operations. Hence to be interested in simulating behavior is to be interested in a range of "how"-questions about behavior that psychological theories built on the nomological-deductive model are not designed to answer. This is a state of affairs which ought to give philosophers of science pause, since it suggests that scientific theories may compete not only in such well-known respects as predictive power, simplicity, and so on, but also in the range of types of questions to which they seek to provide answers.

So, now, the situation is this: not only is it the case that an organism can know how to X only if there is an answer to the question "How do you X?," but also: if an organism knows how to X, then nothing is a simulation of the behavior of the organism which fails to provide an answer to the question "How do you X?"

Now I want to say: if X is something an organism knows how to do but is unable to explain how to do, and if S is some sequence of operations, the specification of which would constitute an answer to the question "How do you X?," and if an optimal simulation of the behavior of the organism X is by running through the sequence of operations specified by S, then the organism *tacitly knows* the answer to the question "How do you X?," and S is a formulation of the organism's tacit knowledge.

This, however, leaves us in a slightly curious conceptual situation.

On the present account, "tacit knowledge" is, *inter alia,* a theoretical term in psychology. The term is introduced by reference to the computational operations of some optimal simulation of an organism, but the relation that the term designates presumably holds between the organism itself and some proposition, rule, maxim, or technique. And this might appear paradoxical. For how could *any* fact about the computational operations of some *machine* (even a machine that optimally simulates the behavior of an organism) provide grounds for asserting that an epistemic relation holds between an organism and a proposition? That is, in attributing tacit knowledge to an organism, we infer from a fact about a simulation of the organism to a fact about the mental life of the organism. And one might reasonably want to know what sort of inference this could possibly be.

This is as much a problem about machines as about organisms. Let us start with the former.

In describing the propositions, maxims, or instructions that a machine employs in the computation of its output, we are *ipso facto* describing the etiology of its output. After all, what happens when a computer "understands" or "executes" a certain set of "instructions" is simply that some very complex physical system changes physical states in a certain characteristic way. A programming language mediates between these physical states and English (roughly) by assigning the machine states to sentences of English in a way that preserves desired logical-mathematical relations among these sentences. (For example, the programming language may assign states of the machine to sentences of English in such fashion that if $S_1, S_2, \ldots, S_n$ is a sequence of machine states and $F_1, F_2, \ldots, F_{n-1}, F_n$ are the formulas of English assigned, respectively to $S_1, S_2, \ldots, S_{n-1}, S_n$, then the machine runs through the sequence of $S_1, S_2, \ldots, S_n$ only if $F_1, F_2, \ldots, F_{n-1}$ constitutes a proof of F_n. Patently, the assignment could be made in some other way; only, if it were, the machine's change of states could ipso facto not be interpreted as proofs.)

In short, a programming language can be thought of as establishing a mapping of the physical states of a machine onto sentences of English such that the English sentence assigned to a given state expresses the instruction the machine is said to be executing when it is in that state. Conversely, if L is a programming language for machine M, then it is a fact about each (computationally relevant) physical state of M that a certain sentence of English is its image under the mapping effect by L. Such facts are, one might say, ontologically kosher. In particular, each (computationally relevant) machine state S_i has a true description of the form: 'is the machine state assigned English formula F_i under the mapping effected by the programming language of the machine.' It follows, then, that to give the sequence of English sentences that the programming language of a machine associates with the physical states the machine runs through in the course of a given computation is ipso facto to give a true description of the causal sequence underlying the machine's production of output. It it thus to give one kind of description of the etiology of the machine's behavior.

Now suppose that there is a machine that optimally simulates the behavior of some organism. Then, first, a given type of behavior appears in the repertoire of the machine if and only if the corresponding type of behavior appears in the repertoire of the organism; and second, for each type of behavior in the repertoire of the machine, there exists a sequence of sentences of English that the programming language of the machine maps onto the sequence of machine states which terminates in that behavior. (I am assuming, for the sake of simplicity and because it doesn't matter, that the machine and the organism have only one way of producing the kind of behavior in question.) Finally, by the argument given above, such a sequence of English sentences is a true description of the etiology of the machine's output.

But, now, the following seems to me to be a reasonable principle of inductive inference. If D is a true description of the etiology of an event e, and if e' is an event numerically distinct from e but of the same kind as e, then it is reasonable to infer, *ceteris paribus*, that D is a true description of the etiology of e'. This is intended to be a formulation of the inductive principle that permits us to infer like causes from like effects. It goes without saying that a serious formulation of that principle would need to be hedged about with *caveats*: as, for example, that D contain only projectable predicates, that some restrictions be placed upon the cases when two events are to be counted as being of the same type, etc. None of this need concern us here, however, since our goal is only the modest one of displaying the inference from the computational character of machines to the tacit knowledge of the organisms they simulate as recognizably similar to orthodox patterns of scientific inference, whatever the detailed analysis of such patterns of inference may turn out to be.

If machines and organisms can produce behaviors of the same type and if descriptions of machine computations in terms of the rules, instructions, etc., that they employ are true descriptions of the etiology of their output, then the principle that licenses inferences from like effects to like causes must license us to infer that the tacit knowledge of organisms is represented by the programs of the machines that simulate their behavior. Of course this inference is analytic only where we know that a given simulation is optimal, and since claims for optimality are always empirical claims, we must run an inductive risk when we infer from the operations of a well-evidenced simulation to the tacit knowledge of an organism. Since the inference from like effects to like causes is an inductive inference, all that a well-evidenced simulation gives us is inductive grounds for believing that we have discovered something about the tacit knowledge of the organism we are studying. What more would it be rational to want? What more would it be possible to have?

Chapter 3

What Psychological States Are Not

(with Ned Block)

As far as anyone knows, different organisms are often in psychological states of exactly the same type at one time or another, and a given organism is often in psychological states of exactly the same type at different times. Whenever either is the case, we shall say of the psychological states of the organism(s) in question that they are *type identical.*

One thing that currently fashionable theories in the philosophy of mind often try to do is characterize the conditions for type identity of psychological states. For example, some varieties of philosophical behaviorism claim that two organisms are in type-identical psychological states if and only if certain of their behaviors or behavioral dispositions are type identical. Analogously, some (though not all) varieties of physicalism claim that organisms are in type-identical psychological states if and only if certain of their physical states are type identical.[1]

Insofar as they are construed as theories about the conditions for type identity of psychological states, it seems increasingly unlikely that either behaviorism or physicalism is true. Since the arguments for this conclusion are widely available in the literature, we shall provide only the briefest review here.[2]

The fundamental argument against behaviorism is simply that

A number of friends and colleagues have read earlier drafts. We are particularly indebted to Professors Richard Boyd, Donald Davidson, Michael Harnish, and Hilary Putnam for the care with which they read the paper and for suggestions that we found useful.

what an organism does or is disposed to do at a given time is a very complicated function of its beliefs and desires together with its current sensory inputs and memories. It is thus enormously unlikely that it will prove possible to pair behavioral predicates with psychological predicates in the way that behaviorism requires— namely, that for each type of psychological state, an organism is in that state if and only if a specified behavioral predicate is true of it. This suggests that behaviorism is overwhelmingly likely to be false simply in virtue of its empirical consequences and independent of its implausibility as a semantic thesis. Behaviorism cannot be true unless mind/behavior correlationism is true, and mind/behavior correlationism is not true.

The argument against physicalism rests upon the empirical likelihood that creatures of different composition and structure, which are in no interesting sense in identical physical states, can nevertheless be in identical psychological states; hence that types of psychological states are not in correspondence with types of physical states. This point has been made persuasively in Putnam's "Psychological Predicates" (1967). In essence, it rests on appeals to the following three kinds of empirical considerations.

First, the Lashleyan doctrine of neurological equipotentiality holds that any of a wide variety of psychological functions can be served by any of a wide variety of brain structures. While the generality of this doctrine may be disputed, it does seem clear that the central nervous system is highly labile and that a given type of psychological process is, in fact, often associated with a variety of distinct neurological structures. For example, though linguistic functions are normally represented in the left hemisphere of right-handed persons, insult to the left hemisphere can lead to the establishment of these functions in the *right* hemisphere. (Of course, this point is not *conclusive,* since there may be some relevant neurological property in common to the structures involved.) Physicalism, as we have been construing it, requires that organisms are in type-identical psychological states if and only if they are in type-identical physical states. Hence, equipotentiality (if true) provides evidence against physicalism.

The second consideration depends on the assumption that the Darwinian doctrine of convergence applies to the phylogeny of psychology as well as to the phylogeny of morphology and of behavior. It is well known that superficial morphological similarities between organisms may represent no more than parallel evolutionary solutions of the same environmental problem: in particular, that they may be the expression of quite different types of physiological structure. The analogous point about behavioral similarities across species has been widely recognized in the ethological literature: organisms of widely differing phylogeny and morphology may nevertheless come to exhibit superficial behavioral similarities in response to convergent environmental pressures. The present point is that the same considerations may well apply to the phylogeny of the psychology of organisms. Psychological similarities across species may often reflect convergent environmental selection rather than underlying physiological similarities. For example, we have no particular reason to suppose that the physiology of pain in man must have much in common with the physiology of pain in phylogenetically remote species. But if there are organisms whose psychology is homologous to our own but whose physiology is quite different, such organisms may provide counterexamples to the psychophysical correlations physicalism requires.

Finally, if we allow the conceptual possibility that psychological predicates could apply to artifacts, then it seems likely that physicalism will prove empirically false. For it seems very likely that given any psychophysical correlation which holds for an organism, it is possible to build a machine which is similar to the organism psychologically, but physiologically sufficiently different from the organism that the psychophysical correlation does not hold for the machine.

What these arguments seem to show is that the conditions that behaviorism and physicalism seek to place upon the type identity of psychological states of organisms are, in a relevant sense, insufficiently abstract. It seems likely that organisms which differ in their behavior or behavioral dispositions can nevertheless be in type-identical psychological states, as can organisms that are in different physical states. We shall presently discuss a "functionalist" approach to type identity which attempts to set the identity criteria at a level more abstract than physicalism or behaviorism acknowledge.

Of course, it is *possible* that the type-to-type correspondences required by behaviorism or by physicalism will turn out to obtain. The present point is that even if behavioral or physical states *are* in one-to-one correspondence with psychological states, we have no current evidence that this is so; hence we have no warrant for adopting philosophical theories that *require* that it be so. The paradox about behaviorism and physicalism is that while most of the arguments that have surrounded these doctrines have been narrowly "conceptual," it seems increasingly likely that the decisive arguments against them are empirical.

It is often suggested that one might meet these arguments by supposing that although neither behavioral nor physical states correspond to psychological states in a one-to-one fashion, they may nevertheless correspond many-to-one. That is, it is supposed that for each type of psychological state, there is a distinct disjunction of types of behavioral (or physical) states, such that an organism is in the psychological state if and only if it is in one of the disjuncts.

This sort of proposal is, however, shot through with serious difficulties. First, it is less than obvious that there is, in fact, a *distinct* disjunction of behavioral (or physical) states corresponding to each psychological state. For example, there is no reason to believe that the class of types of behaviors which, in the whole history of the universe, have (or will have) expressed rage for some organism or other is distinct from the class of types of behaviors which have expressed, say, pain. In considering this possibility, one should bear in mind that practically any behavior might, in the appropriate circumstances, become the conventional expression of practically any psychological state, and that a given organism in a given psychological state might exhibit almost any behavioral disposition depending on its beliefs and preferences. The same kind of point applies, *mutatis mutandis,* against the assumption that there is a distinct disjunction of types of physical states corresponding to each type of psychological state, since it seems plausible that practically any type of physical state could realize practically any type of psychological state in some kind of physical system or other.

But even if there *is* a distinct disjunction of types of behavioral (or physical) states corresponding to each type of psychological state, there is no reason whatever to believe that this correspondence is lawlike; and it is not obvious what philosophical interest would inhere in the discovery of a behavioral (or physical) property that happened, accidentally, to be coextensive with a psychological predicate. Thus, as Davidson (1970) has pointed out, on the assumption that psycho-behavioral correlations are not lawlike, even "if we were to find an open sentence couched in behavioral terms and exactly coextensive with some mental predicate, nothing could reasonably persuade us that we had found it." As Davidson has also pointed out, the same remark applies, *mutatis mutandis,* to physical predicates.

Finally, a theory which says that each psychological predicate is coextensive with a distinct disjunction of behavioral (or physical) predicates[3] is incompatible with what we have been assuming is an obvious truth—namely, that a given behavioral state may express (or a given physical state realize) different psychological states at different times. Suppose, for example, that we have a theory which says that the psychological predicate p_1 is coextensive with the disjunctive behavioral predicate A, and psychological predicate p_2 is coextensive with the disjunctive behavioral predicate B. Suppose further that S_i designates a type of behavior that has sometimes expressed p_1 but not p_2 and at other times expressed p_2 but not p_1. Then S_i will have to be a disjunct of both A and B. But the disjuncts of A are, severally, sufficient conditions for p_1 and the disjuncts of B are, severally, sufficient conditions of p_2 on the assumption that p_1 and A, and p_2 and B, are respectively coextensive. Hence the theory entails that an organism in S_i is in both p_1 and p_2, which is logically incompatible with the claim that S_i expresses p_1 (but not p_2) at some times and p_2 (but not p_1) at others. Of course, one could circumvent this objection by including spatiotemporal designators in the specification of the disjuncts mentioned in A and B. But to do so would be totally to abandon the project of expressing psycho-behavioral (or psycho-physical) correlations by lawlike biconditionals.

II

It has recently been proposed that these sorts of difficulties can be circumvented, and an adequate theory of the conditions on type identity of psychological states can be formulated, in the following way. Let us assume that any system P to which psychological predicates can be applied has a description as a probabilistic automaton. (A probabilistic automaton is a generalized Turing machine whose machine table includes instructions associated with finite positive probabilities less than or equal to one. For a brief introduction to the notion of a Turing machine, a machine table, and related notions, see Putnam (1967). A *description* of P, in the technical sense intended here, is any true statement to the effect that P possesses distinct states S_1, S_2, . . . S_n which are related to one another and to the outputs and inputs of P by the transition probabilities given in a specified machine table. We will call the states S_1, S_2, . . . S_n specified by the *description* of an organism, the "machine table states of the organism" relative to that *description*.

It is against the background of the assumption that organisms are describable as probabilistic automata that the present theory (hereafter "*FSIT*" for "functional state identity theory") seeks to specify conditions upon the type identity of psychological states. In particular, *FSIT* claims that for any organism that satisfies psychological predicates at all, there exists a unique best *description* such that each psychological state of the organism is identical with one of its machine table states relative to that description.

Several remarks about *FSIT* are in order. First, there is an obvious generalization of the notion of a probabilistic automaton in which it is thought of as having a separate input tape on which an "oracle" can print symbols during a computation. *FSIT* presupposes an interpretation of this generalization in which sensory transducers play the role of the "oracle" and in which outputs are thought of as instructions to motor transducers. Such an interpretation must be intended if a *description* of an organism is to provide a model of the mental operations of the organism.

Second, we have presented *FSIT* in the usual way as an *identity* theory[4] —in particular, one which claims that each type of psychological state is identical to (a type of) machine table state. Our aim, however, is to sidestep questions about the identity conditions of abstract objects and discuss only a certain class of biconditionals which type-to-type identity statements entail—that is, statements of the form "O is in such and such a type of psychological state at time t if and only if O is in such and such a type of machine table state at time t."

Third, it is worth insisting that *FSIT* amounts to more than the claim that every organism has a description as a Turing machine or as a probabilistic automaton. For there are a number of respects in which that claim is trivially true; but its truth in these respects does not entail *FSIT*. For example, if we can give a physical characterization of the state of an organism at a time (e.g., in terms of its component elementary particles) and if there is a computable physical state function (whose arguments are the physical state at t_1, the physical inputs between t_1 and t_2, and the value of $t_2 - t_1$; and whose value is the physical state at t_2), then there is a Turing machine capable of simulating the organism (by computing its physical state function) and a corresponding Turing machine description of the organism. But it is not obvious that the states mentioned in this description correspond in any natural way to the psychological states of the organism. Hence it is not obvious that this Turing machine description satisfies the requirements of *FSIT*. (And it does not follow that the organism has a unique best *description* of the sort characterized above.) Second, as Putnam has pointed out (in conversation), *everything* is describable as a realization of what one might call the "null" Turing machine: that is, a machine which has only one state and stays in it, and emits no output, no matter what the input. (The point is, roughly, that whether a system *P* realizes a Turing machine depends, inter alia, on what counts as a change of state in *P* and what counts as an output of *P*. If one counts *nothing* as a change of state in *P*, or as an output of *P*, then *P* is a realization of the null Turing machine.) But again, *FSIT* would not be true if the only true *description* of an organism is as a null Turing machine, since *FSIT* requires that the machine table states of an organism correspond one-to-one with its psychological states under its best description.

There are thus two important respects in which *FSIT* involves more than the claim that organisms which satisfy psychological predicates have *descriptions*. First, *FSIT* claims that such systems have unique best *descriptions*. Second, *FSIT* claims that the types of machine table states specified by the unique best *description* of a system are in correspondence with the types of psychological states that the system can be in. It is this second claim of *FSIT* with which we shall be primarily concerned.

FSIT, unlike either behaviorism or physicalism, is not an

ontological theory: that is, it is neutral about what token psychological states *are,* in that as far as *FSIT* is concerned, among the systems to which psychological predicates are applicable (and which therefore have *descriptions*) might be included persons, material objects, souls, and so forth. This last point suggests how *FSIT* might meet certain of the kinds of difficulties we raised against physicalism and behaviorism. Just as *FSIT* abstracts from considerations of the ontological status of the systems which have *descriptions,* so too it abstracts from physical differences between systems that have their *descriptions* in common. As Putnam has remarked, "the *same* Turing machine (from the standpoint of the machine table) may be physically realized in a potential infinity of ways" (1966, p. 271), and *FSIT* allows us to state type-identity conditions on psychological states in ways that are neutral as between such different realizations.

Similarly, *FSIT* permits us to state such conditions in a way that abstracts from the variety of behavioral consequences which a psychological state may have. It thereby meets a type of objection which, we supposed above, was fatal to behaviorism.

We remarked that the behaviorist is committed to the view that two organisms are in the same psychological state whenever their behaviors and/or behavioral dispositions are identical; and that this theory is implausible to the extent that the behaviors and the behavioral dispositions of an organism are the effects of *interactions* between its psychological states. But *FSIT* allows us to distinguish between psychological states not only in terms of their behavioral consequences but also in terms of the character of their interconnections. This is because the criterion of identity for machine table states acknowledges *their relations to one another* as well as their relations to inputs and outputs. Thus, *FSIT* can cope with the characteristic indirectness of the relation between psychological states and behavior. Indeed, *FSIT* allows us to see how psychological states that have *no* behavioral expressions might nevertheless be distinct.

Finally, it may be remarked that nothing precludes taking at least some of the transitions specified in a machine table as corresponding to causal relations in the system which the table *describes.* In particular, since *FSIT* is compatible with token physicalism, there is no reason why it should not acknowledge that token psychological states may enter into causal relations. Thus any advantages that accrue to causal analyses of the psychological states, or of the relations between psychological states and behavior, equally accrue to *FSIT*.[5]

III

In this section we are going to review a series of arguments which provide one degree or another of difficulty for the claim that *FSIT* yields an adequate account of the type-identity conditions for psychological states. It is our view that, taken collectively, these arguments are fairly decisive against the theory of type identity of psychological states which *FSIT* proposes. In the final section we will suggest some reasons why the attempt to provide substantive type-identity conditions on psychological states so often founders.

(1) Any account of type-identity conditions on psychological states which adheres at all closely to our everyday notion of what types of psychological states there are will presumably have to draw a distinction between dispositional states[6] (beliefs, desires, inclinations, and so on) and occurrent states (sensations, thoughts, feelings, and so on). So far as we can see, however, *FSIT* has no plausible way of capturing this distinction short of abandoning its fundamental principle that psychological states correspond one-to-one to machine table states. Suppose, for example, *FSIT* attempts to reconstruct the distinction between occurrents and dispositions by referring to the distinction between the machine table state that an organism is *in* and all the other states specified by its machine table. Thus one might refine *FSIT* to read: for occurrent states, two organisms are in type-identical psychological states if and only if they are in the same machine table state; and for each dispositional state there is a machine table state such that an organism is in the former if and only if its machine table contains the latter.

This proposal has serious difficulties. Every machine table state of an organism is one which it is possible for the organism to be in at some time and, of course, every machine table state that an organism can be in is among the states that belong to the table of its *description*. Hence, if the present proposal is right, for an organism to be in a dispositional state implies the possibility of its being in the "corresponding" occurrent state and vice versa. But it is hard to see how that proposal could be true. It might be suggested, for example, that what corresponds to the dispositional "believes that p" is the occurrent "is thinking that p." But a moment's consideration shows that must be wrong: it can be false that someone believes that p even though it is true that it is possible for him to think that p. (We do not believe that there are flying saucers, though there are certainly possible circumstances in which we would think there are.) In short: the present account construes a dispositional as a possible occurrent, and a possible occurrent as a state in the table of an organism's *description*. But these identifications cannot be sustained; the first, in particular, is implausible.

Now, we do not mean to deny that necessary and sufficient conditions for the having of dispositional states could be given by reference to some *abstract* property of the organization of machine tables. To take a far-fetched example, given a normal form for *descriptions,* it might turn out that an organism believes that the sun is 93,000,000 miles from the earth if and only if the first n columns in its machine table have some such abstract property as containing only odd integers. Since saying of a machine that the first n columns . . . and so forth does not ascribe a machine table state to it, psychological states that are analyzed as corresponding to this sort of property would not thereby be described as possible occurrent states.

To take this line, however, would be to abandon a fundamental claim of *FSIT*. For while this approach is compatible with the view that two organisms have the same psychology if and only if they have the same machine table, it is *not* compatible with the suggestion that two organisms are in the same (dispositional) psychological state if and only if they have a specified state of their machine tables in common. Hence it is incompatible with the view that psychological states are in one-to-one correspondence with machine table states. Moreover, since we have no way of telling what kinds of abstract properties of machine tables might turn out to correspond to psychological states, the present difficulty much reduces the possibility of using *FSIT* to delineate substantive type-identity conditions on psychological states. To say that psychological states correspond to some property or other of machine tables is to say something very much weaker than that psychological states correspond to machine table states. This is a kind of point to which we will return later in the discussion.

There is, of course, at least one other way out of the present difficulty for *FSIT*. It might be suggested that we ought to give up the everyday notion that there are some dispositional states which are not possible occurrent states (for example, to acknowledge an occurrent, though perhaps nonconscious, state of believing that *p*). Clearly, the possibility that we might some day have theoretical grounds for acknowledging the existence of such states cannot be precluded a priori. But we have no such grounds *now*, and there does seem to us to be a methodological principle of conservatism to the effect that one should resist models which require empirical or conceptual changes that are not independently motivated.

(2) We suggested that *FSIT* allows us to account for the fact that behavior is characteristically the product of interactions between psychological states, and that the existence of such interactions provides a standing source of difficulty for behaviorist theories insofar as they seek to assign characteristic behaviors *severally* to psychological states. It is (empirically) immensely likely, however, that there are *two* kinds of behaviorally efficacious interactions between psychological states, and *FSIT* provides for a natural model of only one of them.

On one hand, behavior can be the product of a *series* of psychological states, and the *FSIT* account shows us how this could be true, and how some of the states occurring in such a series may not themselves have behavioral expressions. On the other hand, behavior can be the result of interactions between *simultaneous* mental states. For example, prima facie, what an organism does at *t* may be a function of what it is feeling at *t* and what it is thinking at *t*. But *FSIT* provides no conceptual machinery for representing this state of affairs. In effect, *FSIT* can provide for the representation of sequential interactions between psychological states, but not for simultaneous interactions. Indeed *FSIT* even fails to account for the fact that an organism can be in more than one occurrent psychological state at a time, since a probabilistic automaton can be in only one machine table state at a time. The upshot of this argument seems to be that if probabilistic automata are to be used as models of an organism, the appropriate model will be a set of intercommunicating automata operating in parallel.

It is again important to keep clear on what the argument does not show about *FSIT*. We have read *FSIT* as claiming that the psychological states of an organism are in one-to-one correspondence with the machine table states postulated in its best *description*. The present argument suggests that if this claim is to be accepted, then the best *description* of an organism must not represent it as a single probabilistic automaton. If organisms, but not single probabilistic automata, can be in more than one state at a time, then either an organism is not a single probabilistic automaton, or the psychological states of an organism do not correspond to machine table states of single probabilistic automata. (It should be remarked that there is an algorithm that will construct a single automaton equivalent to any given set of parallel automata. It cannot be the case, however, that a set of parallel automata and the equivalent single automaton *both* provide best *descriptions* of an organism.)

These remarks are of some importance, since the kind of psychological theory we get on the assumption that organisms are parallel processors will look quite different from the kind we get on the assumption that they are serial processors. Indeed, while the general characteristics of serial processors are relatively well understood, very little is known about the corresponding characteristics of parallel systems.

On the other hand, this argument does not touch the main claim of *FSIT:* even if organisms are in some sense sets of probabilistic automata, it may turn out that each psychological state of an organism corresponds to a machine table state of one or other of the members of the set. In the following arguments, we will assume the serial model for purposes of simplicity and try to show that even on this assumption, psychological states do not *correspond* to machine table states.

(3) *FSIT* holds that two organisms are in psychological states of the same type if and only if they are in the same machine table state. But machine table states are identical if and only if they are identically related to other machine table states and to states of the input and output mechanisms. In this sense, the criterion for identity of machine table states is "functional equivalence." Thus *FSIT* claims that type identity of psychological states is also a

matter of a certain kind of functional equivalence; psychological states are type identical if and only if they share those properties that must be specified to individuate a machine table state.

But it might plausibly be argued that this way of type-identifying psychological states fails to accommodate a feature of at least some such states that is critical for determining their type: namely, their "qualitative" character. It does not, for example, seem entirely unreasonable to suggest that nothing would be a token of the type "pain state" unless it felt like a pain, and that this would be true even if it were connected to all the other psychological states of the organism in whatever ways pain are. It seems to us that the standard verificationist counterarguments against the view that the "inverted spectrum" hypothesis is conceptually coherent are not persuasive. If this is correct, it looks as though the possibility of qualia inversion poses a serious prima facie argument against functionalist accounts of the criteria for type identity of psychological states.

It should be noticed, however, that the inverted qualia argument is *only* a prima facie objection against *FSIT*. In particular, it is available to the proponent of functionalist accounts to meet this objection in either of two ways. On the one hand, he might argue that though inverted qualia, *if they occurred,* would provide counterexamples to his theory, as a matter of nomological fact it is impossible that functionally identical psychological states should be qualitatively distinct: in particular, that anything which altered the qualitative characteristics of a psychological state would alter its functional characteristics. This sort of line may strike one as blatant apriorism, but in the absence of any relevant empirical data, it might be well to adopt an attitude of wait and see.

There is, moreover, another defense open to the proponent of *FSIT*. He might say that, given two functionally identical psychological states, we would (or perhaps should) *take* them to be type identical, independent of their qualitative properties—that is, differences between the qualitative properties of psychological states which do not determine corresponding functional differences are *ipso facto* irrelevant to the goals of theory construction in psychology, hence should be ignored for purposes of type identification.

To see that this suggestion may be plausible, imagine that, it turns out, every person does, in fact, have slightly different qualia (or, better still, grossly different qualia) when in whatever machine table state is alleged to be identical to pain. It seems fairly clear that in this case it might be reasonable to say that the character of an organism's qualia is irrelevant to whether it is in pain or (equivalently) that pains feel quite different to different organisms.

This form of argument may, however, lead to embarrassing consequences. For all that we now know, it may be nomologically possible for two psychological states to be functionally identical (that is, to be identically connected with inputs, outputs, and successor states), even if only one of the states has a qualitative content. In this case, *FSIT* would require us to say that an organism might be in pain even though it is feeling *nothing at all,* and this consequence seems totally unacceptable.

It may be remarked that these "inverted (or absent) qualia" cases in a certain sense pose a deeper problem for *FSIT* than any of the other arguments we shall be discussing. Our other arguments are, by and large, concerned to show that psychological states cannot be functionally defined in a certain way—namely, by being put in correspondence with machine table states. But though they are incompatible with *FSIT,* they are compatible with functionalism in the broad sense of that doctrine which holds that the type-identity conditions for psychological states refer only to their relations to inputs, outputs, and one another. The present consideration, however, might be taken to show that psychological states cannot be functionally defined *at all* and that they cannot be put into correspondence with *any* properties definable over abstract automata. We will ignore this possibility in what follows, since if psychological states are not functional states at all, the question whether they are machine table states simply does not arise.

(4) We remarked that there are arguments against behaviorism and physicalism which suggest that each proposes constraints upon type-identity conditions on psychological states that are, in one way or another, insufficiently abstract. We will now argue that *FSIT* is susceptible to the same kind of objection.

A machine table specifies a state in terms of a set of instructions which control the behavior of the machine whenever it is in that state. By definition, in the case of a deterministic automaton, such instructions specify, for each state of the machine, an associated output and a successor machine state. Probabilistic automata differ only in that any state may specify a *range* of outputs or of successor states, with an associated probability distribution. In short, two machine table states of a deterministic automaton are distinct if they differ either in their associated outputs or in their associated successor state. Analogously, two machine table states of probabilistic automata differ if they differ in their range of outputs, or in their range of successor states, or in the probability distributions associated with either of these ranges.

If, however, we transfer this convention for distinguishing machine table states to the type identification of psychological states, we get identity conditions which are, as it were, too fine-grained. Thus, for example, if you and I differ *only* in the respect that your most probable response to the pain of stubbing your toe is to say "damn" and mine is to say "darn," it follows that the pain you have when you stub your toe is type-distinct from the pain I have when I stub my toe.

This argument iterates in an embarrassing way. To see this, consider the special case of deterministic automata: x and y are type-distinct machine table states of such an automaton if the immediate successor states of x and y are type-distinct. But the immediate successor states of x and y are type-distinct if *their* immediate successor states are type-distinct. So x and y are type-distinct if the immediate successors of their immediate successors are type-distinct; and so on. Indeed, on the assumption that there is a computational path from every state to every other, any two automata that have less than all their states in common will have none of their states in common. This argument generalizes to probabilistic automata in an obvious way.

It is again important to see what the argument does *not* show. In particular, it does not show that psychological states cannot be type-identified by reference to some sort of *abstract* properties of machine table states. But, as we remarked in our discussion of Argument 1, to say that psychological states correspond to some or other property definable over machine table states is to say much less about the conditions upon the type identity of psychological states than *FSIT* seeks to do. And the present argument *does* seem to show that the conditions used to type-identify machine table states per se cannot be used to type-identify psychological states. It is presumably this sort of point which Putnam, for example, has in mind when he remarks that "the difficulty of course will be to pass from models of *specific* organisms to a *normal* form for the psychological description of *organisms*" (1967, p. 43). In short, it may seem at first glance that exploitation of the criteria employed for type-identifying machine table states provides *FSIT* with concepts at precisely the level of abstraction required for type-identifying psychological states. But, in fact, this appears not to be true.

(5) The following argument seems to us to show that the psychological states of organisms cannot be placed in one-to-one correspondence with the machine table states of organisms.

The set of states that constitute the machine table of a probabilistic automaton is, by definition, a list. But the set of mental states of at least some organisms (namely, persons) is, in point of empirical fact, productive. In particular, abstracting from theoretically irrelevant limitations imposed by memory and mortality, there are infinitely many type-distinct, nomologically possible psychological states of any given person. The simplest demonstration that this is true is that, on the assumption that there are infinitely many non-equivalent declarative sentences, one can generate definite descriptions of such states by replacing S with sentences in the schemata A:

A: the belief (thought, desire, hope, and so forth) that S

In short, while the set of machine table states of a Turing machine can, by definition, be exhaustively specified by listing them, the set of mental states of a person can at best be specified by finite axiomatization.

It might be maintained against this argument that not more than a finite subset of the definite descriptions generable by substitution in A do in fact designate nomologically possible beliefs (desires, hopes, or whatever) and that this is true *not* because of theoretically uninteresting limitations imposed by memory and mortality, but rather because of the existence of psychological laws that limit the set of believable (and so forth) propositions to a finite set. To take a farfetched example, it might be held that if you eliminate all such perhaps unbelievable propositions as "2 + 2 = 17," "2 + 2 = 147," and so forth, the residuum is a finite set.

There is no reason at all to believe that this is true, however, and there are some very persuasive reasons for believing that it is not. For example, the infinite set of descriptions whose members are "the belief that 1 + 1 = 2," "the belief that 2 + 2 = 4," "the belief that 3 + 3 = 6," and so forth would appear to designate a set of possible beliefs of an organism ideally free from limitations on memory; to put it the other way around, the fact that there are arithmetical statements that is is nomologically impossible for any person to believe is a consequence of the character of people's memory, not a consequence of the character of their mental representation of arithmetic.

It should be emphasized, again, that this is intended to be an empirical claim, albeit an overwhelmingly plausible one. It is possible to imagine a creature ideally free from memory limitations whose mental representation of arithmetic nevertheless specifies only a finite set of possible arithmetic beliefs. The present point is that it is vastly unlikely that we are such creatures.

Once again it is important to see what the argument does *not* show. Let us distinguish between the *machine table states* of an automaton and the *computational states* of an automaton. By the former, we will mean what we have been meaning all along: states specified by columns in its machine table. By the latter we mean any state of the machine which is characterizable in terms of its inputs, outputs, and/or machine table states. In this usage, the predicates "has just run through a computation involving three hundred seventy-two machine table states," or "has just proved Fermat's last theorem," or "has just typed the *i*th symbol in its output vocabulary" all designate possible computational states of machines.

Now, what the present argument seems to show is that the psychological states of an organism cannot be put into correspondence with the machine table states of an automaton. What it of course does *not* show is that the psychological states of an organism cannot be put into correspondence with the *computational* states of an automaton. Indeed, a sufficient condition for the existence of the latter correspondence is that the possible psychological states of an organism should be countable.[7]

(6) We have argued that since the set of machine table states of an automaton is not productive, it cannot be put into correspondence with the psychological states of an organism. We will now argue that even if such a correspondence could be effected, it would necessarily fail to represent essential properties of psychological states.

It seems fairly clear that there are structural similarities among at least some psychological states, and that a successful theory of such states must represent and exploit such similarities. For example, there is clearly some theoretically relevant relation between the psychological state that someone is in if he believes that P and the psychological state that someone is in if he believes that P & Q. The present point is simply that representing the psychological states as a list (for example, as a list of machine table states) fails to represent this kind of structural relation. What needs to be said is that believing that P is somehow[8] a constituent of believing that P & Q; but the machine table state model has no conceptual resources for saying that. In particular, the notion "is a constituent of" is not defined for machine table states.

It might be replied that this sort of argument is not strictly relevant to the claims of *FSIT;* for it is surely possible, in principle, that there should be a one-to-one correspondence between machine table states and psychological states, even though the vocabulary appropriate to the individuation of the former does not capture the structural relations among the latter.

This reply, however, misses the point. To see this, consider the case with sentences. The reason there are structural parallelisms among sentences is that sentences are constructed from a fixed set of vocabulary items by the iterated application of a fixed set of rules, and the theoretical vocabulary required to analyze the ways in which sentences are structurally similar is precisely the vocabulary required to specify the domain of those rules. In particular, structurally similar sentences share either lexical items or paths in their derivations, or both. Thus one explains structural similarities between sentences in the same way that one explains their productivity—namely, by describing them as a generated set rather than a list.

Our point is that the same considerations apply to the set of psychological states of an organism. Almost certainly, they too are, or at least include, a generated set, and their structural similarities correspond, at least in part, to similarities in their derivation—that is, with psychological states as with sentences, the fact that they are productive and the fact that they exhibit internal structure are two aspects of the same phenomenon. If this is true, then a theory which fails to capture the structural relations within and among psychological states is overwhelmingly unlikely to arrive at a *description* adequate for the purposes of theoretical psychology.

This argument, like 5, thus leads to the conclusion that if we wish to think of the psychology of organisms as represented by automata, then the psychological states of organisms seem to be analogous to the computational states of an automaton rather than to its machine table states.

IV

We have been considering theories in the philosophy of mind which can be construed as attempts to place substantive conditions upon type identity of psychological states. We have argued that none of the major theories currently in the field appears to succeed in this enterprise. It might therefore be advisable to reconsider the whole undertaking.

Suppose someone wanted to know what the criteria for type identity of fundamental physical entities are. Perhaps the best one could do by way of answering is to say that two such entities are type-identical if they do not differ with respect to any fundamental physical magnitudes. Thus, as far as we know, the conditions upon type identification of elementary physical particles do not refer to their distance from the North Pole, but do refer to their charge. But notice that this is simply a consequence of the fact that there are no fundamental physical laws which subsume entities as a function of their distance from the North Pole, and there *are* fundamental physical laws which subsume entities as a function of their charge.

One might put it that the basic condition upon type identity in science is that it makes possible the articulation of the domain of laws. This principle holds at every level of scientific description. Thus what is *relevant* to the question whether two entities at a level will be type-distinct is the character of the laws that subsume entities at that level. But if this is the general case, then it looks as though substantive conditions upon type identity of psychological states will be imposed by reference to the psychological (and perhaps neurological) laws which subsume those states and in no other way.

In the light of these remarks, we can get a clearer view of what has gone wrong with the kinds of philosophical theories we have been rejecting. For example, one can think of behaviorism as involving an attempt to type-identify psychological states just by reference to whatever laws determine their *behavioral* effects. But this would seem, even prima facie, to be a mistake, since there must be laws which govern the interaction of psychological states and there is no reason to believe (and much reason not to believe) that psychological states that behave uniformly vis-à-vis laws of the first kind characteristically behave uniformly vis-à-vis laws of the second kind.

Analogously, what has gone wrong in the case of physicalism is the assumption that psychological states that are distinct in their behavior vis-à-vis neurological laws are *ipso facto* distinct in their behavior vis-à-vis psychological laws. But in all probability, distinct neurological states can be functionally identical. That is, satisfaction of the criteria for type-distinctness of neurological states probably does not guarantee satisfaction of the criteria for type-distinctness of psychological states or vice versa.

In short, the fundamental problem with behaviorism and physicalism is that type identity is being determined relative to, at best, a subset of the laws which must be presumed to subsume psychological states. The only justification for this restriction seems to lie in the reductionist biases of these positions. Once the reductionism has been questioned, we can see that the nomological demands upon type identification for psychological states are likely to be extremely complicated and various. Even what little we already know about psychological laws makes it look implausible that they will acknowledge type boundaries between psychological states at the places where physicalists or behaviorists want to draw them.

The basic failure of *FSIT* is in certain respects analogous to that of behaviorism and physicalism. Of course, *FSIT* is not reductionist in quite the same way, and insofar as it is a species of functionalism, it does invite us to type-identify psychological states by reference to their nomological connections with sensory inputs, behavioral outputs, and one another. But *FSIT* seeks to impose a further constraint on type identity—namely, that the psychological states of an organism can be placed in correspondence with (indeed, identified with) the machine table states specified by the best *description* of the organism. We have argued that this is in fact a substantive constraint and one that cannot be satisfied.

What seems to be left of *FSIT* is this. It may be both true and important that organisms are probabilistic automata. But even if it is true and important, the fact that organisms are probabilistic automata seems to have very little or nothing to do with the conditions on type identity of their psychological states.

Chapter 4

Three Cheers for Propositional Attitudes

The belief that P has fallen upon hard times.[1] Here is how it came about.

Many respectable philosophers used to think that substitution instances of the schema *S: x believes that P,* together with their friends and logical relations, are eliminable from English *salva* the expressive power of the language. Roughly, each sentence generated by substitution in *S* was to be replaced by some (logically equivalent, perhaps synonymous) sentence in which the predicate expresses a form of behavior or a disposition to behave. Insouciance prevailed; nobody actually provided the analyses, and there were those who seemed to glory in not providing them. So, Ryle (if I read him right) held both that talking about propositional attitudes is just a way of talking about behavior or behavioral dispositions *and* that nothing that can be (finitely) said about behavior or behavioral dispositions can, in the general case, exhaust the content of the ascription of a propositional attitude. A darkish doctrine, no doubt, but those were darkish times.

At their very worst, however, the *facticity* of such ascriptions went unimpugned. If, after all, claims about the belief that P are claims about the behaviors of organisms, then surely they are at ontological par with other things that we say about the doings of middle-sized objects. Even if the analysis of such ascriptions should exhibit them as intractably dispositional, it is arguably a fact that salt is soluble: Why should it not be as good a fact that

P-believers are disposed to P-behave (disposed, for instance, to utter tokens of 'I believe that *p*')?

We all know now that this will not work. Not, of course, that it is impossible to find some formula logically equivalent to 'x believes that P' in which 'believes' does not occur: there are expressions in French that would do for that. The point is, rather, that any such expression is itself bound to contain intentional idioms, so if what one had in mind was not so much doing without 'believes' but eliminating intensionality at large, it looks as though the behaviorist program just cannot be carried out. Take uttering 'I believe that P.' Doing that is not (as one used to say) "criterial" for believing that P unless producing the utterance at least constitutes the making of a statement. But statements are utterances intentionally (in the other sense, namely, willfully) uttered: mere random giving voice won't do. And, of course, 'intentional' is intentional. So, by one or the other route, the verbs of propositional attitude bend back upon themselves: they are, perhaps, interdefinable, but there appears to be no way out of the circle of intentional idioms.

"So be it," some philosophers have said, "and so much the worse for the circle of intentional idioms. If believers won't behave, we won't have any." Hence, the view is now widely current among philosophers that the refutation of *logical* behaviorism was tantamount to a demonstration of the *un*facticity of ascriptions of propositional attitudes, and thus to the establishment of a sort of *eliminative* behaviorism. Strictly speaking, according to this new account, there is no question of truth or falsity about what a man believes, hopes, intends, supposes, etc. Strictly speaking, we could encounter all the facts there are and not encounter any facts like these. So, it is all right if we *cannot* express in our purely extensional (or, anyhow, purely nonintentional) language—the language we reserve for such solemnities as formalizing physics—what we *can* express by reference to intentions. Physics is, perhaps, committed to saying all there is to say that is strictly true; but there is nothing strictly true that can be said about propositional attitudes. What can't be said can't be said, and it can't be reduced to physics either.

It is worth emphasizing the difference between this reaction and the one that has been typical among psychologists. The psychologists have reasoned: *statements about mental states and processes are not translatable into statement about behavior. Hence there must be ontologically autonomous facts about mental states and processes. Hence, behaviorism is false.* Whereas, the philosophers have reasoned: *statements about mental states and processes are not translatable into statements about behavior. Hence there must not be ontologically autonomous facts about mental states or processes. Hence behaviorism is true.* Clearly, one or the other of these lines of reasoning must be unsound. This chapter is about which one.

To begin with, if there are no facts about mental states and processes, that is *very* surprising. For the simple facticity of at least *some* ascriptions of propositional attitudes had seemed to be among life's little certainties. So, prior to philosophical instruction, one might have thought it straightout true not only that, say, Carter's name begins with C, but also that one *believes* that Carter's name begins with C. And, one might have thought, there is not much to choose between these truths. After all, Carter's name *does* begin with C, and one knows, more or less, how to spell. So why on Earth should one *not* have the belief when all the evidence conspires to tempt one to it? The burden of argument lies, surely, upon those who say that it is not the case that one believes even what one is strongly disposed to believe that one believes.

Moreover, nobody supposes that the failure of logical behaviorism literally *entails* the unfacticity of propositional attitude ascriptions. "Behaviorism or nothing" will strike the sophisticated as not self-evidently true. If, in short, the burden of argument is to be taken up, supporting considerations will need to be adduced. Such considerations have recently been proposed on several hands. I want to look at some of them in this paper. In particular, I want to consider in detail D. C. Dennett's (1971) account of the role of intentional ascriptions in explanations of behavior. Dennett's theory, if true, would make it clear why it is unreasonable to expect such ascriptions to be more than just heuristic.

Whereas I am inclined to think that, so far at least, the case against propositional attitudes rests unproven. For all that anyone has thus far shown, ascriptions of beliefs, when true at all, are literal. I take it that this conclusion is important if correct. After all, if there are no facts about mental states and processes, then there is, quite literally, nothing for psychology to be about. In this respect, the methodological implications of the new, eliminative behaviorism are even *more* radical than those of the old, reductive behaviorism. On the latter view psychology at least had a subject matter: the organization of behavior. To put it brutally, the psychologist's choice used to be between mentalism and tedium. It is now between mentalism and unemployment.

Dennett recommends that we "Consider the case of a chess-playing computer, and the different strategies or stances one might adopt as its opponent in trying to predict its moves [p. 87]." It may not, at first, be clear why we should *want* to consider a chess-playing computer in the course of considering what underlies our ascriptions of intentional properties to intentional systems: prima facie, a computer is a shaky example of such a system, and it is not beyond doubt that ascriptions of intentional properties to machines rest on relatively dubious analogies to solid paradigms like us. Still, marginal cases can have their philosophical uses, and I suppose that Dennett's strategy is this: In deciding what to say about a marginal case, we shall have to trot out reasons, and that should help clarify what kinds of reasons can, in principle, be alleged in favor of intentional ascriptions.

Moreover, as Dennett sees very clearly, the example serves to illustrate the involvement of intentional ascription in the prediction and explanation of behavior: Our interest in intentional ascriptions is—at least for the present case—part and parcel of our interest in figuring out what the machine is likely to *do*. Dennett says:

> A man's best hope of defeating such a machine in a chess match is to predict its responses by figuring out as best he can what the best or most rational move would be given the rules and goals of chess. That is, one assumes not only (1) that the machine will function as designed, but (2) that the design is optimal as well, that the computer will 'choose' the most rational move. (p. 89)

Now, it is notable, according to Dennett, that the recourse to intentional ascription is not the *only* way that we could, in principle, go about predicting the machine's moves. For, on the one hand, the moves could be predicted from a knowledge of the physical construction of the machine (assuming, as we may for present purposes, that the machine's physical construction determines its moves) and, on the other, the moves could be predicted by reference to the machine's teleological or functional structure. Dennett says that, in making predictions in the first way, we are adopting a "physical stance" towards the machine and that in making predictions in the second way we are adopting a "design stance." "The essential feature of the design stance is that we make predictions solely from knowledge or assumptions about the system's functional design, irrespective of the physical constitution of the innards of the particular object" (p. 88). Design-stance predictions are riskier than are physical-stance predictions, for, presumably, if we have an inference whose premises are physical laws and a specification of the physical state of the machine at t, and whose conclusion is that the machine will do such-and-such at t, then that prediction can go wrongly only insofar as the physics of the machine is not deterministic. Whereas, consider a corresponding inference whose premises are true generalizations about the functional design of the system (e.g., its program) and a specification of its functional state at t. Such an argument will be reliable only when the machine functions as it is designed to function: when, for example, it does not break down, blow out, strip a gear, etc. Failures-to-function yield exceptions to design-stance predictions but not to physical-stance predictions.

The intentional stance is like the others in that we adopt it insofar (perhaps *only* insofar; Dennett does not say) as we are interested in the prediction of behavior. And, like the design stance, it is prone to kinds of fallibility that the physical stance is immune to. When we assume the intentional stance, we figure out what the system will do by figuring out what it would be *rational* to do and then predicting that the system will do *that*. Now, supposing that the system *is* rational, it will still be true that intentional-stance predictions will typically go astray insofar as the system misfunctions, so intentional stance predictions inherit the kinds of fallibility that design-stance predictions are prone to. But, moreover, they have problems of their own since, even if the system does not misfunction—even if no gear strips—it may fail to do the rational thing because it failed to be designed to be entirely rational. Where the, as it were, program of the device is less than optimal, the intentional-stance prediction will be correspondingly less than reliable.

Why, then, resort to the intentional stance at all? For two reasons (both of them, notice, *purely* pragmatic). First, we may know what it would be rational for the system to do even if we do not know what the physical constitution or the program of the system is, so we may be in a position to predict behavior from the intentional stance even when we are not in a position to predict it from the physical or design stances. Second, even if we *do* know what the physics is, or what the functional analysis is, predictions based upon either may become unfeasible in practice when the system is sufficiently complicated. (This is an instance of a tendency of Dennett's that I remarked upon in the Introduction to this volume: explaining *intentionality* in terms of *complexity*). In either case, then, it is essentially practical considerations that force us to intentional ascriptions: in particular, it is *not* considerations of *truth*. Dennett says: "The decision to adopt the strategy is pragmatic and is not intrinsically right or wrong. One can always refuse to adopt the intentional stance, . . . one can switch stances at will . . . etc." (p. 91). We, as it were, adopt the intentional stance towards a system because of facts about *us*, not because of facts about *it*.

So, Dennett's analysis takes us where it was supposed to; it explains the utility (and hence, presumably, the prevalence) of the intentional idiom without assuming that there are facts that intentional ascriptions correspond to. If the analysis is right, then the least hypothesis is, surely, that there are no such facts and that appears to be the conclusion Dennett wants us to endorse.

What, then, can be said in favor of the analysis? Dennett's main argument goes something like this: Since intentional stance predictions will work only insofar as we are dealing with rational systems, an assumption of rationality is implicit in every such prediction. But such assumptions are ours to make or to withhold: i.e., they are themselves heuristic idealizations, justifiable only insofar as they lead, by and large, to true intentional stance predictions. So, we can conclude the unfacticity of propositional attitude ascriptions from the unfacticity of the rationality assumptions that they presuppose.

I do not think that this is a very convincing line of argument, either in the condensed form in which I have just sketched it or in the unpacked version that Dennett gives. Let's now have a look at the details.

Dennett needs to show (a) that some assumption of rationality is implicit in any attempt to predict the behavior of an organism from its intentional states, and (b) that such assumptions are somehow just heuristic. I am going to focus on (a) for the moment; how (b) comes in is something that we'll see as we go along. Let's start with some softening-up arguments.

First, it just is not true that "A man's best hope of defeating a machine in a chess match is to predict its responses by figuring out as best he can what the best or most rational move would be" and predicting that move for the machine. Indeed, the hope one cherishes in playing chess with a machine (or with, for that matter, some better instance of an intentional system—say, a Russian) is that (s)he/it *won't* make the best, most rational, optimal (etc.) move, but will, instead, make the very move that falls for one's little ruses, springs one's little traps, and, in general, exhibits levels of intellectual functioning gratifyingly inferior to one's own. Trap-baiting is itself rational only in the light of such hopes and predictions.

I am not quibbling. Dennett's case is supposed to show us straight-off that our predictions from the intentional stance depend upon postulates of optimal functioning. Whereas, it is precisely from the intentional stance that we hope and fondly expect that our opponent will not *notice* our traps, or that if our traps are noticed they will not be *understood,* or, if they are understood, no way out of them will be *seen, remembered,* or otherwise *conjured up.* These, surely, are intentional idioms par excellence, so it is precisely here that we would expect postulates of optimality to be deployed. For all that, we do not play chess on the assumption that our opponent will make the optimal move; indeed (a small point) in any game much more complicated than, say, tick-tack-toe, one is unlikely to have a clue as to what the optimal move is, or even, indeed, whether one exists. The intentionality of one's opponent's propositional attitudes is not thereby impugned.

These observations point in two directions, and I want to look both ways. First, there is something odd about a theory of intentional ascription which does not explain why intentional idioms have the characteristic properties they do: namely, the property that inferences warranted in transparent contexts *fail* when the context is opaque. Second, it seems clear that intentional explanation works in all sorts of cases where it is precisely *lapses* from optimal rationality that are at issue. These points in order.

1. A theory of intentional ascription ought to explain why intentional predicates are intensional (with-an-'s'), and the theory that assumptions of rationality are at the core of intentional ascriptions does not do so. On the contrary; quite generally, the more rational a system is assumed to be, the more justified we are in substituting in the (syntactic) objects of statements about its propositional attitudes: i.e., in reading such statements *transparently* rather than opaquely. Consider God. God is, I suppose, *fully* rational in the sense of rationality that Dennett explicitly has in mind. That is, God believes the entailments of his beliefs, so that, from 'God believes P' and 'P entails Q', we have the right to infer 'God believes Q'. Whereas, though God's beliefs are closed under the entailment relation, ours very notably are not. It is part and parcel of the opacity of *our* propositional attitudes that the inference from 'we believe P' and 'P entails Q' to 'we believe Q' is not, in general, valid. Suppose, now, that God is not merely rational but also omniscient. Then we have the full transparency of all belief contexts for God; i.e., we have not only the closure of God's beliefs under entailment, but also under material implication; and we have their closure under substitution of coreferring expressions. So, if God believes that Cicero denounced Catiline, and if Cicero = Tully, then God believes that Tully denounced Catiline. Similarly, mutatis mutandis, for God's views about Bernard Ortcutt and the man in the brown hat.

So, the more rational the system, the less opaque its belief contexts. The *more* we assume "optimality of functioning," the *less* intentionality, opacity, etc., we have to deal with.[2] How, one is inclined rhetorically to demand, could it then be that an assumption of rationality and optimality of functioning is somehow built into our ascriptions of intentional predicates?

It may be worth reemphasizing that what holds for God *in excelsis* holds for chess playing machines only *in moderation*. Suppose

I have moved my knight to KB4, and suppose that my knight's being at KB4 = my knight's threatening Black's queen. We assume that Black knows the general principles of chess, whatever those may be. So then, by hypothesis, it follows from what Black knows and notices that the positioning of my knight = (entails) the threatening of Black's Queen. The principle of rationality is, inter alia, the principle that noticings are closed under their entailments. So, if I am assuming Black's rationality, I am assuming, inter alia, that Black notices the threat.

Whereas, what I hope and predict is precisely that the threat will go unmarked. Nor, in so predicting, have I abandoned the intentional stance. On the contrary, I may rationally predict Black's lapse precisely *because* of what I know or believe about Black's intentional states: in particular, about what he is and is not likely to notice. I have, let's suppose, a mini-theory about Black's noticings. Put vulgarly, the theory might be that Black is a sucker for a knight fork. I get my prediction from this theory, and the postulates of the theory reek of intentionality. Where is the assumption of rationality? If to be rational is to believe the consequences of one's beliefs, and if the opacity of propositional attitudes is the failure of closure under the consequence relation, then to ascribe an intentional predicate to a system will often involve postulating its *ir*rationality if the predicate is opaquely construed. Or, to put the moral of the example slightly differently, it is not postulates of rationality that license intentional stance predictions: it is (mini- or maxi-, formal or informal) theories about who is likely to have which propositional attitude when, and what behavioral consequences are likely to ensue.

2. This brings us to the second point, which is precisely that intentional explanations run rampant just where they should not if the postulate of rationality story were true: namely, in the psychology of one or another *dis*function. What I have in mind is not so much the exotic specimens that get retailed in psychoanalytic paperbacks, but rather the psychology of such mundane propositional attitudes as, say, forgetting and misunderstanding. Much of our most respectable cognitive psychology operates in this area, and it operates essentially with intentional predicates. Quite a lot is known, for example, about the kinds of mistakes that people make in deductive reasoning. So, to come to cases, it is known

that one does worse with arguments that contain negative premises than with matched arguments in the affirmative mode (for a review, see Wason & Johnson-Laird, 1972). You will do better, that is to say, with the information that P is true than with the information that not-P is false, and the difference remains when banal variables are controlled away. But, of course, 'information' must be opaquely construed if this generalization is to be so much as stated. The information that P *is* the information that not-P ⊃ F on the transparent construal. And equally, of course, it is all One to God whether P or not (not-P), since belief is closed under entailment for a perfectly rational Being functioning optimally.

Such cases are legion, but I will not provide more here. What I take it that they all come to for our purposes is that ascriptions of intentionality and postulates of optimality are largely independent in precisely the area where it is most important that intentional idioms should be available; namely, in the (formal and informal) psychology of cognition. What *is* characteristic of this area—what I believe *does* explain the opacity of typical psychological idioms—is the relativization of our descriptions of the intentional states of a system to the way that the system represents the objects of its propositional attitudes. That is, however, a very long story, and one that I have tried to tell elsewhere (Fodor, 1975; and Chapter 7, this volume). Suffice it to say here that much of our psychology is the psychology of lapses from optimal rationality, and its typical idioms are opaque all the same.

These were, as I remarked, softening-up arguments. I suspect that, for Dennett's purposes, they could all be met by a judicious pulling in of horns. For—though I doubt this is an option he'd approve—it would be open to Dennett to meet these objections by weaking the assumption of rationality to an assumption of non-irrationality. The discussion has suggested that intentional stance prediction is often compatible with—and sometimes even relies upon—postulating *less than optimal* rationality. But it seems right to say that successful intentional stance predictions do depend on assuming that the system whose behavior is at issue won't act at random or go nuts. I'll take it for granted, then, that it is the dependency of intentional stance predictions upon postulates of non-irrationality (rather than optimal functioning) that Dennett is committed to defending, together with the heuristic status of such postulation. And now we need to see how the defense might go. Since I'm uncertain precisely how Dennett *wants* it to go, I propose to march back and forth over the terrain, trying several different lines of argument and hoping that something will turn up.

I suppose that Dennett's view is this: A typical prediction from the intentional stance rests on (what I shall call) an *intentional argument*. An intentional argument has the form *F*:

> Premise 1: In situation S, a not-irrational agent performs (might perform) action A. (In order for this to be an intentional argument, we must assume that situation S is specified, at least in part, by reference to the propositional attitudes of the agent. For simplicity, I shall assume that it is *entirely* so specified.)
>
> Premise 2: x is in situation S.
>
> Premise 3: x is a not-irrational agent.
>
> Conclusion/prediction: x performs (might perform) action A.

As now construed, Dennett's point is two-fold. First, that our intentional stance theories license (only) generalizations such as premise 1 (as we have seen, Dennett holds that to adopt the intentional stance is to argue from what the system would do if it were rational.) But, second, if this is right, then premises such as 3 figure essentially in intentional arguments. Knowledge of what a not-irrational agent would do in situation S, and knowledge that x is in S, licenses predictions about what x will do in S only insofar as we assume that x is not irrational. So, we appear to have a part, at least, of what we wanted: we have the essential involvement of a rationality premise in any warranted intentional stance prediction, even if we don't yet have the heuristic character of the premise that is so involved. (That this is in fact the line of argument Dennett has in mind is perhaps clearest in his [1978] article "Skinner Skinned," q.v.)

The trouble with this way of proceeding, however, is that it leaves us needing some reason to assume that any predictive scheme which seeks to infer from the propositional attitudes of an organism to its behavior *must* have the form of an intentional argument; viz. must be of form F. Prima facie, there would appear to be plausible alternatives. For example, F*.

> Premise 1: Being in situation S causes (might cause) the performance of action A.
>
> Premise 2: x is in situation S.

Conclusion/prediction: x performs (might perform) action A.

Since, by assumption, being in situation S involves having the relevant propositional attitudes, F* counts as an argument from beliefs to behaviors if F does. But there doesn't seem to be any assumption of rationality essentially operative in F*. What's presupposed by F* is just that beliefs cause behaviors, and do so in ways that can be subsumed by general causal principles.

Of course, it's true about F* that insofar as premise 1 subsumes only non-irrational agents, it will fail to subsume x when x is irrational. And if, as one might suppose, being subsumed by such principles as premise 1 is somehow *constitutive* of being not irrational, then the non-irrationality of a system will follow from the fact that it satisfies arguments like F*. If, however, *that's* what the assumption of rationality amounts to, then the assumption of rationality is harmless. For what we have is only that the soundness of intentional stance predictions entails the rationality of a system insofar as the rationality of a system is a matter of the predictability of its behaviors from its beliefs and desires. Which is to say that the intentional stance prediction of behavior entails the predictability of behavior from beliefs and desires. And that isn't just *true;* it's *truistic.* The moral is this: What we need is not just to show that intentional stance prediction *somehow* involves a postulate of non-irrationality; we need to show that it involves a postulate of non-irrationality in some way that makes the predictive arguments merely heuristic. To discover that a system satisfies arguments like F* is, perhaps, to find out that the system is, to that extent, not irrational. But, so what?

'*Ah, but*', you may say, rather more in the spirit of Quine and Davidson than of Dennett, '*the substitution of F* for F as the format for intentional prediction begs the very question that's at issue. The difference between F* and F is that, whereas 1, F (premise 1 of F) is presumably some sort of framework truth (constitutive, perhaps, of the concept of rationality), 1, F* (premise 1 of F*) purports to be a true (maybe lawlike) causal generalization. But, now, (1, F*) can't be a true causal generalization unless it is possible to identify states of organisms as being states of believing, wanting, intending, . . . etc. that P in ways that are* independent of *the identification of such states as being subsumed by generalizations like (1, F*). And this is* not *possible because, roughly, of the holistic character of the epistemological considerations that* *underlie identifications of propositional attitudes. That is: it is precisely such facts about a state as that it is subsumed by generalizations like (1, F*) which warrant the identification of that state as one of believing that P. So, it is a kind of charade to view (1, F*) as a causal generalization. Viewed in its proper epistemological context, it is more plausible to take it as a conceptual condition upon the identification of such propositional attitudes as figure in S. If, however, it is not a causal generalization, then the important difference between F and F* vanishes and no progress has been made.'*

To which I am inclined to reply as follows: It ought to be a ground rule for discussions of intentional theories that problems which hold for scientific explanations *in general* should not be raised as difficulties for intentional explanations *in particular*. There is, to be sure, a problem about the dependence of the identification of a scientific construct upon the assumption that the theory which employs the construct is true. The tendency of the fundamental generalizations which structure a science to act like implicit definitions of its theoretical terms creates notorious problems about intertheoretical reference; about the distinction between conceptual and empirical truth; and about the nature of empirical confirmation. In extreme cases, it causes terminal Idealism. For all I know, it causes sunspots too. What *hasn't* been shown, however, is that the dependence of identifications of propositional attitudes upon the truth of causal generalizations like (F*, 1) amounts to anything more than a special case of this general difficulty. If it doesn't, then it isn't anything that we ought to worry about here.

One further point along this line: if the identification of propositional attitudes depends essentially on their subsumption by generalizations like (F*, 1) (viz. generalizations couched, by hypothesis, in intentional idiom), then there may be quite a direct argument from the present considerations to the "ineliminability of the intentional". But that would be an argument for the *heuristic* character of the intentional only given precisely the assumption that's at issue: viz. that there is no fact of the matter about intentional states. This is an area in which it is frightfully easy to find oneself arguing backwards.

But maybe this is all beside the point. For Dennett might want to argue as follows: 'It's true that I think a rationality assumption comes in; only I don't think it comes in where you think I think it does. It's not that we postulate rationality in the course of attributing beliefs to agents or in the course of attributing causal efficacy to the agent's beliefs. When the assumption of rationality comes in is when we use our theoretical formalisms to figure out which predictions about the agent's mental processes to make. Suppose we attribute to Jones the belief that P and the belief that if P then Q. Presumably, we will then wish to predict that these beliefs will cause (or at least tend to cause) a belief that Q. But notice that in generating such predictions, we will very often appeal to our knowledge that, in point of logic, Q is derivable from (P & (if P then Q)). What, then, licenses arguing from the point of logic to the causal predictions about the interactions of Jones' mental states? Precisely the assumption that Jones' mental processes are, to this extent, rational processes. Moreover, it's not unreasonable to suppose that the willingness to make this sort of transition— from the logical to the causal facts—is constitutive of being willing to ascribe beliefs at all. Were we to find a kind of system for which such transitions never (or almost never) worked, we would, for that very reason, refuse to think of it as having beliefs.' Dennett sometimes writes in ways that suggest that this is, for him, the crucial point about intentional prediction. "Ask a thousand American mathematicians how much seven times five is, more than nine hundred would respond by saying that it was thirty-five. . . . (this) is not a prediction of human psychology, but of the 'psychology' of Intentional systems generally" (97). That is: it's a prediction that we get just from arithmetic, given the assumption of rationality. It's the aprioricity of this sort of prediction that shows that intentional psychology, though "not totally vacuous" (ibid.), somehow isn't the real thing.

But this is, I think, precisely a case of arguing backwards. If we *start out* by thinking of our intentional stance theories (for example, our logic) as simply computational devices from which predictions about mental phenomena are somehow to be elicited, then the question "What licenses the transition from interformulaic relations in the theory to causal relations in the mind?" surely does arise. And the answer: "It's the assumption of rationality that issues the license" is entirely plausible insofar as one thinks of the intentional theories as implicitly defining—or otherwise constraining—the concept of rationality.

There is, however, an alternative view. To put it crudely, one possible answer to the question "What justifies using an intentional stance theory to generate psychological predictions?" is: it's the assumption that the theory is *true* under the intended (psychological) interpretation; it's the assumption that, in something spiritually similar to the technical sense, the mental processes of the agent constitute a model of the theory. Since Dennett's *conclusion* was supposed to be that psychological deployments of intentional stance theories are heuristic (hence that such theories are *not* literally true under the intended psychological interpretation), he needs an argument that the Realist construal cannot be sustained. We still haven't got such an argument.

What we have got is just the difference between F and F* writ large. According to F, we take the theorems of our intentional theories as constitutive of rationality, and we use the assumption that the agent is rational to infer from the intentional theory to the psychological predictions. According to F*, we interpret interformulaic relations in the theory as expressing causal relations among mental states. So, for example, the derivability of Q from (P & (if P then Q) is interpreted as the claim that if an organism has the belief that P and the belief that if P then Q, then it has the belief that Q. This is, of course, *not* a logical truth; it's an empirical generalization which specifies (presumably causal) relations among mental states by reference to the contents of those states. As such, it will be true only if the mental states, together with their causal relations do, in the intended sense, constitute a model of the logic. What we then need to license the use of the intentional theory to make predictions about, say, Jones', mental states, is just the assumption that such empirical generalizations *are* true.

I suppose, by the way, that we *always* have this sort of choice when we consider the application of a theoretical formalism to an empirical domain; it has nothing to do with the empirical application of intentional theories per se.[3] For example, we predict the combinatorial properties of atoms by appeal to the theory of valences. The theory of valences contains, among other things, certain mathematical principles (let's say, for our purposes, the postulates for summing positive and negative integers). When we appeal to the formalism to derive chemical predictions, we use the mathematical apparatus to compute the valence of complex objects as a function of the valences of their constitutents. Now, how shall we think about this?

One possibility is to view the formalism as simply a computational device which implicitly constrains the (otherwise uninterpreted) concept *has valence n.* On this view, the application of the device to predict chemical interactions proceeds via an "assumption of mathematicity": roughly, the assumption that atoms combine according to the postulates for summing integers. This way of talking is harmless precisely *because* it isn't mandatory. We could equally say that what licenses using the theory to make the predictions is the assumption that the formalism is true under the intended (chemical) interpretation. According to this latter picture, assignments of integer values as valences of atoms correspond to (some or other) claims about the distribution of electrons in their outer orbits; the principles for the summation of valences correspond to laws of electron capture, and so on. On the first account, we apply the theory of valences on the assumption that atomic processes are mathematic; on the second, we apply the theory of valences on the assumption that it is true under chemical interpretation. Similarly, mutatis mutandis, for the application of an intentional theory in a domain of mental processes.

The reader will have noticed that I am simplifying—indeed, trivializing—what are, in fact, dark matters. But I think the moral survives the exposition: there may be general reasons for preferring the first sort of story about valences to the second; but if there are, the very fact that they are *general* makes them irrelevant to the discussion of intentional theories qua intentional theories. Certainly, according to the second picture, there is nothing *specially* puzzling about the way that the assumption of rationality comes into intentional predictions: no empirical domain is a model of a formalism unless it exhibits analogues to the interformulaic relations that structure the formalism. That's all the postulate of rationality (and the postulate of mathematicity) amounts to.

Here, finally, is where push comes to shove. For, I suspect that Dennett would reply like this: *'The asymmetry between the application of the theory of valence to atoms and the application of the logic to our mental states is that we already* know *that our beliefs don't, in the required sense, constitute a model of the theory. Q is derivable from (P & (if P then Q)), but the belief that P and the belief that if P then Q don't invariably and in the general case cause the belief that Q. The causal interactions among beliefs do not bear to modus ponens that relation (whatever that relation is) that the interactions among atoms bear to the principles for summing integers. So, again: intentional theories may be useful for predicting the behavioral outcomes of mental processes; but they aren't ever* true.' The point here, notice, is not just that intentional theories rest on an assumption of rationality; it's that they rest on a *counterfactual* assumption of rationality. And, of course, a theory that entails (or presupposes) a falsehood *can't* be better than heuristic. I do think that this must be the heart of the matter; what's needed to make the case for the heuristic status of the intentional is, surely, an argument that engages the issue of truth; and this is the first such that we have encountered.

Such considerations as, for example, the failure of beliefs to exhibit deductive closure certainly show something: the least they show is that viewing the mental processes of an organism as a model of a logic (or a decision theory, or a grammar, etc.) requires what may amount to very severe idealization. The question, however, is what *that* shows.

For one thing, it might just be that you've got the wrong logic. A number of philosophers have suggested that, whereas standard logics give at best a poor fit to the psychological facts, some *non*-standard logic might be literally satisifed by interactions among beliefs. Since we have seen that optimal rationality (in, say, the sense of believing all of the logical truths and none of the logical falsehoods) is *surely* not a precondition for intentional ascription, a logic might serve to support intentional explanation and still be weaker than standard logics are; only those derivations being licensed which do correspond to "psychologically real" inferential processes. Equivalently for our purposes, one might hold that intentional ascription presupposes that the ascribee believe at least some of the logical truths (and not believe at least some of the logical falsehoods), but that *which* ones are mandatory depends on which inferences are complicated given the psychology of the system being described (see Cherniak, 1977). I'm inclined to think, however, that this is a counsel of despair; a position to which we may have to retreat, but not, at least, in the face of any considerations thus far alleged. Anyhow, I'm prepared to argue for this: the inference from 'intentional theory I applies to system S only under severe idealization' to 'I isn't literally true of S' is unwarranted.

I want to distinguish—if only in a rough and intuitive sort of way—between two kinds of idealization that may be involved in applying a scientific theory in an empirical domain. I think the issues here are actually quite deep, and I don't begin to claim to understand them. But it will do, for our purposes, just to suggest the feel of the thing.

One familiar sort of scientific idealization involves (what one might call) extrapolations to Platonic objects. Paradigm cases of idealizations of this kind (the thermodynamics of ideal gasses, the chemistry of literally pure samples, the mechanics of frictionless planes, etc.) exhibit a very special kind of relation between the parameter values that the theory predicts and the ones that experimentation derives—namely, the latter *approximate* the former. The (presumptive) indispensability of idealization lies, at least in part, in the fact that it is only "in the limit" that we obtain parameter values that precisely satisfy the laws of the theory. Which is to say that, strictly speaking, (and barring accidents), we do not obtain them at all. At best the observations tend to converge upon the ideal values, and we need the idealization because it is only at the point of convergence that the lawful relations that the theory postulates are strictly satisfied. Unless the ideal objects yield the predicted parameter values, nothing does.

What is interesting—and puzzling—about this sort of idealization is that it appears to prescind from ontological commitment to the very objects over which the generalizations of the theory are defined. To put it crudely, nobody thinks that the truth of mechanics depends on the existence of frictionless planes; yet it is at least unobvious whether scientific theories could, in the general case, be so formulated as to avoid Platonic reference without diminution of their explanatory and predictive power. I have precisely nothing to say about this matter; in particular, I don't have an account of the truth conditions upon theories which resort to Platonic

idealization. But I'm prepared to believe—or, anyhow, to concede—
that *if* intentional theories are among them, there may be *some*
sense in which the function of intentional theories in predicting
psychological data is heuristic.

There are, however, other kinds of scientific idealization.
Tuchman (1978) discusses the question why fourteenth-century
investigators had so much trouble understanding the epidemiology
of plague: "The existence of two carriers confused the trail, and
more so because the flea could live and travel independently of
the rat for as long as a month and, if infected by the particularly
virulent septicemic form of the bacillus, could infect humans
without reinfecting itself from the rat. The simultaneous presence
of the pneumonic form of the diesease, which was indeed com-
municated through the air, blurred the problem further" (p. 106).

What's going on here is that the observed facts of contagion
turned out to have been determined by the simultaneous contribution of several different sources of variance, sometimes acting independently and sometimes interacting. To have gotten a viable
theory would therefore have involved a certain epistemic ma-
neuver: idealizing away from—in fact, ignoring—quite a lot of the
data, the latter being viewed, in retrospect, as largely unsystematic
and attributable to the misleading convergence of several distinct
etiologies.

Notice that, prima facie, this second (call it 'epistemic') sort of
idealization is quite different from the Platonic variety. Here the
problem is not that the observations would satisfy the theroetical
predictions only *in the limit;* it's rather that the underlying generalization (say, infected rats transmit plague) explains only *some
of* what at first appear to be the relevant cases: the theory works,
but only barring exceptions attributable to noise from relatively
unsystematic variables. In this sort of situation, the thrust of
idealization is not, then, primarily ontological; on the contrary,
we are clearly and straightforwardly ontologically committed to
the objects and processes over which the generalizations of the
theory are defined. It's just that because the surface variance is
an effect of many different sorts of causes, we have to idealize
away from observations that turn out to be irrelevant to the
character of the underlying generalizations. The point is: whatever
may be the case for Platonic idealization, the fact that applying a

theory involves idealization of this second kind is no argument against the literal truth of its ontological commitments.

I think that Dennett may well be assuming that the kind of idealization involved in intentional prediction is ipso facto Platonic. The line of argument I'm attributing to him would go like this: intentional theories under psychological interpretation do predict mental processes, but only for the case of ideally rational believers. Since there *are* no ideally rational believers (cf. the failure of deductive closure for beliefs), applying such a theory to us rests on a heuristic assumption of rationality. What shows that the assumption *is* heuristic is precisely the fictional—or, anyhow, Platonic—character of the objects over which the generalizations of the intentional theory are defined.

That *is* quite a standard way of understanding claims that intentional theories make. Even so relentlessly Realistic an intentional theorist as Chomsky is prone sometimes to describe the goal of grammar construction as the prediction of the linguistic intuitions of an ideally competent speaker/hearer. (Compare: the logic predicts the inferences acceptable to an ideally rational believer.) In Chomsky's case, however, this Platonic view of intentional idealization cohabits with quite a different sort of account. I'll return to this in the immediate future.

Notice, to begin with, that there is no obvious reason for construing intentional idealization as Platonic rather than epistemic. The problem isn't, after all, that our beliefs tend towards rationality only in the limit; it's rather that our beliefs are rational only *some of the time.* We get, as it were, the parameter values that the intentional theory predicts, but we also get counter-cases due to lapses of attention, failure of computational power, weakness of the flesh and, for that matter, sheer bull-headedness. To consider just one case: it's notoriously hard to get people to accept the *validity* of arguments whose conclusions they know to be false. Everybody makes this sort of mistake some of the time; undergraduates seem to make it *a la folie.* We *could* view such errors as the consequence of accepting non-rational principles of inference, but we certainly don't need to do so. Sometimes—surely at least in the cases where one makes such mistakes oneself—it seems reasonable to accept the account one's dignity demands and think of the errors as the consequence of interactions between two different strategies for assessing arguments, one of which one knows perfectly well is no better than heuristic. But if some of the errors are like this, perhaps many of them are. Perhaps *all* of them are.

To come, finally, to the moral: There is, I think, at least one way of construing the psychological application of intentional theories as involving epistemic rather than Platonic idealization. That is to view intentional theories as accounts of one among the (presumably very many) mechanisms whose interactions eventuate in such psychological processes as reasoning and the fixation of belief. On this account, idealization to optimally rational agents is *not* involved in the formulation of intentional stance theories; the predictions such theories license do *not* concern the mental processes of Platonic individuals; and the theories are literally true of us if they are true of us at all.

Instead of viewing an intentional theory as enumerating the beliefs of an ideal believer (or the intuitions of an ideal speaker/ hearer), we might think of it as explicating what real reasoners know about valid inferences (what real speaker/hearers know about their language; Chomsky's other line). In a nutshell: intentional theories explicate knowledge structures, and knowledge structures are among the psychological mechanisms which interact in mental processes. To claim that the mental processes of an organism are a model of a logic, in the sense of that notion that is now at issue, is thus *not* to claim that there is a belief of the organism corresponding to each theorem of the logic (what beliefs the organism has will depend on how the internal representation of the logic interacts with other psychological mechanisms). It *is* to claim only that the postulates of the logic are mentally represented by the organism, and that this mental representation contributes (in appropriate ways) to the causation of its beliefs. Perhaps, on some construals, it would follow from that that *were* the organism ideally rational, it would believe whatever the logic entails. But that hardly matters, since it's not, as it were, the fact that makes the logic true of the psychology of the organism; what makes the logic true of the psychology of the organism is that the postulates of the logic are internally represented and etiologically involved. A fortiori, the *evidence* for attributing a logic to an organism would not normally be that the organism believes whatever the logic entails. Rather, the appropriate form of argument is to show that the assumption that the organism internally represents the logic, when taken together with independently motivated theories of the character of the other interacting variables, yields the best explanation of the data about the organism's mental states and processes and/or the behaviors in which such processes eventuate.

There may be other ways of viewing intentional idealization as non-Platonic. If, however, we do it this way, we need the notion of mental representation; in particular, we need to be able to make sense of the idea that the postulates of an intentional theory may be represented by (or, more precisely, may express the same information that is expressed by) certain of the mental structures of the organism. I do not know that this notion can be made clear, but then (I suppose) Dennett does not know that it cannot. *If* it can—to summarize—then we may not argue from such facts as the failure of beliefs to exhibit deductive closure to the heuristic character of appeals to logics as psychological models. For, on the present view, an intentional theory isn't about what we believe; it's about *what causes our beliefs.* This consideration does not, of course, show that the Realistic interpretation of intentional ascription is true; it shows only that we have—as yet—no decisive reason for supposing that it is false.

'*Yes, but, as a matter of fact, are any intentional theories true? How plausible is it that any of our intentional theories yield literal (though partial) accounts of the knowledge structures that interact in mental processes?*' Well, as Dennett himself says, Darwinian selection guarantees that organisms either know the elements of logic or become posthumous. (It is slightly odd that Dennett *should* say this, since, if there is no fact of the matter about our beliefs, it could hardly be the consequence of an *empirical* theory that some of our beliefs are rational.) Moreover, it's worth contemplating that no one has ever developed a serious theory in cognitive psychology that was other than intentionalist through-and-through; and common-sense psychological explanation can't get started without intentional ascription. So, what we have in favor of the literal ascription of the belief that P is both the available science and the evidence of our day-to-day experience. Sicitur ad astra. I mean: what better kinds of reasons have we for the belief that there are stars?

For all of which, I doubt that the strength of our attachment to belief/desire psychology can be fully accounted for by reference to the confirmatory evidence. The idea that behavior is explicable in terms of the propositional attitudes of the agent plays, it seems to me, quite a special role in our world view: nobody *seriously* (as opposed to philosophically) doubts it; it seems to be utterly universal (in the way that, say, ontological commitment to enduring physical objects is); and, despite its logical complexity and the elaborateness of its ramifications, it is notably the sort of thing which children pick up untaught. (In fact, the problem with children is to get them to restrict their intentional ascriptions to remotely plausible candidates—hence to forego the impulse to attribute propositional attitudes to dolls, clouds, and, literally, everything else that looks like us or moves. Much the same could be said of overgeneralizations of intentional ascription in the history of science.) Moreover, I think it is probably true that, whereas we could (but wouldn't) maintain *any* scientific theory even in the face of vastly and admittedly recalcitrant data, we actually *would* hold onto intentional explanation come what may. Intentional concepts provide a framework for explanations which are, no doubt, empirical, but which I, at least, can't imagine giving up.

Any sensible ethologist contemplating any *other* species would surely take such considerations as prima facie evidence that the framework of intentional explanation is innate. Indeed, that much of what a social organism believes about the psychology of its conspecifics should prove to be innate is ethologically plausible even independent of such considerations. The more social an organism—and the longer its prematurity—the more its survival depends on having predictively adequate views about how its conspecifics are likely to behave.

It seems to me that that is overwhelmingly plausibly the right story to tell about us. If true, it would explain the intuition that our preference for intentional theory is discernibly stronger than what the evidence would rationally demand. It's not that intentional theory is, in principle, insensitive to empirical confirmation; it's not even that the level of confirmation currently available is less than quite respectable; it's rather that the sources of our adherence to intentional explanation don't really have much to do with the fact that it's well confirmed. It is important, at this point, to avoid the genetic fallacy: the fact that intentional theory is innate would *not* be a reason for supposing it to be untrue.

Realism, nativism, intentionality, and mental representation; the fundamental things apply. Play it again, Sam.

II.
Reduction and Unity of Science

Chapter 5

Special Sciences

A typical thesis of positivistic philosophy of science is that all true theories in the special sciences should reduce to physical theories 'in the long run'. This is intended to be an empirical thesis, and part of the evidence which supports it is provided by such scientific successes as the molecular theory of heat and the physical explanation of the chemical bond. But the philosophical popularity of the reductionist program cannot be explained by reference to these achievements alone. The development of science has witnessed the proliferation of specialized disciplines at least as often as it has witnessed their elimination, so the widespread enthusiasm for the view that there will eventually be only physics can hardly be a mere induction over past reductionist successes.

I think that many philosophers who accept reductionism do so primarily because they wish to endorse the generality of physics vis-à-vis the special sciences: roughly, the view that all events which fall under the laws of any science are physical events and hence fall under the laws of physics.[1] For such philosophers, saying that physics is basic science and saying that theories in the special sciences must reduce to physical theories have seemed to be two ways of saying the same thing, so that the latter doctrine has come to be a standard construal of the former.

In what follows, I shall argue that this is a considerable confusion. What has traditionally been called 'the unity of science' is a much stronger, and much less plausible, thesis than the generality of physics. If this is true, it is important. Though reductionism is an empirical doctrine, it is intended to play a regulative role in scientific practice. Reducibility to physics is taken to be a *constraint* upon the acceptability of theories in the special sciences, with the curious consequence that the more the special sciences succeed, the more they ought to disappear. Methodological problems about psychology, in particular, arise in just this way: The assumption that the subject matter of psychology is part of the subject matter of physics is taken to imply that psychological theories must reduce to physical theories, and it is this latter principle that makes the trouble. I want to avoid the trouble by challenging the inference.

Reductionism is the view that all the special sciences reduce to physics. The sense of 'reduce to' is, however, proprietary. It can be characterized as follows:[2]

Let formula (1) be a law of the special science S.

(1) $S_1 x \rightarrow S_2 y$

Formula (1) is intended to be read as something like 'all events which consist of x's being S_1 bring about events which consist of y's being S_2.' I assume that a science is individuated largely by reference to its typical predicates (see note 2), hence that if S is a special science, 'S_1' and 'S_2' are not predicates of basic physics. (I also assume that the 'all' which quantifies laws of the special sciences needs to be taken with a grain of salt. Such laws are typically *not* exceptionless. This is a point to which I shall return at length.) A necessary and sufficient condition for the reduction of formula (1) to a law of physics is that the formulae (2) and (3) should be laws, and a necessary and sufficient condition for the reduction

(2a) $S_1 x \rightleftharpoons P_1 x$
(2b) $S_2 y \rightleftharpoons P_2 y$
(3) $P_1 x \rightarrow P_2 y$

of S to physics is that all its laws should be so reduced.[3]

'P_1' and 'P_2' are supposed to be predicates of physics, and formula (3) is supposed to be a physical law. Formulae like (2) are often called 'bridge' laws. Their characteristic feature is that they contain predicates of both the reduced and the reducing science.

Bridge laws like formula (2) are thus contrasted with 'proper' laws like formulae (1) and (3). The upshot of the remarks so far is that the reduction of a science requires that any formula which appears as the antecedent or consequent of one of its proper laws must appear as the reduced formula in some bridge law or other.[4]

Several points about the connective '→' are now in order. First, whatever properties that connective may have, it is universally agreed that it must be transitive. This is important because it is usually assumed that the reduction of some of the special sciences proceeds via bridge laws which connect their predicates with those of intermediate reducing theories. Thus, psychology is presumed to reduce to physics via, say, neurology, biochemistry, and other local stops. The present point is that this makes no difference to the logic of the situation so long as the transitivity of '→' is assumed. Bridge laws which connect the predicates of S to those of S^* will satisfy the constraints upon the reduction of S to physics so long as there are other bridge laws which, directly or indirectly, connect the predicates of S^* to physical predicates.

There are, however, quite serious open questions about the interpretation of '→' in bridge laws. What turns on these questions is the extent to which reductionism is taken to be a physicalist thesis.

To begin with, if we read '→' as 'brings about' or 'causes' in proper laws, we will have to have some other connective for bridge laws, since bringing about and causing are presumably *a*symmetric, while bridge laws express symmetric relations. Moreover, unless bridge laws hold by virtue of the *identity* of the events which satisfy their antecedents with those that satisfy their consequents, reductionism will guarantee only a weak version of physicalism, and this would fail to express the underlying ontological bias of the reductionist program.

If bridge laws are not identity statements, then formulae like (2) claim at most that, by law, x's satisfaction of a P predicate and x's satisfaction of an S predicate are causally correlated. It follows from this that it is nomologically necessary that S and P predicates apply to the same things (i.e., that S predicates apply to a subset of the things that P predicates apply to). But, of course, this is compatible with a nonphysicalist ontology, since it is compatible with the possibility that x's satisfying S should not

itself be a physical event. On this interpretation, the truth of reductionism does *not* guarantee the generality of physics vis-à-vis
the special sciences, since there are some events (satisfactions of S
predicates) which fall in the domain of a special science (S) but
not in the domain of physics. (One could imagine, for example, a
doctrine according to which physical and psychological predicates
are both held to apply to organisms, but where it is denied that
the event which consists of an organism's satisfying a psychological predicate is, in any sense, a physical event. The upshot would
be a kind of psychophysical dualism of a non-Cartesian variety;
a dualism of events and/or properties rather than substances.)

Given these sorts of considerations, many philosophers have
held that bridge laws like formula (2) ought to be taken to express
contingent event identities, so that one would read formula (2a) in
some such fashion as 'every event which consists of an x's satisfying S_1 is identical to some event which consists of that x's satisfying P_1 and vice versa'. On this reading, the truth of reductionism
would entail that every event that falls under any scientific law is
a physical event, thereby simultaneously expressing the ontological bias of reductionism and guaranteeing the generality of physics
vis-à-vis the special sciences.

If the bridge laws express event identities, and if every event
that falls under the proper laws of a special science falls under a
bridge law, we get classical reductionism, a doctrine that entails
the truth of what I shall call 'token physicalism'. Token physicalism is simply the claim that all the events that the sciences talk
about are physical events. There are three things to notice about
token physicalism.

First, it is weaker than what is usually called 'materialism'.
Materialism claims *both* that token physicalism is true *and* that
every event falls under the laws of some science or other. One
could therefore be a token physicalist without being a materialist,
though I don't see why anyone would bother.

Second, token physicalism is weaker than what might be called
'type physicalism', the doctrine, roughly, that every *property* mentioned in the laws of any science is a physical property. Token
physicalism does not entail type physicalism, if only because the
contingent identity of a pair of events presumably does not guarantee the identity of the properties whose instantiation constitutes

the events; not even when the event identity is nomologically necessary. On the other hand, if an event is simply the instantiation of a property, then type physicalism does entail token physicalism; two events will be identical when they consist of the instantiation of the same property by the same individual at the same time.

Third, token physicalism is weaker than reductionism. Since this point is, in a certain sense, the burden of the argument to follow, I shan't labor it here. But, as a first approximation, reductionism is the conjunction of token physicalism with the assumption that there are natural kind predicates in an ideally completed physics which correspond to each natural kind predicate in any ideally completed special science. It will be one of my morals that reductionism cannot be inferred from the assumption that token physicalism is true. Reductionism is a sufficient, but not a necessary, condition for token physicalism.

To summarize: I shall be reading reductionism as entailing token physicalism since, if bridge laws state nomologically necessary contingent event identities, a reduction of psychology to neurology would require that any event which consists of the instantiation of a psychological property is identical with some event which consists of the instantiation of a neurological property. Both reductionism and token physicalism entail the generality of physics, since both hold that any event which falls within the universe of discourse of a special science will also fall within the universe of discourse of physics. Moreover, it is a consequence of both doctrines that any prediction which follows from the laws of a special science (and a statement of initial conditions) will follow equally from a theory which consists only of physics and the bridge laws (together with the statement of initial conditions). Finally, it is assumed by both reductionism and token physicalism that physics is the *only* basic science; *viz*, that it is the only science that is general in the sense just specified.

I now want to argue that reductionism is too strong a constraint upon the unity of science, but that, for any reasonable purposes, the weaker doctrine will do.

Every science implies a taxonomy of the events in its universe of discourse. In particular, every science employs a descriptive

vocabulary of theoretical and observation predicates, such that
events fall under the laws of the science by virtue of satisfying
those predicates. Patently, not every true description of an event is
a description in such a vocabulary. For example, there are a large
number of events which consist of things having been transported
to a distance of less than three miles from the Eiffel Tower. I take
it, however, that there is no science which contains 'is transported
to a distance of less than three miles from the Eiffel Tower' as part
of its descriptive vocabulary. Equivalently, I take it that there is
no natural law which applies to events in virtue of their instantiating the property *is transported to a distance of less than three
miles from the Eiffel Tower* (though I suppose it is just conceivable that there is some law that applies to events in virtue of their
instantiating some distinct but coextensive property). By way of
abbreviating these facts, I shall say that the property *is transported
. . .* does not determine a *(natural) kind,* and that predicates which
express that property are not (natural) kind predicates.

If I knew what a law is, and if I believed that scientific theories
consist just of bodies of laws, then I could say that '*P*' is a kind
predicate relative to S if S contains proper laws of the form
'$P_x \to \ldots y$' or '$\ldots y \to P_x$': roughly, the kind predicates of a
science are the ones whose terms are the bound variables in its
proper laws. I am inclined to say this even in my present state of
ignorance, accepting the consequence that it makes the murky
notion of a kind viciously dependent on the equally murky
notions of *law* and *theory.* There is no firm footing here. If we
disagree about what a kind is, we will probably also disagree about
what a law is, and for the same reasons. I don't know how to
break out of this circle, but I think that there are some interesting
things to say about which circle we are in.

For example, we can now characterize the respect in which reductionism is too strong a construal of the doctrine of the unity of
science. If reductionism is true, then *every* kind is, or is coextensive with, a physical kind. (Every kind *is* a physical kind if bridge
statements express nomologically necessary property identities,
and every kind is coextensive with a physical kind if bridge statements express nomologically necessary event identities.) This
follows immediately from the reductionist premise that every
predicate which appears as the antecedent or consequent of a law

of a special science must appear as one of the reduced predicates in some bridge law, together with the assumption that the kind predicates are the ones whose terms are the bound variables in proper laws. If, in short, some physical law is related to each law of a special science in the way that formula (3) is related to formula (1), then every kind predicate of a special science is related to a kind predicate of physics in the way that formula (2) relates 'S_1' and 'S_2' to 'P_1' and 'P_2' respectively.

I now want to suggest some reasons for believing that this consequence is intolerable. These are not supposed to be knock-down reasons; they couldn't be, given that the question of whether reductionism is too strong is finally an *empirical* question. (The world could turn out to be such that every kind corresponds to a physical kind, just as it could turn out to be such that the property *is transported to a distance of less than three miles from the Eiffel Tower* determines a kind in, say, hydrodynamics. It's just that, as things stand, it seems very unlikely that the world *will* turn out to be either of these ways.)

The reason it is unlikely that every kind corresponds to a physical kind is just that (a) interesting generalizations (e.g., counterfactual supporting generalizations) can often be made about events whose physical descriptions have nothing in common; (b) it is often the case that *whether* the physical descriptions of the events subsumed by such generalizations have anything in common is, in an obvious sense, entirely irrelevant to the truth of the generalizations, or to their interestingness, or to their degree of confirmation, or, indeed, to any of their epistemologically important properties; and (c) the special sciences are very much in the business of formulating generalizations of this kind.

I take it that these remarks are obvious to the point of self-certification; they leap to the eye as soon as one makes the (apparently radical) move of taking the existence of the special sciences at all seriously. Suppose, for example, that Gresham's 'law' really is true. (If one doesn't like Gresham's law, then any true and counterfactual supporting generalization of any conceivable future economics will probably do as well.) Gresham's law says something about what will happen in monetary exchanges under certain conditions. I am willing to believe that physics is general *in the sense that it implies that any event which consists of a monetary exchange* (hence any event which falls under Gresham's law) *has a true description in the vocabulary of physics and in virtue of which it falls under the laws of physics.* But banal considerations suggest that a physical description which covers all such events must be wildly disjunctive. Some monetary exchanges involve strings of wampum. Some involve dollar bills. And some involve signing one's name to a check. What are the chances that a disjunction of physical predicates which covers all these events (i.e., a disjunctive predicate which can form the right hand side of a bridge law of the form 'x is a monetary exchange $\rightleftharpoons$ . . .') expresses a physical kind? In particular, what are the chances that such a predicate forms the antecedent or consequent of some proper law of physics? The point is that monetary exchanges have interesting things in common; Gresham's law, if true, says what one of these interesting things is. But what is interesting about monetary exchanges is surely not their commonalities under *physical* description. A kind like a monetary exchange *could* turn out to be coextensive with a physical kind; but if it did, that would be an accident on a cosmic scale.

In fact, the situation for reductionism is still worse than the discussion thus far suggests. For reductionism claims not only that all kinds are coextensive with physical kinds, but that the coextensions are nomologically necessary: bridge laws are *laws*. So, if Gresham's law is true, it follows that there is a (bridge) law of nature such that 'x is a monetary exchange $\rightleftharpoons x$ is P' is true for every value of x, and such that P is a term for a physical kind. But, surely, there is no such law. If there were, then P would have to cover not only all the systems of monetary exchange that there *are,* but also all the systems of monetary exchange that there *could be;* a law must succeed with the counterfactuals. What physical predicate is a candidate for P in 'x is a nomologically possible monetary exchange iff P_x'?

To summarize: An immortal econophysicist might, when the whole show is over, find a predicate in physics that was, in brute fact, coextensive with 'is a monetary exchange'. If physics is general—if the ontological biases of reductionism are true—then there must *be* such a predicate. But (a) to paraphrase a remark Professor Donald Davidson made in a slightly different context, nothing but brute enumeration could convince us of this brute coextensivity, and (b) there would seem to be no chance at all that the physical predicate employed in stating the coextensivity would be a physical kind term, and (c) there is still less chance that the coextension would be lawful (i.e., that it would hold not only for the nomologically possible world that turned out to be real, but for any nomologically possible world at all).[5]

I take it that the preceding discussion strongly suggests that economics is not reducible to physics in the special sense of reduction involved in claims for the unity of science. There is, I suspect, nothing peculiar about economics in this respect; the reasons why economics is unlikely to reduce to physics are paralleled by those which suggest that psychology is unlikely to reduce to neurology.

If psychology is reducible to neurology, then for every psychological kind predicate there is a coextensive neurological kind predicate, and the generalization which states this coextension is a law. Clearly, many psychologists believe something of the sort. There are departments of psychobiology or psychology and brain science in universities throughout the world whose very existence is an institutionalized gamble that such lawful coextensions can be found. Yet, as has been frequently remarked in recent discussions of materialism, there are good grounds for hedging these bets. There are no firm data for any but the grossest correspondence between types of psychological states and types of neurological states, and it is entirely possible that the nervous system of higher organisms characteristically achieves a given psychological end by a wide variety of neurological means. It is also possible that given neurological structures subserve many different psychological functions at different times, depending upon the character of the activities in which the organism is engaged.[6] In either event, the attempt to pair neurological structures with psychological functions could expect only limited success. Physiological psychologists of the stature of Karl Lashley have held this sort of view.

The present point is that the reductionist program in psychology is clearly *not* to be defended on ontological grounds. Even if (token) psychological events are (token) neurological events, it does not follow that the kind predicates of psychology are coextensive with the kind predicates of any other discipline (including physics). That is, the assumption that every psychological event is a physical event does not guarantee that physics (or, a fortiori, any other discipline more general than psychology) can provide an appropriate vocabulary for psychological theories. I emphasize this point because I am convinced that the make-or-break commitment of many physiological psychologists to the reductionist program stems precisely from having confused that program with (token) physicalism.

What I have been doubting is that there are neurological kinds coextensive with psychological kinds. What seems increasingly clear is that, even if there are such coextensions, they cannot be lawful. For it seems increasingly likely that there are nomological-ly possible systems other than organisms (viz., automata) which satisfy the kind predicates of psychology but which satisfy no neurological predicates at all. Now, as Putnam has emphasized (1960), if there are any such systems, then there must be vast numbers, since equivalent automata can, in principle, be made out of practically anything. If this observation is correct, then there can be no serious hope that the class of automata whose psychol-ogy is effectively identical to that of some organism can be de-scribed by *physical* kind predicates (though, of course, if token physicalism is true, that class can be picked out by some physical predicate or other). The upshot is that the classical formulation of the unity of science is at the mercy of progress in the field of computer simulation. This is, of course, simply to say that that formulation was too strong. The unity of science was intended to be an empirical hypothesis, defeasible by possible scientific findings. But no one had it in mind that it should be defeated by Newell, Shaw, and Simon.

I have thus far argued that psychological reductionism (the doctrine that every psychological natural kind is, or is coextensive with, a neurological natural kind) is not equivalent to, and cannot be inferred from, token physicalism (the doctrine that every psychological event is a neurological event). It may, however, be argued that one might as well take the doctrines to be equivalent since the only possible *evidence* one could have for token physical-ism would also be evidence for reductionism: viz., that such evidence would have to consist in the discovery of type-to-type psychophysical correlations.

A moment's consideration shows, however, that this argument

is not well taken. If type-to-type psychophysical correlations would be evidence for token physicalism, so would correlations of other specifiable kinds.

We have type-to-type correlations where, for every n-tuple of events that are of the same psychological kind, there is a correlated n-tuple of events that are of the same neurological kind.[7] Imagine a world in which such correlations are *not* forthcoming. What is found, instead, is that for every n-tuple of type identical psychological events, there is a spatiotemporally correlated n-tuple of type *distinct* neurological events. That is, every psychological event is paired with some neurological event or other, but psychological events of the same kind are sometimes paired with neurological events of different kinds. My present point is that such pairings would provide as much support for token physicalism as type-to-type pairings do *so long as we are able to show that the type distinct neurological events paired with a given kind of psychological event are identical in respect of whatever properties are relevant to type identification in psychology.* Suppose, for purposes of explication, that psychological events are type identified by reference to their behavioral consequences.[8] Then what is required of all the neurological events paired with a class of type homogeneous psychological events is only that they be identical in respect of their behavioral consequences. To put it briefly, type identical events do not, of course, have *all* their properties in common, and type distinct events must nevertheless be identical in *some* of their properties. The empirical confirmation of token physicalism does not depend on showing that the neurological counterparts of type identical psychological events are themselves type identical. What needs to be shown is just that they are identical in respect of those properties which determine what kind of *psychological* event a given event is.

Could we have evidence that an otherwise heterogeneous set of neurological events have those kinds of properties in common? Of course we could. The neurological theory might itself explain why an n-tuple of neurologically type distinct events are identical in their behavioral consequences, or, indeed, in respect of any of indefinitely many other such relational properties. And, if the neurological theory failed to do so, some science more basic than neurology might succeed.

My point in all this is, once again, not that correlations between type homogeneous psychological states and type heterogeneous neurological states would prove that token physicalism is true. It is only that such correlations might give us as much reason to be token physicalists as type-to-type correlations would. If this is correct, then epistemological arguments from token physicalism to reductionism must be wrong.

It seems to me (to put the point quite generally) that the classical construal of the unity of science has really badly misconstrued the *goal* of scientific reduction. The point of reduction is *not* primarily to find some natural kind predicate of physics coextensive with each kind predicate of a special science. It is, rather, to explicate the physical mechanisms whereby events conform to the laws of the special sciences. I have been arguing that there is no logical or epistemological reason why success in the second of these projects should require success in the first, and that the two are likely to come apart *in fact* wherever the physical mechanisms whereby events conform to a law of the special sciences are heterogeneous.

I take it that the discussion thus far shows that reductionism is probably too strong a construal of the unity of science; on the one hand, it is incompatible with probable results in the special sciences, and, on the other, it is more than we need to assume if what we primarily want, from an ontological point of view, is just to be good token physicalists. In what follows, I shall try to sketch a liberalized version of the relation between physics and the special sciences which seems to me to be just strong enough in these respects. I shall then give a couple of independent reasons for supposing that the revised doctrine may be the right one.

The problem all along has been that there is an open empirical possibility that what corresponds to the kind predicates of a reduced science may be a heterogeneous and unsystematic disjunction of predicates in the reducing science. We do not want the unity of science to be prejudiced by this possibility. Suppose, then, that we allow that bridge statements may be of this form,

(4) $Sx \rightleftharpoons P_1 x \vee P_2 x \vee \ldots \vee P_n x$

where $P_1 \vee P_2 \vee \ldots \vee P_n$ is *not* a kind predicate in the reducing science. I take it that this is tantamount to allowing that at least some 'bridge laws' may, in fact, not turn out to be laws, since I take it that a necessary condition on a universal generalization being lawlike is that the predicates which constitute its antecedent and consequent should be kind predicates. I am thus assuming that it is enough, for purposes of the unity of science, that every law of the special sciences should be reducible to physics by bridge statements which express true empirical generalizations. Bearing in mind that bridge statements are to be construed as species of identity statements, formula (4) will be read as something like 'every event which consists of x's satisfying S is identical with some event which consists of x's satisfying some or other predicate belonging to the disjunction $P_1 \lor P_2 \lor \ldots \lor P_n$'.

Now, in cases of reduction where what corresponds to formula (2) is not a law, what corresponds to formula (3) will not be either, and for the same reason: viz., the predicates appearing in the antecedent and consequent will, by hypothesis, not be kind predicates. Rather, what we will have is something that looks like Figure 1. That is, the antecedent and consequent of the reduced law will each be connected with a disjunction of predicates in the reducing science. Suppose, for the moment, that the reduced law is exceptionless, viz., that no S_1 events satisfy P'. Then there will

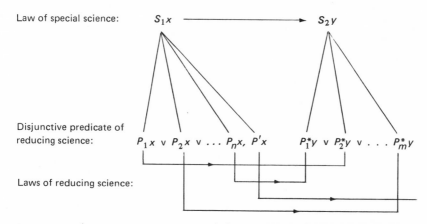

*Figure 1. Schematic representation of the proposed relation between the re-
duced and the reducing science on a revised account of the unity of science.
If any S_1 events are of the type P', they will be exceptions to the law $S_1 x \rightarrow
S_2 y$. See text.*

be laws of the reducing science which connect the satisfaction of *each* member of the disjunction associated with the antecedent of the reduced law with the satisfaction of some member of the disjunction associated with the consequent of the reduced law. That is, if $S_1 x \to S_2 y$ is exceptionless, then there must be some proper law of the reducing science which either states or entails that $P_1 x \to P^*$ for some P^*, and similarly for $P_2 x$ through $P_n x$. Since there must be such laws, and since each of them is a 'proper' law in the sense of which we have been using that term, it follows that each disjunct of P_1 v P_2 v ... v P_n is a kind predicate, as is each disjunct of P^*_1 v P^*_2 v ... v P^*_n.

This, however, is where push comes to shove. For it might be argued that if each disjunct of the P disjunction is lawfully connected to some disjunct of the P^* disjunction, then it follows that formula (5) is itself a law.

(5) $P_1 x$ v $P_2 x$ v ... v $P_n x \to P^*_1 y$ v $P^*_2 y$ v ... v $P^*_n y$

The point would be that the schema in Figure 1 implies $P_1 x \to P^*_2 y$, $P_2 x \to P^*_m y$, etc., and the argument from a premise of the form $(P \supset R)$ *and* $(Q \supset S)$ to a conclusion of the form $(P$ v $Q) \supset (R$ v $S)$ is valid.

What I am inclined to say about this is that it just shows that 'it's a law that ——' defines a nontruth functional context (or, equivalently for these purposes, that not all truth functions of kind predicates are themselves kind predicates); in particular, that one may not argue from: 'it's a law that P brings about R' and 'it's a law that Q brings about S' to 'it's a law that P or Q brings about R or S'. (Though, of course, the argument from those premises to 'P or Q brings about R or S' *simpliciter* is fine.) I think, for example, that it is a law that the irradiation of green plants by sunlight causes carbohydrate synthesis, and I think that it is a law that friction causes heat, but I do not think that it is a law that (either the irradiation of green plants by sunlight or friction) causes (either carbohydrate synthesis or heat). Correspondingly, I doubt that 'is either carbohydrate synthesis or heat' is plausibly taken to be a kind predicate.

It is not strictly mandatory that one should agree with all this, but one denies it at a price. In particular, if one allows the full range of truth-functional arguments inside the context 'it's a law that ——', then one gives up the possibility of identifying the kind predicates of a science with the ones which constitute the antecedents or consequents of its proper laws. (Thus formula (5) would be a proper law of physics which fails to satisfy that condition.) One thus inherits the need for an alternative construal of the notion of a kind, and I don't know what that alternative would be like.

The upshot seems to be this. If we do not require that bridge statements must be laws, then either some of the generalizations to which the laws of special sciences reduce are not themselves lawlike, or some laws are not formulable in terms of kinds. Whichever way one takes formula (5), the important point is that the relation between sciences proposed by Figure 1 is weaker than what standard reductionism requires. In particular, it does not imply a correspondence between the kind predicates of the reduced and the reducing science. Yet it does imply physicalism given the same assumption that makes standard reductionism physicalistic: viz., that bridge statements express token event identities. But these are precisely the properties that we wanted a revised account of the unity of science to exhibit.

I now want to give two further reasons for thinking that this construal of the unity of science is right. First, it allows us to see how the laws of the special sciences could reasonably have exceptions, and, second, it allows us to see why there are special sciences at all. These points in turn.

Consider, again, the model of reduction implicit in formulae (2) and (3). I assume that the laws of basic science are strictly exceptionless, and I assume that it is common knowledge that the laws of the special sciences are not. But now we have a dilemma to face. Since '→' expresses a relation (or relations) which must be transitive, formula (1) can have exceptions only if the bridge laws do. But if the bridge laws have exceptions, reductionism loses its ontological bite, since we can no longer say that every event which consists of the satisfaction of an S-predicate consists of the satisfaction of a P-predicate. In short, given the reductionist model, we cannot consistently assume that the bridge laws and the basic laws are exceptionless while assuming that the special laws are not. But we cannot accept the violation of the bridge laws unless we are willing to vitiate the ontological claim that is the main point of the reductionist program.

We can get out of this (*salve* the reductionist model) in one of two ways. We can give up the claim that the special laws have exceptions or we can give up the claim that the basic laws are exceptionless. I suggest that both alternatives are undesirable—the first because it flies in the face of fact. There is just no chance at all that the true, counterfactual supporting generalizations of, say, psychology, will turn out to hold in strictly each and every condition where their antecedents are satisfied. Even when the spirit is willing the flesh is often weak. There are always going to be behavioral lapses which are physiologically explicable but which are uninteresting from the point of view of psychological theory. But the second alternative is not much better. It may, after all, turn out that the laws of basic science have exceptions. But the question arises whether one wants the unity of science to depend on the assumption that they do.

On the account summarized in Figure 1, however, everything works out satisfactorily. A nomologically sufficient condition for an exception to $S_1 x \rightarrow S_2 y$ is that the bridge statements should identify some occurrence of the satisfaction of S_1 with an occurrence of the satisfaction of a P-predicate which is not itself lawfully connected to the satisfaction of any P^*-predicate (i.e., suppose S_1 is connected to P' such that there is no law which connects P' to any predicate which bridge statements associate with S_2. Then any instantiation of S_1 which is contingently identical to an instantiation of P' will be an event which constitutes an exception to $S_1 x \rightarrow S_2 y$). Notice that, in this case, we need assume no exceptions to the laws of the *reducing* science since, by hypothesis, formula (5) is not a law.

In fact, strictly speaking, formula (5) has no status in the reduction at all. It is simply what one gets when one universally quantifies a formula whose antecedent is the physical disjunction corresponding to S_1 and whose consequent is the physical disjunction corresponding to S_2. As such, it will be true when $S_1 x \rightarrow S_2 y$ is exceptionless and false otherwise. What does the work of expressing the physical mechanisms whereby n-tuples of events conform, or fail to conform, to $S_1 x \rightarrow S_2 y$ is not formula (5) but the laws which severally relate elements of the disjunction P_1 v P_2 v . . . v P_n to elements of the disjunction P^*_1 v P^*_2 v . . . v P^*_m . Where there *is* a law which relates an event that satisfies one of the P

disjuncts to an event which satisfies one of the $P*$ disjuncts, the pair of events so related conforms to $S_1 x \rightarrow S_2 y$. When an event which satisfies a P-predicate is not related by law to an event which satisfies a $P*$-predicate, that event will constitute an exception to $S_1 x \rightarrow S_2 y$. The point is that none of the laws which effect these several connections need themselves have exceptions in order that $S_1 x \rightarrow S_2 y$ should do so.

To put this discussion less technically: We could, if we liked, *require* the taxonomies of the special sciences to correspond to the taxonomy of physics by insisting upon distinctions between the kinds postulated by the former whenever they turn out to correspond to distinct kinds in the latter. This would *make* the laws of the special sciences exceptionless if the laws of basic science are. But it would also likely loose us precisely the generalizations which we want the special sciences to express. (If economics were to posit as many *kinds* of monetary systems as there are physical realizations of monetary systems, then the generalizations of economics *would* be exceptionless. But, presumably, only vacuously so, since there would be no generalizations left for economists to state. Gresham's law, for example, would have to be formulated as a vast, open disjunction about what happens in monetary system$_1$ or monetary system$_n$ under conditions which would themselves defy uniform characterization. We would not be able to say what happens in monetary systems *tout court* since, by hypothesis, 'is a monetary system' corresponds to no kind of predicate of physics.)

In fact, what we do is precisely the reverse. We allow the generalizations of the special sciences to *have* exceptions, thus preserving the kinds to which the generalizations apply, But since we know that the *physical* descriptions of the members of these kinds may be quite heterogeneous, and since we know that the physical mechanisms which connect the satisfaction of the antecedents of such generalizations to the satisfaction of their consequents may be equally diverse, we expect both that there will be exceptions to the generalizations and that these will be 'explained away' at the level of the reducing science. This is one of the respects in which physics really is assumed to be bedrock science; exceptions to *its* generalizations (if there are any) had better be random, because there is nowhere 'further down' to go in explaining the mechanism whereby the exceptions occur.

This brings us to why there are special sciences at all. Reductionism, as we remarked at the outset, flies in the face of the facts about the scientific institution: the existence of a vast and interleaved conglomerate of special scientific disciplines which often appear to proceed with only the most casual acknowledgment of the constraint that their theories must turn out to be physics 'in the long run'. I mean that the acceptance of this constraint often plays little or no role in the practical validation of theories. Why is this so? Presumably, the reductionist answer must be *entirely* epistemological. If only physical particles weren't so small (if only brains were on the *out*side, where one can get a look at them), *then* we would do physics instead of paleontology (neurology instead of psychology, psychology instead of economics, and so on down). There is an epistemological reply: viz., that even if brains were out where they could be looked *at,* we wouldn't, as things now stand, know what to look *for.* We lack the appropriate theoretical apparatus for the psychological taxonomy of neurological events.

If it turns out that the functional decomposition of the nervous system corresponds precisely to its neurological (anatomical, biochemical, physical) decomposition, then there are only epistemological reasons for studying the former instead of the latter. But suppose that there is no such correspondence? Suppose the functional organization of the nervous system cross-cuts its neurological organization. Then the existence of psychology depends not on the fact that neurons are so depressingly small, but rather on the fact that neurology does not posit the kinds that psychology requires.

I am suggesting, roughly, that there are special sciences not because of the nature of our epistemic relation to the world, but because of the way the world is put together: not all the kinds (not all the classes of things and events about which there are important, counterfactual supporting generalizations to make) are, or correspond to, physical kinds. A way of stating the classical reductionist view is that things which belong to different physical kinds ipso facto can have none of their projectable descriptions in common:[9] that if x and y differ in those descriptions by virtue of which they fall under the proper laws of physics, they must differ in those descriptions by virtue of which they fall under any laws at all. But why should we believe that this is so? Any pair of entities, however different their physical structure, must nevertheless converge in indefinitely many of their properties. Why should there not be, among those convergent properties, some whose lawful interrelations support the generalizations of the special sciences? Why, in short, should not the kind predicates of the special sciences *cross-classify* the physical natural kinds?[10]

Physics develops the taxonomy of its subject matter which best suits its purposes: the formulation of exceptionless laws which are basic in the several senses discussed above. But this is not the only taxonomy which may be required if the purposes of science in general are to be served: e.g., if we are to state such true, counterfactual supporting generalizations as there are to state. So there are special sciences, with their specialized taxonomies, in the business of stating some of these generalizations. If science is to be unified, then all such taxonomies must apply *to the same things*. If physics is to be basic science, then each of these things had better be a physical thing. But it is not further required that the taxonomies which the special sciences employ must themselves reduce to the taxonomy of physics. It is not required, and it is probably not true.

Chapter 6

Computation and Reduction

Introduction

Nobody loses all the time; a fitful and negative glimmer illuminates the philosophy of mind. We now know that the program of behavioristic reduction of psychological theories cannot, in general, be carried through. And we know why. Let a behaviorist be someone who claims, at a minimum, that there must be a reference to behavior in any logically perspicuous specification of a psychological state. Then whatever else may be wrong with the behaviorist program (no doubt plenty else is wrong), it is blocked by the intensionality of typical psychological terms.[1] So, for example, there is a *sense* in which there is a reference to whistling (to, as psychologists inelegantly say, Dixie-whistling behavior) in such English formulae as 'Ψ = John's intention to whistle a snatch of Dixie', and perhaps there would be a similar sort of reference to, say, avoidance behavior in any adequately perspicuous specification of John's pains. Perhaps, that is, John's having a pain profoundly involves his intending or desiring to avoid a painful stimulus. But, of course, that would not be good enough to make the behaviorist's case. For such "references to behavior" as are, in *this* sense, involved in logically perspicuous specifications of psychological states occur (only) in intensional contexts; which is to say that they are not, in any full-blooded sense, references to behavior at all. Briefly, whatever is required to make it true that John's intention to whistle a snatch of *Dixie* is such and such does not in general, involve the actual occurrence of any *Dixie*-whistling, and whatever is required to make it true that John's pain is such and such does not, in general, involve the actual occurrence of any avoidance behavior. Similarly, mutatis mutandis, for other psychological states and processes.

This is all familiar territory, and I mention these points only in order to set them to one side. My present interest is the following. Although it is fairly clear what kinds of problems phenomena of intentionality raise for *behavioristic* reductions of psychological predicates, very little is understood about the problems they raise for *physicalistic* reductions of the sort often contemplated by central-state identity theorists. In fact, it often happens in the standard literature on mind/body identity that this question is not so much as aired.[2] Perhaps this is due to the continuing influence of an early version of the identity theory, which was physicalist about *sensations* but behaviorist about propositional attitudes (see, for example, Place, 1956, and Smart, 1957). On that view, physicalism presupposes behavioral analyses for those psychological predicates which most evidently establish intensional contexts: verbs like "hopes," "thinks," "intends," "feels that," "believes," etc. The identity theory is thus left free to operate in the account of sensations, an area where issues of intensionality seem less pressing.

But however one construes the history, it now seems clear that behavioristic analyses of propositional attitudes will not be forthcoming, so physicalist theories will have to decide what to do about their intensionality. And it also seems clear that the problems intensionality poses for physicalism are likely to be quite different from the ones it posed for behaviorism. The reason for this is that, prima facie, what the behaviorist requires of reduction is quite different from what the physicalist requires. Behaviorism will not do unless for every true sentence in an (ideally completed) psychology there exists a canonical *paraphrase* in a proprietary vocabulary. Nonlogical expressions in this vocabulary are to be behavioral (whatever, precisely, that is supposed to mean), and all contexts in canonical paraphrases are to be extensional.

It is a good deal less clear what the physicalist wants. *Not* a paraphrase, surely, because on no plausible account does a physicalistic sentence say what the corresponding mentalistic sentence means. But, on the other hand, the physicalist presumably wants something more than an extensional sentence materially equivalent to each intensional sentence, since that is available by merest stipulation. Let 'Alfred = John's intention to whistle a snatch of *Dixie*' be a stipulated equivalence. Then, for 'John intends to whistle a s. of D.' we get, roughly, 'Here's Alfred,' which satisfies none of the traditional tests for opacity. Nor will it content the physicalist to find an extensional sentence equivalent to each intensional one such that the equivalence is nomologically necessary since, presumably, a psychophysical parallelist or epiphenomenalist could grant him that without granting him what he primarily wants. Nor, I think, would the physicalist be content with the de facto identity of the things that mental terms name with those that physical terms name since, as we shall see, there are several respects in which he might get that and not get the substantive reduction of psychology to neurology (or any more basic science). In fact, it seems difficult to me to say just what the physicalistic reductionist *does* want. In this paper, in any event, I shall consider what, in the light of the intensionality of typical psychological predicates, he is likely to get, and what it is likely to cost him.

My strategy will be the following. I shall say a few things about reduction and a few things about psychological explanation. I shall then argue that, given the notions of reduction and psychological explanation at issue, the reduction of psychology could probably be purchased only at the expense of its explanatory power. I shall suggest, too, that this situation is probably specific to psychology as opposed to other special sciences. That is, reducing psychology to (say) neurology would probably lose us something that reducing meterology to (say) mechanics would probably not lose us. This argument will turn on the special role that intensional expressions play in psychological theories. Finally, I shall discuss very briefly how we could strengthen the notion of reduction so as to guarantee that, if psychology is reducible in this stronger sense, then it *is* reducible without loss of explanatory power.

I shall not, however, argue for or against the blanket contention that psychology is reducible to neurology or physics. Indeed, it is hard to see how a sensible argument to either conclusion *could* be mounted in the present state of play. For, not only are there straightforwardly empirical questions that are pertinent and un-answered, but also what we say about the reducibility of psychol-ogy depends on what we think psychological theories should be like and what we require reduction to preserve. And we do not know much about what psychological theories should be like or about which constraints on reduction are justifiable.

Reduction

In what follows, I shall be taking "reduction" in quite a special-ized sense; the sense that (if I read the literature correctly) in-formed much positivistic thinking about the relation between physics and the special sciences. It will be one of my points that this notion of reduction is not the only one compatible with the ontological assumptions of physicalism. But I shall start with it because it is widely known and because the considerations that are likely to make psychological theories recalcitrant to reduction in this special sense would also hold on many other construals, as far as I can tell. So as not to have to write "reduction in this special sense", whenever I wish to refer to reduction in this special sense, I shall adopt the practice of calling it simply "re-duction." But the reader is encouraged to bear the qualifier in mind.

In the first place, then, "reduces to" names a relation between *theories.* When that relation holds between a pair of theories, say T_1 and T_0, T_0 is said to be a *reducer* of T_1. The reduction relation is transitive and asymmetrical, hence irreflexive. By the "unity of science" I shall mean the doctrine that all sciences except physics reduce to physics. By "physicalistic reductionism" I shall mean a certain claim that is entailed by, but does not entail, the unity of science; viz., the claim that psychology reduces to physics (pre-sumably via neurology).

I do not know whether theories are sets of sentences, and I do not wish to prejudice that question. However, some of the condi-tions on reduction constrain properties of the syntax and vocabu-lary of expressions in the reduced and reducing sciences. So, in what follows, I shall take "theory" to mean "theory in normal form." A theory in normal form *is* a set of sentences by stipula-tion. I shall also sometimes write as though all the sentences that belong to a theory in normal form are universal generalizations.

The interesting problems about reduction persist on this assumption, and it helps with the exposition.

Let each sentence of the set T_1 be the universal closure of a formula of the form $A_x \rightarrow B_y$ (read: it is a law that x's being A is causally sufficient for y's being B). Let each sentence of the set T_0 be the universal closure of a formula of the form $\Phi_x \rightarrow \Psi_y$. Then the crucial conditions on T_0 reducing T_1 are these.

a) (At least some) items in the vocabulary A, B . . . are not in the vocabulary Φ, Ψ. . . .

b) Let the "projected" predicates of a science be the ones that appear essentially in its laws. Then T_0 reduces T_1 only if nomologically necessary and sufficient conditions for the satisfaction of the projected predicates of T_1 can be framed in the vocabulary of T_0.

So, for example, theories in whose laws the expression 'water' (or its cognates) occurs will reduce to chemistry only if (a') chemistry contains some expression other than 'water' (say 'H_2O') such that (b') '(x) (x is water if x is H_2O)' expresses a law.

c) Let T_2 be the set whose members are T_0 together with such laws. Then T_0 reduces T_1 only if every consequence of T_1 is a consequence of T_2.[3]

Formulae like the one quoted in (b') are said to express "bridge" laws; we can call them *bridge formulae*. For our purposes, the essence of standard reductionism is the suggestion that bridge formulae link reduced sciences to their reducers. Viewed as principles of inference, bridge formulae permit us to substitute expressions in the vocabulary of T_0 for expressions in the vocabulary of T_1 preserving nomological necessity. That is, if G is a generalization in the vocabulary of T_1, and G' is the formula derived from G by replacing every expression of T_1 by the T_0 expression that is related to it by some bridge formula, then if G is nomologically necessary, G' will be too. For essentially this reason, it is plausible to claim that any event causally explained by G is also causally explained by G'.

There are many difficulties with this notion of reduction, but I shall not pursue them here. Suffice it to mention only the following rather general points. First, on this account, reducibility involves a good deal more than the ontological claim that things that satisfy descriptions in the vocabulary of T_1 also satisfy descriptions in the vocabulary of T_0 (e.g., that every event that falls under a law of psychology satisfies a physical description). I have stressed this point in Chapter 5, above, but it may be worth repeating here in passing. Since the present account requires that bridge formulae be lawlike, it entails not only that their antecedents and consequents be expressions of the reduced and reducing science respectively, but also that they be *projectible* expressions of the reduced and reducing sciences respectively. (This is of a piece with the remark made above, that substitution under the equivalences specified by bridge formulae is supposed to preserve nomological necessity.) That this condition is stronger than the ontological requirement that whatever falls under the generalizations of T_1 should also fall under those of T_0 can be seen from the consideration that the latter could be satisfied even if bridge formulae expressed (not laws but) mere true empirical generalizations; but the requirement that nomological necessity be preserved under the substitutions that bridge formulae license would presumably *not* be satisfied in this case.

Second, if the present account is correct, there is an important sense in which *syntax* is preserved under reduction; on this view, the pertinent difference between a reduced generalization of T_1 and its reducing counterpart in T_0 lies just in the (nonlogical) *vocabulary* of the two formulae. To put this point the other way around, if we look only at the *form* of the sentences that constitute T_0 and T_1, disregarding such expressions as belong to the nonlogical vocabularies of the two theories, then there will not, in general, be any way of telling the sentences of T_0 and T_1 apart. Fundamentally, standard reduction just consists in substituting expressions in the nonlogical vocabulary of T_0 for expressions in the nonlogical vocabulary of T_1 under the equivalences which the bridge formulae specify.

It connects with the latter observation that the *point* of standard reduction (insofar as the point is not merely ontological) is primarily to exhibit the generalizations of T_1 as special cases of the generalizations of T_0. The idea is roughly this: events fall under the generalizations of T_1 by virtue of satisfying descriptions in the vocabulary of T_1. Reduction permits us to *re*describe these events in the vocabulary of T_0, hence to express their conformity to the generalizations of T_0. Since it is assumed that the generalizations of T_0 will normally hold in a domain that properly includes the domain of T_1 (e.g., physics is true of everything that psychology is true of, and physics is true of other things as well), progress in reduction should permit us to subsume phenomena under laws of increasing generality. But since it is said that the generality of laws is an index of the explanatory power of the theories that express them, progress in reduction turns out to be progress toward theories of increasing explanatory power. The unity of science was, perhaps, initially construed as just a way of expressing the ontological claim that everything is the kind of thing that physics is about. But we can now see that the unity of science expressed an epistemological claim as well: the claim that physical explanation subsumes explanation in the special sciences.[4]

I want to consider the application of this picture of reduction to certain kinds of theories typical of current work in cognitive psychology. In order to do so, however, I shall first have to say something about the structure of such theories.

Computation

I am interested, for present purposes, in psychological theories that propose "computational" or "information flow" accounts of mental processes. Not all psychological theories do propose such accounts; indeed, not all mental processes provide appropriate domains for theories of this kind. Roughly, and to put the cart before the horse, mental states are computationally related only when they are related in content. Psychological theories of information flow model such relations of content by (a) providing a descriptive vocabulary in which the content of a mental state can be perspicuously represented, and (b) specifying transformations over formulae in that vocabulary which predict mental states and processes of the organism—in particular, its propositional attitudes. I have elsewhere discussed such theories at considerable length (Fodor, 1975), so in this paper I shall work largely from examples.

Consider learning. I suppose that cases of learning (or, in any event, cases of learning that . . . , where what fills the blank is approximately a sentence) are typically cases of environmentally determined alterations of epistemic state. In particular, what happens when someone learns that so and so is typically that (a) what he knows or believes changes, and (b) the change is a causal consequence (inter alia) of his transactions with his environment. So, for example, you can learn that Minneapolis is in Minnesota by looking at a map of Minnesota and noticing that Minneapolis is on it, or by hearing someone say (in a language one understands) that Minneapolis is in Minnesota, or by drawing the pertinent inference from the observation that Minneapolis is in the same state as St. Paul and that St. Paul is in Minnesota, etc. In general, in such cases, certain things happen to one and, as a more or less direct consequence, what one knows or believes is altered in certain ways. I assume that "consequence" is to be construed causally here since, as far as I can see, no other way of construing it will suit the case.

But not every case of environmentally caused alteration in knowledge or belief is a case of learning. Suppose, for example, that someone were to invent a pill which, when swallowed, induces a mastery of Latin. One takes the pill and eo ipso acquires the relevant beliefs about what "eo ipso" means, how "cogitare" is conjugated, and so on. Moreover, the acquisition of these beliefs is, let us suppose, a causal consequence of taking the pill: the events of taking the pill and acquiring the beliefs fall, respectively, under the antecedent and consequent of a causal law, etc. Still, acquiring Latin by taking the pill is not *learning* Latin, any more than coming to speak the way aphasics do as a consequence of traumatic insult to Broca's area counts as learning aphasic. What is missing?

Intuitively, what is missing is this: the relation between what is acquired when one acquires Latin this way and the experiences that causally occasion the acquisition is, though nomological by hypothesis, notably arbitrary. (This contrasts with the case in which, e.g., one learns what "eo ipso" means by being told what "eo ipso" means, or by inducing its meaning from observations of occasions on which people say "eo ipso," etc.) A way to exhibit the arbitrariness is this: but for the hypothetical causal laws involved, one could imagine the situation to be reversed, so that it is insult to Broca's area that occasions the acquisition of Latin and swallowing the pill that induces aphasia. This situation seems no less gratuitous than the one we imagined initially. It is, in this sense, just an accident—or better, just a brute fact—that the pills are connected with Latin rather than with aphasia; there is, as it were, nothing in a perspicuous description of what one learns when one learns Latin that connects it with what happens when one swallows a pill. But it is surely *not* just an accident that being told what "eo ipso" means is connected with learning what "eo ipso" means, or, for that matter, that it is English (and not Latin, Urdu, or aphasic) that children reared in English-speaking environments eventually learn to speak.[5]

Take another case. A man sees many gray elephants and, as a consequence of what he sees, comes to believe that elephants are gray. One wants to say there is a difference between this situation and one in which a man sees many gray elephants and, as a consequence of what he sees, comes to believe, say, that two is a prime number. What *kind* of difference? Well, not that the relation between seeing what he saw and coming to believe what he came to believe is causal, for we can imagine that to be true in *both* cases. Still, one wants to say, the first man learned (from his experiences) that elephants are gray, whereas the second man simply had certain experiences and came to believe that two is a prime number as a result of having had them. The relation between the second man's beliefs and his experiences is, in some important sense, arbitrary, whereas the relation between the first man's beliefs and his experiences, in the same important sense, is not. (It is, of course, connected with this that the experiences from which one can learn that so and so are often the experiences one can appeal to in justifying the belief that so and so.)

One more example, and then I shall try to say something about what the examples are examples of. A man sees many gray elephants and, as a causal consequence, comes to believe that elephants are gray. But, although each of the things he saw (the seeing of which contributed causally to the fixation of his beliefs that elephants are gray) was, in fact, a gray elephant, still what he *took* each of these things to be was, say, a very small, brown camel. Such a case is, of course, doubly grotesque; one wants to ask why a man should take elephants to be camels and why, having done so, he should come to believe that elephants are gray as a consequence of the putative camel-sightings. My point is that there need be no answer to these questions beyond adverting to the facts about the man's physical constitution and the way the world happens to impinge upon him. One can, in short, imagine a man so constructed and so situated that his experiences come to fix the right belief about the color of elephants by, as it were, the wrong route. But I think we should want to add that, prima facie, that sort of fixation of belief would not be learning.[6] For learning one needs a nonarbitrary relation (not just between the facts about the experiences and the content of the beliefs they determine, but also) between the content of the beliefs and what the man *takes* the facts about the experiences to be.

To a first approximation, then: in paradigmatic cases of learning, there is a relation of content between the belief that is acquired and the events that causally determine its acquisition. But this is a poor first approximation, because events do not, in general, have contents, although beliefs, in general, do. A better procedure is to relativize to descriptions and say that, in paradigmatic cases of learning, there is a relation of content between the belief acquired, under its theoretically pertinent description, and the events that causally determine the learning, under *their* theoretically pertinent descriptions. That is: one imagines an account of fixation of beliefs at large (hence of learning in particular) such that descriptions in some canonical language are assigned to the beliefs and to such organism/environment interactions as causally occasion the having of them. One further assumes that, under this assignment, it will sometimes turn out that there are relations of content between the former descriptions and the latter. Presumably all cases of learning will be cases of this kind. Indeed, one might take it to be a condition upon the adequacy of canonical psychological descriptions that this should, in general, be true.

But this is not good enough either. For, as we have seen, there could be cases in which experiences that are correctly described as experiences of gray elephants fix beliefs that are correctly described as beliefs that elephants are gray, yet the required relations of content do not hold between the experiences and the beliefs they fix. What is "transparently" an experience of gray elephants may be taken as an experience of brown camels: if such an experience fixes a belief about elephant colors, the relations between the belief and the experience is, in the relevant sense, arbitrary (see note 6). This is a way of saying what psychologists have in mind when they emphasize the theoretical centrality of the *proximal representation* of the stimulus (as opposed to the distal stimulus per se) in any but the most superficial accounts of learning. (See the discussion in Dennett, 1978.)

We can fix this up as follows. We continue to reconstruct the notion of learning (as distinct from undifferentiated causal fixation of belief) in terms of content relations between experiences and beliefs, both taken under their theoretically pertinent descriptions. But we construe theoretical pertinency as requiring an appropriate correspondence between the description the *psychological theory* assigns to the experience and the description the *subject* assigns to it. In effect, we construe theoretical pertinency of a description as requiring its psychological reality. If the subject internally represents what are in fact experiences of gray elephants as experiences of brown camels, then it is the latter description that enters into the psychological account of the relation between his experience and his beliefs. Descriptions of mental states are, of course, read opaquely for the purposes of constructing such accounts.[7]

I have been considering the kinds of conceptual mechanisms a psychological theory will need if it is to preserve the distinction between learning that so and so and merely acquiring the belief that so and so. It appears, if the sketch I have given is even more or less correct, that at the heart of this distinction are certain constraints upon relations of content between beliefs and the experiences that fix them. It seems to follow that a psychology of learning will have to respect those constraints if it is to *be* a theory of learning; a fortiori, it will have to be able to represent the properties of mental states in virtue of which they have the content they do.

Now it may be thought that this sort of argument makes a great deal rest upon the preservation of a bit of ordinary language taxonomy; viz., on preserving the distinction between learning and mere causal fixation of belief. However, that is not even slightly the sort of point I have in mind. I assume, rather, that the linguistic distinction probably corresponds to a fact *in rerum natura;* roughly, to the fact that there are generalizations that hold for learning but not for arbitrary cases of fixation of belief. I assume, moreover, that to state these generalizations we shall need to advert to the content of what is learned and to the content of the experiences that causally occasion the learning. To put the same claim the other way around, I assume that if we taxonomize mental states by their contents we shall be able to state general truths about them that we shall not be able to state otherwise; such truths, as, for example, that general beliefs tend to be fixed by experiences of their instances.[8]

I think it is, to put it mildly, very plausible that there *are* generalizations about mental states that hold in virtue of their contents, but I am not going to argue that claim here. Suffice it to emphasize its centrality not only in current approaches to the psychology of learning, but also in such adjacent fields as the psychology of perception, problem-solving, action, etc. In each case, theory construction proceeds by assigning canonical descriptions to mental states and by specifying functions from one such state to another. In each case, whether the theory represents a given mental state as falling under such a function depends on the canonical description the theory assigns to the state; the adequacy of the canonical description depends, in turn, on the accuracy with which it specifies the content of the mental state it applies to. A causal chain of mental states (e.g., the chains that run from experience to beliefs) thus gets a special sort of representation in this kind of theory: viz., a representation as a sequence of formulae related by content.

The explanatory power of such a treatment lies in its ability to predict the content of some mental states, given knowledge of the content of other, causally connected mental states. So, given a canonical representation of sensory contents, we should be able to predict the content of the percepts they give rise to. Given a canonical representation of a percept, we should be able to predict the memories it engenders; and so on, mutatis mutandis, wherever causally related mental states *are* related by content, viz., nonarbitrarily related. If, rather tendentiously, we take "coherent" to be the contradictory of "arbitrary," then the interest of computational psychological theories lies in their ability to explicate the principles according to which causally related mental states are also coherently related.

We have thus far been developing a picture of computational psychological theories as, in effect, treating causal relations among mental states as though they were derivational relations among formulae. It is, however, of prime importance to insist upon a point we encountered above: the interformulaic relations that such a theory articulates typically hold only insofar as the canonical descriptions of mental states are, as it were, construed opaquely.[9] So, for example, suppose it is true that general beliefs tend to be fixed by experiences of their instances. Then a theory of learning might tell us how John's belief that elephants are gray is fixed by (what John takes to be) his experiences of gray elephants; e.g., given, as datum, that John took n of his experiences to be gray-elephant experiences, the theory might predict that John's belief that elephants are gray is fixed to degree m. But now 'elephant' is nonreferential in 'John believes elephants are gray' and in 'John took e to be a gray-elephant experience,' and 'gray' is nonextensional in those contexts. This is patently essential if the theory of learning is to be remotely plausible, since it seems clear that the very same experiences that fix the belief that elephants are gray may be neutral to the belief that pachyderms reflect light of such and such a wavelength, and this may be true even though *for* elephants to be gray just *is* for pachyderms to reflect light of that wavelength. Whether a given belief is fixed by a given experience notoriously depends on how the belief and the experience are represented.

I have been arguing for the following contentions: on the one hand, information flow theories reconstruct content relations among mental states as computational relations among canonical descriptions; and on the other, because canonical descriptions function to specify the contents of mental states, they must be read opaquely. One way of putting the situation is this: if the general account of computational psychological theories I have sketched is right, then the possibility of constructing such theories depends on a certain approach to formulae embedded to verbs of propositional attitude in canonical psychological descriptions. Such formulae must be viewed as nonextensional but not as "fused."[10] To make this clear, I shall have to say a little about what fusion is supposed to be.

'Dog' is nonreferential in 'dogmatic.' But that is a bad way of putting it since "dog" (I mean the *word* 'dog' as opposed to the sequence of letters 'd' 'o' 'g') does not so much as *occur* in 'dogmatic.' Similarly, according to the fusion story, 'elephant' is non-referential in 'John believes elephants are gray,' because the word 'elephant' does not so much as occur in 'John believes elephants are gray.' Rather, 'believes-elephants-are-gray' is a fused expression, analogous to a one-word predicate or an idiom, so that the logical form of 'John believes elephants are gray' is simple $FJohn$, indistinguishable from the logical form of, say, 'John is purple.' It is worth remarking, for later reference, that this is a two-step story. The nonreferentiality of 'elephant' is explained by the assumption that it is not a term in 'believes elephants are gray,' and the denial of termhood is then rationalized by appeal to the notion of fusion. One can imagine alternative accounts on which 'elephant' is not construed as a term in 'believes elephants are gray' but on which verbs of propositional attitude are nevertheless *not* construed as fused with their objects. We shall return to this further on.

The present point, in any event, is this: fusion will certainly account for failures to refer; in something like the way being dead accounts for failures to be loquacious. But it is a kind of account that is not compatible with the development of psychological theories of the kind I have been describing. Suppose "believes elephants are gray" is a fused expression. Then a fortiori the canonical representation of John's mental state when he believes that elephants are gray bears no more intimate relation to the canonical representation of his mental state when he takes himself to sight a gray elephant than it does to the canonical representation of his mental state when, say, he takes himself to have sighted a brown camel.[11] Fusion is precisely a way specifying propositional attitudes *without* representing their contents; a fortiori without representing the relations of content that they bear to one another.

Whereas, of course, the whole point of appealing to a notion of canonical psychological representation in the first place was to permit the development of, e.g., principles of fixation of belief that *are* sensitive to the way that mental states are related in virtue of content. So, in particular, the theory was to reconstruct the intuitive notion that there is a relation of content between experiences of elephants and beliefs about the color of elephants, and that the experiences tend to fix the beliefs in virtue of this relation. But if this whole strategy is to succeed, then it had better be that in canonical descriptions like 'believes elephants are gray' the syntactic object of 'believes' is somehow connected with the generalization *elephants are gray,* and in canonical descriptions like 'takes himself to see a gray elephant' the syntactic object of 'takes himself to see' is somehow connected with a singular statement about an elephant. Unless this condition is satisfied, we shall not have succeeded in representing John's belief that elephants are gray *as* a general belief: a fortiori, we shall not have succeeded in representing the fixation of that belief as falling under the principle that general beliefs tend to be fixed by experiences of their instances. Conversely, if this condition *is* satisfied, then, by that very fact, it follows that the canonical representations of situations in which *a* has such and such a propositional attitude cannot, in general, be of the form *Fa.* In short, *we can have fusion or we can have computation, but we cannot have both.*

I take it to be the moral that any operation on canonical descriptions that has the effect of fusing the expressions they deploy will thereby deprive us of the very formal mechanisms on which the (presumed) explanatory power of computational psychological theories rests. My strategy in the rest of this paper will assume this is true. I shall argue (a) that the conditions on standard reduction could be satisfied even if canonical neurological representations of mental states are fused, hence (b) that the satisfaction of the conditions upon standard reduction does *not* guarantee the subsumption of psychological explanation by neurological explanation. The form of argument is thus that since fusion is a sufficient condition for loss of explanatory power and since standard reduction is compatible with fusion, the success of standard reduction would not, in and of itself, ensure that the kinds of explanations that computational psychological theories yield can be reconstructed in the vocabulary of the neurological theories that reduce them. One can look at such an argument as showing that there is something wrong with the standard notion of reduction (since standard reduction turns out to be compatible with loss of explanatory power). Alternatively, one can hold to the standard notion of reduction and abandon the claim that explanation in a reduced science is subsumed by explanation in the reducing science. My own inclination, for present purposes, is to take the former line and strengthen the constraints on the neurological reducers of psychological theories; I shall return to this in the last section.

Computation and Reduction

I remarked above that, in paradigm cases of classical reduction, mapping the sentences of T_1 onto sentences of T_0 is primarily a matter of replacing items in the vocabulary of the former with items in the vocabulary of the latter, such replacements being mediated by the lawful coextensions (or identities; the distinction is not germane to the present argument) that bridge laws express. But it should now be clear that this will *not* be the case in the reduction of (computational) psychological theories to, say, neurology. For, as we have seen, computational psychological theories contain canonical descriptions that make serious use of a formulae in which sentences are embedded to opaque verbs ("serious" in the sense that the generalizations the theory articulates depends critically on the form and vocabulary of such embedded sentences); whereas at least on the usual assumptions about neurology (and, a fortiori, about physics) those sciences do not employ descriptions of that kind. So the reduction of psychology to neurology (unlike, say, the reduction of meteorology to mechanics) involves alteration of the syntax of the reduced formulae, and it is easy to see from examples that the effect of such alteration will typically be the fusion of expressions that specify the objects of propositional attitudes.

Consider the reduction to neurology of a psychological theory containing the formula 'John believes elephants are gray.' Given the usual assumptions, there will be a sentence of neurological theory (say 'John is N') such that 'John believes elephants are gray iff John is N' is nomologically necessary. So let us suppose that 'John believes elephants are gray' reduces to 'John is N,' and similarly, mutatis mutandis, for 'John takes e to be a gray elephant experience,' which comes out under reduction to be, let us say, 'John is M.' Given this much, the classical constraints upon the reduction of psychology to neurology are satisfied insofar as they apply to these two sentences. And if, as we may suppose, 'John's being M brings about John's being N' instantiates a causal law, then we have a causal explanation, in the vocabulary of neurology, of the contingency of John's belief about elephant colors upon John's experiences of colored elephants. So far, so good.

Except, of course, that fusion has already occurred (taking, as the criterion of fusion, the failure of canonical—now neurological

—descriptions to specify the content of the mental states they apply to). To see this, imagine that, by some or other causal quirk, not only (putative) experiences of gray elephants, but also some experiences that do not have contents (like swallowing pills) or some experiences that have the "wrong" contents (like putative sightings of camels) happen to be causally sufficient for fixing beliefs about the color of elephants. Then, presumably, there will be an expression E that is (a) in the language of neurology, (b) such that 'John is E' is true if John swallows the pill (takes himself to sight the camel), and (c) such that 'John's being E brings about John's being N' is *also* an instance of a causal law. That is, once we go over to neurological descriptions, there need be nothing to choose between the way the theory represents the case in which John's coming to believe elephants are gray is consequent upon his sighting gray elephants and the case in which John's coming to believe elephants are gray is consequent upon his swallowing blue pills. Looked at formally, this is due to the fact that reduction permits the fusion of 'believes elephants are gray' (and/or 'takes himself to sight a gray elephant'), where the mechanism that accomplishes fusion is the substitution of some (possibly elementary) neurological expression for a psychological expression in which a verb of propositional attitude has scope over a formula that specifies the content of a propositional attitude. Looked at substantively, what has been lost is a representation that expresses the relation of content between beliefs about elephants and elephant-experiences. If, then, there are generalizations that hold of mental states in virtue of the content relations between them (if, for example, there are generalizations that relate the content of beliefs to the content of the experiences that fix them), the conditions on reduction may be satisfied even though such generalizations (statable by assumption in the psychological vocabulary) are not statable in the vocabulary of the reducing science. In short, insofar as there is any explanatory power to be gained by resort to a computational psychology, reduction is in danger of losing it for us.

I had better, at this point, make as clear as I can what I am *not* claiming. To begin with, I do not deny that there could be a truth of neurological theory that applies to exactly the cases in which say, a general belief is fixed by its instances. On the contrary, if

the truths of psychology are to follow from the truths of neurology plus bridge laws, there had *better* be a neurological state necessary and sufficient for having any given belief, and a neurological
state necessary and sufficient for having any given belief-fixing
experience; and the neurological theory had better say (or, anyhow, entail) that states of the latter kind are causally sufficient
for bringing about the states of the former kind. Nor am I denying
that the neurological expressions that specify such states might be
projectible; I think that is perhaps unlikely (see Chapter 5), but
that is *not* the point I'm now concerned to stress. The difficulty is
rather that since the *contents* of the beliefs and experiences presumably will not be specified by their neurological descriptions, it
is only when we are given their *psychological* descriptions that we
will be able to predict the contents of the beliefs *from* the contents of the experiences. I am saying, in effect, that beliefs and
experiences reduce to neurological entities, but the contents of
beliefs and experiences—the things that our beliefs and experiences
relate us to—do not reduce to anything; psychological representations of content simply fuse under neurological description of
mental states. So, to put it rather misleadingly, although neurology can, in principle, say anything that needs to be said about the
contingency of beliefs upon experiences, it has no mechanisms
whatever for talking about the contingency of the contents of
beliefs upon the contents of experiences. Yet there are, it appears,
such contingencies, and there are interesting things to be said
about them.

It might nevertheless be held with some justification that this
line of argument is unfair, if not to the spirit of standard reductionism, then at least to the letter. For, on the reductionist view,
T_0 will not reduce T_1 unless all the consequences of T_1 are consequences, not of T_0 alone, but of T_0 together with the bridge laws.
Now, if there are bridge laws of the form: (x) (x has a general
belief [of the appropriate content] iff N_x), and (y) (y has a belief-
fixing experience [of the appropriate content] iff M_y), and if 'M
brings about N' expresses a law of neurology, then neurology
together with the bridge laws *does* entail whatever psychology
entails about the fixation of beliefs by experiences.

Still, the present case if quite unlike what the classical reduction
paradigm envisions. True, in the standard examples, we need not

only T_0 but also the bridge laws to recover the entailments of T_1. But that is only for the relatively uninteresting reason that the bridge laws provide access to the (nonlogical) *vocabulary* of T_1, which is, by assumption, not included in the vocabulary of T_0. (Chemistry can entail "H_2O is wet," but only chemistry plus the bridge laws can entail "Water is wet.") Whereas the curious thing about the psychology/neurology case is that here the bridge laws provide access not just to the vocabulary of the reduced science but also to an *explanatory construct*—content—for which the reducing science offers no counterpart. Specifically, we shall need the bridge laws to unpack the fused objects of verbs of propositional attitude if, as I have argued, fusion deprives us of the appropriate theoretical mechanisms for specifying the domains in which generalizations about cognitive processes hold.

In short, we are back where we started. I have argued, *not* that the classical constraints upon reduction cannot be met in the psychology/neurology case, but rather that they fail to provide sufficient conditions for the subsumption of psychological explanations by neurological explanations. And examination of that case has shown precisely that it is possible for a pair of theories to meet the classical constraints (T_0 plus the bridge laws entails whatever T_1 does) even though intuitively (and by the fusion test) the explanations of T_1 are not subsumed by T_0. Requiring that T_0 together with the bridge laws yield the entailments of T_1 does not ensure that the explanations available in T_1 have counterparts in T_0, Q.E.D.

I have been issuing caveats. Here is another: the present argument is not that reduction *must* lose the advantages that psychological models gain; only that it *can* do so compatibly with the satisfaction of such conditions, ontological and methodological, as standard views of reduction impose. This is due to the fact that nothing in those conditions prohibits fusion as the consequence of reduction. On the contrary, in the absence of further constraints upon reduction, fusion would be its *natural* consequence, as can be seen from the following.

Reduction required, in effect, that for every psychological state of John's there exist a coextensive (or token-identical) neurological state of John's, and that every psychological sentence that attributes the former state to him should be replaced by a neurological sentence that attributes the latter state to him. But consider again the sentence, 'John believes elephants are gray.' The shortest stretch of that sentence that can be construed as expressing a state (property, etc.) of *anything* is surely 'believes elephants are gray,' since, in particular, in this sentence the occurrence of 'elephants' is nonreferential and 'are gray' does not express a property of elephants. In short, if we are to substitute neurological-state expressions for psychological-state expressions, the natural choice is to make the substitution in the frame: 'John . . .', i.e., to substitute simultaneously for the verb of propositional attitude and its object. And since the classical construals of reduction do not do anything like requiring that the content of propositional attitudes can be specified by neurological representations of mental states, the consequence of substitution in this frame is likely to be, precisely, fusion.

I have a strong suspicion that this chapter would do well to stop here. For I suspect the moral just drawn is essentially the right one: reduction will probably require fusion, and fusion will entail the loss of the explanatory power that computational psychological theories are constructed to obtain. If this is true, it suggests that we will have to be very much more pluralistic about scientific explanation than classical views of the unity of science supposed. In particular, nothing in the discussion has jeopardized the ontological claim that mental states are neurological states; on the contrary, the whole argument can be run on the standard assumptions of the mind/body identity theory. But what turns out *not* to be true is that explanation in a reduced science is invariably subsumed by explanation in its reducer. Rather, we shall have to say something like this: Mental states have canonical psychological descriptions in virtue of which they fall under the generalizations expressed by computational principles, and they have canonical neurological descriptions in virtue of which they fall under the generalizations expressed by causal laws. Quite possibly there never will be a state of science which we can, as it were, do neurology *instead of* psychology because, quite possibly, it will never be possible to express in the vocabulary of neurology those generalizations about relations of content that computational psychological theories articulate. Psychologists have lots of things to worry about, but technological unemployment is not likely to be one of them.

It may, however, be worth forging on. I want to sketch, very rapidly and incompletely, a way that psychology and neurology might turn out so as to make possible reduction without fusion. I am not going to defend the claim that either psychology or neurology *will* turn out that way. My primary interest is still just to make clear how much more than correlation (or contingent identity) of psychological and neurological states the substantive reduction of psychology to neurology would require.

Reduction without Fusion

What we have said so far amounts to this: we want a psychological theory that at least provides canonical descriptions of mental states, and we want canonical descriptions to reconstruct the contents of the mental states they apply to. Insofar as such a theory is formalized, its generalizations will apply to mental states in virtue of features of their canonical representations. Such a theory should therefore suffice to represent the causal sequences that constitute the mental life of an organism by sequences of transformations of canonical representations. To contemplate the substantive reduction of computational psychology is, in effect, to suppose that such theories can operate solely with neurological constructs. To put this last point slightly differently, it is to suppose that the descriptions in virtue of whose satisfaction psychological states fall under principles of computation are descriptions in the same vocabulary as those in virtue of whose satisfaction psychological states fall under neurological laws. The question is whether we can imagine a reduction of psychology to neurology that makes this true.

We have seen that the basic methodological problem is to find a way of representing the contents of mental states that avoids recourse to fusion while doing justice to the nonreferentiality of terms occurring in typical psychological contexts. There is a classical proposal here that, as far as I can see, may well point in the direction in which we ought to look: take verbs of propositional attitude to express relations between organisms and *formulae*. In particular, on this view, to believe that elephants are gray is to be related, in a certain way, to some such formula as 'elephants are gray'; to take oneself to see a gray elephant is to be related in a certain (different) way to some such formula as 'I see a gray elephant,' etc.[12]

There is a well-known difficulty with this suggestion, but I think it has been overplayed: viz., believing that elephants are gray *cannot* be being related (in whatever way) to the formula 'elephants are gray,' since, if it were, it would presumably follow that monolingual English speakers cannot have the same beliefs as, say, monolingual French speakers. And it would also presumably follow that infraverbal organisms (cats, dogs, and human infants, inter alia) can have no beliefs at all.

The most that this objection shows, however, is not that believing cannot be being related to a formula, but only that, if it is, then all organisms that can have shared beliefs must have some shared language.[13] I am convinced, for reasons I have elaborated elsewhere (see Chapter 7 and Fodor, 1975), that we would be well advised to take that suggestion seriously; in fact, that it is quite impossible to make sense of the notion of a computational psychology unless some such suggestion is endorsed. The idea is, roughly, that all organisms that have a mental life at all have access to some system of internal representations; that insofar as the mental life of organisms is homogeneous (e.g., insofar as people and animals, or, for that matter, people and machines, instantiate the same psychology) there must be corresponding homogenieties between their internal representational systems; and that a major goal of information flow theories must be to characterize this system of representations and provide necessary and sufficient conditions for the having of propositional attitudes by reference to relations between organisms and the formulae of the system. On this view, for example, to believe that elephants are gray is to be in a certain relation to whatever internal formula translates the English sentence, 'Elephants are gray'; if there is a content relation between that belief and certain of the experiences that are causally responsible for fixing it, then that relation is expressed by generalizations defined over whichever internal representations are implicated in the having of the belief and experiences. In effect, there is a language of thought, and content relations among propositional attitudes are to be explicated as relations among formulae of that language.[14]

Correspondingly, the canonical representations of mental states deployed by a computational psychology are assumed to contain structural descriptions of internal formulae. Mental states fall under the generalizations articulated by psychological theories because they satisfy their canonical representations, so John's believing that elephants are gray makes true a certain psychological sentence; viz., a sentence of the form R John, SD. In that sentence, SD is the structural description of an internal representation (in particular of the internal representation which translates "elephants are gray") and R is a relation between John and that internal representation (in particular, whichever relation to an internal representation is nomologically necessary and sufficient for believing what it expresses).

For the benefit of those keeping score, we note that the following pieces are now in play. There are (a) internal representations. These are formulae in an internal language, and it is assumed that they are the immediate objects of propositional attitudes. In particular, nomologically necessary and sufficient conditions for the having of a propositional attitude are to be formulated in terms of (presumably computational) relations that the organism bears to internal representations.

There are also (b) structural descriptions of internal representation. These are formulae in the vocabulary of an (ideally completed) psychological theory. Structural descriptions are canonical names of internal representations (see below). A propositional attitude has the content that it does because the internal representation that constitutes its immediate object satisfies the structural description that it does.

There are also (c) English sentences like 'Elephants are gray.' For heuristic purposes, we use such sentences to form definite (but noncanonical) descriptions of internal representations. We do this because we do not know what the structural descriptions of internal representations are like. That is: ideally completed psychological theories refer to internal representations via their structural descriptions. We refer to them as, e.g., the internal representation that translates 'elephants are gray.' We do so faut de mieux.

Finally, there are (d) structural descriptions of English sentences. Structural descriptions of English sentences specify properties in virtue of which *they* have the content that they have. Roughly, structural descriptions are specifications of sentence types couched in an ambiguity-free notation. If what most psycholinguists now believe is true, the structural descriptions of English sentences must themselves function as internal representations. For, on current views, structural descriptions are normally (among) the ones that speakers intend their utterances to satisfy and that hearers recover in the course of construing the utterances of speakers. That is: in the theoretically interesting cases, the internal representation of an English sentence *is* its structural description.

We are so far from having a developed cognitive psychology that it is hard to give untendentious examples. But consider the propositional attitude *remembering,* and suppose (for once *not* contrary to fact) that psychology acknowledges a relation of *storing* that holds between organisms and internal representations. Then the following might be among the sentences that psychology entails: 'John remembers (the fact) that elephants are gray iff John stores the formula SD', where what substitutes for 'SD' is the structural description of the internal translation of 'elephants are gray.' Note that the biconditional is extensional for the object of 'stores.' That is, it remains true whatever name of the internal formula one substitutes for 'SD.'

However, structural descriptions (unlike other kinds for names) play a special role in this sort of theory, and this connects with the fact that, strictly speaking, structural descriptions are not *names* at all. What they are, of course, is descriptions. So, suppose that 'Alfred' is a name of the internal formula SD. Then, although we preserve *truth* if we substitute 'Alfred' for a structural description of SD in psychological sentences containing the canonical representation of SD, we *do not,* in general, preserve canonicalness. A canonical representation of a mental state must determine its content. We get such determination (ceteris paribus) insofar as the canonical representation of a mental state contains the structural description of an internal formula, but we do not get it (ceteris paribus) when it contains a noncanonical name of that formula like 'Alfred.' The general idea is that internal representations (like, for that matter, English sentences) express the content they do because they satisfy the structural descriptions they do. Structural descriptions specify those properties of a formula that determine its syntactic and semantic behavior—those properties by virtue of which a formula constitutes an expression in a language.

The assumption that canonical psychological representations typically contain structural descriptions of internal formulae allows us some of the advantages of fusion theories without their most obvious vices. In particular, if the canonical counterpart of 'John believes elephants are gray' is of the form R John, SD, it is not surprising that the canonical counterpart of 'elephant' fails to refer to elephants when it occurs within the scope of the canonical counterpart of 'believes.' Roughly, the present account agrees with the fusion story in holding that 'elephant' is not a term in 'John believes elephants are gray.' But it provides a different rationale for the denial of termhood. Since the immediate epistemic objects of propositional attitudes are taken to be formulae, the syntactic objects of verbs of propositional attitude are taken to be structural descriptions of formulae; the word 'elephant' is not a term in 'believes elephants are gray,' but the name of that word is.

The difference between this view and the fusion story should not be minimized. Structural descriptions are unfused expressions: qua names, they purport to refer, and qua descriptions, they purport to determine their referents in virtue of the properties of their referents. Correspondingly, verbs of propositional attitude are construed relationally on the present account; in particular, they express relations between organisms and the referents of structural descriptions; i.e., relations between organisms and formulae of the internal representational system. Such relations are ontologically kosher. No fusion theory can make that statement.

Suppose, then, that canonical psychological representations turn out to contain structural descriptions of internal formulae. Is there any way of reducing this sort of psychology to neurology without committing fusion at the point of reduction? If the line of analysis we have been pursuing is correct, that is what the issue about the possibility of substantive reduction—reduction without loss of explanatory power—boils down to in the case of cognitive psychology.

I suppose the answer goes like this: substantive reduction would at least require (1) that token computational processes turn out to be token neurological processes (storing a formula turns out to be a neurological process, etc.); (2) token internal representations turn out to be token neurological states (a token internal representation that translates 'elephants are gray' turns out to be some neurological configuration in, roughly, the way this sentence token is a configuration of ink marks on this page); and (3) canonical names of internal formulae (viz., their structural descriptions) are specifiable in the vocabulary of neurology.

I take it that (1) and (2) are just consequences of applying the usual ontological conditions upon reduction to the special case of psychological theories that acknowledge internal representations. They do not, that is, distinguish substantive reduction from standard reduction. It is (3) that does the work. In effect, (3) requires that the canonical *neurological* description of a mental state (of a's) be of the form $R_{a, SD}$, (and not, for example, of the form $R_{a, Alfred}$). So the question that has to be faced is: what would have to be the case in order for (3) to be satisfied? Heaven knows, I am unclear about how that question should be answered, but what I *think* it comes to is this: for psychology to be substantively reducible to neurology, it must turn out that neurological entities constitute a code, and that the canonical neurological representation of such entities specifies the properties in virtue of which they constitute formulae in that code. Since the properties in virtue of which a formula belongs to a code are the ones in virtue of which it satisfies its structural description, and since the properties in virtue of which a formula satisfies its structural description are the ones in virtue of which it has the content it has, we can summarize the whole business by saying that neurology will not reduce psychology unless neurological descriptions determine the content of internal formulae. (Compare the standard view, in which what specifies the content of a mental state is its canonical neurological representation *together with the relevant bridge laws,* and in which the specification is couched in the vocabulary of the reduced rather than the reducing science.)

I have gone about as far as I can, but it is worth remarking that the notion that some neurological states do constitute a code is not exactly foreign to the speculative literature on brain and behavior. So, one might suppose, neurons are relays and canonical names of neurological states are specifications of levels of neural excitation. For this to be true, it would have to turn out that to specify the state of excitation of a set of neurons is to fix the content of a token formula, just as specifying the structural description of an English sentence fixes the content of its tokens. I do not have the foggiest idea whether anything like that *is* true, but the following, at least, is clear: if neurological representations specify those properties of states of the central nervous system in virtue of which they constitute formulae belonging to a code, then the descriptions that such states receive in sciences still more basic than neurology almost certainly do not. (Think what a particle description of a token neurological state—or, for that matter, a token English sentence—would actually look like; then try to imagine specifying, in *that* vocabulary, such properties as those in virtue of which a sentence token like 'elephants are gray' is content-related to a sentence token like 'there's a gray elephant.' To specify such relations, we need, e.g., notions like 'quantifier' and 'general term.' Is it plausible that such notions should be express-ible in the vocabulary of particle physics? The more reason we have for thinking that neurology might substantively reduce psychology, the less reason we have for thinking that physics might substantively reduce neurology.[15]

We have come quite a long way from the suggestion that what we need to reduce psychology to neurology is just correlation (or token identity) of psychological and neurological states. And, as we anticipated at the start, it is the intensionality of psychological predicates that primarily confounds that suggestion. On the one hand, terms in formulae embedded to psychological verbs are typi-cally nonreferential, but, on the other, it is precisely such formulae that express the contents of mental states; and, in the theoretically interesting cases, mental states are related in virtue of their con-tent. Insofar as reduction leads to fusion, it thereby results in the failure to represent the generalizations about mental life that structure such relations. But these generalizations are, as we re-marked above, involved in the very rationality of mental life. (It is constitutive of the rationality of John's beliefs about the color of elephants that they are fixed by, e.g., his elephant-sightings and not, e.g., by swallowing pills, or sighting camels, or having his cor-tex surgically rewired.) Small wonder that antireductionists have often held that to replace psychological explanations by neurolog-ical explanations is to lose precisely what a theory of the mind ought to be about. Given the standard notion of reduction, this objection seems to me entirely pertinent.

There is, however, an undefended premise in this whole argu-ment, and I had better say something about it before I stop. I have argued that neurological representations will, quite possibly, fail to provide the appropriate format for such generalizations as hold in virtue of content-relations of mental states. But it might be replied that there are, in fact, no such generalizations; that the distinction between believing elephants are gray because of all those gray elephants and believing elephants are gray because of all those blue pills is not a distinction that a scientifically disciplined theory of mental states would recognize. Of course we, pretheoretic as we are, like to draw such distinctions; and of course, insofar as they come to anything at all, there will be distinctions between causal mechanisms corresponding to (viz., coextensive with) what we take to be distinctions among relations of content. But a theory of content-relations per se would not be formulable in a first-class conceptual system. What counts, in such a system, is those descriptions under which events (including mental events) instantiate the laws of basic science. And nothing else counts.

Underlying this objection (if I understand it correctly) is the observation that no behavioral or neurological (or physical) description of an organism will uniquely determine an assignment of propositional attitudes to that organism. Any such assignment, however plausible in the light of the behavioral and neurological data, is to that extent an interpretation that we place upon the physical facts and hence not something to be mentioned in even the most exhaustive catalogue of the physical facts themselves.[16] (That assignments of propositional attitudes are interpretations of the physical facts would itself not be mentioned in such a catalogue; interpretation is not a physical category either.) But if there are not any facts about propositional attitudes, then a fortiori there is not the fact that internal formulae are nomologically implicated in the having of propositional attitudes; this also is true however plausible it turns out to be to treat neurological states as tokens in a code and however much such a treatment seems to rationalize the behavioral observations. We need internal formulae to account for propositional attitudes, and we need propositional attitudes if we are to represent such facts as that organisms act out of their beliefs and utilities. But if there are no such facts the whole pattern of explanation is otiose.

Whatever else there is to be said on this issue, however, it is essential to distinguish it from the question of the substantive reducibility of psychology. For the latter is, by hypothesis, an

empirical matter, whereas the whole point about the underdeter-
mination of mental ascriptions by physics is that, if it is true at all,
it is true *however* the physics and the psychology turn out. Suppose our evidence for treating a certain neurological state as a
token of a certain linguistic type were as good as our evidence for
treating 'it's raining' as a token of the English type *it's raining*.
That would not advance the case one jot since, on the present
view, the assignment of token inscriptions to English sentences is
also just a gloss upon the physical facts. There must be indefinitely
many ways of associating objects of the physical form "it's raining" with linguistic objects *salve* the totality of physically characterizable facts about the organisms which produce such tokens.

On the other hand, there is nothing in this line of argument that
stops our evidence for the linguistic analysis of token neurological
states from being as good as—indeed, of the same kind as—our
evidence for the linguistic analysis of English inscriptions, and,
skeptical worries to one side, it is hard to believe the latter evidence is other than pretty good. There is thus room for a program
of empirical research this side of skepticism: show that *if* there is
good reason for treating (some) inscriptions as linguistic tokens,
then there is *equally* good reason for treating (some) neurological
states as linguistic tokens. It would, in short, be enormously impressive to show that neurological objects satisfy relevant necessary
conditions for interpretation as a code, even if it turns out that
nothing could show *which* code they (or anything else) belong
to.[17] Such a demonstration would be tantamount to the substantive reduction of computational psychological theories. My point
throughout has been that nothing less will do.

III.
Intensionality and Mental Representation

Chapter 7

Propositional Attitudes

Some philosophers (Dewey, for example, and maybe Austin) hold that philosophy is what you do to a problem until it's clear enough to solve it by doing science. Others (Ryle, for example, and maybe Wittgenstein) hold that if a philosophical problem succumbs to empirical methods, that shows it wasn't *really* philosophical to begin with. Either way, the facts seem clear enough: questions first mooted by philosophers are sometimes coopted by people who do experiments. This seems to be happening now to the question "What are propositional attitudes?" and cognitive psychology is the science of note.

One way to elucidate this situation is to examine theories that cognitive psychologists endorse, with an eye to explicating the account of propositional attitudes that the theories presuppose. That was my strategy in Fodor (1975). In this paper, however, I'll take another tack. I want to outline a number of a priori conditions which, on my view, a theory of propositional attitudes (PAs) ought to meet. I'll argue that, considered together, these conditions pretty clearly demand a treatment of PAs as relations between organisms and internal representations; precisely the view that the psychologists have independently arrived at. I'll thus be arguing that we have good reasons to endorse the psychologists' theory even aside from the empirical exigencies that drove them to it. I take it that this convergence between what's plausible a priori and what's demanded ex post facto is itself a reason for believing that the theory is probably true.

Three preliminary remarks: first, I'm not taking 'a priori' all that seriously. Some of the points I'll be making are, I suppose, strictly conceptual, but others are merely self-evident. What I've got is a set of glaring facts about propositional attitudes. I don't doubt that we might rationally adopt an account of the attitudes which contravenes some or maybe even all of them. But the independent evidence for such an account would have to be extremely persuasive or I, for one, would get the jitters. Second, practically everything I'll say about the attitudes has been said previously in the philosophical literature. All I've done is bring the stuff together. I do think, however, that the various constraints that I'll discuss illuminate one another; it is only when one attempts to satisfy them all at once that one sees how univocal their demands are. Finally, though I intend what I say to apply, mutatis mutandis, to PAs at large, I shall run the discussion pretty much exclusively on beliefs and wants. These seem to be the root cases for a systematic cognitive psychology; thus learning and perception are presumably to be treated as varieties of the fixation of belief, and the theory of action is presumably continuous with the theory of utility.[1] Here, then, are my conditions, with comments.

I. Propositional attitudes should be analyzed as relations. In particular, the verb in a sentence like 'John believes it's raining' expresses a relation between John and something else, and a token of that sentence is true if John stands in the belief-relation to that thing.[2] Equivalently, for these purposes, 'it's raining' is a term in 'John believes it's raining'.[3] I have three arguments for imposing condition I, all of them inconclusive.

(I-a) It's intuitively plausible. 'Believes' looks like a two-place relation, and it would be nice if our theory of belief permitted us to save the appearances.

No doubt, appearances sometimes deceive. The "'s" in 'Mary's sake' looks as though it's expressing a relation (of possession) between Mary and a sake; but it doesn't, or so we're told. In fact, 'Mary's sake' doesn't look *very* relational, since *x's sake* would surely qualify as an idiom even if we had no ontological scruples to placate. There's something syntactically wrong with: 'Mary's sake is *F*er than Bill's', 'Mary has a (little) sake', etc. For that matter, there's something syntactically wrong with 'a sake' *tout* *court.* Yet we'd expect all such expressions to be well formed if 'Mary's sake' contained a true possessive. 'Mary's sake' doesn't bear comparison with 'Mary's lamb'.

Still, there are some cases of *non*-idiomatic expressions which appear to be relational but which, upon reflection, maybe aren't. 'Mary's voice' goes through the transformations even if 'Mary's sake' does not (Dennett, 1969). Yet there aren't, perhaps, such *things* as voices; and, if there aren't, 'Mary's voice' can't refer in virtue of a relation between Mary and one of them.[4] I think it is fair to view the "surface" grammar as ontologically misleading in *these* cases, but only because we know how to translate into more parsimonious forms. 'Mary has a good voice (bad voice; little voice; better voice than Bill's)' goes over, pretty much without residue, into 'Mary sings well (badly, weakly, less well than Bill)'. If, however, we were *un*able to provide (or, anyhow, to envision providing) the relevant translations, what right would we have to view such expressions as ontologically promiscuous? 'Bill believes it's raining' is not an idiom, and there is, so far as anybody knows, no way of translating sentences nominally about beliefs into sentences of reduced ontological load. (Behaviorists used to think such translations might be forthcoming, but they were wrong.) We must, then, either take the apparent ontological commitments seriously or admit to playing fast and loose.

(I-b) Existential Generalization applies to the syntactic objects of verbs of propositional attitude; from 'John believes it's raining' we can infer 'John believes something' and 'there is something that John believes' (viz., that it's raining). *EG* may not be *criterial* for ontological commitment, but it is surely a straw in the wind.[5]

(I-c) The only known alternative to the view that verbs of propositional attitude express relations is that they are (semantically) "fused" with their objects, and that view would seem to be hopeless.[6]

The fusion story is the proposal that sentences like 'John believes it's raining' ought really to be spelled 'John believes-it's-raining'; that the logical form of such sentences acknowledges a referring expression ('John') and a one-place predicate with no internal structure ('believes-it's-raining'). 'John believes it's raining' is thus an atomic sentence, similar *au fond* to 'John is purple'.

Talk about counter-intuitive! Moreover:

1. There are infinitely many (semantically distinct) sentences of the form *a believes complement*. If all such sentences are atomic, how is English learned? (Davidson, 1965).

2. Different propositional attitudes are often "focused" on the same content; for example, one can both fear and believe that it will rain on Tuesday. But on the fusion view, 'John fears that it will rain on Tuesday' has nothing in common with 'John believes that it will rain on Tuesday' save only the reference to John. In particular, it's an *accident* that the form of words 'it will rain on Tuesday' occurs in both.

3. Similarly, different beliefs can be related in such ways as the following: John thinks Sam is nice; Mary thinks Sam is nasty. Under ordinary English representation these beliefs overlap at the 'Sam' position, so the notation sustains the intuition that John and Mary disagree about Sam. But, if the fusion view is correct, 'John thinks Sam is nice' and 'Mary thinks Sam is nasty' have no more in common at the level of canonical notation than, say, 'John eats' and 'Mary swims'. Talk about imperspicuous! In respect of saving the intuitions, the recommended reconstruction does *worse* than the undisciplined orthography that we started with.[7] (For that matter, there's nothing in 'believes-that-S' to suggest that it's about believing. Here, too, 'believes that S' does much better.)

4. It could hardly be an accident that the declarative sentences of English constitute the (syntactic) objects of verbs like 'believe'. Whereas, on the fusion view it's *precisely* an accident; the complement of 'believes' in 'John believes it's raining' bears no more relation to the sentence 'It's raining' than, say, the word 'dog' bears to the first syllable of 'dogmatic'.

5. On the fusion view, it's a sheer accident that if 'John believes it's raining' is true, then what John believes is true if 'it's raining' is true. But this, surely, is one accident too many. Surely the identity between the truth conditions on John's belief when he believes Fa, and those on the corresponding sentence 'a is F' must be what connects the theory of sentence interpretation with the theory of PAs (and what explains our using 'it's raining', and not some other form of words, to specify *which* belief John has when he believes it's raining).

It's the mark of a bad theory that it makes the data look

fortuitous. I conclude that the fusion story is not to be taken very seriously; that neither the philosophy of language nor the philosophy of mind is advanced by proliferating hyphens. But the fusion story is (de facto) the only alternative to the view that 'believe' expresses a relation. Hence, first blush, we had better assume that 'believe' *does* express a relation and try to find an account of propositional attitudes which comports with that assumption.

II. A theory of PAs should explain the parallelism between verbs of PA and verbs of saying. ("Vendler's Condition").

Rather generally, the things we can be said to *believe* (want, hope, regret, etc.) are the very things that we can be said to *say* (assert, state, etc.). So John can either believe or assert that it's about to blow; he can either hope that or inquire whether somebody has reefed the main; he can either doubt or demand that the crew should douse the Jenny. Moreover, as Vendler (1972) has shown, there are interesting consequences of classifying verbs of PA (on the one hand) and verbs of saying (on the other) by reference to the syntax of their object complements. It turns out that the taxonomies thus engendered are isomorphic down to surprisingly fine levels of grain. Now, of course, this *could* be just an accident, as could the semantic and syntactic parallelisms between the complements of verbs of PA and free standing declaratives (see above). Certainly, it's a substantial inference from the syntactic similarities that Vendler observes to the conclusion he draws: that the object of assertion is identical with the object of belief. Suffice it for now to make the less ambitious point: we should prefer a theory that explains the facts to one that merely shrugs its shoulders; viz. a theory that satisfies Vendler's condition to a theory that does not.

III. A theory of propositional attitudes should account for their opacity ("Frege's Condition").

Thus far, I have stressed logico-syntactic analogies between the complements of belief clauses and the corresponding free-standing declaratives. However, it has been customary in the philosophical literature since Frege to stress one of their striking *dis*analogies: the former are, in general, opaque to inferential operations to which the latter are, in general, transparent. Since this aspect of the behavior of sentences that ascribe propositional attitudes has so dominated the philosophical discussion, I shall make the point quite briefly here. Sentences containing verbs of PA are not, normally, truth functions of their complements. Moreover, contexts subordinated to verbs of PA are normally themselves nontruth functional, and *EG* and substitution of identicals may apply at syntactic positions in a free-standing declarative while failing at syntactically comparable positions in belief sentences. A theory of PAs should explain why all this is so.

It should be acknowledged that, however gross the inadequacies of the fusion view, it does at least provide an account of propositional attitudes which meets Frege's condition. If *S* doesn't so much as occur in 'John believes S', it's hardly surprising that the one should fail to be a truth function of the other; similarly, if 'Mary' doesn't occur in 'Bill believes that John bit Mary', it's hardly surprising that the sentence doesn't behave the way it would if 'Mary' occurred referentially. The methodological moral is, perhaps, that Frege's condition under-constrains a theory of PAs; ideally, an acceptable account of opacity should follow from a theory that is independently plausible.

IV. The objects of propositional attitudes have logical form ("Aristotle's Condition").

Mental states (including, especially, token havings of propositional attitudes) interact causally. Such interactions constitute the mental processes that eventuate (inter alia) in the behaviors of organisms. Now, it is crucial to the whole program of explaining behavior by reference to mental states that the propositional attitudes belonging to these chains are typically *non*-arbitrarily related in respect to their content (taking the "content" of a propositional attitude, informally, to be whatever it is that the complement of the corresponding PA-ascribing sentence expresses).

This is not an a priori claim, though perhaps it is a transcendental one. For though one can imagine the occurrence of causal chains of mental states which are not otherwise related (as, e.g., a thought that two is a prime number, causing a desire for tea, causing an intention to recite the alphabet backwards, causing an expectation of rain) and though such sequences doubtless actually occur (in dreams, say, and in madness), still if *all* our mental life were like this, it's hard to see what point ascriptions of contents to mental states would have. Even phenomenology presupposes some correspondence between the content of our beliefs and the content of our beliefs about our beliefs; else there would be no coherent introspections for phenomenologists to report.

The paradigm situation—the grist for the cognitivist's mill—is the one where propositional attitudes interact causally and do so *in virtue of* their content. And the paradigm of this paradigm is the practical syllogism. Since it is part of my point that the details matter not at all, I shall take liberties with Aristotle's text.

John believes that it will rain if he washes his car. John wants it to rain. So John acts in a manner intended to be a car-washing.

I take it that this might be a true, if informal, etiology of John's "car-washing behavior"; the car washing is an effect of the intention to car-wash, and the intention to car-wash is an effect of the causal interaction between John's beliefs and his utilities. Moreover, the etiological account might be counterfactual-supporting in at least the following sense: John wouldn't have car-washed had the content of his beliefs, utilities, and intentions been other than they were. Or, if he did, he would have done so unintentionally, or for different reasons, or with other ends in view. To say that John's mental states interact causally *in virtue of* their content is, in part, to say that such counterfactuals hold.

If there are true, contingent counterfactuals which relate mental state *tokens* in virtue of their contents, that is presumably because there are true, contingent generalizations which relate mental state *types* in virtue of their contents. So, still following Aristotle at a distance, we can schematize etiologies like the one above to get the underlying generalization: if x believes that A is an action x can perform; and if x believes that a performance of A is sufficient to bring it about that Q; and if x wants it to be the case that Q; then x acts in a fashion intended be a performance of A.

I am not, for present purposes, interested in whether this is a plausible decision theory, still less in whether it is the decision theory that Aristotle thought plausible. What interests me here is rather: (a) that any decision theory we can now contemplate will surely look rather like this one, in that (b) it will entail generalizations about the causal relations among content-related beliefs, utilities, and intentions; and (c) such generalizations will be specified by reference to the form of the propositional attitudes which instantiate them. (This remains true even if, as some philosophers suppose, an adequate decision theory is irremediably in need of ceteris paribus clauses to flesh out its generalizations. See, for example, Grice, 1975.) So, in particular, we can't state the theory-relevant generalization that is instantiated by the relations among John's mental states unless we allow reference to beliefs of the form *if X then Y;* desires of the form *that Y;* intentions of the form *that X should come about;* and so forth. Viewed one way (material mode), the recurrent schematic letters require identities of content among propositional attitudes. Viewed the other way (linguisitcally), they require formal identities among the complements of the PA-ascribing sentence which instantiate the generalizations of the theory that explains John's behavior. Either way, the form of the generalization determines how the theory relates to the events that it subsumes. There is nothing remarkable about this, of course, except that form is here being ascribed *inside* the scope of verbs of PA.

To summarize: our common-sense psychological generalizations relate mental states in virtue of their content, and canonical representation does what it can to reconstruct such content relations as relations of form. "Aristotle's condition" requires that our theory of propositional attitudes should rationalize this process by construing verbs of PA in a way that permits reference to the form of their objects. To do this is to legitimize the presuppositions of common-sense psychology and, for that matter, of real (viz. cognitive) psychology as well. (See Fodor, 1975).

In fact, we can state (and satisfy) Aristotle's condition in a still stronger version. Let anything be a *belief sentence* if it is of the form *a believes that S.* Define the *correspondent* of such a sentence as the formula that consists of S standing alone (i.e. the sentence #S#).[8] We remarked above that there is the following relation between the truth conditions on the belief that a belief sentence ascribes and the truth conditions on the correspondent of the belief sentence: the belief is true if the correspondent is. This is, presumably, at least part of what is involved in viewing the correspondent of a belief sentence as *expressing* the ascribed belief.

It should not be surprising, therefore, to find that our intuitions about the form of the belief ascribed by a given belief sentence are determined by the logical form of its correspondent. So, intuitively, John's belief that Mary and Bill are leaving is a conjunctive belief (cf. the logical form of 'Mary and Bill are leaving'); John's belief that Alfred is a white swan is a singular belief (cf. the logical form of 'Alfred is a white swan'); and so on. It is, of course, essential that we understand 'belief' *opaquely* in such examples; otherwise, the belief that P will have the logical form of any sentence equivalent to P. But this is as it should be: it is in virtue of its *opaque* content that John's belief that P plays its systematic role in John's mental life—e.g., in the determination of his actions and in the causation of his other mental states. Hence it is the opaque construal that operates in such patterns of explanation as the practical syllogism and its spiritual heirs (see below, Chapter 9).

We are now in position to state Aristotle's condition in its strongest (and final) version. A theory of propositional attitudes should legitimize the ascription of form to the objects of propositional attitudes. In particular, it should explain why the form of a belief is identical to the logical form of the correspondent of a sentence which (opaquely) ascribes that belief.[9]

I digress: One may feel inclined to argue that the satisfaction of Aristotle's condition is incompatible with the satisfaction of Frege's condition; that the opacity of belief sentences shows the futility of assigning logical form to their objects. The argument might go as follows. Sentence have logical form in virtue of their behavior under logical transformations; the logical form of a sentence is that aspect of its structure in virtue of which it provides a domain for such transformations. But Frege shows us that the objects of verbs of propositional attitude are inferentially inert. Hence, it's a sort of charade to speak of the logical form of the objects of PAs; what's the force of saying that a sentence has the form $P \& Q$ if one must also say that simplification of conjunction does not apply?

Perhaps some such argument supplies the motive force of fusion theories. It is, in any event, misled. In particular, it muddles the distinction between what's entailed by what's believed, and what's entailed by believing what's believed. Less cryptically: if John believes that P & Q, then what John believes entails that P and what John believes entails that Q. This is surely incontestible; P & Q is what John believes, and P & Q entails P, Q. Full stop. It would thus be highly ill-advised to put Frege's condition as "P & Q is semantically inert when embedded in the context 'John believes. . .'";

for this makes it sound as though P & Q sometimes doesn't entail P, viz. when it's in the scope of "believes". (A parallel bad argument: P & Q sometimes doesn't entail P, viz. when it's in the scope of the operator 'not'.) What falls under Frege's condition, then, is not the sentence that expresses what John believes (viz. P & Q) but the sentence that expresses John's believing what he believes (viz. the sentence 'John believes that P & Q'). Note that the inertia of this latter sentence isn't an exception to simplification of conjunction, since simplification of conjunction isn't defined for sentences of the form *a believes that P & Q;* only for sentences of the form *P & Q.*

"Still," one might say, "if the form of words 'P & Q' is logically inert when embedded in the form of words 'John believes . . .', what's the *point* of talking about the logical form of beliefs?" This isn't an argument, of course, but it's a fair question. Answers: (a) because we may want to satisfy Aristotle's condition (e.g., in order to be in a position to state the practical syllogism); (b) because we may want to compare beliefs in respect of their form (John's belief that (x) Fx→Gx is a generalization of Mary's belief that a is F and G; Sam's belief that P is incompatible with Bill's belief that not-P; etc.); (c) because we may wish to speak of the consequences of a belief, even while cheerfully admitting that the consequences of a belief may not themselves be objects of belief (viz. believed in). Indeed, we need the notion of the consequences of a belief if only in order to say that belief isn't closed under the consequence relation.

I cease to digress.

V. A theory of propositional attitudes should mesh with empirical accounts of mental processes.

We want a theory of PAs to say what (token) propositional attitudes *are,* or, at least, what the facts are in virtue of which PA ascriptions are true. It seems to me self-evident that no such theory could be acceptable unless it lent itself to explanations of the data—gross and commonsensical or subtle and experimental—about mental states and processes. This is not, of course, to require that a theory of PAs legitimize our *current* empirical psychology; only that it comport with some psychology or other that is independently warranted. I hear this as analogous to: the theory that water is H_2O couldn't be acceptable unless, taken together with appropriate empirical premises, it leads to explanations of the macro- and micro-properties of water. Hence, I hear it as undeniable.

I think, in fact, that the requirement that a theory of propositional attitudes should be empirically plausible can be made to do quite a lot of work—much more work than philosophers have usually realized. I'll return to this presently, when we have some theories in hand.

Those, then, are the conditions that I want a theory of propositional attitudes to meet. I shall argue that, taken together, they strongly suggest that propositional attitudes are relations between organisms and formulae in an internal language; between organisms and internal sentences, as it were. It's convenient, however, to give the arguments in two steps; first, to show that conditions I-V comport nicely with the view that the objects of PAs are sentences, and then to show that these sentences are plausibly internal.

I begin by anticipating a charge of false advertising. The arguments to be reviewed are explicitly non-demonstrative. All I claim for the internal language theory is that it works (a) surprisingly well, and (b) better than any of the available alternatives. The clincher comes at the end: even if we didn't need internal sentences for purposes of I-V, we'd need them to do our psychology. Another non-demonstrative argument, no doubt, but one I find terrifically persuasive.

Carnap's Theory

Carnap suggested, in *Meaning and Necessity* (1947), that PAs might be construed as relations between people and sentences they are disposed to utter; e.g., between people and sentences of English. What Carnap had primarily in mind was coping with the opacity problem, but it's striking and instructive that his proposal does pretty well with *all* the conditions I've enumerated. Consider:

I. If propositional attitudes are relations to sentences, then they are relations *tout court*. Moreover, assume that the relations ascribed by a sentence of the form *a believes* . . . holds between the individual denoted by 'a' and the correspondent of the complement clause. It is then immediately clear why the belief ascribed to *a* is true if the correspondent is; the correspondent is the *object* of the belief (i.e., the correspondent is what's believed-true) if Carnap's story is right.

II. Vendler's condition is presumably satisfiable, though how the details go will depend on how we construe the objects of verbs of saying. A natural move for a neo-Carnapian to make would be to take 'John said that P' to be true in virtue of some relation between John and a token of the type P. Since, on this account, saying that P and believing that P involve relations to tokens of the very same sentence, it's hardly surprising that formulae which express the object of the *says-that* relation turn out to be logico-syntactically similar to formulae which express the object of the *believes-that* relation.

III. Frege's condition is satisfied; the opacity of belief is construed as a special case of the opacity of quotation. To put it slightly differently; 'John said "Bill bit Mary"' expresses a relation between John and a (quoted) sentence, so we're unsurprised by the fact that John may bear *that* relation to *that* sentence, while not bearing it to some arbitrarily similar but distinct sentence, e.g., to the sentence 'somebody bit Mary' or to the sentence 'Bill bit somebody', etc. But ditto, *mutatis mutandis,* if 'John believes Bill bit Mary' *also* expresses a relation between John and a quoted sentence.

IV. Aristotle's condition is satisfied in the strong form. The logical form of the object of a belief sentence is inherited from the logical form of the correspondent of the belief sentence. Of course it is, since on the Carnap view, the correspondent of the belief sentence *is* the object of the belief.

V. Whether you think that Carnap's theory can claim empirical plausibility depends on what you take the empirical facts about propositional attitudes to be and how ingenious you are in exploiting the theory to provide explanations of the facts. Here's one example of how such an explanation might go.

It's plausible to claim that there is a fairly general parallelism between the complexity of beliefs and the complexity of the sentences that express them. So, for example, I take it that 'the Second Punic War was fought under conditions which neither of the combatants could have desired or forseen' is a more complex sentence than, e.g., 'it's raining'; and, correspondingly, I take it that the thought that the Second Punic War was fought under conditions which neither of the combatants could have desired or forseen is a more complicated thought than the thought that it's raining. Carnap's theory provides for this parallelism,[10] since, according to the theory, what makes a belief ascription true is a relation between an organism and the correspondent of the belief-ascribing sentence. To hold the belief that the Second Punic War . . . , etc. is thus to be related to a more complex sentence than the one you are related to when you hold the belief that it's raining, and it's quite plausible that being disposed to utter a complex sentence should be a more complex state than being disposed to utter a simple sentence, ceteris paribus.

Some people need to count noses before they will admit to having one. In which case, see the discussion of "codability" in Brown and Lenneberg (1954) and Brown (1976). What the experiments showed is that the relative complexity of the descriptions which subjects supply for color chips predicts the relative difficulty that the subjects have in identifying the chips in a recognition-recall task. Brown and Lenneberg explain the finding along strictly (though inadvertently) Carnapian lines: complex descriptions correspond to complex memories because it's the description which the subject (opaquely) remembers when he (transparently) remembers the color of the chip.

We can now begin to see *one* of the ways in which Condition V is supposed to work. A theory of propositional attitudes specifies a construal of the objects of the attitudes. It tells for such a theory if it can be shown to mesh with an independently plausible story about the "cost accounting" for mental processes. A cost accounting function is just a (partial) ordering of mental states by their relative complexity. Such an ordering is, in turn, responsive to a variety of types of empirical data, both intuitive and experimental. Roughly, one has a "mesh" between an empirically warranted cost accounting and a theory of the objects of PAs when one can predict the relative complexity of a mental state (or process) from the relative complexity of whatever the theory assigns as its object (or domain). (So, if Carnap is right, then the relative complexity of beliefs should be predictable from the relative linguistic complexity of the correspondents of belief-ascribing sentences.)

There's a good deal more to be said about all this than I have space for here. Again, roughly: to require that the complexity of the putative objects of PAs predict the cost accounting for the attitudes is to impose empirical constraints on the *notation* of (canonical) belief-ascribing sentences. So, for example, we would clearly get different predictions about the relative complexity of beliefs if we take the object of a PA to be the correspondent of the belief ascribing sentence than if we take it to be, e.g., the correspondent transformed into disjunctive form. The fact that there are empirical consequences of the notation we use to specify the objects of PAs is, of course, part and parcel of the fact that we are construing the attitude ascriptions *opaquely;* it is precisely under opaque construal that we distinguish (e.g.,) the mental state of believing that P & Q from the mental state of believing that neither not-P nor not-Q.

In short, Carnap's theory fares rather well with conditions I-V; there's more to be said in its favor than one might gather from the muted enthusiasm which philosophers have generally accorded it. Nevertheless, I think the philosophical consensus is warranted; Carnap's theory won't do. Here are some of the reasons.

1. Carnap has a theory about the objects of the propositional attitudes (viz., they're sentences) and a theory about the character of the relation to those objects in virtue of which one has a belief, desire, etc. Now, the latter theory is blatantly behavioristic; on Carnap's view, to believe that so-and-so is to be disposed (under presumably specifiable conditions) to utter tokens of the correspondent of the belief-ascribing sentence. But, patently, beliefs aren't behavioral dispositions; a fortiori, they aren't dispositions to utter. Hence, something's wrong with at least part of Carnap's account of the attitudes.

I put this objection first because it's the easiest to meet. So far as I can see, nothing prevents Carnap from keeping his account of the *objects* of belief while scuttling the behavioristic analysis of the belief relation. This would leave him wanting an answer to such questions as: what relation to the sentence 'it's raining' is such that you believe that it's raining if you and the sentence are in that relation? In particular, he'd want some answer other than the behavioristic: "It's the relation of being disposed to utter tokens of that sentence when . . ."

The natural solution would be for Carnap to turn functionalist; to hold that to believe it's raining is to have a token of 'it's raining' play a certain role in the causation of your behavior and of your (other) mental states, said role eventually to be specified in the course of the detailed working out of empirical psychology . . . etc., etc. This is, perhaps, not much of a story, but it's fashionable, I know of nothing better, and it does have the virtue of explaining why propositional attitudes are opaque: You wouldn't expect to be able to infer from 'tokens of the sentence S_1 have the causal role R' to 'tokens of the sentences S_2 have the causal role of R' on the basis of any logical relation between S_1 and S_2 (except, of course, identity). More generally, so far as I can see, a functionalist account of the way quoted sentences figure in the having of PAs will serve as well as a disposition-to-utter account in coping with all of conditions I-V. From now on, I'll take this emendation for granted.

2. The natural way to read the Carnap theory is to take type identity of the correspondents of belief-ascribing sentences as necessary and sufficient for type identity of the ascribed beliefs; and it's at least arguable that this cuts the PAs too thin. So, for example, one might plausibly hold that 'John believes Mary bit Bill' and 'John believes Bill was bitten by Mary' ascribe the same belief (see note 9, page 327). In effect, this is the sinister side of the strategy of inheriting the opacity of belief from the opacity of quotation. The strategy fails whenever the identity conditions on beliefs are *different* from the identity conditions on sentences.

A way to cope would be to allow that the objects of beliefs are, in effect, *translation sets* of sentences; something like this seems to be the impetus for Carnap's doctrine of intentional isomorphism. In any event, the problems in this area are well-known. It may well be, for example, that the right way to characterize a translation relation for sentences is by referring to the communicative intentions of speaker/hearers of whatever language the sentences belong to. (S_1 translates S_2 if the two sentences are both standardly used with the same communicative intentions.) But, of course, we can't both identify translations by reference to intentions and individuate propositional attitudes (including, n.b., intentions) by reference to translations. This problem holds quite independent of epistemological worries about the facticity of ascriptions of propositional attitudes, the determinacy or otherwise of translations, etc., which suggests that it may be serious.

3. You can believe that it's raining even if you don't speak English. This is a variant of the thickness of slice problem just mentioned; it again suggests that the appropriate objects of belief are translation sets and raises the specters that haunt that treatment.

4. You can, surely, believe that it's raining even if you don't speak any language at all. To say this is to say that at least *some* human cognitive psychology generalizes to infra-human organisms; if it didn't, we would find the behavior of animals *utterly* bewildering, which, in fact, we don't.

Of course, relations are cheap; there must be *some* relation which a dog bears to 'it's raining' iff the dog believes that it's raining; albeit, perhaps, some not very interesting relation. So, why not choose *it* as the relation in virtue of which the belief-ascription holds of the dog? The problem is condition V. It would simply be a miracle if there were a relation between dogs and tokens of 'it's raining' such that any of the empirical facts about the propositional attitudinizing of dogs proved explicable in terms of that relation. (We can't, for example, choose any functional/causal relation because the behavior of dogs is surely not in any way caused by tokens of English sentences.) To put it generally if crudely, satisfying condition V depends on assuming that whatever the theory takes to be the object of a PA plays an appropriate role in the mental processes of the organism to which the attitude is ascribed. But English sentences play no role in the mental life of dogs. (Excepting, perhaps, such sentences as 'Down, Rover!' which, in any event, don't play the kind of role envisaged.)

5. We argued that the truth conditions on beliefs are inherited from the truth conditions on the correspondents of belief-ascribing sentences, but this won't work if, for example, there are inexpressible beliefs. This problem is especially serious for behaviorist (or functionalist) accounts of the belief relation; to believe that P can't be a question of being disposed to utter (or of having one's behavior caused by) tokens of the sentence P if, as a matter of fact, there is no such sentence. Yet it is the appeal to quoted sentences which does the work in such theories: which allows them to satisfy I-V.

6. We remarked that there's a rough correspondence between the complexity of thoughts and the complexity of the sentences which express them, and that the (neo-) Carnapian theory provides

for this; more generally, that the view that the objects of PAs are natural-language sentences might mesh reasonably well with an empirically defensible cost accounting for mental states and processes. Unfortunately this argument cuts both ways if we assume—as seems entirely plausible—that the correspondence is no better than partial. Whenever it fails, there's prima facie evidence *against* the theory that sentences are the objects of propositional attitudes.

In fact, we can do rather better than appealing to intuitions here. For example: we noted above that the "codability" (viz., mean simplicity of descriptions in English) of colors predicts their recallability in a population of English speakers, and that this comports with the view that what one remembers when one remembers a color is (at least sometimes) its description—i.e., with the view that descriptions are the objects of (at least some) propositional attitudes. It thus comes as a shock to find that codability *in English* also predicts recall for a monolingual Dani subject population. We can't explain this by assuming a correlation between codability-in-English and codability-in-Dani (i.e., by assuming that the colors that English speakers find easy to describe are the ones that Dani-speakers also find easy to describe), since, as it turns out, Dani has no vocabulary *at all* for chromatic variation; all such variation is *infinitely* uncodable in Dani. This comes close to being the paradox dreaded above: how could *English* sentences be the objects of the propositional attitudes of the Dani? And, if they are not, how could a property defined over English sentences mesh with a theory of cost accounting for the mental processes of the Dani? It looks as though either (a) some propositional attitudes are *not* relations to sentences, or (b) if they are—if English sentences are somehow the objects of Dani PAs—then sentences which constitute the objects of PAs need play no functional/causal role in the having of the attitudes. (For discussion of the cross-cultural results on codability, see Brown (1976). For details of the original studies, see Heider (1972) and Berlin and Kay (1969).)

7. If (token) sentences of a natural language are the objects of propositional attitudes, how are (first) languages learned? On any theory of language learning we can now imagine, that process must involve the collection of data, and the decision about which of the hypotheses the data best confirm. That is, it must involve such

mental states and processes as beliefs, expectations and perceptual integrations. It's important to realize that *no* account of language learning which does not thus involve propositional attitudes and mental processes has ever been proposed by anyone, barring only behaviorists. And behaviorist accounts of language learning are, surely, not tenable. So, on pain of circularity, there must be *some* propositional attitudes which are not functional/causal relations to natural language sentences. I see no way out of this which isn't a worse option than rejecting the Carnap theory.

So, the situation looks discouraging. On the one hand, we have a number of plausible arguments in favor of accepting the Carnap story (viz., I-V) and, on the other, we have a number of equally plausible arguments in favor of not (viz. 1–7). Never mind; for, at second blush, it seems we needn't accept the whole Carnap theory to satisfy I-V and we needn't reject the whole Carnap theory to avoid 1–7. Roughly, all that I-V require is the part of the story that says that the objects of PAs are *sentences* (hence have logical forms, truth conditions, etc.). Whereas what causes the trouble with 1–7 is only that part of the story which says that they are *natural language* sentences (hence raising problems about non-verbal organisms, first language learning, etc.). The recommended solution is thus to take the objects of PAs to be sentences of a *non*-natural language; in effect, formulae in an Internal Representational System.

The first point is to establish that this proposal does what it is supposed to: copes with I-V without running afoul of 1–7. In fact, I propose to do less than that, since, so far as I can see, the details would be extremely complicated. Suffice it here to indicate the general strategy.

Conditions I and III are relatively easy to meet. I demands that propositional attitudes be relations, and so they are if they are relations to internal representations. III demands a construal of opacity. Carnap met this demand by reducing the opacity of belief to the opacity of quotation, and so do we: the only difference is that, whereas for Carnap, 'John believes it's raining' relates John to a sentence of English, for us it relates John to an internal formula.

Conditions II and IV stress logico/syntactic parallelism between the complements and the correspondents of belief-ascribing sentences; such relations are epitomized by the identity between the truth conditions on 'it's raining' and those on what is believed when it's believed that it's raining. (Neo-) Carnap explained these symmetries by taking the correspondents of belief ascriptions to be the objects of beliefs. The present alternative is spiritually similar but one step less direct: we assume that the correspondent of a belief-ascriber inherits its logico-semantic properties from the same internal formula which functions as the object of the belief ascribed.

There are three pieces in play: there are (a) *belief-ascribers* (like 'John believes it's raining'); (b) *complements* of belief ascribers (like 'it's raining' in 'John believes it's raining'); and (c) *correspondents* of belief ascribers (like 'it's raining' standing free). The idea is to get all three to converge (though, of course, by different routes) on the same internal formula (call it 'F (it's raining)'),[11] thereby providing the groundwork for explaining the analogies that II and IV express.

To get this to work out right would be to supply detailed instructions for connecting the theory of PAs with the theory of sentence interpretation, and I have misplaced mine. But the general idea is apparent. Belief-ascribers are true in virtue of functional/causal (call them 'belief making') relations between organisms and tokens of internal formulae. Thus, in particular, 'John believes it's raining' is true in virtue of a belief-making relation between John and a token of F (it's raining). It is, of course, the complement of a belief-ascriber that determines *which* internal formula is involved in its truth conditions; in effect 'it's raining' in 'John believes it's raining' functions as an index which picks out F (it's raining) and not, for example, F (elephants have wings), as the internal formula that John is related to iff 'John believes it's raining' is true.

So, viewed along one vector, the complement of a belief-ascriber connects it with an internal formula. But, viewed along another vector, the complement of a belief ascriber connects it to its correspondent: if the correspondent of 'John believes it's raining' is 'it's raining', that is because the form of words 'it's raining' constitutes its complement. And now we can close the circle, since, of course, F (it's raining) is *also* semantically connected with the correspondent of 'John believes it's raining' viz., by the principle that 'it's raining' is the sentence that English speakers use when they are in the belief-making relation to a token of F (it's raining) and wish to use a sentence of English to say what it is that they believe.

There are various ways of thinking about the relation between internal formulae and the correspondents of belief-ascribers. One is to think of the conventions of a natural language as functioning to establish a pairing of its verbal forms with the internal formulae that mediate the propositional attitudes of its users; in particular, as pairing the internal objects of beliefs with the form of words that speaker/hearers use to express their beliefs. This is a natural way to view the situation if you think of a natural language as a system of conventional vehicles for the expression of thoughts (a view to which I know of no serious objections). So in the present case, the conventions of English pair: 'it's raining' with F (it's raining) (viz., with the object of the belief that it's raining); 'elephants have wings' with F (elephants have wings) (viz., with the object of the belief that elephants have wings); and, generally, the object of each belief with the correspondent of some belief-ascribing sentence.[12]

Another option is to assume that F (it's raining) is distinguished by the fact that its tokens play a causal/functional role (not only as the object of the belief that it's raining, but also) in the production of linguistically regular utterances of 'it's raining'. Indeed, this option would plausibly be exercised in tandem with the one mentioned just above, since it would be reasonable to construe "linguistically regular" utterances as the ones that are produced in light of the speaker's knowledge of the linguistic conventions. The basic idea, in any event, would be to implicate F (it's raining) as the object of the communicative intentions that utterances of 'it's raining' standardly function to express; hence, as among the mental causes of such utterances. I take it that, given this relation, it ought to be possible to work out detailed tactics for the satisfaction of conditions II and IV, but this is the bit I propose to leave to the ingenuity of the reader. What I want to emphasize here is the way the linguistic structure of the complement of a belief ascriber connects it with free declaratives (in one direction) and with internal formulae (in the other). Contrary to the fusion story, it's no accident that 'it's raining' occurs in 'John believes it's raining'. Rather, the availability of natural languages for saying *both* what one believes *and* that one believes it turns on the exploitation of this elegant symmetry.

What about condition V? I shall consider this in conjunction with 2–7, since what's noteworthy about the latter is that they all register *empirical* complaints against the Carnap account. For example, 3, 4 and 6 would be without force if only everybody (viz., every subject of true propositional attitude ascriptions) talked English. 2 and 5 depend upon the empirical likelihood that English sentences fail to correspond one to one to objects of propositional attitudes. 7 would be met if only English were innate. Indeed, I suppose an ultra hard-line Neo-Carnapian might consider saving the bacon by claiming that—appearances to the contrary nonwithstanding—English *is* innate, universal, just rich enough, etc. My point is that this is the right *kind* of move to make; all we have against it is its palpable untruth.

Whereas, it's part of the charm of the internal language story that, since practically nothing is known about the details of cognitive processes, we can make the corresponding assumptions about the internal representational system risking no more than gross implausibility at the very worst.

So, let's assume—what we don't, at any event, *know* to be false —that the internal language is innate, that it's formulae correspond one to one with the contents of propositional attitudes (e.g., that 'John bit Mary' and 'Mary was bitten by John' correspond to the same "internal sentences"), and that it is *as* universal as human psychology; viz., that to the extent that an organism shares our mental processes, it also shares our system of internal representations. On these assumptions, everything works. It's no longer paradoxical, for example, that codability *in English* predicts the relative complexity of the mental processes of the Dani; for, by assumption, it's not *really* the complexity of English sentences that predicts *our* cost accounting; we wouldn't expect *that* correspondence to be better than partial (see objection 6). What really predicts our cost accounting is the relative complexity of the internal representations that we use English sentences to express. And, again by assumption, the underlying system of internal representations is common to the Dani and to us. If you don't like this assumption, try and find some other hypothesis that accounts for the facts about the Dani.

Notice that to say that we can have our empirical assumptions isn't to say that we can have them for free. They carry a body of empirical commitments which, if untenable, will defeat the internal representation view. Imagine, for example, that cost accounting for English speakers proves utterly unrelated to cost accounting for (e.g.,) speakers of Latvian. (Imagine, in effect, that the Whorf-Sapir hypothesis turns out to be more or less true.) It's then hard to see how the system of internal representations could be universal. But if it's not universal, it's presumably not innate. And if it's not innate, it's not available to mediate the learning of first languages. And if it's not available to mediate the learning of first languages, we lose our means of coping with objection 7. There are plenty of ways in which we could find out that the theory's wrong if, in fact, it is.

Where we've got to is this: the general characteristics of propositional attitudes appear to demand sentence-like entities to be their objects. And broadly empirical conditions appear to preclude identifying these entities with sentences of *natural* languages—hence internal representations and private languages. How bad is it to have got here? I now want to argue that the present conclusion is independently required because it is presupposed by the best—indeed the only—psychology that we've got. Not just, as one philosopher has rather irresponsibly remarked, that "some psychologists like to talk that way," but that the best accounts of mental processes we have are quite unintelligible unless something like the internal representation story is true.

The long way of making this point is via a detailed discussion of such theories, but I've done that elsewhere and enough is enough. Suffice it here to consider a single example—which is, however, prototypical. I claim again that the details don't matter, that one could make the same points by considering phenomena drawn from any area of cognitive psychology that is sufficiently well worked out to warrant talk of a theory *in situ*.

So, consider a fragment of contemporary (psycho)linguistics; consider the explanation of the ambiguity of a sentence like 'they are flying planes' (hereinafter, frequently, S). The conventional story goes as follows: the sentence is ambiguous because there are two ways of grouping the word sequence into phrases, two ways of "bracketing" it. One bracketing, corresponding to the reading of the sentence which answers 'what are those things?', goes: (they) (are) (flying planes)—viz., the sentence is copular, the main verb is 'are', and 'flying' is an adjectival modifier of 'planes'. Whereas, on the other bracketing—corresponding to the reading on which the sentence answers 'What are those guys doing?'—the bracketing goes: (they) (are flying) (planes)—viz. the sentence is transitive, the main verb is 'flying', and 'are' belongs to the auxiliary. I assume without argument that something like this is, or at least contributes to, the explanation of the ambiguity of S. The evidence for such treatments is overwhelming, and there is, literally, no alternative theory in the field.

But what could it mean to speak of S as "having" two bracketings? I continue to tread the well-worn path: S has two bracketings in that there exists a function (call it G-proper) from (as it might be) the word 'sentence' onto precisely those bracketed word strings which constitute the sentences of English. And both '(they) (are) (flying planes)' and '(they) (are flying) (planes)' are in the range of that function. (Moreover, no other bracketing of that word sequence is in the range of G-proper . . . etc.)

Now, the trouble with this explanation, as it stands, is that it is either enthymemic or silly. For, one wants to ask, how *could* the mere, as it were Platonic, existence of G-proper account for the facts about the ambiguity of English sentences? Or, to put it another way, sure there is, Platonically, a function under which S gets two bracketings. But there is also, Platonically, a function G' under which it gets sixteen; and a function G'' under which it gets seven; and a function G''' under which it gets none. Since G', G'', and G''' are all, qua functions, just as good as G-proper, how could the mere *existence* of the latter explain the linguistic properties of S; (You may feel inclined to say: "Ah, but G-proper is the (or perhaps is *the*) grammar of English, and that distinguishes it from G', G'', and the rest." But this explanation takes one nowhere, since it invites the question why does the grammar of English play a special role in the explanation of English sentences? Or, to put the same question minutely differently: call G' the schmamar of English. We now want to know how come it's the bracketing assigned by English grammar and not the bracketing assigned by English schmamar, which predicts the ambiguity of 'they are flying planes'?)

So far as I can see, there's only one way such questions can conceivably be answered—viz., by holding that G-proper (not only exists but) specifies the very system of (internal (what else?)) representations that English speaker/hearers use to parse the sentences of their language. But, then, if we accept this, we are willy-nilly involved in talking of at least *some* mental processes (processes of understanding and producing sentences) as involving at least some relations to at least some internal representations. And, if we have to have internal representations anyhow, why not take them to be the objects of propositional attitudes, thereby placating I-V? I say "if we accept this"; but really we have no choice. For the account is well evidenced, not demonstrably incoherent, and, again, it's the only one in the field. A working science is ipso facto in philosophical good repute.

So, by a series of non-demonstrative arguments: there are internal representations and propositional attitudes are relations that we bear to them. It remains to discuss two closely related objections.

Objection 1: Why not take the object of propositional attitudes to be *propositions?*

This suggestion has, no doubt, a ring of etymological plausibility; in fact, for all I know, it may be right. The mistake is in supposing it somehow conflicts with the present proposal.

I am taking seriously the idea that the system of internal representations constitutes a (computational) language. Qua language, it presumably has a syntax and a semantics; specifying the language involves saying what the properties are in virtue of which its formulae are well-formed, and what relations(s) obtain between the formulae and things in the (non-linguistic) world. I have no idea what an adequate semantics for a system of internal representations would look like; suffice it that, if propositions come in at all, they come in here. In particular, nothing stops us from specifying a semantics for the IRS by saying (inter alia) that some of its formulae express propositions. If we do say this, then we can make sense of the notion that propositional attitudes are relations to propositions—viz., they are *mediated* relations to propositions, with internal representations doing the mediating.

This is, quite generally, the way that representational theories of the mind work. So, in classical versions, thinking of John (construed opaquely) is a relation to an "idea"—viz., to an internal representation of John. But this is quite compatible with its also being (transparently) construable as a relation *to John.* In particular, when Smith is thinking of John, he (normally) stands in relation to John and does so *in virtue* of his standing in relation to an idea of John. Similarly, mutatis mutandis, if thinking that it will rain is standing in relation to a proposition, then, on the present account, you stand in that relation in virtue of your (functional/causal) relation to an internal formula which expresses the proposition. No doubt, the "expressing" bit is obscure; but that's a problem about propositions, not a problem about internal representations.

"Ah, but if you are going to allow propositions as the *mediate* objects of propositional attitudes, why bother with internal representations as their immediate objects? Why not just say: 'propositional attitudes are relations to propositions. Punkt!'" There's a small reason and a big reason. The small reason is that propositions don't have the right properties for our purposes. In particular, one anticipates problems of cost-accounting. Condition V, it will be remembered, permits us to choose among theories of PAs in virtue of the lexico-syntactic form of the entities they assign as objects of the attitudes. Now, the problem with propositions is that they are the sorts of things which don't, in the relevant respects, *have* forms. Propositions neutralize the lexico-syntactic differences between various ways of saying the same thing. That's what they're *for.* I say that this is a small problem, but it looms prodigious if you hanker after a theory of the object of PAs which claims empirical repute. After all, it's not just cost-accounting that is supposed to be determined by formal aspects of the objects of PAs; it's *all* the mental processes and properties that cognitive psychology explains. That's what it *means* to speak of a *computational* psychology. Computational principles are ones that apply in virtue of the form of entities in their domain.

But my main reason for not saying "propositional attitudes are relations to propositions. Punkt." is that I don't understand it. I don't see how an organism can stand in an (interesting epistemic) relation to a proposition except by standing in a (causal/functional) relation to some token of a formula that expresses the proposition. I am aware that there is a philosophical tradition to the contrary. Plato says (I think) that there is a special intellectual faculty (theoria) wherewith one peers at abstract objects. Frege says that one *apprehends* (what I'm calling) propositions, but I can find no doctrine about what apprehension comes to beyond the remark (in "The Thought") that it's not sense perception because its objects are abstract and it's not introspection because its objects aren't mental. (He also says that grasping a thought isn't much like grasping a hammer. To be sure.) As for me, I want a *mechanism* for the relation between organisms and propositions, and the only one I can think of is mediation by internal representations.[13]

Objection 2: Surely it's *conceivable* that propositional attitudes are *not* relations to internal representations.

I think it is; the theory that propositional attitudes are relations to internal representations is a piece of empirical psychology, not an analysis. For there might have been angels, or behaviorism might have been true, and then the internal representation story would have been false. The moral is, I think, that we ought to give up asking for analyses; psychology is all the philosophy of mind that we are likely to get.

But, moreover, it may be *empirically* possible that there should be creatures that have the same propositional attitudes we do (e.g., the same beliefs) but *not* the same system of internal representations; creatures that, as it were, share our epistemic states but not our psychology. Suppose, for example, it turns out that Martians, or porpoises, believe what we do but have a very different sort of cost accounting. We might then want to say that there are translation relations among systems of internal representation (viz., that formally distinct representations can express the same proposition). Presumably *which* proposition an internal representation expresses—what content it has—would be complexly determined by its functional role in the organism's mental life, including, especially, the way it is connected to stimulations and responses. Functional identity of internal representations would then be criterial for their intertranslatability. Whether we can actually make sense of this sort of view remains to be seen; we can barely think about the question prior to the elaboration of theories about how representational systems are semantically interpreted; and as things now stand, we haven't got semantic theories for natural languages, to say nothing of languages of thought. Perhaps it goes without saying that it's no objection to a doctrine that it *may* run us into incoherencies. Or, rather, if it is an objection, there's an adequate reply: "Yes, but also it may not."

I'll end on the note just sounded. Contemporary cognitive psychology is, in effect, a revival of the representational theory of the mind. The favored treatment of PAs arises in this context. So, in particular, the mind is conceived of as an organ whose function is the manipulation of representations and these, in turn, provide the domain of mental processes and the (immediate) objects of mental states. That's what it is to see the mind as something like a computer. (Or rather, to put the horse back in front of the cart, that's what it is to see a computer as something like the mind. We give sense to the analogy by treating selected states of the machine as formulae and by specifying which semantic interpretations the formulae are to bear. It is in the context of such specifications that we speak of machine processes as computations and of machine states as intensional.)

If the representational theory of the mind is true, then we know what propositional attitudes are. But the net total of philosophical problems is surely not decreased thereby. We must now face what has always been *the* problem for representational theories to solve: what relates internal representations to the world? What is it for a system of internal representations to be semantically interpreted? I take it that this problem is now the main content of the philosophy of mind.[14]

Chapter 8

Tom Swift and His
Procedural Grandmother

1. Introduction

Rumor has it that, in semantics, AI is where the action is. We hear not only that computational (hereafter 'procedural') semantics offers an alternative to the classical semantics of truth, reference, and modality,[1] but that it provides what its predecessor so notably lacked: clear implications for psychological models of the speaker/hearer. Procedural semantics is said to be 'the psychologist's' theory of meaning, just as classical semantics was 'the logician's'. What's bruited in the by-ways is thus nothing less than a synthesis of the theory of meaning with the theory of mind. Glad tidings these, and widely credited.

But, alas, unreliable. I shall argue that, soberly considered:

(a) The computer models provide no semantic theory *at all*, if what you mean by a semantic theory is an account of the relation between language and the world. In particular, procedural semantics doesn't supplant classical semantics, it merely begs the questions that classical semanticists set out to answer. The begging of these questions is, of course, quite inadvertent; we shall consider at length how it comes about.

(b) Procedural semantics does provide a theory about what it is to know the meaning of a word. But it's not a brave new theory. On the contrary, it's just an archaic and wildly implausible form of verificationism. Since practically nobody except procedural semanticists takes verificationism seriously any more, it will be of some interest to trace the sources of their adherence to the doctrine.

(c) It's the verificationism which connects the procedural theory of language to the procedural theory of perception. The consequence is a view of the relation between language and mind which is not significantly different from that of Locke or Hume. The recidivism of PS theorizing is among the most striking of the ironies now to be explored.

2. Use and mention

Perhaps the *basic* idea of PS is this: providing a compiler for a language is tantamount to specifying a semantic theory for that language. As Johnson-Laird (1977) puts it, the "artificial languages which are used to communicate programs of instructions to computers, have both a syntax and a semantics. Their syntax consists of rules for writing well-formed programs that a computer can interpret and execute. The semantics consists of the procedures that the computer is instructed to execute" (page 189). Johnson-Laird takes this analogy between compiling and semantic interpretation quite seriously: "we might speak of the intension of a program as the procedure that is executed when the program is run" (page 192). And Johnson-Laird is not alone. According to Winograd (1971), "the program [which mediates between an input sentence and its procedural translation] operates on a sentence to produce a representation *of its meaning* in some internal language" (page 409; my emphasis)".

Now, there is no principled reason why this analogy between compiling and semantic interpretation should not be extended from artificial languages (for which compilers actually exist) to natural languages (for which semantic theories are so badly wanted). If compilers really are species of semantic theories, then we could provide a semantics for English if only we could learn to compile *it*. That's the PS strategy in a nutshell.

Since the strategy rests upon the assumption that the compiled (e.g. Machine Language)[2] representation of a sentence is eo ipso a representation of its meaning, it will pay to consider this assumption in detail. It will turn out that there's a sense in which it's true and a sense in which it's not, and that the appearance that PS offers a semantic theory depends largely upon sliding back and forth between the two.

To begin cheerfully: if we take programming languages to be

the ones that we are able to compile (thereby excluding natural languages de facto but not in principle), then there *is* a sense in which programming languages are ipso facto semantically interpreted. This is because compiling is translation into ML, and ML is itself an interpreted language. If, then, we think of a compiler for PL_i, as a semantic theory for PL_i, we are thinking of semantic interpretation as consisting of translation into a semantically interpreted language.

Now, this needn't be as circular as it sounds, since there might be (indeed, there clearly are) two different notions of semantic interpretation in play. When we speak of ML as an interpreted language, we have something like the *classical* notion of interpretation in mind. In this sense of the term, an interpretation specified denotata for the referring expressions, truth conditions for the sentences (or, better, 'compliance conditions', since many of the sentences of ML are imperative), etc. Whereas, when we speak of interpretation of PL_i, we have in mind (not classical interpretation but) translation into a language that is itself classically interpreted (e.g. translation into ML).

It's entirely possible that this is the *right* notion of interpretation for a natural language; that, for one reason or another, it would be a bad research strategy to attempt to classically interpret a natural language 'directly' and a good research strategy to attempt to interpret it 'mediately' (viz. via its translation into some other, classically interpreted, formalism). This idea is quite widespread across the disciplines, the mediating language being called 'logical syntax' in philosophy, 'internal representation' in psychology, and 'ML' in AI. I'm inclined to endorse this strategy, and I'll return to it toward the end of this paper. But what's important for present purposes is this: if we see the PS strategy as an attempt to interpret English by translating it into a classically interpreted ML, then we see straight off that PS isn't an alternative to classical semantics. Rather, PS is parasitic on CS. Translation into ML is semantic interpretation only if ML is itself semantically interpreted, and when we say of ML that it is semantically interpreted, we mean not that ML is translated into a semantically interpreted language, but that ML is *classically* semantically interpreted. Translation has got to stop somewhere.

So, there's *a sense* in which compiling is (or might be) semantic interpretation. Hence, there's *a sense* in which a programming language has a semantics if it is compiled. That's what is right about the PS approach. But there is also a sense in which compilable languages are *not* ipso facto interpreted; a sense in which compiling need not—and normally does not—give the 'intension' of a program. The point is that the interpretation assigned a PL sentence by the compiler is not, normally, its 'intended interpretation'; it's not, normally, the interpretation that specifies *what the sentence means.* One might put it even stronger: machines typically don't know (or care) what the programs that they run are about; all they know (or care about) is how to run their programs. This may sound cryptical or even mystical. It's not. It's merely banal.

You can see the point at issue by considering an example (suggested to me by Professor Georges Rey, in conversation). Imagine two programs, one of which is a simulation of the Six Day War (so the referring expressions designate, e.g., tank divisions, jet planes, Egyptian soldiers, Moshe Dayan, etc., and the relational terms express bombing, surrounding, commanding, capturing, etc.): and the other of which simulates a chess game (so the referring expressions designate knights, bishops, pawns, etc., and the relational terms express threatening, checking, controlling, taking, etc.). It's a possible (though, of course, unlikely) accident that these programs should be *indistinguishable when compiled;* viz. that the ML counterparts of these programs should be identical, so that the internal career of a machine running one program would be identical, step by step, to that of a machine running the other.

Suppose that these programs were written in English. Then it's possible that the sentence "Israeli infantry surround a tank corps" and the sentence "pawns attack knight" should receive the same ML 'translations'. Yet, of course, the sentences don't mean anything like the same; the compiled versions of the sentences don't, therefore, specify their intensions. Or, if you're dubious about intensions, then: the sentences don't have the same compliance conditions (if they're imperatives) or truth conditions (if they're declaratives); and there is nothing in common between the entities that their referring expressions designate or the relations that their predicates express.[3] In the sense of "interpretation" we are likely to have in mind when we speak pretheoretically of a semantic theory as interpreting English sentences, these sentences are *not* interpreted when they are compiled. Equivalently: the *programmer* knows the interpretation; he knows which interpretation he intends, and, probably, he cares about the program largely because he cares about the (intended) interpretation. But the machine doesn't know the intended interpretation. Nor does it care what the intended interpretation is, *so long as it knows the interpretation in ML.*

How could it be that a compiled sentence is interpreted in one sense yet not interpreted in the other? The answer has partly to do with the nature of computers, and partly to do with the *point* of compiling.

Computers are devices for doing jobs we set; in particular, devices for following orders. What we need for instructing a computer is a language in which we can tell it what jobs we want it to do. What the computer needs to do its job is instructions in a language that it can understand. Machine Language satisfies both these conditions. In one way of looking at things, it is a very powerful language, since, in a useful sense of "precisely", any job that can be specified precisely can be specified in ML (assuming, as I shall do throughout, that ML is at least rich enough to specify a Turing machine). But, looked at another way—and this is the essential point—it is a very *weak* language. For the things you can talk about in ML are just the states and processes of the machine (viz. the states and processes that need to be mentioned in specifying its jobs). So, the referring expressions of ML typically name, for example, addresses of the machine, formulae stored or storable at addresses, etc. And the relational terms typically express operations that the machine can perform (e.g. writing down symbols, erasing symbols, comparing symbols, moving symbols from address to address, etc.). Whereas, prima facie, the semantic apparatus of a natural language is incomparably richer. For by using a natural language, we can refer not just to symbols and operations on them, but also to Moshe Dayan and tank divisions, cabbages, kings, harvestings, and inaugurations. Of course, it's conceptually possible that anything that can be said in a *prima facie* rich language like English can be *translated into* (not just *paired with*) formulae of ML. But, patently, from the mere assertion that English might be compiled in ML and that compiled languages are *ipso facto* interpreted, it does not follow that the meaning of English sentences can be expressed in ML. *A fortiori* it does not follow that a compiler for English would *ipso facto* capture (what I'm calling) the intended semantic interpretations of the sentences of English.

Why, then, do procedural semanticists think that compiling is an interesting candidate for semantic interpretation? I think part of the answer is that when procedural semanticists talk informally about the compiled representation of English sentences, they allow themselves to forget that ML is interpreted *solely* for machine states, processes, etc. and speak as though we knew how to interpret ML for much richer semantic domains—in fact, for the world at large. That is, they talk as though the semantics of ML constituted a theory of language-and-the world, whereas, in fact, it provides only a theory of language-and-the-insides-of-the-machine.

This equivocation is very widespread indeed in the PS literature. Thus, for example, Winograd remarks that (in PLANNER) "we can represent such facts as 'Boise is a city'. and 'Noah was the father of Jafeth'. as: (CITY BOISE) (FATHER-OF NOAH JAFETH). Here, BOISE, NOAH and JAFETH are specific objects, CITY is a property which objects can have, and FATHER-OF is a relation" (page 207).[4] To which one wants to reply: 'Who says they are?' In particular, neither Winograd (nor PS at large) supply anything remotely resembling an account of the relation between a symbol (say, 'BOISE') and a city (say, Boise) such that the former designates the latter in virtue of their standing in that relation. Nor, of course, does the eventual ML translation of 'BOISE IS A CITY' provide the explication that's required. On the contrary, ML has no resources for referring to Boise (or to cities) *at all*. What it *can* do (and *all* that it can do that's relevant to the present purposes) is refer to the *expression* 'BOISE' and say of that expression such things as that it appears at some address in the machine (e.g. at the address labeled by the expression 'CITY'). But, of course, the sentence (capturable in ML) "the expression 'BOISE' appears at the address CITIES" is not remotely a translation of the sentence "Boise is a city". To suppose that it is is to commit a notably unsubtle version of the use/mention fallacy.

Or consider Miller and Johnson-Laird (1976). They provide an extended example (circa page 174) of how a procedural system might cope with the English question: 'Did Lucy bring the dessert? The basic idea is that the question is "translated" into instructions in accordance with which "[episodic memory] is searched for memories of Lucy . . ." The memories thus recovered are sorted through for reference to (e.g.) chocolate cakes, and how the device answers the question is determined by which such memories it finds. The details are complicated, but they needn't concern us; our present point is that the authors simply have no right to this loose talk of memories *of* Lucy and internal representations *of* chocolate cakes. This is because nothing is available in their theory to reconstruct such (classical) semantic relations as the one that holds between 'Lucy' and Lucy, or between 'chocolate cake' and chocolate cakes. Strictly speaking, all you can handle in the theory is what you can represent in ML. And all you can represent in ML is an instruction to go to the *address* labeled 'Lucy' (but equally well—and perhaps less misleadingly—labeled, say, '#959' or 'BOISE' or 'The Last Rose of Summer') and see if you find at that address a certain formula, viz. the one which is paired, under compiling, with the English predicate 'brought a cake'. Of course, the theorist is welcome—if he's so inclined—to construe the formulae he finds at Lucy (the address) as information about Lucy (the person); e.g. as the information that Lucy brought a cake. But PS provides no account of this aboutness relation, and the machine which realizes the Lucy-program has no access to this construal.

Remember that, though ML is, in the strict sense, an interpreted language,[5] the interpretation of 'Lucy' (the ML expression) yields as denotatum not Lucy-the-girl but only Lucy-the-address (viz. the address that the machine goes to when it is told to go to Lucy and it does what it is told). In short, the semantic relations that we care about, the one between the name and the person and the one between the predicate 'bring the desert' and the property of being a dessert bringer, just aren't reconstructed *at all* when we represent 'Did Lucy bring dessert?' as a procedure for going-to-Lucy-and-looking-for-formulae. To reconstruct *those* relations, we need a classical semantic theory of names and predicates, which PS doesn't give us and which, to quote the poet, in our case we have not got. In effect, then, a machine can compile 'Did Lucy bring dessert?' and have not the foggiest idea that the sentence asks about whether Lucy brought dessert. For the ML "translation" of that sentence—the formula which the machine does, as it were, understand—*isn't* about whether Lucy brought dessert. It's about whether a certain formula appears at a certain address.

We get a clearer idea of what has happened if we forget about computers entirely; the brilliance of the technology tends to dazzle the eye. So, suppose somebody said: 'Breakthrough! The semantic interpretation of "Did Napoleon win at Waterloo?" is: *find out whether the sentence "Napoleon won at Waterloo" occurs in the volume with Dewey decimal number XXX, XXX in the 42nd St. branch of the New York City Public Library*'. So far as I can see, the analogy is exact, except that libraries use a rather more primitive storage system than computers do. "'But', giggled Granny, 'if that was what 'Did Napoleon win at Waterloo?" meant, it wouldn't even be a question about *Napoleon*'. 'Aw, shucks', replied Tom Swift".

3. Verificationism

I have stressed the use/mention issue, not because I think that use/mention confusions are what PS is all about, but because, unless one avoids them, one can't get a clear view of what the problems are. However, I doubt that anybody really thinks that you can translate English into ML, taking the latter to be a language just rich enough to specify sequences of machine operations. If you put it *that* way (and that's the way you *should* put it), no procedural semanticist would endorse the program. What is, I believe, widely supposed is that you can translate English into an *enriched* ML; that there is some ML rich enough to say whatever you can say in English, and some machine complicated enough to use that language. So reconstructed, the PS research strategy is to find the language and build the machine.

Of course, you don't want the language to be *too* rich; because (a) it's no news (and no help) that you can translate English into very rich languages like (e.g.) French (or, for that matter, English); and (b) translation isn't interpretation unless it's translation into a (classically) interpreted language, and if ML gets too rich, we won't know how to interpret *it* any more than we now know how to interpret English. That is, to repeat, the very heart of the problem. A compiler would be a semantic theory only if it took us into a very rich ML; i.e., into a language rich enough to paraphrase the sentences of English. But we do not know how to interpret very rich languages, and we do not have anything approaching a clue about what it is to be able to *use* a rich, interpreted language (e.g. what it is to be able to use 'Lucy' to refer to Lucy or what it is to be able to use the internal representation of chairs to think about chairs). PS provides us with no insight at all into either of these questions; indeed, precious few of its practitioners seem to understand that these *are* questions where insight is needed.

Nevertheless, I think that many procedural semanticists think that they have found a middle road. Suppose, in particular, that we equip our machine with sensory transducers and correspondingly enrich ML with names of the transducer input and output states. This enriched ML (which I'll call MLT) still talks about only machine states and processes, but now they are states and processes of something more than a computer: at best a robot and at worst a sort of creepy-feely. Let's assume, also, that MLT has linguistic mechanisms for introducing definitions; e.g. it has a list of dummy names and rules of elimination which allow it to replace complex expressions (including, of course, expressions which contain names of states of the transducers) by single expressions consisting of dummy names. The question is whether the machine language of *this* device is rich enough to translate English.

It seems to me that many, many researchers in AI believe that the answer to this question is 'yes'. Indeed, I think that they had better think that since (a) compiling is translating only when the target language is classically interpreted; and (b) so far, there is no suggestion from PS about how to interpret a target language which is enriched beyond what you get by taking standard ML and adding the names of transducer states (together with the syntactic mechanisms of eliminitive definition). So, if the procedural semanticists don't think that English can be paraphrased in MLT, they owe us some alternative account of how the target language is to be classically interpreted. And if they don't think the target language can be classically interpreted, they lose their rationale for taking compilers to be semantic theories in *any* sense of that notion.

Be that as it may, the historical affinities of this program are all too clear. They lie, of course, with the Empiricist assumption that *every* nonlogical concept is reducible to sensation concepts (or, in trendier versions, to sensation plus motor concepts) via coordinating definitions. I do not want to comment on this program besides saying that, Heaven knows, the Empiricists tried. Several hundred years of them tried to do without 'thing' language by getting reductions to 'sense datum' language. Several decades of verificationists tried (in very similar spirit) to do without 'theoretical' terms by getting reductions to 'observation' terms. The near-universal consensus was that they failed and that the failure was principled: they failed because it can't be done. (For an illuminating discussion of why it can't be done, see Chisholm, 1957).

My own view, for what it's worth, is that the permissible moral is a good deal stronger: not only that you can't reduce natural language to ML-plus-transducer language, but really, that you can't hardly reduce it at all. I think, that is, that the vocabulary of a language like English is probably not much larger than it needs to be given the expressive power of the language. I think that's probably why, after all those years of work, there are so few good *examples* of definitions of English words (in sensation language or otherwise). After we say that 'bachelor' means 'unmarried man' (which perhaps it does) and that 'kill' means 'cause to die' (which it certainly does not), where are the *other* discoveries to which reductionist semantics has led? Surely it should worry us when we find so few cases for our theories to apply to? Surely the world is trying to tell us something? (Of course, there are lots of *bad* examples of definitions; but it's uninteresting that one can get pairings of English words with formulae to which they are *not* synonymous. To get some idea of how hard it is to do the job right, see J. L. Austin's "Three Ways of Spilling Ink" (1966), a lucid case study in the non-interdefinability of even semantically closely related terms. For further discussion of the role of definitions in theories of natural language, see below, Chapter 10.)

I want to be fairly clear about what claims are at issue. For the reductionist version of the PS strategy to work, it must be true not only that (a) many words of English are definable, but also that (b) they are definable in a primitive basis consisting of ML plus transducer vocabulary; in effect, in sensation language, (a) is dubious but not beyond rational belief. But (b) requires not just that there be definitions, but also that there be an epistemologically interesting *direction* of definition—viz. that the more definitions we apply, the closer we get to MLT. There is, however, no reason *at all* to believe that this is true, and the bankruptcy of the Empiricist program in epistemology provides considerable prima facie evidence that it is not.

Semantic reduction is the typical PS strategy for interpreting the nonsyntactic vocabulary of a rich programming language—viz. semantic reduction to formulae in MLT. In this respect, there is simply no difference between the typical PS view and that of, say, John Locke. However, as I remarked above, in the standard PS analysis, compiled programs tend to emerge as sequences of *instructions,* and this fact puts a characteristic twist on PS versions of Empiricism. In particular, it burdens PS with a form of verificationism.

For if 'that's a chair' goes over into instructions, it must be instructions to *do* something. Sometimes procedural semanticists suggest that the instruction is to add (the ML translation of) 'that's a chair' to memory. But it's closer to the spirit of the movement to take it to be an instruction to confirm 'that's a chair', viz. by checking whether that (whatever it is) has the transducer features in terms of which 'chair' is procedurally defined. Indeed, one just about has to take the latter route if one is going to argue that procedures capture intensions, for *nobody* could suppose that 'that's a chair' means 'remember that that's a chair'; whereas it's at least *possible* to believe that 'that's a chair' means 'that's something that has the observable features F' where 'F' operationally defines 'chair'. So, once again, it's the verificationism that turns out to be critical to the claim that compiling captures meaning; if 'chair' can't be defined in operational terms, then we have no way of interpreting MLT for chairs. And if we can't interpret MLT for chairs, then we have no way of capturing the meaning of 'that's a chair' in MLT.

Some procedural semanticists admit to being verificationists and some do not. Miller and Johnson-Laird (1976), for example, deny the charge both frequently and vehemently, but the grounds of their denial are obscure. Interpreting liberally, I take it that their point is this: to give procedural reductions of 'chair', 'grandmother', 'dessert', or whatever, you usually need not only transducer vocabulary but also primitive terms which express quite abstract notions like 'is possible', 'intends', 'causes', and heaven knows what more. Miller and Johnson-Laird (quite correctly) doubt that such abstract notions can be reconstructed in MLT. Hence they hold that there is no operational analysis for such English sentences as contain words defined in terms of 'intends', 'causes', and the rest. Hence they claim not to be verificationists.

Given a dilemma, you get to choose your horn. Miller and Johnson-Laird do, I think, avoid verificationism, but at an exorbitant price (as should be evident from the discussion in section 2, above). In particular, they have no semantic theory for most of the sentences of English. For consider the sentence E, which goes over into a (compiled) representation of the form '........ causes ....'. The internal expression 'causes' isn't part of ML proper, since it isn't interpreted by reference to the states and processes of the machine; and it isn't part of MLT either, since, by hypothesis, 'causes' isn't operationally definable. But the domain in which MLT is semantically interpreted is exhausted by what can be operationally defined; i.e. by what can be defined in terms of machine states and transducer states. So 'causes' is *un*interpreted in the internal representation of E. So Miller and Johnson-Laird don't have a semantic theory for E.

Some procedural semanticists prefer to be impaled upon the *other* horn. One of the few explicit discussions of the relation between PS and CS is to be found in Woods (1975). Woods takes a classical semantic theory to be a mechanism for projecting the (roughly) truth conditions of syntactically complex sentences from a specification of the semantic properties of their constituent atomic sentences. However, "they [classical semantic theories] fall down on the specification of the semantics of the basic 'atomic' propositions [*sic;* surely Woods means 'atomic sentences'] " (page 39). Enter procedural semantics: "In order for an intelligent entity to know the meaning of such sentences it must be the case that it has stored somehow an effective set of criteria for deciding in a given possible world whether such a sentence is true or false" (ibid.). It's a bit unclear how Woods wants his quantifiers ordered here; whether he's claiming that there exists a procedure such that for every possible world........, or just that for every possible world there exists a procedure such that........ Even on the latter reading, however, this must be about the strongest form of verificationism that anybody has ever endorsed anywhere. Consider, for example, such sentences as: 'God exists,' 'positrons are made of quarks,' 'Aristotle liked onions,' 'I will marry an Armenian,' 'the set of English sentences is RE,' 'Procedural semantics is true,' 'there are no secondary qualities,' 'Nixon is a crook,' 'space is four dimensional,' etc. According to Woods, I am, at this very moment and merely by virtue of having learned English, in possession of an algorithm ("an effective set of criteria", yet!) for determining the truth value of each of these sentences. Whereas, or so one would have thought, one can know English and *not* know how to tell whether God exists or what positrons are made of. Good grief, Tom Swift: if all us English speakers know how to tell whether positrons are made of quarks, why doesn't somebody get a grant and find out?[6]

It is of some interest that, having announced that enunciating "such procedures for determining truth or falsity [of atomic sentences]" is the goal of procedural semantics, what Woods actually discusses in the body of his (very interesting) paper is something quite else.

4. PS as perceptual psychology

Thus far, I've argued as follows:

(a) Compilers won't be semantic theories unless they take us into an interpreted target language.

(b) It's patent that the intended interpretation of English sentences can't be captured in ML proper.

(c) The proposal that we should compile into MLT is the only recommendation that procedural semanticists have made for coping with the semantic poverty of ML.

(d) It's adherence to that suggestion which gives PS its characteristic Empiricist-verificationist cast.

Essentially similar remarks apply to PS treatments of perception; having gone this far, their major theoretical options are, to all intents and purposes, forced. Suppose that F is a formula in MLT such that F expresses the meaning of 'chair'. It presumably follows that determining that 'a is F' is true is a sufficient condition for determining that a is a chair. But now, the (nonsyntactic) vocabulary of F is, by hypothesis, exclusively transducer (viz. sensory) vocabulary; so that the normal way of determining that 'a is F' is true would be by reference to the sensory properties of a. However, determining that something is a chair by reference to its sensory properties is a plausible candidate for *perceiving* that it's a chair.[7] So we have an easy bridge from an atomistic view of the semantics of the lexicon ('chair' is proceduraly definable in MLT) to an atomistic view of perception (the 'percept' chair is constructed from sensations; constructed, indeed, by precisely the operations that procedural definitions specify). Semantic reductions thus emerge as perception recipes.

In saying that the options are forced, I don't mean to imply that procedural semanticists generally resist this line of thought; on the contrary, they generally rush to embrace it. The advertising for PS standardly includes the claim that it provides a theory of the interface between language and perception. So far as I can tell, the theory proposed *always* runs along the lines just sketched: semantic decomposition of the lexicon parallels sensory decomposition of percept; the 'translation' of 'chair' into semantic features corresponds to the analysis of chairs into perceptual features.

This isn't the place for a diatribe against atomistic views of perception (though I admit to being tempted). Suffice it to make three points:

In the first place, it's notable that—whether or not such views are right—they're remarkably old news. Once again, PS offers no theoretical advance over Locke and Hume (except that, whereas the Empiricists had to use association to stick sensations together, the procedural semanticists can avail themselves of a rather more powerful combinatorial apparatus borrowed from list processing, logic, or set theory). I think this point to be worth emphasizing, since the flossy technology of computer implementation may make it look as though PS offers an approach to the language-and-perception problem that's importantly novel in kind. To the contrary: if there are reasons for believing that the Locke-Hume program was fundamentally wrong about perception, there are the *same* reasons for believing that the PS program is fundamentally wrong about perception; it's the *same* program. Nothing has changed except the gadgets.

The second point is that, so far as I can tell, no new *arguments* for the Locke-Hume program have been forthcoming from the PS camp.[8] This is unsurprising if, as I've been arguing, it's not facts about perception but facts about computers that are forcing the procedural semanticists' hand. Data processes specified in ML won't reconstruct perception unless ML is an interpreted language. And the only interpretation that we currently know how to provide for ML embraces assignments to its terms of (strictly) computational states and relations, together with what can be defined over the names of the transducer states. The perception we can simulate is, therefore, the reduction of complex percepts to transducer outputs. There is, however, no reason for believing that percepts *are* reducible to transducer outputs except that, if they're not, the PS theory of perception won't be true. The fact is that, for some three hundred years, Empiricists have been playing 'heads I win, tails you loose' with the principle that perceptual states reduce to sensory states.[9] The proof that the reductions are possible consists of an appeal to the principle. The proof of the principle is that, were it false, the reductions wouldn't be possible. No workable examples are *ever* given. PS is playing exactly the same game, only it started later.

Now, this last remark may strike you as a smidgen unfair. For—you might ask—doesn't the Winograd program (for example) provide precisely the kind of illustrations of successful reductionistic analyses that are here said not to exist?

Answer: no. The whole point about the Winograd program, the trick, as it were, that makes it work, is that the block world that SHRDLU (nominally) lives in is constructed *precisely, so as to satisfy the epistemological and ontological requirements of verificationism;* in particular, each object is identifiable with a set of features, each feature is either elementary or a construct out of the elementary ones, and the elementary features are (by assumption) transducer-detectible. What the Winograd program shows, then, is at most that verificationism is logically possible; there are possible worlds, and possible languages, such that verificationism would be a good semantics for those languages in those worlds (and, *mutatis mutandis,* such that reductionism would be a good theory of the way that percepts are related to sensations in those worlds). The problem, however, is that nobody has ever doubted that verificationism is *consistent;* what there is considerable reason to doubt is that it's *true.* The Winograd program would bear on this latter question if somebody could figure out how to generalize a verificationist semantics for Block World into a verificationist semantics for English. So far, to the best of my knowledge, there are no bids.

The final point is that there *are* alternatives to reductionistic theories of perception, though you'd hardly know it from the PS literature. In particular, it doesn't *follow* from the fact that we are able to recognize (some) chairs (sometimes) that there must be procedures for recognizing chairs, either in the Empiricist sense of sensory checklists or, for that matter, in any sense *at all.* To see why this is so will require a (very brief) excursis into the philosophy of science.

The conventional wisdom in the philosophy of science these days is that there is a principled reason why verificationism won't work. It's the following. The question whether that thing over there is an electron isn't settled by crucial experiment but by adjudication between the demands that observation and theoretical conservatism jointly impose upon rational belief. We can't give a feature list for 'electron' because, given enough pull from simplicity and conservatism of theory, we may have to decide that it's an electron even if it fails our feature lists, and we may have to decide that it's not one even if it satisifies them. Notice that this is Gestaltism in one sense but not another; there *is* an emphasis on the influence of our *whole* science on the determination of truth value for any given sentence that our science contains. But, *of course,* it doesn't follow that there are no tests relevant to deciding whether something is an electron. On the contrary, this (roughly Quinean) account explains, really for the first time in the philosophy of science, why good experiments are so intellectually satisfying and so hard to devise. If there were feature lists semantically associated with theoretical terms, then verifying theories would be a relatively dull matter of finding out whether the defining features are satisfied. Whereas, the present account suggests that inferences from observation to theory are typically *non-*demonstrative and *anything we know* (or think we know) could, in principle and given sufficient experimental ingenuity, be brought to bear on the confirmation of any bit of our science. A sufficiently clever experimenter might be able to connect the question whether that's an electron with the annual rainfall in Philadelphia (via, of course, an enormous amount of mediating theory). In which case, more power to him! If the experiment works, we'll have learned something important about electrons (and about Philadelphia).

Now that, of course, is 'philosophy', not 'psychology'. Unless, however, psychology is that way too. It may be that there is no procedural analysis of the concept *chair* precisely because perceptual recognition is fundamentally like scientific problem solving (they are, after all, both means to the rational fixation of belief). On this view, in the limiting case, perception would involve bringing to bear our *whole* cognitive resources on the determination of how the world is (what 'perceptual categories' it instantiates). And, of course, every intermediate position is *also* open. It may be that some (but not all) of our cognitive resources are available for perceptual integration—that perceptual integration can be distinguished from problem solving at some interesting point that we don't yet know how to specify. (I think it's likely that this *is* the case; else how explain the persistence of perceptual illusions even when the subject knows that the percept is illusory?) My present point is just that there is a vast range of empirically respectable alternatives to PS atomism. These alternatives suggest the possibility (in some unimaginable and euphoric future) of an integration of the philosophy of science with the psychology of perception, so that 'the logician' can lie down with 'the psychologist' at last. It is, in any event, a reason for worrying about PS that if it *were* philosophy of science, it would be *bad* philosophy of science.

5. What is PS *really* about?

I've thus far argued that PS suffers from verificationism, operationalism, Empiricism, reductionism, recidivism, atomism, compound fractures of the use/mention distinction, hybris, and a serious misunderstanding of how computers work. What, then, is *wrong* with PS? Basically that it confuses semantic theories with theories of sentence comprehension.

There is a philosophical insight—which goes back at least to

Russell and Frege, and, in a certain way of looking at things, perhaps to Aristotle—that can be put like this: the surface form of a sentence is a bad guide to many of the theoretically interesting aspects of its behavior. If, therefore, you want a theory whose principles formally determine the behavior of a sentence, your best strategy is (a) to pair the sentence with some representation more perspicuous than its surface form; and then (b) to specify the theoretical principles over this more perspicuous representation. So, for example, if you want a theory that formally determines the way a sentence behaves in valid arguments, the way to proceed is (a) to pair the sentence with a representation of its 'logical form' (e.g. a paraphrase in a canonical logical notation) and then (b) specify the valid transformations of the sentence over that representation. For reasons too complicated to rehearse here, philosophers have usually taken it that representations of logical form would be appropriate candidates for the domain of rules of (classical) semantic interpretation.

In any event, recent work in the 'cognitive sciences' has added three wrinkles to the basic idea of canonical paraphrase. First, there's no particular reason why the canonical representation of a sentence should be sensitive *only* to its logico-semantic properties. In principle, we might want a representation of a sentence which captures not just its logical form (in the proprietary sense sketched above) but which also provides an appropriate domain for principles which govern syntactic transformation, or memory storage, or interaction with perceptual information, or learning, or whatever. The more we think of the construction of a theory of canonical paraphrase as a strategy in psychology, the more we shall want to extend and elaborate such constraints. There's no a priori argument that they *can* be satisfied simultaneously, but there's also no a priori argument that they can't. Trade-offs, moreover, are not out of the question; we are open to negotiation.

The second important recent idea about canonical paraphrase is that it might be effected more or less algorithmically: there might be computational principles which associate each sentence with its appropriate canonical representation (or representations, if that's the way things turn out). This is quite different from what Russell and Aristotle had in mind; they were content to leave the mapping from a sentence to its logical form relatively *in*explicit, so long as the logico-semantic behavior of the sentence was formally determined given its canonical representation.

The third idea is that the theory which maps sentences onto their canonical paraphrases (which, as it were, compiles them) might be construed as a model—more or less realistic and more or less real-time—for what the speaker/hearer does when he *understands* a sentence. That is, we might think of a speaker/hearer as, to all intents and purposes, realizing a function from canonical paraphrases (taken, now, as mental representations) onto forms of utterance. Patently, the more kinds of constraints internal representations can be made to satisfy qua domains for mental operations, and the more real-time-like computations of the function from canonical paraphrases to surface forms can be shown to be, the more reason we shall have to take this sort of model of speaker/hearers as empirically plausible.

I take it that this general approach is common to *all* current work on cognition, barring only Gibsonians and eccentrics.[10] That is, it's common ground to AI, PS, linguistics, cognitive psychology, psycholinguistics, and, for that matter, me. What's special about PS is only a bundle of proclivities within this strategic commitment: procedural semanticists tend to emphasize that canonical paraphrases should be constrained to provide domains for principles which specify the interactions between sentential and contextual information; they tend to emphasize real-time constraints on the recovery and coding of canonical representations; they tend to countenance trade-offs which buy feasibility at the price of generality; they tend to be relatively uninterested in constraining canonical representations by considerations of linguistic plausibility. Such proclivities amount, in effect, to an implicit research strategy within the general cognitivist camp. Like any such strategy, it is to be judged by its pay-off. My own view, for what it's worth, is that the pay-off has, thus far, been negligible; that, so far, practically nothing has been learned about language processes from the PS models, whereas quite a lot has been learned by investigators who have taken opposed views of how a theory of internal representation might best be constrained. That, however, is as it may be.

My present point is two-fold. First, if I'm right about what PS and the rest of us are up to, then there's no new account of language (or of language-and-the-mind) explicit or implicit in PS; there's simply a set of recommended tactics for approaching the problem we *all* take ourselves to be dealing with: how should we best model the speaker/hearer, given the assumption that the speaker/hearer is to be viewed as a function from utterances onto canonical internal representations. That is what we *all* are doing in trying to provide *a model of sentence comprehension* (/production); a model which says (a) what the speaker/hearer has in his head insofar as having *that* in his head constitutes understanding a sentence; and (b) which explains how whatever he has in his head when he understands a sentence manages to get there.

The second, and final, point is that what *none* of us is doing (including NB, PS) is providing a semantics for a natural (or any other) language: a theory of language-and-the-world. What we're all doing is really a kind of logical syntax (only psychologized); and we all very much hope that when we've got a reasonable internal language (a formalism for writing down canonical representations), someone very nice and very clever will turn up and show us how to interpret it; how to provide it with a semantics. What has disguised this fact from the procedural semanticists is that everybody else has given up supposing that the semantics will be verificationist. This difference *makes* a difference, as we've seen. In particular, it has allowed the procedural semanticists to suppose that a theory of how you understand a sentence can do double duty as a theory of what the sentence means; to confuse compiling with semantic interpretation, in short.

Whereas, because the rest of us are *not* verificationists, we can live with the fact that 'chair' refers to chairs; we don't have to go around supposing that 'chair' refers to bundles of sense data. It is, of course, not very *interesting* to say that 'chair' refers to chairs, since we have no *theory* of reference and we have no *mechanism* to realize the theory.[11] A fortiori, we don't know how to build a robot which can *use* 'chair' to refer to chairs. But, though "'chair' refers to chairs" isn't very interesting, we don't mind that so much, since reference isn't what we're working on. We're working on logical syntax (psychologized). Moreover, "'chair' refers to chairs" has one striking advantage over 'chairs are made of sense data'; it's not interesting, but at least it's *true*.

So, Tom Swift, here is how things stand: understanding a

natural language sentence *may* be sort of like compiling. That is, it may be a matter of translating from the natural language into a paraphrase in some canonical target language. If so, the target language must have a very rich semantics (nothing like MLT) and must be syntactically perspicuous in a way that natural languages are not. Nobody has the foggiest idea of how to connect this system to the world (how to do the semantics of internal representations), but that's OK because there are lots of other constraints that we can impose and maybe even meet; constraints inherited from logic, linguistics, psychology, and the theory of real-time computation. It might be instructive to try to build a machine which meets some of these constraints. Qua computer, such a machine would carry out sequences of operations upon the (de facto uninterpreted) formulae of some canonical language. Qua simulation, it would provide a psychological model insofar as mental processes can be construed as sequences of formal operations upon mental representations. But do not, Tom Swift, mistake this machine for a semantic theory. *A fortiori, DO NOT MISTAKE IT FOR YOUR GRANDMOTHER.*

Right, Tom Swift: back to the drawing board.[12]

Chapter 9

Methodological Solipsism Considered as a Research Strategy in Cognitive Psychology

> . . . to form the idea of an object and to form an idea simply is the same thing; the reference of the idea to an object being an extraneous denomination, of which in itself it bears no mark or character.
>
> —Hume, *Treatise,* Book I

Your standard contemporary cognitive psychologist—your thoroughly modern mentalist—is disposed to reason as follows. To think (e.g.,) that Marvin is melancholy is to represent Marvin in a certain way; viz., as being melancholy (and not, for example, as being maudlin, morose, moody, or merely moping and dyspeptic). But surely we cannot represent Marvin as being melancholy except as we are in some or other relation to a representation of Marvin; and not just to *any* representation of Marvin, but, in particular, to a representation the content of which is *that* Marvin is melancholy; a representation which, as it were, expresses the proposition that Marvin is melancholy. So, a fortiori, at least some mental states/processes are or involve at least some relations to at least some representations. Perhaps, then, this is the *typical* feature of such mental states/processes as cognitive psychology studies; perhaps all such states can be viewed as relations to representations and all such processes as operations defined on representations.

I've had a lot of help with this one. I'm particularly indebted to: Professors Ned Block, Sylvain Bromberger, Janet Dean Fodor, Keith Gunderson, Robert Richardson, Judith Thomson; and to Mr. Israel Krakowski.

This is, prima facie, an appealing proposal, since it gives the psychologist two degrees of freedom to play with and they seem, intuitively, to be the right two. On the one hand, mental states are distinguished by the *content* of the associated representations, so we can allow for the difference between thinking that Marvin is melancholy and thinking that Sam is (or that Albert isn't, or it sometimes snows in Cincinnati); and, on the other hand, mental states are distinguished by the *relation* that the subject bears to the associated representation (so we can allow for the difference between thinking, hoping, supposing, doubting, and pretending that Marvin is melancholy). It's hard to believe that a serious psychology could make do with fewer (or less refined) distinctions than these, and it's hard to believe that a psychology that makes these distinctions could avoid taking the notion of mental representation seriously. Moreover, the burden of argument is clearly upon anyone who claims that we need *more* degrees of freedom than just these two: the least hypothesis that is remotely plausible is that a mental state is (type) individuated by specifying a relation and a representation such that the subject bears the one to the other.[1]

I'll say that any psychology that takes this line is a version of the *representational theory of the mind.* I think that it's reasonable to adopt some such theory as a sort of working hypothesis, if only because there aren't any alternatives which seem to be even remotely plausible and because empirical research carried out within this framework has, thus far, proved interesting and fruitful.[2] However, my present concern is neither to attack nor to defend this view, but rather to distinguish it from something other—and stronger—that modern cognitive psychologists *also* hold. I shall put this stronger doctrine as the view that mental states and processes are *computational.* Much of what is characteristic of cognitive psychology is a consequence of adherence to this stronger view. What I want to do in this paper is to say something about what this stronger view is, something about why I think it's plausible, and, most of all, something about the ways in which it shapes the cognitive psychology we have.

I take it that computational processes are both *symbolic* and *formal.* They are symbolic because they are defined over representations, and they are formal because they apply to representations in virtue of (roughly) the *syntax* of the representations. It's the second of these conditions that makes the claim that mental processes are computational stronger than the representational theory of the mind. Most of this paper will be a meditation upon the consequences of assuming that mental processes are formal processes.

I'd better cash the parenthetical "roughly." To say that an operation is formal isn't the same as saying that it is syntactic since we could have formal processes defined over representations which don't, in any obvious sense, *have* a syntax. Rotating an image would be a timely example. What makes syntactic operations a species of formal operations is that being syntactic is a way of *not* being semantic. Formal operations are the ones that are specified without reference to such semantic properties of representations as, for example, truth, reference, and meaning. Since we don't know how to complete this list (since, that is, we don't know what semantic properties there are), I see no responsible way of saying what, in general, formality amounts to. The notion of formality will thus have to remain intuitive and metaphoric, at least for present purposes: formal operations apply in terms of the, as it were, shapes of the objects in their domains.[3]

To require that mental processes be computational (viz., formal-syntactic) is thus to require something not very clear. Still, the requirement has some clear consequences, and they are striking and tendentious. Consider that we started by assuming that the *content* of representations is a (type) individuating feature of mental states. So far as the *representational* theory of the mind is concerned, it is possibly the *only* thing that distinguishes Peter's thought that Sam is silly from his thought that Sally is depressed. But, now, if the *computational* theory of the mind is true (and if, as we may assume, content is a semantic notion par excellence) it follows that content alone cannot distinguish thoughts. More exactly, the computational theory of the mind requires that two thoughts can be distinct in content only if they can be identified with relations to formally distinct representations. More generally: fix the subject and the relation, and then mental states can be (type) distinct only if the representations which constitute their objects are formally distinct.

Again, consider that accepting a formality condition upon mental states implies a drastic narrowing of the ordinary ontology of the mental; all sorts of states which look, prima facie, to be mental states in good standing are going to turn out to be none of the psychologist's business if the formality condition is endorsed. This point is one that philosophers have made in a number of contexts, and usually in a deprecating tone of voice. Take, for example, knowing that such-and-such, and assume that you can't know what's not the case. Since, on that assumption, knowledge is involved with truth, and since truth is a semantic notion, it's going to follow that there can't be a psychology of *knowledge* (even if it is consonant with the formality condition to hope for a psychology of *belief*). Similarly, it's a way of making a point of Ryle's to say that, strictly speaking, there can't be a psychology of perception if the formality condition is to be complied with. Seeing is an achievement; you can't see what's not there. From the point of view of the representational theory of the mind, this means that seeing involves relations between mental representations *and their referents;* hence, semantic relations within the meaning of the act.

I hope that such examples suggest (what, in fact, I think is true) that even if the formality condition isn't very clear, it is quite certainly very strong. In fact, I think it's not all *that* anachronistic to see it as the central issue that divides the two main traditions in the history of psychology: "Rational psychology" on the one hand, and "Naturalism" on the other. Since this is a mildly eccentric way of cutting the pie, I'm going to permit myself a semi-historical excursus before returning to the main business of the paper.

Descartes argued that there is an important sense in which how the world is makes no difference to one's mental states. Here is a well-known passage from the *Meditations:*

> At this moment it does indeed seem to me that it is with eyes awake that I am looking at this paper; that this head which I move is not asleep, that it is deliberately and of set purpose that I extend my hand and perceive it. . . . But in thinking over this I remind myself that on many occasions I have been deceived by similar illusions, and in dwelling on this reflection I see so manifestly that there are no certain indications by which we may clearly distinguish wakefulness from sleep that I am lost in astonishment. And my astonishment is such that it is almost capable of persuading me that I now dream. (Descartes, 1931)

At least three sorts of reactions to this kind of argument are distinguishable in the philosophical literature. First, there's a long tradition, including both Rationalists and Empiricists, which takes it as axiomatic that one's experiences (and, a fortiori, one's beliefs) might have been just as they are even if the world had been quite different from the way that it is. See, for example, the passage from Hume which serves as an epigraph to this paper. Second, there's a vaguely Wittgensteinian mood in which one argues that it's just *false* that one's mental states might have been what they are had the world been relevantly different. For example, if there had been a dagger there, Macbeth would have been *seeing*, not just hallucinating. And what could be more different than that? If the Cartesian feels that this reply misses the point, he is at least under an obligation to say precisely which point it misses; in precisely *which* respects the way the world is is irrelevant to the character of one's beliefs, experiences, and so on. Finally there's a tradition which argues that—epistemology to one side—it is at best a strategic mistake to attempt to develop a psychology that individuates mental states without reference to their environmental causes and effects (e.g., which counts the state that Macbeth *was* in as type-identical to the state he would have been in had the dagger been supplied). I have in mind the tradition which includes the American Naturalists (notably Pierce and Dewey), all the learning theorists, and such contemporary representatives as Quine in philosophy and Gibson in psychology. The recurrent theme here is that psychology is a branch of biology, hence that one must view the organism as embedded in a physical environment. The psychologist's job is to trace those organism/environment interactions which constitute its behavior. A passage from William James (1890, p. 6) will serve to give the feel of the thing:

On the whole, few recent formulas have done more service of a rough sort in psychology than the Spencerian one that the essence of mental life and of bodily life are one, namely, 'the adjustment of inner to outer relations.' Such a formula is vagueness incarnate; but because it takes into account the fact that minds inhabit environments which act on them and on which they in turn react; because, in short, it takes mind in the midst of all its concrete relations, it is immensely more fertile than the old-fashioned 'rational psychology' which treated the soul as a detached existent, sufficient unto itself, and assumed to consider only its nature and its properties.

A number of adventitious intrusions have served to muddy the issues in this long-standing dispute. On the one hand, it may well be that Descartes was relying on a specifically introspectionist construal of the claim that the individuation of mental states is independent of their environmental causes. That is, Descartes's point may have been that (a) mental states are (type) identical if and only if (iff) they are introspectively indistinguishable, and (b) introspection cannot distinguish (e.g.) perception from hallucination, or knowledge from belief. On the other hand, the naturalist, in point of historical fact, is often a behaviorist as well. He wants to argue not only that mental states are individuated by reference to organism/environment relations, but also that such relations constitute the mental. In the context of the present discussion, he is arguing for the abandonment not just of the formality condition, but of the notion of mental representation as well.

If, however, we take the computational theory of the mind as what's central to the issue, we can reconstruct the debate between rational psychologists and naturalists in a way that does justice to both their points; in particular, in a way that frees the discussion from involvement with introspectionism on the one side and behaviorism on the other.

Insofar as we think of mental processes as computational (hence as formal operations defined on representations), it will be natural to take the mind to be, inter alia, a kind of computer. That is, we will think of the mind as carrying out whatever symbol manipulations are constitutive of the hypothesized computational processes. To a first approximation, we may thus construe mental operations as pretty directly analogous to those of a Turing machine. There is, for example, a working memory (corresponding to a tape) and there are capacities for scanning and altering the contents of the memory (corresponding to the operations of reading and writing on the tape). If we want to extend the computational metaphor by providing access to information about the environment, we can think of the computer as having access to "oracles" which serve, on occasion, to enter information in the memory. On the intended interpretation of this model, these oracles are analogs to the senses. In particular, they are assumed to be transducers, in that what they write on the tape is determined solely by the ambient environmental energies that impinge upon them. (For elaboration of this sort of account, see Putnam [1960]; it is, of course, widely familiar from discussions in the field of artificial intelligence.)

I'm not endorsing this model, but simply presenting it as a natural extension of the computational picture of the mind. Its present interest is that we can use it to see how the formality condition connects with the Cartesian claim that the character of mental processes is somehow independent of their environmental causes and effects. The point is that, so long as we are thinking of mental processes as purely computational, the bearing of environmental information upon such processes is exhausted by the formal character of whatever the oracles write on the tape. In particular, it doesn't matter to such processes whether what the oracles write is *true;* whether, for example, they really are transducers faithfully mirroring the state of the environment, or merely the output end of a typewriter manipulated by a Cartesian demon bent on deceiving the machine. I'm saying, in effect, that the formality condition, viewed in this context, is tantamount to a sort of methodological solipsism. If mental processes are formal, then they have access only to the formal properties of such representations of the environment as the senses provide. Hence, they have no access to the *semantic* properties of such representations, including the property of being true, of having referents, or, indeed, the property of being representations *of the environment.*

That some such methodological solipsism really is implicated in much current psychological practice is best seen by examining what researchers actually do. Consider, for example, the well-known work of Terry Winograd. Winograd was primarily interested in the computer simulation of certain processes involved in the handling of verbal information; asking and answering questions, drawing inferences, following instructions and the like. The form of his theory was a program for a computer which "lives in" and operates upon a simple world of blocklike geometric objects (see Winograd 1971). Many of the capacities that the device exercises vis-à-vis its environment seem impressively intelligent. It can arrange the blocks to order, it can issue "perceptual" reports of the present state of its environment and "memory" reports of its past states, it can devise simple plans for achieving desired environmental configurations, and it can discuss its undertakings (more or less in English) with whoever is running the program.

The interesting point for our purposes, however, is that the machine environment which is the nominal object of these actions and conversations actually isn't there. What actually happens is that the programmer so arranges the memory states of the machine that the available data are whatever they would be *if* there were objects for the machine to perceive and manipulanda for it to operate upon. In effect, the machine lives in an entirely notional world; all its beliefs are false. Of course, it doesn't matter to the machine that its beliefs are false since falsity is a semantic property and, qua computer, the device satisfies the formality condition; viz., it has access only to formal (nonsemantic) properties of the representations that it manipulates. In effect, the device is in precisely the situation that Descartes dreads; it's a mere computer which dreams that it's a robot.

I hope that this discussion suggests how acceptance of the computational theory of the mind leads to a sort of methodological solipsism as a part of the research strategy of contemporary cognitive psychology. In particular, I hope it's clear how you get that consequence from the formality condition alone, without so much as raising the introspection issue. I stress this point because it seems to me that there has been considerable confusion about it among the psychologists themselves. People who do machine simulation, in particular, very often advertise themselves as working on the question how thought (or language) is related to the world. My present point is that, whatever else they're doing, they certainly aren't doing *that*. The very assumption that defines their field—viz., that they study mental processes *qua* formal operations on symbols —guarantees that their studies won't answer the question how the symbols so manipulated are semantically interpreted. You can, for example, build a machine that answers baseball questions in the sense that (e.g.) if you type in "Who had the most wins by a National League pitcher since Dizzy Dean?" it will type out "Robin Roberts, who won 28." But you delude yourself if you think that a machine which in this sense answers baseball questions, is thereby answering questions *about* baseball (or that the machine has somehow referred to Robin Roberts). If the *programmer* chooses to interpret the machine inscription "Robin Roberts won 28" as a statement about Robin Roberts (e.g., as the statement that he won 28), that's all well and good, but it's no business of the machine's. The machine has no access to that interpretation, and its computations are in no way affected by it. The machine doesn't know what it's talking about, and it doesn't care; *about* is a semantic relation.[4]

This brings us to a point where, having done some sort of justice to the Cartesian's insight, we can also do some sort of justice to the naturalist's. For, after all, mental processes are supposed to be operations on representations, and it is in the nature of representations to represent. We have seen that a psychology which embraces the formality condition is thereby debarred from raising questions about the semantic properties of mental representations; yet surely such questions ought *somewhere* to be raised. The computer which prints out "RR won 28" is not thereby referring to RR. But, surely, when I think: *RR won 28,* I *am* thinking about RR, and if not in virtue of having performed some formal operations on some representations, then presumably in virtue of something else. It's perhaps borrowing the least tendentious fragment of causal theories of reference to assume that what fixes the interpretation of my mental representations of RR is something about the way that he and I are embedded in the world; perhaps not a causal chain stretching between us, but anyhow *some* facts about how he and I are causally situated; *Dasein,* as you might say. Only a *naturalistic* psychology will do to specify these facts, because here we are explicitly in the realm of organism/environment transactions.

We are on the verge of a bland and ecumenical conclusion: that there is room both for a computational psychology—viewed as a theory of formal processes defined over mental representations— *and* a naturalistic psychology, viewed as a theory of the (presumably causal) relations between representations and the world which fix the semantic interpretations of the former. I think that, in principle, this is the right way to look at things. In practice, however, I think that it's misleading. So far as I can see, it's overwhelmingly likely that computational psychology is the only one that we are going to get. I want to argue for this conclusion in two steps. First, I'll argue for what I've till now only assumed: that we must *at least* have a psychology which accepts the formality condition. Then I'll argue that there's good reason to suppose that that's the most that we can have; that a naturalistic psychology isn't a practical possibility and isn't likely to become one.

The first move, then, is to give reasons for believing that at least *some* part of psychology should honor the formality condition. Here too the argument proceeds in two steps. I'll argue first that it is typically under an *opaque* construal that attributions of propositional attitudes to organisms enter into explanations of their behavior; and second that the formality condition is intimately involved with the explanation of propositional attitudes so construed: roughly, that it's reasonable to believe that we can get such explanations only within computational theories. *Caveat emptor:* the arguments under review are, in large part, nondemonstrative. In particular, they will assume the perfectibility in principle of the kinds of psychological theories now being developed, and it is entirely possible that this is an assumption contrary to fact.

Thesis: when we articulate the generalizations in virtue of which behavior is contingent upon mental states, it is typically an opaque construal of the mental state attributions that does the work; for example, it's a construal under which believing that *a is F* is logically independent from believing that *b is F,* even in the case where $a = b$. It will be convenient to speak not only of opaque construals of propositional attitude ascriptions, but also of *opaque taxonomies* of mental state types; e.g., of taxonomies which, inter alia, count the belief that the Morning Star rises in the east as type distinct from the belief that the Evening Star does. (Correspondingly, *transparent* taxonomies are such as, inter alia, would count these beliefs as type identical). So, the claim is that mental states are typically opaquely taxonomized for purposes of psychological theory.[5]

The point doesn't depend upon the examples, so I'll stick to the most informal sorts of cases. Suppose I know that John wants to meet the girl who lives next door, and suppose I know that this is true when "wants to" is construed opaquely. Then, given even rough-and-ready generalizations about how people's behaviors are contingent upon their utilities, I can make some reasonable predictions (guesses) about what John is likely to do: he's likely to say (viz., utter), "I want to meet the girl who lives next door." He's likely to call upon his neighbor. He's likely (at a minimum, and all things being equal) to exhibit next-door-directed behavior. None of this is frightfully exciting, but it's all I need for present purposes, and what more would you expect from folk psychology?

On the other hand, suppose that all I know is that John wants to meet the girl next door where "wants to" is construed transparently; i.e., all I know is that it's true of the girl next door that John wants to meet her. Then there is little or nothing that I can predict about how John is likely to proceed. And this is *not* just because rough-and-ready psychological generalizations want *ceteris paribus* clauses to fill them in; it's also for the deeper reason that I can't infer from what I know about John to any relevant description of the mental causes of his behavior. For example, I have no reason to predict that John will say such things as "I want to meet the girl who lives next door" since, let John be as cooperative and as truthful as you like, and let him be utterly a native speaker, still, he *may* believe that the girl he wants to meet languishes in Latvia. In which case, "I want to meet the girl who lives next door" is the last think it will occur to him to say. (The contestant wants to say "suspender," for "suspender" is the magic word. Consider what we can predict about his probable verbal behavior if we take this (a) opaquely and (b) transparently. And, of course, the same sorts of points apply, mutatis mutandis, to the prediction of *non*verbal behavior).

Ontologically, transparent readings are stronger than opaque ones; for example, the former license existential inferences which the latter do not. But psychologically opaque readings are stronger than transparent ones; they tell us more about the character of the mental causes of behavior. The representational theory of mind offers an explanation of this anomaly. Opaque ascriptions are true in virtue of the way that the agent represents the objects of his wants (intentions, beliefs, etc.) *to himself.* And, by assumption, such representations function in the causation of the behaviors that the agent produces. So, for example, to say that it's true *opaquely* that Oedipus did such-and-such because he wanted to marry Jocasta, is to say something like (though not, perhaps, *very* like; see Chapter 7: "Oedipus said to himself, 'I want to marry Jocasta,' and his so saying was among the causes of his behavior." Whereas to say (only) that it's true transparently that O. wanted to marry J. is to say no more than that among the causes of his behavior was O.'s saying to himself "I want to marry . . ." where the blank was filled by *some* expression that denotes J.[6] But now, what O. *does,* how he in the proprietary sense behaves, will depend on which description he (literally) had in mind.[7] If it's "Jocasta," courtship behavior follows *ceteris paribus.* Whereas, if it's "my Mum," we have the situation towards the end of the play and Oedipus at Colonus eventually ensues.

I dearly wish that I could leave this topic here, because it would be very convenient to be able to say, without qualification, what I strongly implied above: the opaque readings of propositional attitude ascriptions tell us how people represent the objects of their propositional attitudes. What one would like to say, in particular, is that if two people are identically related to formally identical mental representations, then they are in opaquely type-identical mental states. This would be convenient because it yields a succinct and gratifying characterization of what a computational cognitive psychology is about: such a psychology studies propositional attitudes opaquely taxonomized.

I think, in fact, that this is *roughly* the right thing to say since what I think is *exactly* right is that the construal of propositional attitudes which such a psychology renders is nontransparent. (It's nontransparency that's crucial in all the examples we have been considering). The trouble is that nontransparency isn't quite the same notion as opacity, as we shall now see.

The question before us is: "What are the relations between the pretheoretic notion of type identity of mental states opaquely construed and the notion of type identity of mental states that you get from a theory which strictly honors the formality condition?" And the answer is: complicated. For one thing, it's not clear that we have *a* pretheoretic notion of the opaque reading of a propositional attitude ascription: I doubt that the two standard tests for opacity (failure of existential generalization and failure of substitutivity of identicals) even pick out the same class of cases.

But what's more important are the following considerations. While it's notorious that extensionally identical thoughts may be opaquely type distinct (e.g., thoughts about the Morning Star and thoughts about the Evening Star) there are nevertheless some semantic conditions on opaque type identification. In particular:

(a) there are some cases of formally distinct but coextensive thoughts which count as tokens of the same (opaque) type (and hence as identical in content at least on one way of individuating contents); and

(b) *non*coextensive thoughts are, ipso facto, type-distinct (and differ in content, at least on one way of individuating contents).

Cases of type (a): 1. I think I'm sick and you think I'm sick. What's running through my head is "I'm sick"; and what's running through your head is "he's sick." But we are both having thoughts of the same (opaque) type (and hence of the same content).

2. You think: "that one looks edible"; I think: "this one looks edible." Our thoughts are opaquely type-identical if we are thinking about the same one.

It connects with the existence of such cases that pronouns and demonstratives are typically (perhaps invariably) construed as referring, even when they occur in what are otherwise opaque constructions. So, for example, it seems to me that I can't report Macbeth's hallucination by saying: "Macbeth thinks that's a dagger" if Macbeth is staring at nothing at all. Which is to say that "that's a dagger" doesn't report Macbeth's mental state even though "that's a dagger" may be precisely what is running through Macbeth's head (precisely the representation his relation to which is constitutive of his belief).

Cases of type (b): 1. Suppose that Sam feels faint and Misha knows he does. Then what's running through Misha's head may be "he feels faint." Suppose too that Misha feels faint and Alfred knows he does. Then what's running through Alfred's head, too, may be "he feels faint." I have no, or rather no univocal, inclination to say, in this case, that Alfred and Misha are having type identical thoughts even though the principle of type individuation is, by assumption, opaque and even though Alfred and Misha have the same things running through their heads. But if this is right, then formal identity of mental representations cannot be sufficient for type identity of opaquely taxonomized mental states.[8] (There is an interesting discussion of this sort of case by Geach (1957). Geach says that Aquinas says that there is no "intelligible difference" between Alfred's thought and Misha's. I don't know whether this means that they are having the same thought or that they aren't).

2. Suppose that there are two Lake Eries (two bodies of water so-called). Consider two tokens of the thought "Lake Erie is wet," one of which is, intuitively speaking about the Lake Erie in North America and one of which is about the other one. Here again, I'm inclined to say that the aboriginal, uncorrupted pretheoretical notion of type-wise same thought wants these to be tokens of *different* thoughts and takes these thoughts to differ in content. (Though in this case, as in the others, I think there's also a countervailing inclination to say that they count as type-identical—and as identical in content—for some relevant purposes and in some relevant respects. How like aboriginal, uncorrupted, pretheoretical intuition!)

I think, in short, that the intuitive opaque taxonomy is actually what you might call "semitransparent." On the one hand, certain conditions of coreference are in force (Misha's belief that he's ill is type distinct from Sam's belief that *he's* ill and my thought *this is edible* may be type identical to your thought *that is edible*.) On the other hand, you don't get free substitution of co-referring expressions (beliefs about the Morning Star are type-distinct from beliefs about the Evening Star) and existential generalization doesn't go through for beliefs about Santa Claus.

Apparently, then, the notion of same mental state that we get from a theory which honors the formality condition is related to, but not identical to, the notion of same mental state that unreconstructed intuition provides for opaque construals. And it would certainly be reasonable to ask whether we actually need both. I think that the answer is probably: yes, if we want to capture *all* the intuitions. For if we restrict ourselves to either one of the taxonomies, we get consequences that we don't like. On the one hand, if we taxonomize *purely* formally, we get identity of belief compatible with difference of truth value. (Misha's belief that he's ill will be type-identical to Sam's belief that *he's* ill, but one may be true while the other is false.) On the other hand, if we taxonomize solely according to the pretheoretic criteria, we get trouble with the idea that people act out of their beliefs and desires. We need, in particular, some taxonomy according to which Sam and Misha have the *same* belief in order to explain why it is that they exhibit the same behaviors. It is, after all, *part* of the pretheoretic notion of belief that difference in belief ought *ceteris paribus* to show up in behavior *somewhere;* ("ceteris paribus" means "given relevant identities among other mental states"). Whereas, it's possible to construct cases where differences like the one between Misha's belief and Sam's can't show up in behavior even in principle (see note 8). What we have, in short, is a tension between a partially semantic taxonomy and an entirely functional one, and the recommended solution is to use both.

Having said all this, I now propose largely to ignore it and use the term "opaque taxonomy" for principles of type individuation according to which Misha and Sam are in the same mental state when each believes himself to be ill. When I need to distinguish this sense of opaque taxonomy from the pretheoretic one, I'll talk about *full* opacity and fully opaque type identification.

My claim has been that, in doing our psychology, we want to attribute mental states fully opaquely because it's the fully opaque reading which tells us what the agent has in mind, and it's what the agent has in mind that causes his behavior. I now need to say something about how, precisely, all this is supposed to constitute an argument for the formality condition.

Point one: it's just as well that it's the fully opaque construal of mental states that we need since, patently, that's the only one that the formality condition permits us. This is because the formality condition prohibits taxonomizing psychological states by reference to the semantic properties of mental representations and, at bottom, transparency is a semantic (viz., nonformal; viz., non-syntactic) notion. The point is sufficiently obvious: if we count the belief that the Evening Star is F as (type) identical to the belief that the Morning Star is F, that must be because of the co-reference of such expressions as "the Morning Star" and "the Evening Star." But coreference is a semantic property, and not one which could conceivably have a formal doppelganger; it's inconceivable, in particular, that there should be a system of mental representations such that, in the general case, coreferring expressions are formally identical in that system. (This might be true for God's mind, but not, surely, for anybody else's—[and not for God's either unless He is an Extentionalist; which I doubt.]) So if we want transparent taxonomies of mental states, we will have to give up the formality condition. So it's a good thing for the computational theory of the mind that it's not transparent taxonomies that we want.

What's harder to argue for (but might, nevertheless, be true) is point two: that the formality condition *can* be honored by a theory which taxonomizes mental states according to their content. For, barring caveats previously reviewed, it may be that mental states are distinct in content only if they are relations to formally distinct mental representations; in effect, that aspects of content can be reconstructed as aspects of form, at least insofar as appeals to content figure in accounts of the mental causation of behavior. The main thing to be said in favor of this speculation is that it allows us to explain, within the context of the representational theory of mind, how beliefs of different content *can* have different behavioral effects, even when the beliefs are transparently type-identical. The form of explanation goes: it's because different content implies formally distinct internal representations (via the formality condition) and formally distinct internal representations can be functionally different—can differ in their causal roles. Whereas, to put it mildly, it's hard to see how internal representations could differ in causal role *unless* they differed in form.

To summarize: transparent taxonomy is patently incompatible with the formality condition; whereas taxonomy in respect of content *may* be compatible with the formality condition, plus or minus a bit. That taxonomy in respect of content *is* compatible with the formality condition, plus or minus a bit, is perhaps *the* basic idea of modern cognitive theory. The representational theory of mind and the computational theory of mind merge here for, on the one hand, it's claimed that psychological states differ in content only if they are relations to type-distinct mental representations; and, on the other, it's claimed that only formal properties of mental representations contribute to their type individuation for the purposes of theories of mind/body interaction. Or, to put it the other way 'round, it's allowed that mental representations affect behavior in virtue of their content, but it's maintained that mental representations are distinct in content only if they are also distinct in form. The first clause is required to make it plausible that mental states are relations to mental representations and the second is required to make it plausible that mental processes are computations. (Computations just *are* processes in which representations have their causal consequences in virtue of their form.) By thus exploiting the notions of content and computation *together,* a cognitive theory seeks to connect the *intensional* properties of mental states with their *causal* properties vis-à-vis behavior. Which is, of course, exactly what a theory of the mind ought to do.

As must be evident from the preceding, I'm partial to programmatic arguments: ones that seek to infer the probity of a conceptual apparatus from the fact that it plays a role in some prima facie plausible research enterprise. So, in particular, I've argued that a taxonomy of mental states which honors the formality condition seems to be required by theories of the mental causation of behavior, and that that's a reason for taking such taxonomies very seriously.

But there lurks, within the general tradition of representational theories of mind, a deeper intuition: that it is not only *advisable* but actually *mandatory* to assume that mental processes have access only to formal (nonsemantic) properties of mental representations; that the contrary view is not only empirically fruitless but also conceptually unsound. I find myself in sympathy with this intuition, though I'm uncertain precisely how the arguments ought to go. What follows is just a sketch.

I'll begin with a version that I *don't* like, an epistemological version:

Look, it makes no *sense* to suppose that mental operations could apply to mental representations in virtue of (e.g.) the truth or falsity of the latter. For, consider: truth value is a matter of correspondance to the way the world is. To determine the truth value of a belief would therefore involve what I'll call 'directly comparing' the belief with the world; i.e., comparing it with the way the world *is,* not just with the way the world is represented as being. And the representational theory of mind says that we have access to the world only *via* the ways in which we represent it. There is, as it were, nothing that corresponds to looking around (behind? through? what's the right metaphor?) one's beliefs to catch a glimpse of the things they represent. Mental processes can, in short, compare representations, but they can't compare representations with what they're representations of. Hence mental processes can't have access to the truth value of representations or, mutatis mutandis, to whether they denote. Hence the formality condition.

This line of argument could, certainly, be made a good deal more precise. It has been in, for example, some of the recent work of Nelson Goodman (see especially Goodman 1978). For present purposes, however, I'm content to leave it *im*precise so long as it sounds familiar. For I suspect that all versions of the argument suffer from a common deficiency: they assume that you can't run a *correspondence* theory of truth together with a *coherence* theory of evidence. Whereas I see nothing compelling in the inference from "truth" is a matter of the correspondence of a belief with the way the world is" to "*ascertaining* truth is a matter of 'directly comparing' a belief with the way the world is." Perhaps we ascertain the truth of our beliefs by comparing them with one another, appealing to inference to the best explanation whenever we need to do so.

Anyhow, it would be nice to have a *non*epistemological defence of the formality condition; one which saves the intuition that there's something conceptually wrong with its denial but doesn't acquire the skeptical/relativistic commitments with which the traditional epistemic versions of the argument have been encumbered. Here goes:

Suppose, just for convenience, that mental processes are algorithms. So, we have rules for the transformation of mental representations, and we have the mental representations that constitute their ranges and domains. Think of the rules as being like hypothetical imperatives; they have antecedents which specify conditions on mental representations, and they have consequents which specify what is to happen if the antecedents are satisfied. And now consider rules (a) and (b):

(a) Iff it's the case that P, do such and such.
(b) Iff you believe it's the case that P, do such and such.

Notice, to begin with, that the compliance conditions on these injunctions are quite different. In particular, in the case where P is *false but believed true*, compliance with (b) consists in doing such and such, whereas compliance with (a) consists in *not* doing it. But despite this difference in compliance conditions, there's something *very* peculiar (perhaps *pragmatically* peculiar, whatever precisely that may mean) about supposing that an organism might have different ways of going about attempting to comply with (a) and (b). The peculiarity is patent in (c). To borrow a joke from Robert Jagger, (c) is a little like the advice: "buy low, sell high." One knows just what it would be *like* to comply with either, but somehow knowing that doesn't help much.

(c) Do such and such iff it's the case that P, *whether or not* you believe that it's the case that P.[9]

The idea is this: when one has done what one can to establish that the belief that P is warranted, one has done what one can to establish that the antecedent of (a) is satisfied. And, conversely, when one has done what one can to establish that the antecedent of (a) is satisfied, one has done what one can to establish the warrant of the belief that P. Now, I suppose that the following is at least *close* to being true: to have the belief that P is to have the belief that the belief that P is warranted; and conversely, to have the belief that the belief that P is warranted is to have the belief that P. And the upshot of *this* is just the formality condition all over again. Given that mental operations have access to the fact that P is believed (and hence that the belief that P is believed to be warranted, and hence that the belief that the belief that P is warranted is believed to be warranted, . . . etc.) there's nothing further left to do; there is nothing that corresponds to the notion of a mental operation which one undertakes to perform just in case one's belief that P is *true*.

This isn't, by the way, any form of skepticism, as can be seen from the following: there's nothing wrong with Jones having one mental operation which he undertakes to perform iff it's the case that P and another *quite different* mental operation which he undertakes to perform iff *Smith* ($\neq$ Jones) believes that it's the case that P. (Cf. "I promise . . . though I don't intend to . . ." vs. "I promise . . . though Smith doesn't intend to . . .") There's a first person/third person asymmetry here, but it doesn't impugn the semantic distinction between "P is true" and "P is believed true." The suggestion is that it's the tacit recognition of this pragmatic asymmetry that accounts for the traditional hunch that you can't both identify mental operations with transformations on mental representations and at the same time flout the formality condition; that the representational theory of mind and the computational theory of mind are somehow conjoint options.

So much, then, for the formality condition and the psychological tradition which accepts it. What about Naturalism? The first point is that none of the arguments *for* a rational psychology is, in and of itself, an argument *against* a Naturalistic psychology. As I remarked above, to deny that mental operations have access to the semantic properties of mental representations is *not* to deny that mental representations *have* semantic properties. On the contrary, beliefs are *just* the kinds of things which exhibit truth and denotation, and the Naturalist proposes to make science out of the organism/environment relations which (presumably) fix these properties. Why, indeed, should he not?

This all *seems* very reasonable. Nevertheless, I now wish to argue that a computational psychology is the only one that we are likely to get; that qua research strategy, the attempt to construct a *naturalistic* psychology is very likely to prove fruitless. I think that the basis for such an argument is already to be found in the literature, where it takes the form of a (possibly inadvertent) reductio ad absurdum of the contrary view.

Consider, to begin with, a distinction that Hilary Putnam introduces in "The Meaning of Meaning" (1975) between what he calls "psychological states in the wide sense" and "psychological states in the narrow sense." A psychological state in the *narrow* sense is one the ascription of which does not "(presuppose) the existence of any individual other than the subject to whom that state is ascribed" (p. 10). All others are psychological states in the wide sense. So, for example, *x's jealousy of y* is a schema for expressions which denote psychological states in the wide sense since such expressions presuppose the existence, not only of the *x*s who are in the states, but also of the *y*s who are its objects. Putnam remarks that methodological solipsism (the phrase, by the way, is his) can be viewed as the requirement that only psychological states in the narrow sense are allowed as constructs in psychological theories.

Whereas, it's perhaps Putnam's main point that there are at least *some* scientific purposes (e.g., semantics and accounts of intertheoretical reference) which demand the wide construal. Here, rephrased slightly, is the sort of example that Putnam finds persuasive.

There is a planet (call it "Yon") where things are very much like here. In particular, by a cosmic accident, some of the people on Yon speak a dialect indistinguishable from English and live in an urban conglomerate indistinguishable from the Greater Boston Area. Still more, for every one of our Greater Bostonians, there is a doppelganger on Yon who has precisely the same neurological structure down to and including microparticles. We can assume that, so long as we're construing "psychological state" narrowly, this latter condition guarantees type identity of our psychological states with theirs.

However, Putnam argues, it doesn't guarantee that there is a corresponding identity of psychological states, hither and Yon, if we construe "psychological state" *widely*. Suppose that there is this difference between Yon and Earth; whereas, over here, the stuff we call "water" has the atomic structure H_2O, it turns out that the stuff that they call "water" over there has the atomic structure XYZ ($\neq H_2O$). And now, consider the mental state *thinking about water*. The idea is that, so long as we construe that state widely, it's one that we, but not our doppelgangers, can reasonably aspire to. For, construed widely, one is thinking about water only if it is water that one is thinking about. But it's water that one's thinking about only if it is H_2O that one's thinking about; water *is* H_2O. But since, by assumption, they never think about H_2O over Yon, it follows that there's at least one wide psychological state that we're often in and they never are, however neurophysiologically like us they are, and however much our narrow psychological states converge with theirs.

Moreover, if we try to say what they speak about, refer to, mention, etc.; if, in short, we try to supply a semantics for their dialect, we will have to mention XYZ, not H_2O. Hence it would be wrong, at least on Putnam's intuitions, to say that they have a word for water. A fortiori, the chemists who work in what they call "M.I.T." don't have theories about *water,* even though what runs through their heads when they talk about XYZ may be identical to what runs through our heads when we talk about H_2O. The situation is analogous to the one that arises for demonstratives and token reflexives, as Putnam insightfully points out.

Well, what are we to make of this? Is it an argument against methodological solipsism? And, if so, is it a *good* argument against methodological solipsism?

To begin with, Putnam's distinction between psychological states in the narrow and wide sense looks to be very intimately related to the traditional distinction between psychological state ascriptions opaquely and transparently construed. I'm a bit wary about this since what Putnam *says* about wide ascriptions is only that they "presuppose the existence" of objects other than the ascribee; and, of course *a believes Fb and b exists* does not entail *b is such that a believes F of him,* or even *∃x (a believes Fx).* Moreover, the failure of such entailments is notoriously important in discussions of quantifying in. For all that, however, I don't *think* that it's Putnam's intention to exploit the difference between the existential generalization test for transparency and the presupposition of existence test for wideness. On the contrary, the burden of Putnam's argument seems to be precisely that "John believes (widely) that water is F" is true only if water (viz., H_2O) is such that John believes it's F. It's thus unclear to me why Putnam gives the weaker condition on wideness when it appears to be the stronger one that does the work.[10]

But whatever the case may be with the wide sense of belief, it's pretty clear that the narrow sense must be (what I've been calling) fully opaque. (This is because only full opacity allows type identity of beliefs that have different truth conditions [Sam's belief that he's ill with Misha's belief that *he* is; Yon beliefs about XYZ with hither beliefs about H_2O.]) I want to emphasize this correspondence between narrowness and full opacity, and not just in aid of terminological parsimony. Putnam sometimes writes as though he takes the methodological commitment to a psychology of narrow mental states to be a sort of vulgar prejudice: "Making this assumption is, of course, adopting a *restrictive program*—a program which deliberately limits the scope and nature of psychology to fit certain mentalistic preconceptions or, in some cases, to fit an idealistic reconstruction of knowledge and the world" (p. 137). But, in light of what we've said so far, it should be clear that this is a methodology with malice aforethought. Narrow psychological states are those individuated in light of the formality condition; viz., without reference to such semantic properties as truth and reference. And honoring the formality condition is part and parcel of the attempt to provide a theory which explains (a) how the belief that the Morning Star is F could be different from the belief that the Evening Star is F despite the well-known astronomical facts; and (b) how the behavioral effects of believing that the Morning Star is F could be different from those of believing that the Evening Star is F, astronomy once again apparently to the contrary notwithstanding. Putnam is, of course, dubious about this whole project: ". . . The three centuries of failure of mentalistic psychology is tremendous evidence against this procedure, in my opinion" (p. 137). I suppose this is intended to include everybody from Locke and Kant to Freud and Chomsky. I should have such failures.

So much for background. I now need an argument to show that a naturalistic psychology (a psychology of mental states transparently individuated; hence, presumably, a psychology of mental states in the wide sense) is, for practical purposes, out of the question. So far as I can see, however, Putnam has given that argument. For, consider: a naturalistic psychology is a theory of organism/environment transactions. So, to stick to Putnam's example, a naturalistic psychology would have to find some stuff S and some relation R such that one's narrow thought that water is wet is a thought about S in virtue of the fact that one bears R to S. Well, *which* stuff? The natural thing to say would be: "Water, of course." Notice, however, that if Putnam is right, it may not even be *true* that the narrow thought that water is wet is a thought about water; it *won't* be true of tokens of that thought which occur on Yon. Whether the narrow thought that water is wet is about water depends on whether it's about H_2O; and whether it's about H_2O depends on "how science turns out"—viz., on what chemistry is true. (Similarly, mutatis mutandis, 'water' refers to was is *not*, on this view, a truth of any branch of linguistics; it's chemists who tell us what it is that "water" refers to.) Surely, however, characterizing the objects of thought is methodologically prior to characterizing the causal chains that link thoughts to their objects. But the theory which characterizes the objects of thought is the theory of *everything;* it's all of science. Hence, the methodological moral of Putnam's analysis seems to be: the naturalistic psychologists will inherit the Earth, but only after everybody else is finished with it. No doubt it's all right to have a research strategy that says "wait awhile". But who wants to wait *forever?*

This sort of argument isn't novel. Indeed, it was anticipated by Bloomfield (1933). Bloomfield argues that, for all practical purposes, you can't do semantics. The reason that you can't is that to do semantics you have to be able to say, for example, what "salt" refers to. But what "salt" refers to is NaCl, and that's a bit of chemistry, not linguistics:

> The situations which prompt people to utter speech include every object and happening in their universe. In order to give a scientifically accurate definition of meaning for every form of a language, we would have to have a scientifically accurate knowledge of everything in the speaker's world. The actual extent of human knowledge is very small compared to this. We can define the meaning of a speech-form accurately when this meaning has to do with some matter of which we possess scientific knowledge. We can define the names of minerals, as when we say that the ordinary meaning of the English word *salt* is 'sodium chloride (NaCl),' and we can define the names of plants or animals by means of the technical terms of botany or zoology, but we have no precise way of defining words like *love* or *hate,* which concern situations that have not been accurately classified. . . . The statement of meanings is therefore the weak point in language-study, and will remain so until knowledge advances very far beyond its present state. (pp. 139–140)

It seems to me as though Putnam ought to endorse all of this *including the moral:* the distinction between wanting a naturalistic semantics (psychology) and not wanting any is real but academic.[11]

The argument just given depends, however, on accepting Putnam's analysis of his example. But suppose that one's intuitions run the other way. Then one is at liberty to argue like this:

1. They do too have water over Yon; all Putnam's example shows is that there could be two kinds of water, our kind ($=H_2O$) and their kind ($=XYZ$).

2. Hence, Yon tokens of the thought that water is wet are thoughts about water after all.

3. Hence, the way chemistry turns out is irrelevant to whether thoughts about water are about water.

4. Hence, the naturalistic psychology of thought need not wait upon the sciences of the objects of thought.

5. Hence, a naturalistic psychology may be in the cards after all.

Since the premises of this sort of reply may be tempting (since, indeed, they may be *true*) it's worth presenting a version of the argument which doesn't depend on intuitions about what XYZ is.

A naturalistic psychology would specify the relations that hold between an organism and an object in its environment when the one is thinking about the other. Now, think how such a theory would have to go. Since it would have to define its generalizations over mental states on the one hand and environmental entities on the other, it will need, in particular, some canonical way of referring to the latter. Well, *which* way? If one assumes that what makes my thought about Robin Roberts a thought *about Robin Roberts* is some causal connection between the two of us, then we'll need a description of RR such that the causal connection obtains in virtue of his satisfying that description. And *that* means, presumably, that we'll need a description under which the relation between him and me instantiates a law.

Generally, then, a naturalistic psychology would attempt to specify environmental objects in a vocabulary such that environment/organism relations are law-instantiating when so described. But here's the depressing consequence again: we have no access to such a vocabulary prior to the elaboration (completion?) of the nonpsychological sciences. "What Granny likes with her herring" isn't, for example, a description under which salt is law-instantiating; nor, presumably, is "salt." What we need is something like "NaCl," and descriptions like "NaCl" are available only *after* we've done our chemistry. What this comes down to is that, at a minimum, "x's being F causally explains . . ." can be true only when "F" expresses nomologically necessary properties of the xs. Heaven knows it's hard to say what *that* means, but it presumably rules out both "Salt's being what Granny likes with herring . . ." and "Salt's being salt" . . . ; the former for want of being necessary, and the latter for want of being nomological. I take it, moreover, that Bloomfield is right when he says (a) that we don't know relevant nomologically necessary properties of most of the things we can refer to (think about) and (b) that it isn't the linguist's (psychologist's) job to find them out.

Here's still another way to put this sort of argument. The way Bloomfield states his case invites the question: "Why *should* a semanticist want a definition of 'salt' that's 'scientifically accurate' in your sense? Why wouldn't a 'nominal' definition do?" There is, I think, some point to such a query. For example, as Hartry Field has pointed out (1972), it wouldn't make much difference to the way that truth-conditional semantics goes if we were to say only "'salt' refers to whatever it refers to." All we need for this sort of semantics is some way or other of referring to the extension of "salt"; we don't, in particular, need a "scientifically accurate" way. It's therefore pertinent to do what Bloomfield notably does not: distinguish between the goals of *semantics* and those of a naturalistic psychology of language. The latter, by assumption, purports to explicate the organism/environment transactions in virtue of which relations like reference hold. It therefore requires, at a minimum, lawlike generalizations of the (approximate) form: *X's utterance of 'salt' refers to salt iff X bears relation R to ___.* Since this whole thing *is* supposed to be lawlike, what goes in for "___" must be a projectible characterization of the extension of "salt." But, in general, we discover which descriptions are projectible only *a posteriori;* in light of how the sciences (including the nonpsychological sciences) turn out. We are back where we started. Looked at this way, the moral is that we can do (certain kinds of) semantics if we have a way of referring to the extension of "salt." But we can't do the naturalistic psychology of reference unless we have some way of saying what salt *is;* which of its properties determine its causal relations.

It's important to emphasize that these sorts of arguments do *not* apply to the research program embodied in "Rational psychology"; viz., to the program which envisions a psychology that honors the formality condition. The problem we've been facing is: under what description does the object of thought enter into scientific generalizations about the relations between thoughts and their objects? It looks as though the naturalist is going to have to say: under a description that's law-instantiating; e.g., under physical description. Whereas the rational psychologist has a quite different answer. What *he* wants is *whatever description the organism has in mind* when it thinks about the object of thought, construing "thinks about" fully opaquely. So, for a theory of psychological states narrowly construed, we want such descriptions of Venus as, e.g., "the Morning Star," "the Evening Star," "Venus," etc., for it's these sorts of descriptions which we presumably entertain when we think that the Morning Star is *F*. In particular, it's our relation to these sorts of descriptions that determines what psychological state type we're in insofar as the goal in taxonomizing psychological states is explaining how they affect behavior.

A final point under the general head: the hopelessness of naturalistic psychology. Practicing naturalistic psychologists have been at least dimly aware all along of the sort of bind that they're in. So, for example, the "physical specification of the stimulus" is just about invariably announced as a requirement upon adequate formulations of S–R generalizations. We can now see why. Suppose, wildly contrary to fact, that there exists a human population (e.g., English speakers) in which pencils are, in the technical sense of the notion, discriminative stimuli controlling the verbal response "pencil." The point is that, even if some such generalization were true, it wouldn't be among those enunciated by a naturalistic psychology; the generalizations of naturalistic psychology are presumably supposed to be nomological, and there aren't any *laws* about pencils *qua* pencils. That is: expressions like "pencil" presumably occur in no true, lawlike sentences. Of course, there presumably is *some* description in virtue of which pencils fall under the organism/environment laws of a naturalistic psychology, and everybody (except, possibly, Gibson) has always assumed that those descriptions are, approximately, physical descriptions. Hence, the naturalist's demand, perfectly warranted by his lights, that the stimulus should be physically specified.

But though their theory has been consistent, their practice has uniformly not. In practice, and barring the elaborately circumscribed cases that psychophysics studies, the requirement that the stimulus be physically specified has been ignored by just about *all* practitioners. And, indeed, they were well advised to ignore it; how else could they get on with their job? If they really had to wait for the physicists to determine the description(s) under which pencils are law-instantiators, how would the psychology of pencils get off the ground?

So far as I can see, there are really only two ways out of this dilemma:

1. We can fudge, the way that learning theorists usually do. That is, we can "read" the description of the stimulus from the character of the organism's response. In point of historical fact, this has led to a kind of naturalistic psychology which is merely a solemn paraphrase of what everybody's grandmother knows: e.g., to saying "pencils are discriminative stimuli for the utterance of 'pencil' where Granny would have said 'pencil' refers to pencils." I take it that Chomsky's review of *Verbal Behavior* (1959) demonstrated, once and for all, the fatuity of this course. What *would* be interesting—what would have surprised Grandmother—is a generalization of the form Δ *is the discriminative stimulus for utterances of "pencil"* where Δ is a description which picks out pencils in some projectible vocabulary (e.g., in the vocabulary of physics). Does anybody suppose that such descriptions are likely to be forthcoming in, say, the *next* three hundred years?

2. The other choice is to try for a computational psychology, which is, of course, the burden of my plaint. On this view, what we can reasonably hope for is a theory of mental states fully opaquely type-individuated. We can try to say what the mental representation is, and what the relation to a mental representation is, such that one believes that the Morning Star is F in virtue of bearing the latter to the former. And we can try to say how that representation, or that relation, or both, differ from the representation and the relation constitutive of believing that the Evening Star is F. A naturalistic psychology, by contrast, remains a sort of ideal of pure reason; there must *be* such a psychology since, presumably, we do sometimes think of Venus and, presumably, we do so in virtue of a causal relation between it and us. But there's no practical hope of making science out of this relation. And, of course, for methodology, practical hope is *everything*.

One final point, and then I'm through. Methodological solipsism isn't, of course, solipsism *tout court*. It's not part of the enterprise to assert, or even suggest, that you and I are actually in the situation of Winograd's computer. Heaven only knows what relation between me and Robin Roberts makes it possible for me to think of him (refer to him, etc.), and I've been doubting the practical possibility of a science whose generalizations that relation instantiates. But I *don't* doubt that there *is* such a relation or that I do sometimes think of him. Still more: I have reasons not to doubt it; precisely the sorts of reasons I'd supply if I were asked to justify my knowledge claims about his pitching record. In short: it's true that Roberts won twenty-eight, and it's true that I know that he did, and nothing in the preceding tends to impugn these truths. (Or, contrariwise, if he didn't and I'm mistaken, then the reasons for my mistake are philosophically boring; they're biographical, not epistemological or ontological). My point, then, is *of course* not that solipsism is true; it's just that truth, reference and the rest of the semantic notions aren't psychological categories. What they are is: they're modes of *Dasein*. I don't know what *Dasein* is, but I'm sure that there's lots of it around, and I'm sure that you and I and Cincinnati have all got it. What more do you want?

IV.
Nativism

Chapter 10

The Present Status
of the Innateness Controversy

Plato says in Phaedo that our 'imaginary ideas' arise from the preexistence of the soul, are not derivable from experience—read monkeys for preexistence.

—Charles Darwin

Introduction

Disclaimers first. Many of you may have been misled by the title of this paper to suppose that it is about the current status of the innateness controversy. Well, barely. In fact, my topic is restricted to questions about the innateness—or otherwise—of *concepts.* I shall therefore have nothing whatever to say about the issue of the innate determination—or otherwise—of differences in mental traits and capacities. (I assume that the psychology of individual differences is largely vacuous for our species, as it patently is for every other.) I shall also have nothing to say about the current controversy over the innateness of *beliefs,* except insofar as the holding of certain beliefs may be thought to be constitutive of the attainment of certain concepts. (For example, it might be held that you can't, in point of logic, have the concept BACHELOR unless you

I have borrowed several of the ideas in this paper—and a few of the jokes—from Fodor, Garrett, Walker and Parkes', "Against definitions" (1980). My indebtedness to my co-authors is hereby gratefully acknowledged. Much of this material was first presented as the 1979 Walker-Ames Lectures at the University of Washington. I am most grateful to friends and colleagues there—and especially to Professor Charles Marks—for their stimulating comments and discussion.

have the belief that bachelors are unmarried. If this is true, then the question whether the concept BACHELOR is innate willy nilly involves the question whether the belief that bachelors are unmarried is.) It does seem to me that Chomsky's demonstration that there is serious evidence for the innateness of what he calls 'General Linguistic Theory' is *the* existence proof for the possibility of a cognitive science; indeed, that it is quite possibly the only important result in the field to date. But I shan't discuss either Chomsky's claim or his evidence beyond remarking that if he's right, then the innateness of *some* concepts—viz. the ones that figure in the innate beliefs—follows trivially. You can't have innately the belief that, say, transformations must apply in cycles (or, for that matter, the belief that they must not) unless you have innately the concepts TRANSFORMATION and CYCLE.

I should also confess that, though some of the following may *sound* like philosophy—especially to nonphilosophers—it is really only a kind of speculative psychology. The issues I'll deal with are empirical issues (or so I'll maintain) and quite a lot of the apparatus of current cognitive psychology will be assumed without argument; without explication even. I'll assume, for example, that the mentalistic notion of a concept can be made clear enough to be scientifically respectable, since, if it can't, the question whether any concepts are innate won't be worth discussing. I assume this, moreover, in the teeth of prevailing philosophical opinion to the contrary. My excuse is that I can't imagine a serious psychology which dispenses with that notion, and neither, apparently, can the psychologists.

So much for the disclaimers. What I propose to do in this paper is to consider the innateness issue as it arises in the context of a certain broad class of theories of concept attainment which I will call *classical* theories of concept attainment. Not all conceivable theories of concept attainment are classical theories, and the assumptions that classical theories share are philosophically—and otherwise—tendentious. Still, in point of historical fact, just about every theory of concept attainment that any psychologist or philosopher has succeeded in taking seriously, barring only behavioristic theories, counts as classical by my criteria. So it would be interesting to show—what I propose to maintain—that the most plausible classical theories are Nativistic. At a minimum, I'll try to convince you that the issue between Nativist and Empiricist versions of classical theory has been widely misrepresented and that when one sees what the issue really is, one sees that the Nativist account is distinctly in the running.

I need, by way of stage setting, to say something about what makes a theory of concept attainment a classical theory of concept attainment. Since I don't propose to defend the classical theory, and since I want to fish with a big net, the account I'll give will be rough and sketchy.

To begin with, classical theories are ipso facto species of the Representational Theory of Mind (RTM). The Representational Theory of Mind holds either that propositional attitudes are relations between organisms and mental representations or that such relations are nomologically necessary for having a propositional attitude. (That is, RTM may be, but needn't be, held as an ontological doctrine.) Mental representations are mental objects: RTM quantifies over them like mad. Typical claims that RTM (hence classical theories) makes about mental representations are these: there is an infinite set of mental representations, an infinite proper subset of which are internally structured; mental representations exhibit such semantic properties as truth and reference; mental representations constitute the domain of mental processes.

So, for example, a well known version of RTM had it that mental representations are mental images; that mental images refer to what they resemble; that to believe that such and such is to bear a certain kind of relation to a mental image of such and such; that some mental images have other mental images as proper parts; and that associative processes apply to mental images in virtue of relations of co-occurrence, resemblance, etc., that hold among the images. I suppose that Hume held RTM in something like this form; it seems certain that some of Clark Hull's followers did.

A second thing you have to accept to hold a classical theory of concept acquisition is that concepts are mental entities; in particular, that concepts are species of mental representations. *Roughly,* a concept is that sort of mental representation which *expresses a property* and *is expressed by an open sentence.* So, for example, if you hold the classical theory (hence RTM) on the image version, you will think of the concept DOG as (a) an image of a dog; (b) expressing the property of *dogness* (and hence applying to dogs); and (c) as being the mental representation normally evoked by utterances of the form of words ' ... is a dog.'

That's as precise as I propose to get, this being Cognitive Science. It is worth emphasizing, however, that the mental entity account of concepts is independent of, not incompatible with, Frege's view that a concept is an abstract entity: a Sense.[1] Qua mental representations, concepts have semantic properties. It is thus open to you, if you're so inclined, to run RTM (hence classical theory) on a Fregean line. To wit: the word 'dog' expresses the concept DOG; the concept DOG expresses the sense *dog* (i.e. expresses a certain Fregean concept); the relation *expresses* is transitive. On this account (to which I am, in fact, partial) expressing a Fregean concept is a semantic property par excellence, and the formulae of natural language inherit their semantic properties from those of mental representations. From now on, when I speak of attaining a concept I shall have the mental-object sense of "concept" in mind. It is an agreeable suggestion that *attaining* a concept (mental-object sense) is de facto a necessary condition of becoming *acquainted with* a concept (Fregean sense); i.e. that our acquaintance with Fregean concepts is mediated by our mental representations. But classical theories of concept attainment are not, per se, required to endorse this suggestion.

All classical theories of concept attainment are species of the RTM, and they all take concepts to be species of mental representations. Classical theories of concept attainment come in two varieties: the Empiricist and the Nativist. So far I have been concerned with what these two varieties of classical theories of concept attainment have in common. In the following Section, we'll start to see what distinguishes between them.

Where Do Concepts Come from?

A concept is what an open sentence of a natural language expresses. If we fix the language (choosing, say, English), we can distinguish between *lexical concepts* and *phrasal concepts*. By stipulation, a lexical concept is one that is expressible, in English, by an open sentence with a morphologically simple—viz. a monomorphemic—predicate term. (So, for example, GREEN is a lexical concept, since it is expressible by the open sentence '... is green'. I shall stretch a point in favor of predicate nominals and consider BACHELOR to be a lexical concept because it is expressible by the open sentence '... is a bachelor.') Whereas, a phrasal concept is one that is expressible, in English, only by an open sentence with a morphologically *complex* predicate term. (So, for example, the concept LIVES IN CHICAGO AND EATS MANGLEWORTS is a phrasal concept, since, to put it roughly, there is no one-word predicate term of English which means *lives in Chicago and eats mangleworts.* and IS UNCOMMUNICATIVE is phrasal because 'uncommunicative' is multimorphemic).

For a number of reasons, the lexical/phrasal distinction won't bear much theoretical weight. For example, we would presumably get a different partitioning of the concepts if we changed the reference language; for all I know, some concepts that are expressible only by phrases in English are expressible monomorphemically in, e.g., Urdu. And, for all I know, some concepts aren't expressible in English *at all,* so perhaps the lexical/phrasal distinction isn't exhaustive. Never mind; I only want the distinction for heuristic purposes. We'll see how to dispense with it as the discussion goes along.

We arrive at the first consideration of substance: all theories of concept attainment assume that there are infinitely many phrasal concepts which are acquired by the application of constructive procedures to a basis of lexical concepts. Among the governing considerations are these:

(1) It seems clear that the semantic properties of phrasal concepts are typically inherited from the semantic properties of the corresponding lexical concepts. So, patently, the concept expressed by, say, 'the cat on the mat' inherits its semantic properties from (inter alia) those of the concept expressed by 'cat'. It's thus plausible to think of the latter concept as literally a constituent of the former (conversely, to think of the former concept as literally a construct out of the latter) thereby preparing the groundwork for explaining why nothing satisfies THE CAT ON THE MAT unless it satisfies CAT.

(2) Not only do the semantic properties of phrasal concepts typically depend on the semantic properties of corresponding lexical ones, but the dependence appears to be determined by general and regular principles: on the one hand, THE CAT ON THE MAT differs from THE DOG ON THE MAT in much the same way as THE CAT differs from THE DOG; and, on the other hand, the semantic properties of THE CAT ON THE MAT seem to depend on the semantic properties of THE CAT in much the

NATIVISM

same way that the semantic properties of THE DOG IN THE MANGER depend on the semantic properties of THE DOG. All of which suggests that the principles that construct phrasal concepts from lexical concepts are fairly general in application—in particular, that they can be formulated without listing the concepts they apply to.

(3) A conceptualist theory of language comprehension will presumably want to say that understanding an utterance involves entertaining the concept that it expresses. It comports with that sort of treatment to suppose that the concept expressed by a phrase is a construct out of the concepts expressed by the lexical constituents of that phrase. Attainment of the appropriate lexical concepts, and of the principles of construction, will then constitute a sufficient basis for attaining the corresponding phrasal concepts. Indeed, it's natural to suppose that the "logical syntax" of a phrase exhibits the internal structure of the concept it expresses: that it exhibits the relation of the phrasal concept to the lexical concepts it's constructed from.

This is all familiar stuff and, so far as I know, it's untendentious given the framework of RTM. I'll assume, therefore, that all theories of concept attainment tell more or less the same story about phrasal concepts: there is a (finite) basis of lexical concepts and there is a constructive apparatus. Phrasal concepts are constructed from lexical concepts by application of combinatorial rules. Phrasal concepts are thus reducible to lexical concepts, *salve* their semantic properties. Since the rules of construction are recursive (in the sense of 'iterative'), the set of phrasal concepts is productive.

The various classical theories of concept attainment differ (inter alia) in their formulations of the constructive principles. Some earlier versions take them to be principles of association; some later ones borrow them from the logical theory of quantification or from the syntax of computer languages. For present purposes, however, such differences needn't much concern us. What does bear emphasis is that, on any such account, attaining a phrasal concept will involve actually performing the relevant logical construction: to attain the concept BROWN COW will involve actually assembling it from the constituent concepts BROWN and COW. (Someone who has attained the latter concepts but has *not* performed the construction will have the former concept only potentially). Similarly, thinking about brown cows will involve entertaining a complex mental representation of which the concepts BROWN and COW are constituents in whatever sense of constituency the theory favors.

In short, the phrasal concepts are the closure of the lexical concepts under some combinatorial apparatus. What about the lexical concepts? It is here that interesting differences between Empiricist and Nativist treatments begin to emerge. I want to spell out what I take to be the Empiricist view at some length.

For the Empiricist, the lexical concepts are a mixed lot. Just as phrasal concepts are patently complex relative to their constituent lexical concepts, so, on the Empiricist story, very many *lexical* concepts are complex relative to a set of mental representations that we can call the *primitive conceptual basis*. Some of the essential Empiricist claims in this area might be put as follows:

(4) All concepts—lexical and phrasal—are either primitive or constructed from primitive concepts by a combinatorial apparatus. It's usually assumed that the same combinatorial apparatus that constructs phrasal concepts from lexical ones also operates to construct complex lexical concepts from the primitive ones. It's thus a typical Empiricist view that the internal structure of complex lexical concepts mirrors the internal structure of phrasal concepts. Indeed, it's usual to suppose that there are some—possible many—cases in which a word and a phrase express the *same* concept; "bachelor" and "unmarried man" are both said to express the concept UNMARRIED MAN, and, in general, each definable word is said to express the same concept as the phrase that defines it.

(5) Whereas the distinction between lexical and phrasal concepts is largely accidental—many lexical concepts have internal structure, just as phrasal concepts do—the distinction between primitive concepts and complex concepts is epistemologically principled. That is, we can pick out the primitive concepts by some epistemologically interesting criterion, and it will turn out that those, and only those, concepts which satisfy the criterion are the ones that lack internal structure.

(6) The primitive conceptual basis is *much* smaller than the set of concepts that are lexicalized by any natural language; for example, it is much smaller than the set of concepts that happen

to be expressed by morphemically simple predicate terms in English.

Empiricists disagree as to precisely how one ought to formulate the criterion that picks out the primitive (hence internally unstructured) concepts. But the rough idea is that *primitive concepts are sensory*. Let's, for the moment, not worry very much about what that comes to. I'll simply assume that every organism whose mental states are worth discussing has a *sensorium*—perhaps a set of receptive mechanisms that satisfy the technical notion of a transducer—and that the primitive concepts are the possible outputs of the sensorium across the range of inputs that it responds to.[2] That is, specify the possible outputs of the sensorium and you have the primitive concepts that the organism can potentially entertain. Take the closure of the primitive concepts under the combinatorial apparatus, and you have *all* the concepts that the organism can potentially entertain.

Figure 1 gives a schematic representation of the Empiricist story about the space of concepts potentially available to an organism. Every concept is either sensory (hence primitive, hence internally unstructured, hence the output of the sensorium for some specifiable input) or constructable from the primitive concepts by application of the combinatorial apparatus. Since this disjunction is exhaustive, the "Empiricist maxim" follows: nothing is in the mind except what is first in the senses. The complex concepts include lexical and phrasal concepts indiscriminately, except that no primitive concept is phrasal. (Remember that the logical syntax of a phrase displays the internal structure of the concept it expresses. A concept with no internal structure cannot, therefore, be phrasal, since every phrase has a logical syntax—excepting only idioms.)

The space of potentially available concepts is fixed given an

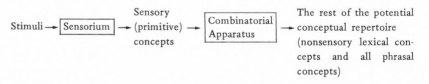

Fig. 1. The origin of the potential conceptual repertoire according to the Empiricist view.

enumeration of the sensory concepts and a specification of the combinatorial mechanisms. I might equally have said: the space of potentially available concepts is fixed given a specification of the combinatorial mechanisms *and a characterization of the sensorium.* From our point of view, a sensorium is simply the realization of a function from stimuli onto primitive concepts. Since the Empiricist assumes that primitive concepts can arise *only* via activation of the sensorium, we can think of a theory of the sensorium as exhaustively specifying the causal occasions for the availability of any primitive concept: the structure of the sensorium determines what sort of stimulation is causally necessary and sufficient for the attainment of each such concept. It's going to be an important difference between Empiricist and Nativist accounts that, according to the latter, primitive (viz. internally unstructured) concepts may become available by means *other than* the activation of the sensorium.

It's important to understand that Figure 1 represents the Empiricist doctrine about what concepts are potentially available to an organism, *not* the Empiricist doctrine about how concepts are attained. Figure 1 says: Here's the class of stimuli which can, in point of nomological fact, affect the conceptual repertoire of the organism; and here's the class of concepts which the organism can, in point of nomological fact, entertain in consequence of such stimulations. Whereas a theory of concept attainment must explain *how* the concepts that an organism actually acquires are determined by the stimuli that it actually encounters: it specifies the mechanisms in virtue of which the conceptual repertoire of an organism varies as a function of its experience. It's this latter sort of theory that we are primarily concerned with in what follows.

Empiricist theories of concept attainment distinguish sharply between the mechanisms postulated to explain the acquisition of primitive concepts and those postulated for the acquisition of complex concepts (be they lexical or phrasal). We've seen that the account of the former mechanisms is, in effect, embodied in the theory of the sensorium. What about the acquisition of complex concepts?

It's here that the concept-attainment models familiar from the psychological and AI literature come into play. Perhaps the best way to understand this literature is to consider what happens in the sorts of experiments that psychologists use to study what they call "concept learning". (Terminological note: from here on, I shall use 'concept learning' as a technical term for the acquisition of a concept as a result of the particular mental processes now to be described. I shall use 'concept acquisition'—or 'concept attainment'—for *any* mental processes which eventuate in the availability of a concept to an organism. The terminology thus means to leave it open that some (many, all) concepts might be acquired but not learned).

A typical concept learning experiment goes as follows (for purposes of exposition, you get to be the Subject): You arrive in the experimental environment. The experimenter says to you something like, "I have here a pack of stimulus cards. Each stimulus card displays a colored geometrical figure. There are some red triangles, there are some green squares, there are some yellow circles, there are some red rectangles, and so on. Now, some of these cards are *flurg* and some of them are *non-flurg* and (for convenience) every card is *either* flurg *or* non-flurg. Your job is to figure out which cards are which. And I am here to help you. For, though I will not tell you which ones the flurg cards are, still I will let you examine any card you like and guess whether *it* is flurg. And I will tell you if your guess is right. Proceed".

You proceed. That is, you examine a card (say it is a green triangular one) and you guess (say you guess flurg). Now, unbeknownst to you, the experimenter has in mind a criterion for correct responding: for example, that the response "flurg" is correct iff the card is either green or square. Since the card you drew *was* either green or square (it was green and triangular), and since you guessed flurg, the experimenter says "Right you are" and you are allowed to go on to the next card. You continue in this wise until, mirabile dictu, your performance "reaches criterion"; e.g. until you say "flurg" for all green or square cards and "non-flurg" for all the rest on, as it might be, twenty consecutive trials. You are then said to have learned (a fortiori attained) the concept *flurg* and you are allowed to go home.

Various aspects of this scenario are inessential to its being a concept-learning experiment. For example, the stimuli didn't have to be colored shapes; they could, in principle, have been any discriminable array. It's also inessential that the criterial property be a Boolean function of the stimulus features; the experimenter could have said "right" depending upon the ordinal position of the stimulus card in the series. It's also inessential that the experimenter uses a verbal signal to tell you which of your responses are correct; he could equally well nod and smile, or supply you with an M & M, or shock you when you get it wrong. Indeed, so far as the basic paradigm is concerned, it's inessential that you're a person. You might have been a pigeon, in which case we would have called it a "discrimination-learning" experiment and we'd have replaced the verbal instructions by some procedure which "shapes" a response (say, pecking the chosen card) that you could then use to indicate which stimulus belongs in which class. The point is that the general structure of this experiment informs practically all the psychological work on concept attainment which the Empiricist tradition has inspired. Much of what we now know about concept learning has consisted in determining how the organism's ability to achieve criterion varies as a function of variation in (e.g.) the character of the stimuli, the character of the reinforcement (feedback signal), the scheduling of the reinforcement, the species, age, sex, IQ, traumatic impairment, etc., of the organism, and so forth.

That, then, is the concept-learning experiment. I assume that the artifactual features are eliminable: that the experimental situation does, indeed, engage the mechanisms of concept learning insofar as the concept is complex and insofar as it is learned "from experience".[3] What, then, is available by way of a theory of the organism's performance in the concept-learning experiment?

So far as I know, only one such theory has ever been seriously proposed (though a variety of rather different vocabularies have been used to express it). The theory is this: concept learning involves the inductive fixation of certain beliefs, and the mechanisms of concept learning are realizations of some species of inductive logic. In particular, they involve the formulation and confirmation of hypotheses about the identity of the concept being learned.

So, for example, what goes on in your head in the experimental situation we've imagined might be something like this: You make your first guess—the green and triangular card is flurg—at random. (For all you know it might just as well be non-flurg, but you have to start somewhere, so why not flip a coin?) Since, as it turned out, that guess was right, you have evidence for any of a range of hypotheses: e.g. that the flurg cards are the green ones; that the flurg cards are the triangular ones; that the flurg cards are the green and triangular ones; that the flurg cards are the green or square ones; that the flurg cards are the non-red ones ... etc. You pick one (or, perhaps a set) of these hypotheses and you try it. For example, you pick the hypothesis that the flurg cards are the green ones. Then, if the next card is a red square, you say "non-flurg" and the experimenter says "wrong". The range of hypotheses compatible with your data (i.e. with the outcomes of past trials) is now altered: for example, the hypothesis *flurg = green* is out, though the hypothesis *flurg = red or triangle* is still in. So you pick one of the hypotheses compatible with this expanded set of data and you try *it;* and so on till you find a hypothesis that's compatible with the old data and which further trials decline to disconfirm. You carry on with this new hypothesis until criterion is achieved.

In short, each trial provides inductive evidence pro or con a hypothesis of the form: *the concept being learned is the concept of something which is ...,* where what goes in the blank is a candidate specification of those properties of a stimulus in virtue of which it satisfies the concept: e.g. *circular and orange, ((not red) and rectangular), fifth stimulus in the series,* or whatever. The mechanisms of concept learning—insofar as concept learning is assumed to occur in the concept-learning experiment—are thus seen to be the mechanisms of inductive inference.[4]

About which a fair bit is known. A mechanism for performing inductive inferences is ipso facto a (realized) inductive logic. As such, it must have access to at least the following:

(7) A source of hypotheses to be tested; which in turn presupposes a canonical format and vocabulary for the specification of the hypotheses.

(8) A canonical format and vocabulary for the representation of the data (e.g. on trial *n* the card was circular and the response "non-flurg" was rewarded.)

(9) An a priori ranking of the hypotheses in order of relative simplicity. (Roughly because, barring such a ranking, a body of data bestows equal confirmation on all of the infinitely many

nonequivalent hypotheses with which it is formally compatible.)

(10) A confirmation metric: roughly, a function from pairs consisting of hypotheses and data sets onto numbers that express the level of confirmation of the hypothesis relative to the data.

Let me emphasize that 7–10 are *presupposed* by an induction machine; they represent minimal structural commitments for a device that can learn by the projection and confirmation of hypotheses. It is, for example, because bricks do not have functional components corresponding to 7–10, whereas pigeons presumably do, that pigeons but not bricks can learn things.

The present claims are, then, as follows:

(11) All Empiricist theories hold that the concept-learning experiment typifies situations in which (complex) concepts are learned from experience.

(12) All Empiricist theories view performance in the concept-learning experiment as mediated by hypothesis formation and confirmation.

(13) All Empiricist theories are therefore committed to the view that the mechanisms of concept learning constitute a realized inductive logic. (Take-home exercise: Convince yourself that 11–13 are true of, inter alia, "habit-strength" models of associative learning.)

At this point, you may be feeling tempted to argue like this: "Look, if *that's* the Empiricist's model of concept acquisition, then the Empiricist *has* no model of concept acquisition. For consider: on this view, learning the concept FLURG is learning that a certain hypothesis is true; viz. the hypothesis that the concept FLURG is the concept of something that is green or square. But learning that that hypothesis is true is in turn said to be a matter of entertaining that hypothesis and comparing it with the data. But that hypothesis itself *contains* the concept GREEN OR SQUARE. Now, surely, if a concept is available to you for hypothesis formation, then you *have* that concept. And if you have to have a concept in order to perform the concept-learning task, then what goes on in the concept-learning task cannot be the learning of that concept. So the concept-learning task is not a task in which concepts are learned, and the theory of the concept-learning task is not a theory of concept attainment".

This is a temptation to which, I think, one ought to succumb.

I did so in *The Language of Thought,* where I argued that if there *is* an Empiricist theory of concept acquisition, it must consist of an account of the origin of the hypotheses which (by assumption) get inductively confirmed in the concept-learning task. And, de facto, there exists no such theory. (This is hardly surprising; standard accounts of inductive inference *presuppose* a range of hypotheses to be evaluated, the source of these hypotheses being unspecified. That is one reason why inductive logics are viewed as theories of *confirmation,* not theories of scientific *discovery.*)

What has happened is that the Empiricist story recruits what is really a theory of the fixation of belief to do double duty as a theory of the attainment of concepts. This strategy doesn't work, and the strain shows in all sorts of places. For example, it's surely clear that any normal adult would have acquired such workaday concepts as GREEN OR SQUARE long before he encountered a concept-learning experiment; hence, achieving criterion in such experiments *couldn't,* in the general case, require that any concept be acquired in the course of performing the experimental task. What the subject would have learned in the case described above, for example, is not GREEN OR SQUARE, but only the fact that the experimenter has decided to call things that are green or square "flurg" for the duration of the run—a fact that is interesting only because it controls the distribution of rewards.

I really do think that the Empiricist will have to admit all this: inductive logics are question-begging when proposed as theories of concept attainment, however illuminating they may be as theories of the experiential fixation of belief. Still, having conceded the spirit of his account, the Empiricist might make a reply that would preserve something of its letter. I want to consider this because it raises a point that's important in the context of the innateness issue. (To which, I promise, we shall presently return. Patience.)

The argument three paragraphs back turned on the assumption that "if a concept is available to you for hypothesis formation, then you *have* that concept". And, though there is a sense in which this surely has to be admitted, there is also a sense in which it might be denied. So, it could be held that concept learning does *sometimes* occur in the concept-learning task, and that when it does, what happens is that a concept previously available to the organism *only* for the formation of inductive hypotheses then *becomes* available for a wider range of cognitive tasks (e.g. in reasoning, in the organization of memory, in perceptual identification, etc.). Assume, for example, that there is a sort of 'faculty of hypothesis formation' (perhaps it's a department in the faculty of imagination mentioned in note 3). Concepts like GREEN OR SQUARE must be available to this faculty for purposes of projecting candidate hypotheses in the concept-learning task. Insofar as these concepts are "learned from experience" in the course of performing that task, what happens is that they are made available for *general* cognitive employment as a causal consequence of the operation of such inductive mechanisms as 7–10 enumerate.

I have no idea whether anything like this is true. I mention the point partly because it saves the Empiricist story from the charge of utter logical vacuity, but also, more importantly, because it serves to emphasize a characteristic difference between the Empiricist treatment of complex concepts on the one hand and of primitive ones on the other. The point to notice is that the Empiricist story about concept learning, even in this revised form, could in principle apply *only* to the acquisition of *complex* concepts. This is important because it's going to be one of my main morals that there isn't, and couldn't be, a coherent story according to which *primitive* concepts are learned.

Learning a complex concept by hypothesis confirmation presupposes the availability of the concept for the expression of the relevant hypothesis. But it's at least plausible that *it needn't presuppose the availability of that concept for the canonical representation of the data base.*[5] Consider FLURG again. The concept FLURG is the concept GREEN OR SQUARE. To learn the concept FLURG is to learn that the hypothesis *the concept FLURG is the concept of something that is green or square* is true. This hypothesis is confirmed, inter alia, by such observations as *stimulus No. 1 is green and is positive; stimulus No. 1 is square and is positive; stimulus No. 7 is red and is negative;* etc. The point is that we presumably *don't* need, in order to express the data base, such observation statements as: *stimulus 1 is green or square and is positive.* If we *did* need such statements, then we would need the concept being "learned" even to express the observations that fix the relevant hypothesis, and the learning model would be entirely vacuous. Another way of putting this is that the constructive apparatus which generates complex concepts out of primitive ones patently must be available to determine the space of hypotheses that the inductive logic confirms; but perhaps it needn't also be available to specify the observation base that figures in the inductions. Perhaps, for the latter purposes, the primitive conceptual basis will do.

Now consider the analogous case for learning *primitive* concepts. Suppose that RED is a primitive concept. Then the hypothesis that has to be confirmed will be: *the concept being learned is the concept of something which is RED* and will thus, as usual, contain the concept whose acquisition is to be explained. But worse, consider the experiences which fix that hypothesis. They will presumably have to be of the form *stimulus No. 1 was red and was positive; stimulus No. 2 was green and was negative,* etc. That is, the availability of the concept being acquired will have to be presupposed even to give canonical expression to the experiences that fix that concept. The point is that hypotheses which contain complex concepts can (maybe) be inductively confirmed by a data base in which only primitive concepts figure. But a data base which contains not even primitive concepts is empty and confirms nothing.

Perhaps for this reason, Empiricist models invariably do assume that the concept-learning story applies *only* to the acquisition of *complex* concepts, primitive concepts being acquired in some other way. In fact, we have already seen what this "other way" is: whereas complex concepts are acquired by a process of hypothesis formation and confirmation, primitive concepts are assumed to be sensory, and their acquisition is occasioned by the activation of the sensorium.

This difference between the treatment of complex and primitive concepts is highly characteristic of Empiricist theorizing about concept attainment. While the processes which occasion the availability of primitive concepts are, as it were, viewed as *merely* causal—whether a given pattern of stimulation occasions the availability of a given primitive concept being simply a matter of the structure of the sensorium—the processes which give rise to the acquisition of complex concepts are typically viewed as *rational* in that the experiences which eventuate in the availability of such a concept are held to bear a confirmation relation to some hypothesis which specifies the internal structure of the concept.

To summarize: the Empiricist model says that there are two sorts of causal processes at play in concept acquisition: in the case of the primitive concepts there are, one might say, brute-causal processes. The structure of the sensorium is such that certain inputs trigger the availability of certain concepts. Punkt. Whereas, in the case of the attainment of complex concepts, there are, as one might say, rational-causal processes: the psychological mechanisms which mediate the availability of such concepts realize an inductive logic, and the experiences of the organism stand in a confirmation relation to the concepts whose availability they occasion.

So much for the Empiricist account of concept acquisition. The Nativist account (I shall sometimes say: 'the *Rationalist* account', since it received its clearest exposition in the hands of philosophers like Descartes) is very much simpler. To a first approximation, a Nativist says that the mechanism underlying the acquisition of *all* lexical concepts is brute-causal. Or, to put the same claim slightly otherwise, whereas the Empiricist says that many lexical concepts are logical constructs out of primitive concepts which are, in turn, made available by the activation of the sensorium, the Nativist says that the triggering of the sensorium is, normally, causally necessary and sufficient for the availability of all concepts except those that are patently phrasal.

So, for example, an Empiricist might give the following ontogeny for the concept TRIANGLE. Primitive concepts of line and angle are available as the causal consequence of sensory stimulation. The concept TRIANGLE is a logical construct out of these primitive concepts. Learning the concept TRIANGLE is a matter of confirming some such hypothesis as *the concept TRIANGLE is the concept of something which is ...,* where the blank is filled by something tantamount to a definition of "triangle". Whereas, the Nativist story might go like this: there are trigger stimuli sufficient to occasion the availability of such concepts as LINE and ANGLE; and there are *also* trigger stimuli sufficient to occasion the availability of such concepts as TRIANGLE. Insofar as one acquires the concept TRIANGLE "from experience", one normally does so as a consequence of being exposed to triggering stimuli of this latter kind. It may be that the concept TRIANGLE can be viewed as a logical construct out of the concepts LINE and ANGLE, but even if it is, *performing* the construction (e.g. confirming a hypothesis that exhibits the structure of the concept) is not part of the learning of the concept.

I'm not entirely happy with this way of putting the issue between Nativist and Empiricist accounts, for reasons that will be made clear later. But suffice it for the moment to notice this: the Empiricist story can't be right unless many concepts that are *de facto* lexical (concepts like TRIANGLE, BACHELOR, TRUMPET, CIGAR, ELECTRON, and literally tens of thousands of others) are structurally complex. In fact, the unvarnished Empiricist story requires that all *de facto* lexical concepts except the ones that are sensory (hence primitive) must be structurally complex. Whereas, it's compatible with the Nativist story that all lexical concepts are primitive. This is, I think, close to the heart of the matter, and we'll return to it presently.

First, let's consider in some detail what the Nativist and Empiricist stories do *not* disagree about; what I want to emphasize is that the point of the controversy has been widely misrepresented and still more widely misunderstood.

(14) Both theories acknowledge a distinction between primitive and complex concepts, and both assume that complex concepts are built out of primitive ones by the operation of some sort of combinatorial apparatus. For example, on both stories, a concept like PEOPLE WHO LIVE IN CHICAGO AND EAT MANGLE-WORTS is patently complex, and it inherits its semantic properties from such constituent concepts as PEOPLE, LIVE IN, CHICAGO, MANGLEWORTS, and so forth. For reasons previously considered, both theories will also assume that if a concept is phrasal, it's likely to be complex.

(15) Both theories assume that the availability of primitive concepts is a function of environmental stimulation. In particular, they both assume that the acquisition of such concepts is contingent upon the activation of the sensorium. As Descartes frequently emphasized, it is *not* part of the Rationalist program to claim that your repertoire of primitive concepts is independent of the character of your experience. On the contrary, just as there are presumably triggering experiences that are nomologically necessary for the acquisition of sensory-primitive concepts like RED, so are

there presumably triggering experiences that are nomologically necessary for the acquisition of *non*-sensory primitive concepts like TRIANGLE. In either case, if you don't encounter the trigger, you don't get the concept.

(16) Both stories assume that primitive concepts are, in a certain sense, unlearned, indeed that they are, in a certain sense, innate.

There are two points to consider here: First, we've seen that the mechanisms of "concept learning" in the technical sense of that notion apply, at best, *only* to the acquisition of complex concepts. Now there are, in principle, many ways other than learning in which the repertoire of mental representations available to an organism might be affected by its experiences. Think of being hit on your head, or of having your cortex surgically rewired, etc. If you are prepared to suppose—what seems to me quite plausible—that the distinguishing characteristic of concept *learning*, in the *non*-technical, *pre*-theoretic sense of that notion, is the existence of a rational relation between the concept acquired and the experience that occasions its availability, then it will follow on *both* the Empiricist and the Nativist model that primitive concepts are ipso facto unlearned. According to the Empiricist, complex concepts are learned *from* experience; but even the Empiricists hold that primitive concepts are merely triggered *by* experience. And triggering is a non-rational, hence non-learning, mechanism.

If this sounds too much like a terminological quibble, consider the following. On all standard theories, including Empiricist theories, the structure of the sensorium is taken to be innately fixed. It is, for example, just a fact about the way that we are put together that the sensory concepts we have are dependent in the ways that they are upon the particular stimulations which occasion them: if our sensoria were differently constructed, we would have a different repertoire of sensory concepts. So, for example, as Empiricists use the notion "sensory concept", blind men have no sensory concept of red. Nor can they *learn* that concept; their sensory mechanisms fail to respond to the relevant stimulations. Similarly, in the intended sense of "sensory concept", none of us have sensory concepts of ultrahigh frequency sounds; hence, for none of us is ULTRAHIGH FREQUENCY SOUND a primitive concept. There are, to be sure, imaginable organisms (bats, dolphins,

Martians)—organisms whose sensoria are constructed differently from our own—which do have sensory concepts in this area, and for them ULTRAHIGH FREQUENCY SOUND is primitive for all we know.

This is a kind of point on which classical Empiricists tend to be quite explicit, and none more so, perhaps, than Locke: ". . . though we cannot believe it impossible to God, to make a Creature with other organs and more ways to convey into the understanding the notice of corporeal things, than those five . . . which he has given to Man: Yet I think it is *not possible,* for any one *to imagine* any other *qualities* in bodies, howsoever constituted, whereby they can be taken notice of, besides sounds, tastes, smells, visible and tangible qualities. And had Mankind been made with but four senses, the qualities then, which are the object of the fifth sense, had been as far from our notice, imagination and conception, as now any belonging to a sixth, seventh, or eighth sense can possible be: which, whether yet some other creatures, in some other parts of this vast and stupendious (sic) universe, may not have, will be a great presumption to deny" (Locke, 1975, p. 120). Once again, on all standard theories the sensorium is an innately specified function from stimuli onto primitive concepts. The range of potentially available primitive-sensory concepts is thus fixed when you specify the biological endowment of the organism, as is the range of stimulations which can occasion the availability of those concepts.

Attributing to the Empiricists—of all people—the doctrine that primitive concepts are innate may strike you as Quixotic; but I think that is because the nature of the Empiricist/Rationalist controversy has been generally misconstrued in modern readings of the texts. In fact, the idea of the innateness of primitive concepts is widely articulated in the *Empiricist* literature. Here's Hume: ". . . understanding by *innate* what is original or copied from no precedent perception, then may we assert that all our impressions are innate, and our ideas not innate" (1909, p. 22). In interpreting this fragment, bear in mind that for Hume simple ideas are *mere copies* of the corresponding impressions; so, if the latter are innate, so too must be the content of the former.

And William James, whom, surely nobody could accuse of wild-eyed Nativism, is still more explicit: "The first thing I have to say is that all schools (however they otherwise differ) must allow that the *elementary qualities* of cold, heat, pleasure, pain, red, blue, sound, silence, etc., are original, innate or *a priori* properties of our subjective nature, even though they should require the touch of experience to waken them into actual consciousness, and should slumber to all eternity without it" (1890, Vol. 2, p. 618).

Let me reiterate what I take to be the central point. Primitive concepts are, ipso facto, not learned; and both the range of potentially available primitive concepts and the ways in which their actual availability depends upon triggering stimulation are determined by the innate structure of the sensorium. In these respects, all Empiricists accept the innateness of the primitive conceptual repertoire. What Empiricists don't accept—what, in fact, *nobody* accepts—is that the availability of primitive concepts is independent of the character of the organism's experience. What causes the confusion about what the Empiricists believed is the bad habit of reading "occasioned by experience" as entailing "learned" when, in fact, the inference is valid only in the opposite direction.

To complete our survey of the issues on which Empiricist and Nativist accounts of concept acquisition agree:

(17) Both sides assume that the space of concepts potentially available to any given organism is completely determined by the innate endowment of that organism. This follows from the assumptions that (a) the set of potentially available concepts is the closure of the primitive concepts under the combinatorial mechanisms; (b) the set of potentially available primitive concepts is innately fixed; and (c) the combinatorial mechanisms available are themselves innately specified.

I hope that, given the previous discussion, only (c) will now strike you as tendentious, and I think it's clear that (c) will have to be accepted. I won't try to set out the details, but the governing considerations should by now sound familiar: if concept learning is hypothesis confirmation, and if you need the combinatorial apparatus to specify the hypotheses that are available for the organism to confirm, then the one thing that *can't* be a consequence of concept learning is the availability of the combinatorial apparatus. This dilemma is conceptual, and loose talk about bootstrapping will buy you nothing. (For elaboration, see Fodor, 1975, especially chapter 2.)

I am being a little cavalier but only because, in point of historical fact, this issue isn't in dispute. It was, for example, presumably because they dreaded the sort of regress I've just alluded to that theorists who held that the combinatorial structure of complex concepts is associative *also* held that the principles of association express unlearned, innate, congenital properties of mental processing. Hume again: Association is "a kind of *attraction,* which in the mental world will be found to have as extraordinary effects as in the natural, and to show itself in as many and as various forms. Its effects are everywhere conspicuous; but as to its causes, they are mostly unknown and must be resolved into *original* qualities of human nature, which I pretend not to explain" (p. 321; Hume's emphasis). But, now, if you hold that the primitive concepts are innate (see above), and if you hold that every concept is either primitive or complex, and if you hold that the complex concepts are the closure of the primitive concepts under some innate combinatorial apparatus, then you'd bloody well better hold that the set of potentially available concepts is innately fixed. And, of course, the Empiricists *did* hold that; it was precisely because their theory guaranteed the exhaustiveness of the disjunction *sensory concept or complex concept reducible to sensory constitutents* that they were able to derive the Empiricist maxim as, as it were, a theorem of their psychology. "Nothing can be in the mind except what's first in the senses" *because* the potentially available conceptual repertoire is exhausted by the closure of the primitive concepts under the combinatorial apparatus.

Well, then, what—insofar as Nativist and Empiricist theories of concept attainment *dis*agree—do they disagree about? I want to answer this question twice: first roughly, by way of scouting out the logical geography; and then more precisely, by way of seeing the issue in detail.

Roughly, what Empiricists and Nativists disagree about is the structure of lexical concepts. For the Empiricist, lexical concepts normally have internal structure. This is because lexical concepts are normally constructs out of primitive concepts, and the primitive concepts are a small subset of the ones that lexical items express. So, in particular, on the assumption that only sensory concepts are primitive—and on the assumption that "sensory" is being used in even a remotely disciplined way—it must be that

concepts like TRIANGLE, BACHELOR, XYLOPHONE, CHICA-
GO, HAND, HOUSE, HORSE, ELECTRON, GRANDMOTHER,
CIGAR, TOMORROW, etc. are all internally complex. The Empiricist must hold this because, by stipulation, the Empiricist view
is that the attainment of non-sensory concepts involves learning
the truth of a hypothesis that exhibits their internal structure.
Patently, if a concept *has* no internal structure, its acquisition
cannot be the consequence of that sort of process.

Whereas, it is open to the Nativist to hold either that (a) all or
most lexical concepts have *no* internal structure, or (b), if they
are internally structured, nevertheless the fact that they are plays
no role in the explanation of their acquisition.[6] To put the same
point another way, according to the Nativist view the story that
Empiricists tell about *sensory* concepts also holds for a wide
range of *non*-sensory lexical concepts: viz. that they are triggered
but unlearned. That Nativists do indeed hold this is clear enough
from the texts. For example, Descartes argues that if the acquisition of concepts requires sensory stimulation, that is not because
"these extraneous things (distal stimuli) transmitted the ideas
themselves to our minds through the organs of sense, but because
they transmitted something which gave the mind occasion to form
these ideas, by means of an innate faculty, at this time rather than
at another . . . Hence it follows that the ideas of . . . movements
and figures are themselves innate in us. So much the more must be
the ideas of pain, colour, sound and the like be innate, that our
mind may, on the occasion of certain corporeal movements en-
visage these ideas" ("Notes Against A Certain Program," quoted
in Adams, 1975, p. 770).

This underlying disagreement about the structure—or otherwise
—of lexical concepts has, of course, a wide range of consequences.
Notice, for starters, that Nativists and Empiricists disagree on the
extent to which the acquisition of lexical concepts is a rational
process. In respect of this disagreement, the traditional nomen-
clature of "Rationalism vs Empiricism" could hardly be more
misleading. It is the *Empiricist* view that the relation between a
lexical concept and the experiences which occasion its acquisition
is normally rational—in particular, that the normal relation is that
such experiences bestow inductive warrant upon hypotheses which
articulate the internal structure of the concepts. Whereas, it's the

Rationalist view that the normal relation between lexical concepts and their occasioning experiences is brute-causal, i.e. "merely" empirical: such experiences function as the innately specified triggers of the concepts which they—to borrow the ethological jargon—"release."

Indeed, the ethological precedents from other species suggest that such relations may often be *extremely* arbitrary. There are fledgling ducks for which the operative rule seems to be: if it moves, it's mother. The fact that this experience triggers this concept is surely to be understood on a Darwinian model and not on the model of concept learning. In particular, the observation that the stimulus moves is surely *not* functioning as data confirmatory of some universal duckish hypothesis about the internal structure of MOTHERHOOD. The point is that the Nativist view allows for any amount of this sort of arbitrariness that you like.

Since the Nativist ipso facto doubts that ambient stimulation must provide inductive support for the concepts it occasions, it is open to him to predict the emergence of the species specific conceptual repertoire across a wide variety of nomologically possible environments. *All* that these environments need to have in common is that they provide the relevant triggers. It is thus a very characteristic Rationalist move—you'll find it from Descartes to Chomsky—to emphasize that the environment of the developing organism actually provides a *poor* inductive basis for the concepts that the organism acquires. "You learn your language on the basis of a fragmentary and impoverished sample" is one of those sentences that *has* been uttered more than once. The logic of this argument should now be apparent: if much of the conceptual repertoire is triggered, it's understandable that it should be invariant over wide—and relatively chaotic—variation in the individual histories of organisms belonging to the same species. To put it crudely: the concept isn't coming from the environment, it's coming from the organism. All the environment does is provide the triggers that release the information.

It is also characteristic of Rationalist theorizing to emphasize the degree to which the conceptual repertoire of the human species does seem to be largely invariant across variation in experience—for example, that the range of scientific hypotheses ever seriously entertained is vastly undetermined by the data that

choose among them. From the Rationalist point of view, the problem posed by the history of science is to explain why there is so much less disagreement than there ought to be, and why such disagreements as there are are resolved by evidence for which "logically inconclusive" is an epithet that puts it mildly. I think that this is a very interesting way of looking at the history of science. I think it's probably the right way. But this is now pure digression, and I *will* get back to work.

I don't quite like the way that the exposition has gone so far, for it makes the dispute about concept attainment primarily a dispute about lexical concepts (the ones that are, de facto, expressed by non-phrasal predicates of English), and, as I remarked at the outset, it's reasonable to doubt that the lexical/phrasal distinction will bear much weight. Indeed, on the Empiricist account, it's an accident—a mere fact about the history of the language—that a given concept *is* lexical; or, if it's not an accident, it's the consequence of the functioning of such unremarkable mechanisms as Zipf's Law. Similarly, though a Nativist might reasonably take the fact that a concept it lexicalized as prima facie evidence that it's primitive—and would thus be led to predict (what seems plausible in view of the data) that the lexical/phrasal distinction should be drawn in largely similar ways across historically unrelated languages—still, it's open to a Nativist to admit that *some* lexical items do, in fact, express complex concepts. He could thus hold that though (*pace* Empiricists) the primitive/complex distinction isn't nearly coextensive with the sensory/nonsensory distinction, it may nevertheless be a fair way from being coextensive with the lexical/phrasal distinction, too. Briefly: the Nativist probably will claim that many de facto lexical concepts are internally unstructured, but that's not the heart of his position. Nativism isn't, primarily, a thesis about *language;* still less is it primarily a thesis about English.

So, let's kick away the ladder. We could simply put it that the dispute is over *which* concepts are primitive, the Nativist claim being that there are very many unstructured (hence primitive, hence unlearned) concepts which are, nevertheless *non*-sensory. This would be a good way of putting it except that even many Empiricists now doubt that the sensory/non-sensory distinction will survive serious scrutiny. Certainly it is unreconstructed as things now stand, so it's not much use as a machine for clarifying other issues.

What might be closer to the point is to characterize the Nativist as denying that the primitive concepts constitute an *epistemologically interesting* set. From the Nativist point of view, which concepts are the triggered ones is basically a biological matter. It would be no surprise—indeed, it would be just what you'd expect —if that set looked unprincipled from the epistemologist's point of view. A Nativist would thus be quite comfortable with its including lots of middle-sized object concepts (FOOD, MOTHER), lots of explanatory concepts (CAUSES, INTENDS), as well as lots of sensory concepts, and God knows what all else.

There are, however, two things wrong with this way of putting the issue. In the first place, some Nativists, including especially many Cartesian Rationalists, *have* sought to make epistemological mileage out of the innate/learned distinction. Descartes agreed with Locke and Hume that the innate ideas can be picked out by an epistemological criterion; what they differed over was just which epistemological criterion was the one to use. Descartes took it that it was clarity and distinctness whereas, as we've seen, the Empiricist's view was that the innate ideas are the ones that are immediately occasioned by sensory stimulation. I think it was a serious mistake on the part of the Rationalists to thus muddle their epistemology with their ethology, but it seems to be the fact that muddle them they did.

The second point is that, while latter-day Empiricists continue to suspect that the primitive concepts have a special epistemological centrality (so that verificationism is epidemic in AI), many have ceased to believe that they form an epistemologically *homogeneous* collection. Typical contemporary formulations allow as primitive not just a sensory basis and a logical syntax, but also a heterogeneous and largely unspecified body of "framework" concepts, from which the mass of de facto lexical concepts are alleged to be constructed. (For a useful example, see Miller and Johnson-Laird, 1976, p. 14). This is a bit of a nuisance because it means that while classical Empiricism was a principled doctrine ('I'll tell you which concepts I claim are primitive: it's all the sensory ones and only those'), modern Empiricism tends to be in the nature of a research program ('The primitive concepts are the ones whose attainment I can't eventually account for by appeal to the me-

attainment I can't eventually account for by appeal to the mechanisms of concept learning. I don't yet know which those concepts are, though I very much doubt that they include XYLOPHONE or GRANDMOTHER. Ask me again later.') Viewed this way, the Nativist/Empiricist controversy is a disagreement about how this research program will turn out. The Empiricist bets that there will prove to be lots of interesting reductions of *prima facie* uncomplex concepts (e.g. of de facto lexical concepts); whereas the Nativist bets that the successes of reduction will be unsystematic and thin on the ground, that we aren't going to be able to display the internal structure of most concepts because, simply, most concepts don't have any internal structure.

I propose to leave it here. This formulation allows that the disagreement is, after all, largely quantitative (*how many* concepts will prove to be reducible?). It allows that the disagreement would be principled if the Empiricist could get his act together to the extent of deciding what precisely the epistemologically interesting characteristic of primitive concepts is supposed to be. And, most importantly, it puts the emphasis at a place where empirical considerations can be brought to bear: it puts the emphasis on the question whether, and which, concepts have internal structure. Let me reemphasize this last clause. The Empiricist story about the acquisition of concepts can, in principle, hold only for those concepts which have internal structure—those concepts which can be viewed as in some sense logical constructs out of a primitive basis in which they are not themselves contained. If it turns out that most concepts cannot be so viewed, then the Empiricist story will have to be abandoned.

The State of the Evidence

I am now going to wave my hands in lieu of providing a really systematic survey of the data. It seems to me that the burden of the empirical evidence overwhelmingly favors the view that most concepts are internally unstructured. Indeed, it seems to me to be among the most important findings of philosophical and psychological research over the last several hundred years (say, since Locke first made the reductionist program explicit) that attempts at conceptual analysis practically always fail.

Consider, for example, the failure of the reductionist program within the study of language. As we've seen, it's characteristic of the Empiricist to claim that an adequate primitive basis for the concepts expressible in English would be much smaller than the set of de facto lexicalized concepts of English. On the further assumption that English is capable of expressing the primitive concepts themselves (an assumption you're likely to grant if, for example, you hold that primitive concepts are sensory), you get what I'll call the *Definition Hypothesis:* (a, weak version) that many de facto lexical concepts are definable; and (b, strong version) that they are definable in a vocabulary of sensory-terms-plus-logical-syntax.

It's simply notorious that the stronger version of this claim has proved to be untenable. There are, I think, *no* cases where it has been possible to show that a prima facie non-sensory term (like, say, 'table' or 'grandmother' or 'electron' or, for that matter, 'bachelor' or 'triangle') is analyzable (i.e. definable) in a reduction base where the non-logical vocabulary is—even prima facie—sensory. That's *why* the Empiricist program, which was healthy as recently as the Logical Atomist movement, is now effectively a dead issue in philosophy. But what's equally true, and considerably more striking, is that the evidence seems to bear against the definition hypothesis even in the weak version; if there are no plausible cases of definition in a sensory vocabulary, there are also remarkably few plausible examples of definition in a *non*-sensory vocabulary, one indication of which is the striking paucity of working examples in the standard literature. There is 'bachelor', which is supposed to mean 'unmarried man'; there are the causative verbs, of which the analysis is vastly in dispute; there are jargon terms, which are explicitly and stipulatively defined ('ketch': 'a two-masted sailing vessel, such that . . .' (See Chapman and Maloney (1977)); there are kinship terms, which are also in dispute; there is a handful of terms which belong to real, honest-to-God axiomatic systems ('triangle', 'prime' as in 'prime number'); and then there are the other half million or so lexical items that the OED lists. About these last apparently nothing much can be done.

Not for lack of trying. The attempt to axiomatize the vocabulary of, say, ethics (i.e. by showing that you can get by with a reduction base which includes, perhaps, 'ought' and 'good' but not 'right') constitutes a sustained and serious contribution to the philosophical literature. The trouble is the one that John Austin pointed out (in a pregnant paper called, "Three Ways of Spilling

Ink" (1966)): there seem always to be counterexamples to the proposed definitions. This observation, if true, needn't be mysterious. Suppose that the vocabulary of English is not much larger than the minimum you would require to make the distinctions that English can encode—i.e. that, far from being vastly redundant, the vocabulary of English is just about adequate to its expressive power. Then you'd expect to find that programs of definitional elimination keep running into trouble with the examples. My claim is that that is what we *do* find, practically everywhere we look; and that this is inductive evidence (by affirmation of the consequent) that most of the morphemically simple expressions of English are undefinable. (I once heard Professor Gilbert Harman remark that it would be *surprising* if "know" were definable, since nothing else is. Precisely.)

The only way to convince yourself of the truth—or otherwise—of this claim is to try actually working through some cases. While we can't do that in any systematic way here, it may be worth looking at one example (chosen more or less arbitrarily from the current literature) just to give a little of the feel of the thing.

In a recent (1978) paper, in which the definition construct is heavily exploited, George Miller makes the following claim (p. 104): "When nouns of Type M are used as verbs, the meaning of x Ms y is to be construed as 'x covers the surface of y with M'." Miller takes the noun 'paint' as his paradigm of the type M, though he mentions a number of others as well: *butter, color, dye, enamel, grease*, etc.

What we have here is a proposal for defining the transitive verb 'paint$_{tr}$' in terms of the noun 'paint$_n$', together with some further conceptual apparatus (COVER, SURFACE, and WITH), and what I claim is that the definition doesn't work; *x covers y with paint* may be a necessary condition for *x paints y* but it is certainly not a sufficient condition. (It is, by the way, quite usual for putative definitions to fail in this particular way; it is very much easier to provide logically necessary conditions for the application of a term than to provide logically necessary and sufficient conditions.)

The first point is that the reason that the definition doesn't work has nothing to do with whether the verb 'paint$_{tr}$' is vague, though that's a red herring that often swims by about here. For example, someone might say 'x covers the wall with paint' isn't necessary for 'x paints the wall' since, surely, you could have painted the wall even if there were a little tiny bit up there in the top left hand corner that you'd missed, hence *failed* to cover with paint. In that case, it might be that you'd painted the wall carelessly, or imperfectly, or not very well; but, nevertheless, you'd have painted it.

But the (presumptive) fact that 'paint$_{tr}$' is vague is *not* a reason for believing that it is undefinable; all it shows is that whatever phrase defines 'paint$_{tr}$' must *also* be vague, and in the right ways. In fact, the definition in terms of 'cover' does the job quite nicely; for if you can be said to have painted a wall even though you missed a spot, you can also be said to have covered the wall with paint even though you missed a spot. The vagueness of definiens and definiendum, as it were, match; and so long as they do so, vagueness is not an argument against definability.

What's wrong with the definition isn't that 'paint$_{tr}$' is vague; it's that there are clear counterexamples to the coextensivity of 'x paints y' with 'x covers y with paint.' To start with a fairly crude point, consider the case where the paint factory explodes and covers the spectators with paint. This may be good fun, but it is not a case of the paint factory (or the explosion) painting the spectators. What we need to patch up the definition is at least the condition that what goes in for '*x*' must denote an *agent.* I don't know what an agent is (nor does anybody else), but it must at least be such as to include John in 'John painted the wall' and to exclude the paint factory in 'the paint factory exploded and covered the spectators with paint.' Notice, by the way, that in adding this condition, we are enriching the presumed reduction base for 'paint$_{tr}$'—hence increasing the range of concepts that our theory about 'paint$_{tr}$' claims that a child has to have mastered *before* he can master that verb. It goes without saying that the more such apparatus we have to add to the reduction base for defining 'paint$_{tr}$', the more elaborately nativistic is the theory which says that learning the verb is learning the definition. In the limiting case, we say that the concept PAINT$_{TR}$ belongs to the reduction base for the verb 'paint$_{tr}$', at which point the theory that learning the verb is learning its definition is equivalent to the theory that the concept PAINT$_{TR}$ is innate, and argument ceases.

It might be argued, however, that conceding AGENT in the

reduction base for 'paint$_{tr}$' isn't really so bad since, when you come to think of it, AGENT is a very abstract concept and a very general one, and is presupposed by the idea of an *action,* which itself turns up as a constituent of lots and lots of the concepts that children have to master. So perhaps we should live with presupposed unanalyzed AGENT and revise the definition of 'paint$_{tr}$' to read something like '*x paints y* iff *x is an agent and x covers the surface of y with paint.*' The trouble is that this definition doesn't work either.

Consider that Michelangelo, though an agent, was not a house-painter. In particular, when he covered the ceiling of the Sistine Chapel with paint, he was not painting the ceiling; he was painting a picture *on* the ceiling. Similarly, when Jackson Pollock flung the pigments about, he wasn't painting his canvases; he was painting a picture ("making an image"?) *on* the canvases. Compare Tom Sawyer and his fence.

What's gone wrong here is maybe this: it's not good enough that you cover the *y* with paint. It's not even good enough that you cover the *y* with paint *intentionally* (though that's clearly necessary since, if you knock over the paint bucket, thereby covering the surface of the floor with paint, you have not thereby painted the floor). It's got to be that when you cover the *y* with paint, what you primarily have in mind to do (the description, as it were, under which you intend your act) is that *y* should be covered with paint in consequence of your activity. If, like Michelangelo, what you primarily have in mind is not (just) that the surface should become covered with paint in consequence of your activity, but that there should be a picture on the surface in consequence of your activity, then what you're doing when you cover the surface with paint doesn't count as painting the surface.

So perhaps we should try something like: '*x paints y*' means '*x* is an agent and *x* covers the surface of *y* with paint, and *x*'s primary intention in covering the surface of *y* with paint was that the surface of *y* should be covered with paint in consequence of *x*'s having so acted upon it.' I pause to remark (a) that the concept PRIMARY INTENTION OF AN ACT is quite unanalyzed; (b) that it is vastly unlikely that children have access to that concept prior to their learning of the concept PAINT$_{TR}$; and (c) that any way you look at it, the definition of 'paint$_{tr}$'—the amount of subsidiary apparatus you need to define it in terms of 'paint$_n$'—is getting sort of hairy.

Anyhow, this definition doesn't work either. For consider that when Michelangelo dipped his brush into Cerulian Blue, he thereby covered the surface of his brush with paint and did so with the primary intention that his brush should be covered with paint in consequence of his having so dipped it. But MICHELANGELO WAS NOT, FOR ALL THAT, PAINTING HIS PAINTBRUSH. (He was just putting paint *on* his paintbrush.)

I don't know where we go from here. For all I know—for all *anybody* knows—'paint$_{tr}$' is undefinable; for all I know, you can't eliminate it even in terms of such a very closely related term as 'paint$_n$'. Or perhaps it *is* definable, but only in a reduction base that includes 'dinasour' and 'Chlorodent'. Either way, the present point is that Miller's example doesn't work. That's not surprising; when it comes to definitions, the examples almost always don't work.

Now consider the case of the definition construct psycholinguistics. If you think that most lexical concepts are complex, you presumably suppose that entertaining a complex concept is normally part and parcel of comprehending (token) utterances in your language. In particular, you will assume this even in the case of utterances of morphemically simple forms, so long as the monomorpheme uttered is definable. A fair amount of experimental work has recently been devoted to testing this assumption—for example, by trying to show that the relative complexity of the state of mind you are in when you grasp a prima facie definable expression is predictable from the relative complexity of the definition. I think it's fair to say that this enterprise has been quite uniformly unsuccessful. (For discussion, see Fodor et al., 1980). There *is* some evidence that the state of mind you're in when you hear an expression is sometimes in a certain sense close to the one you're in when you hear a term that figures in its definition; e.g. that when you hear "cat" you're in a state of mind closely related to the one you're in when you hear "animal" (see particularly Meyer and Schvanetveld, 1971). What's lacking are any empirical grounds for claiming that the latter state of mind is, as it were, a constituent of the former: that understanding "cat" involves entertaining ANIMAL. We'll see presently that this point is not novel; the lack of evidence for such constituency was noticed relatively early by Empiricist theorists, and it occasioned something of a crisis in the history of Associationism.

To put it briefly: when viewed from the perspective of the theory of language, the idea that many terms express concepts that have internal structure is tantamount to the idea that many terms have definitions. This latter doctrine is abstract but empirical: the relevant demonstration would involve exhibiting the alleged definitions and showing that they do play a role in the psychological processes that mediate the use of language. I'm claiming that—ever so many texts to the contrary notwithstanding —the evidence for this doctrine is not good; that, on balance, the attempts to apply the program of conceptual reduction to the study of the lexicons of natural languages have not been fruitful.

It would, however, be a serious mistake to attempt to evaluate the empirical status of that program solely by reference to its application in lexicography and psycholinguistics. On the contrary, what seems to me impressive—what ought to *worry* an Empiricist— is the *range* of enterprises in which conceptual reduction has been tested and, so far at least, found wanting.

I shall scarcely do more than mention the failure of such undertakings in Positivistic philosophy of science. Having convinced themselves that the warrant of inductively founded beliefs turns on the possibility of reducing the theoretical concepts of a science to its observation base, the Positivists undertook a sustained and extremely ingenious attempt to provide—or at least to schematize —the required reductions. It is now, I think, practically universally conceded that this attempt was unsuccessful and, indeed, cannot in principle be carried through. Philosophers disagree about why, precisely, the Positivist program failed; but I doubt that anyone now believes that concepts like ELECTRON are fruitfully viewed as constructs out of an epistemologically specifiable primitive basis.

What is perhaps closer to the heart of a cognitive scientist is the vicissitudes of the program of conceptual reduction in its application to theories of perception. It's usual, in the context of representational theories of mind, to think of perception as the application of a concept to one of its instances. If you think that most concepts are constructs out of a (more or less) sensory basis, then a fortiori you think that sufficient conditions for the application of a concept can be specified in (more or less) sensory terms. Perception can then be viewed as a process in which the organism determines whether the sensory criteria for the application of a concept are satisfied in a given stimulus array. On this view, *the internal structure of a concept determines the flow of information through the perceptual mechanisms when the concept is applied:* If the concept is conjunctive, perceptual processing is the search for stimulus properties which satisfy each of the conjuncts; if it is disjunctive, perceptual processing is the search for stimulus properties which satisfy either of the disjuncts, and so on.

This determination of information flow by conceptual structure is, of course, only very approximate, the possibility of much heuristic shortcutting being conceded on all hands. Nevertheless, in point both of logic and historical fact, people who hold the reductionist view of conceptual structure typically do and ought to hold a basically bottom-to-top view of perceptual analysis. In the limiting case, the internal structure of a concept tells you what you have to know—and all you have to know—to determine whether the concept applies. So in the limiting case the application of a complex concept ought to reduce to the determination of the applicability of its primitive constituents. The flow of information in perception ought, fundamentally, to go in one direction: from the application of sensory concepts, via processes of logical construction, to the application of complex concepts. (Compare the Empiricist theory of confirmation: certitude flows upward, via logical construction, from the observation base of a science to its theoretical sentences; the logical constructions involved are those exhibited by reductive definitions of the theoretical concepts).

My point is that, insofar as the Empiricist view of concepts is wedded to the bottom-to-top view of perceptual processing, the quite general failure of research programs based on the latter doctrine is ipso facto an argument against the former. The relevant consideration is not just that it's hard to specify an adequate sensory basis for perceptual integration, to specify logically sufficient sensory conditions for the application of perceptual concepts. What's more important is that information seems to flow in *every* direction in normal perceptual processing. For all that the study of perception shows us, every concept could be a primitive node in a conceptual network, and *any* connection between nodes might be exploited, at one time or another, in constraining hypotheses about which concepts are satisfied in the stimulus domain. The analogy between theories of perception and theories of confirmation is once again instructive: empirical warrant may be inherited in *any* direction through a network of empirical theory. It's as likely that we accept a datum because it comports with abstract principle as that we accept an abstract principle because it comports with our data. That, as Hume pointed out, is why we don't believe reports of miracles.

I think one could go on to make very similar points about the way that the internal structure story has come to grief in the study of conceptual development in children. But I won't; I now propose to stop waving my hands. Quite a useful book might be written about how the idea that concepts have internal structure has determined the shape of several centuries of research in philosophy, psychology, lexicography, and, most recently, in AI. My own view is that the moral is surprisingly clear: all such programs have failed, and they have failed in just the respects you would expect them to if the doctrine that concepts have internal structure is untrue. But I don't suppose that the preceding fragments will have convinced anyone of this, and I'm content to settle for mere willing suspension of disbelief. In what follows, I'll assume that the evidence is, in any event, not overwhelmingly in favor of the conceptual reduction program and that it might, therefore, be interesting to consider some alternatives. In particular, I want to look at two doctrines—one modern and one traditional—which are prepared to abandon *some* aspects of the standard reduction account, but which seek to block the inference from the failure of conceptual reduction to the Rationalist view of concept attainment. I'll argue that while both these doctrines have interesting lessons to teach, neither succeeds in its primary objective: upon examination, one of them proves to *be* a kind of closet Rationalism, and the other offers a theory of concepts which is inadequate on grounds independent of the ones that Empiricists and Rationalists disagree about. I shall consider these proposals in reverse chronological order. At the end I'll say a little—a *very* little—about what a developed Rationalist theory of concept attainment might eventually look like.

Mental Chemistry and After

The logic of the argument so far has been like this:

(18) Unstructured concepts are ipso facto unlearned.

(19) The primary evidence that most lexical concepts are unstructured is that most lexical items are undefinable.[7]

(20) It's thus presupposed that complexity implies definability, where definability in turn entails identity of semantic properties between the defined term and the defining phrase.

Now, much of what has recently been said about lexical concepts in the philosophical and psychological literature accepts—indeed, insists upon—their undefinability. But it seeks to block the inference from *undefinable* to *unlearned* by showing how a concept might be both *undefinable* and *complex*—hence by showing that undefinable concepts are not ipso facto primitive. In particular, the idea is that complex concepts are typically organized around (not definitions but) *prototypes. Qua* mental representation, a prototype is a complex object: it's a specification of a set of prototypical properties. But specifications of prototypical properties express (roughly) central tendencies of the extension of a concept rather than the logical constituency of the concept. So, to come to cases, the prototype structure of DIAMOND might include such properties as: *brilliant, expensive, durable,* etc. And DIAMOND might itself function (in a slightly different sense of the prototype notion) as the prototype for a higher level concept like GEM. But it's not supposed to follow from these assumptions that all diamonds are expensive, and still less is it supposed to follow that all gems are diamonds. To say that a mental representation has prototype structure is to say that the properties which are internally represented as belonging to the concept do *not* determine its extension. That is, unlike definitions, prototypes do not express logically necessary and sufficient conditions for the application of a concept.

There are, then, two morals to be drawn. One that Hilary Putnam likes is that if meanings are what determine extensions, then meanings aren't in the head (see Putnam, 1975). The other is that there are some undefinable concepts which may nevertheless be learned: undefinable concepts with prototype structure could be learned by (roughly) any device that can estimate central tendencies.

Now, what is striking about prototypes as opposed to definitions is that, whereas the evidence for the psychological reality of the latter is, as we've seen, exiguous, there is abundant evidence for the psychological reality of the former. Eleanor Rosch (1975) and her colleagues, in particular, have provided striking demonstrations that the prototype structure of a concept determines much of the variance in a wide variety of experimental tasks, chronometric and otherwise. So, for example, you can estimate the prototype structure of a concept by asking subjects for the first instance of that concept which occurs to them. (If I say: "Tell me the first kind of gem you can think of" you will probably say "diamond" and you probably will not say "topaz". Similarly, mutatis mutandis, if I say: "Tell me the first property of diamonds you can think of" you will probably say "hard" or "expensive" and you will probably not say "treasured by Armenians"; not even if you believe that Armenians do, in fact, treasure diamonds.) It turns out that such estimates of prototype structure reliably predict speed and/or accuracy of performance in a variety of experimental tasks like:

    —say *"true"* or *"false"* to *"a diamond is a gem".* ("Diamond" is
                        "a topaz is a gem"

faster than "topaz".)

    —say *"true"* or *"false"* to *"diamonds are hard".* ("Hard" is
                      "are treasured by Armenians"

faster.)

Similarly, estimates of its prototype structure reliably predict the relative frequency of lexical items which express a concept ("diamond" is more frequent, in English, than "topaz" is). They reliably predict order of lexical acquisition (children learn "diamond" before they learn "topaz" (Anglin, 1970); and they surely learn that diamonds are hard before they learn that Armenians like them.) Estimates of prototype structure reliably predict some of the facts about 'semantic' priming (a superordinate concept differentially primes its high-prototypicality instances). And so on.

Insofar as theses get established in cognitive psychology, I think we can take the reality of prototype structures as read. The question is: what does this fact show us about the question of concept attainment? One view, currently much in the air, (see Putnam (1975)) goes like this:

Many de facto lexical concepts are really quasi-indexical. In particular, what you actually learn when you learn a concept like TIGER is that a tiger is an animal of the same kind as *this,* where the "this" indicates an ostensive introduction. That sort of mental representation is able to function in (e.g.) mediating communication with the word "tiger" and in the perceptual recognition of tigers because a psychological counterpart to the notion of *same kind* is provided by a tiger prototype. You learn this prototype when you acquire the concept and you share it, more or less, with other members of your speech community—that is, what the ostensively introduced tiger has in common with other tigers, insofar as what tigers have in common is internally represented by people who have the TIGER concept, is just that it's a reasonable fit to the prototype. What is *not* internally represented—or, anyhow, what needn't be—is the defining properties of tigers; properties which all and only tigers share in virtue of being tigers. Those properties —if there are any—have to do with biological or genetic structure and are matters for scientific discovery in *zoology,* not in psychology.

I'm inclined to think there is more than a grain of truth in this (Putnam/Kripke) account, in particular that the proposal that natural-kind concepts are often quasi-indexical is correct and important. What I want to consider here, however, is whether the idea that concepts have prototype structure—that what are in the head are prototypes rather than meanings—will do the work that a theory of concepts needs to do.

Notice, to begin with, that in principle the claim that kind concepts are quasi-indexical comes unstuck from the claim that what's in the head doesn't determine extensions. After all, if what I'm pointing at is a tiger, then the formula '. . . is of relevantly similar kind to what I'm pointing at' does, in fact, determine the extension of "tiger": all and only the tigers satisfy that formula.[8] What makes the Putnam/Kripke story incompatible with the idea that concepts determine extensions isn't the stuff about their being quasi-indexical; it's the stuff about their having prototype structure.

Second, the experimental evidence that prototype structure is psychologically real certainly isn't *incompatible* with the claim that mental representations determine extensions; it isn't even incompatible with the claim that mental representations have the form of definitions. As several investigators (Armstrong et al., forthcoming; Wanner (1979)) have recently remarked, concepts like GRANDMOTHER and TRIANGLE, which are definable concepts *par excellence,* and where, often enough, the subject *can tell you what the definition is,* nevertheless exhibit the characteristic range of prototype phenomena. (The prototypical grandmother is elderly and has white hair; the prototypical triangle is equilateral, etc.) Since prototype structure can, patently, comport with definitional structure, the inference from *many concepts have prototype structure* to *many concepts are complex though undefinable* is, at best, risky.

'Still,' you may say, 'the prototype idea shows how concepts *could* be complex but undefinable, and this lets the wind out of the Rationalist's sails. In particular, we now see that evidence for its undefinability just won't do to make the case that a concept is primitive; and it's primitiveness you need if you are to infer that a concept is unlearned. 'And anyhow,' you may add, in one of your Wittgensteinian moods, 'doesn't it seem *plausible* that the internal representation of a word is typically more or less of a mess? Isn't what games and tigers and typewriters have in common, each with each, more like a family resemblance than like the mutual satisfaction of defining properties? Isn't a language really sort of like a city? Or a rope? Or a fountain? Or something?'

Well, maybe. But there is a principled argument against the prototype story, and unless or until that argument can be met, I see no way of taking prototypes as serious candidates for identification with concepts-qua-mental-representations. The objection goes like this:

The classical mentalist view is that postulating concepts answers three questions; (a) what does a term in a natural language express; (b) what determines the extension of a term in a natural language; and (c) what does a term in a natural language contribute to the semantics of the complex expressions in which it occurs. The beauty of the classical story is that it provides the *same* answer for all three of these questions: in particular, the very thing which determines the extension of a term *is also what the term contributes to the (syntactically) complex expressions that contain it.* So, for example: the concept COW determines the extension of "cow". "Cow" expresses COW, and it contributes the concept it expresses to, for example, the internal representation of "brown cow". Since "brown cow" inherits COW from "cow" (and, of course, inherits BROWN from "brown"), and since concepts determine extensions, it's possible to compute the semantic properties of "brown cow" from the semantic properties of its constituent terms. It is because it's possible to compute the semantic properties of complex expressions from the semantic properties of their constituent terms *that it is possible to understand an infinite language given knowledge of a finite basis.* It's worth adding that this general account is not proprietary to the mentalistic reading of "concept"; the Fregean program in semantics runs along precisely the same line.

So, in short, the idea that concepts determine extensions is part and parcel of the classical theory of how the productivity problem is to be solved. Moreover, I find it hard to imagine a solution to the productivity problem that doesn't share the form of the classical one; one that doesn't say that there is productivity because semantic properties are inherited from terms to phrases (or, equivalently for our purposes, from lexical concepts to phrasal concepts). Contrapositively, nothing could be the meaning of a word unless it's what phrases in which the word occurs inherit from the word's occurrence. The anti-prototype point is just that if that generalization stands, then prototypes *can't* be word meanings.

The argument is blessedly short: the only obvious way in which prototypes could be inherited under combination would be for the prototypes of complex expressions to be determined by the prototypes of their constituents (just as the meanings—hence extensions —of complex expressions were classically supposed to be inherited from the meanings of their constituents). But you can't play *that* game with prototypes because, by and large—i.e. in infinitely many cases—*complex expressions don't have prototypes.* There may, for example, be prototypical *cities* (London, Athens, Rome, New York); there may even be prototypical *American cities* (New York, Chicago, Los Angeles), but there are surely no prototypical *American cities situated on the East Coast just a little south of*

Tennessee. Similarly, there may be prototypical *grandmothers* (Mary Worth) and there may be prototypical *properties of grandmothers* (*good, old* Mary Worth). But there are surely no prototypical properties of, say, *Chaucer's grandmothers,* and there are no prototypical properties of *grandmothers most of whose grandchildren are married to dentists.* Or, if there are, it's clear that knowing the prototypes can't be required to understand the phrases.

Since phrases typically do not have prototypes, it cannot be that the combinatorial inheritance of semantic properties is a matter of the determination of phrasal prototypes by lexical prototypes. And it cannot be that understanding a phrase is a matter of knowing how its prototype is determined by those of its constituents. And since a serious theory of concepts must say what lexical items contribute to phrases, I infer that the prototype story is not a serious theory of concepts.

Or not, at least, so far. For it is, of course, possible that the combinatorial problem could be solved in some way compatible with the idea that lexical concepts are prototypes—i.e. in some way other than the one I have just sketched. It's unfortunately highly characteristic of the neo-Wittgensteinian line in lexicography that the problem of squaring the prototype story with the demands that the problem of linguistic productivity imposes simply isn't broached. Indeed, it's highly characteristic of these texts, from the *Investigations* to "The meaning of meaning" inclusive, not to mention the productivity problem at all. My point has been that lexicography so pursued is lexicography unconstrained.

It is worth pausing to block a possible misunderstanding of the argument just proposed. There exist formal mechanisms which might, at least in principle, permit prototype theories to handle the combinatorial problem for the *extensions* of terms. Indeed, it is a standard assumption among many friends of prototypes that some variant of "fuzzy set theory" could do the job: "cow" expresses a fuzzy set, "brown" expresses a fuzzy set, and the combinatorial mechanisms exhibit "brown cow" as expressing their fuzzy intersection. There are serious problems about characterizing these combinatorial mechanisms (see Osherson and Smith, in press) but that is not the difficulty that I want to emphasize here. The present problem is to give some account of the *sense* (as opposed to the extension) of "brown cow," assuming that the senses of "brown" and "cow" are taken to be prototypes. It appears that this problem could be solved only if prototypes have some sort of combinatorial structure; and, so far as anybody knows, they don't.

To return to the main discussion, my point *hasn't* been, of course, that there are definitions *rather than* prototypes. The current state of the argument is this:

•Rationalists say that lexical concepts are typically undefinable, hence typically unstructured, hence typically primitive, hence typically unlearned.

•The Empiricist counters: you can't infer from *undefinable* to *unstructured*. Perhaps lexical concepts typically have *prototype* structure.

•The Rationalist replies: if prototypes offered a serious account of conceptual structure, then the inference from *undefinable* to *unstructured* would indeed be jeopardized. You have thus shown, at least, that the inference is not apodictic. But (a) the prototype story is *not* a serious account of conceptual structure (see above), and (b) I never thought the inference was apodictic (or, if I did, I shouldn't have). My argument was (or should have been) just that there's no evidence *for* conceptual structure and there's some evidence (apparent undefinability) *against* it. If there is no structure inside lexical concepts, that would *explain* their apparent undefinability. So far, no other plausible explanation suggests itself. In particular, the explanation that goes "lexical concepts are complex but do not determine extensions" apparently won't do.

And there, for the moment at least, the argument comes to rest.

In intellectual history, everything happens twice, first as philosophy and then as cognitive science. It turns out that several of the points in the preceding discussion were anticipated by the "mental chemistry" movement in British Associationism. I want to comment on this movement, since the ideas are of considerable intrinsic interest and some of their implications appear to have been widely misunderstood, even by the philosophers who espoused them.

I think many readers may be laboring under a minor terminological misapprehension of which I was myself only recently disabused: when 'mental chemistry' is discussed in the contemporary literature, the phrase is often used as simply a shorthand for the view that de facto lexical concepts have internal structure. To pick a text practically at random, Harris Savin says in one of his papers: "A mental chemistry of concepts is an attractive program *because most concepts are obviously composite*" (1973, p. 234; my emphasis). Now in point of historical fact the situation is entirely otherwise. The idea of mental chemistry enters the Empiricist tradition as a way of explaining the observation that most concepts *don't* appear to be composite; in particular, many de facto lexical concepts do not.

This wants some spelling out. There are, according to Empiricist doctrine, two tests for the "compositeness" of concepts which ought, in general, to pick out the same class of cases. A concept is composite *by the logical test* if its instantiation "semantically entails" the instantiation of some *other* concept. The doctrine of semantic entailment, and the related doctrines of analyticity and and conceptual necessity are, no doubt, obscure; but it is alleged that there are paradigm cases. So, for example, the instantiation of BACHELOR semantically entails the instantiation of UNMARRIED; the instantiation of GRANDMOTHER semantically entails the instantiation of FEMALE; and so on. Whereas, a concept is "composite" *by the psychological test* if to entertain that concept is to entertain a complex mental object. Hence, derivatively, a concept is composite by the psychological test if to entertain that concept is to be in a complex mental state.

The reason why the logical and psychological tests are supposed to pick out the same cases is this: It's the internal structure of a concept that is supposed to explain its semantic entailments. BACHELOR semantically entails UNMARRIED because the concept UNMARRIED is a *part of* (specifically, a *conjunctive* part of) the concept BACHELOR; GRANDMOTHER entails FEMALE because the concept FEMALE is a part of the concept GRANDMOTHER; and so on. If, however, UNMARRIED is part of the concept BACHELOR, then, a fortiori, the concept BACHELOR *has* parts, and entertaining the concept must be entertaining a structurally composite mental representation.

Now, one can plausible read the mental chemistry literature as responding to the prima facie *failure* of these two tests to coextend—in particular, to the fact that introspection—then the preferred technique for the empirical investigation of mental states—often fails to find psychological structure in concepts in which semantic analysis discovers logical complexity. The germ of the problem, and of the proposed solution, can be found quite early in the Empiricist literature. So, for example, David Hartley—who is approximately a contemporary of Hume's, writes as follows:

> If the number of simple ideas which compose the complex one be very great, it may happen, that the complex idea shall not appear to bear any relation to these its compounding parts, nor to the external senses upon which the original sensations, which gave birth to the compounding ideas, were impressed. The reason of this is, that each simple idea is overpowered by the sum of all the rest, as soon as they are all intimately united together. Thus, in very compound medicines, the several tastes and flavors of the separate ingredients are lost and overpowered by the complex one of the whole mass: so that this has a taste and flavor of its own, which appears to be simple and original, and like that of a natural body."   (Hartley, 1966, p. 75)

Notice two things: (a) the distinction between the properties that philosophical analysis predicts that a concept *ought* to have and the ones that psychological (viz. introspective) analysis finds that it *does* have; and (b) the proposal that the disparity be explained by appeal to some form of interaction among simple ideas other than mere summation (other, that is, than what we've been calling logical construction). These are the leitmotifs of mental chemistry.

If, however, Hartley prefigures the doctrine, J. S. Mill epitomizes it. I quote from Howard C. Warren's useful book, *A History of the Association Psychology* (1967, p. 165):

> The way out of this difficulty appears plain enough to the younger Mill. It involves merely abandoning the mechanical view of association for the chemical analogy. According to him, association produces experiences which are really unitary, in the sense that they are not separable into parts by introspection. Introspection does not break the experience up into elements . . . but it does reveal the elements which the act of association has brought together to form this new product. Association does

more than unite—it transforms . . . what James Mill considered *ingredients* in a complex experience are really its *antecedents* . . . the resulting experience is not so much a complex state as a *derivative* state, which is introspectively as simple as it appears. Thus the perception of an orange or the concept HORSE are really simple, though derived from primitive elements.

This may all seem a little quaint, since latter-day Empiricists will surely say that what Mill ought to have done is hold onto both the logical *and* the psychological complexity of HORSE and give up the infallibility of introspection. As Warren points out, Mill seems to have viewed his problem as precisely a paradox of infallibility: if introspection always delivers truths, how can the results of analysis show that introspectively simple concepts are in fact complex? Or, to put it another way, one has no right to speak, as Hartley does, of a complex concept as merely *appearing* to be simple; the appearance/reality distinction doesn't apply to the objects of an infallible faculty. As Warren remarks, "if introspection declares a certain experience to be simple, how can another introspection prove this introspection to be false?"

But, in fact, the introspection issue is—as usual—a red herring, and Mill's problem is very much our own. If introspection isn't always right, it isn't always wrong either; and, in the present case, the current psychological evidence tends to support the earlier intuitions. There is, if anything, rather less reason to accept the psychological complexity of HORSE now than there was when Mill wrote his *Logic*.

What's interesting is that Mill, having once taken the introspective data seriously, was able to see that they called for a major revision of Empiricist theorizing. And what's still more interesting is that even Mill apparently failed to see how much taking these data seriously was going to cost him. Here is the relevant passage from Mill's *System of Logic*, (1974, Vol. 3, pp. 853–854):

the effect of concurring causes is not always precisely the sum of the effects of those causes when separate, nor even always an effect of the same kind with them . . . the laws of the phenomena of mind are sometimes analogous to mechanical, but sometimes also to chemical laws. When many impressions or ideas are operating in the mind together, there sometimes takes

place a process of a similar kind to chemical combination . . .
the ideas sometimes melt and coalesce with one another and appear not several ideas but one; in the same manner as, when the
seven prismatic colours are presented to the eye in rapid suc-
cession, the sensation produced is that of white. But in this last
case it is correct to say that the seven colours when they rapidly
follow one another *generate* white, but not that they actually
are white; so it appears to me that the Complex Idea, formed by
the blending together of several simple ones, should, when it is
really simple (that is, when the separate elements are not con-
sciously distinguishable in it) be said to *result from,* or *be
generated by,* the simple ideas, not to *consist* of them. Our idea
of an orange really *consists of* the simple ideas of a certain
colour, a certain form, a certain taste and smell, etc., because
we can, by interrogating our consciousness, perceive all these
elements in the idea. But we cannot perceive, in so apparently
simple a feeling as our perception of the shape of an object by
the eye, all those multitudes of ideas derived from other senses,
without which it is well ascertained that no such visual perception would ever have had existence; nor, in our idea of Extension, can we discover those elementary ideas of resistance,
derived from our muscular force, in which it has been conclu-
sively shown that the idea originates. Therefore these are cases
of mental chemistry: in which it is proper to say that the simple
ideas generate, rather than that they compose, the complex
ones.

There are, I think, two things that need to be said about this.
We need to note the magnitude of the concessions, which amounts
—as I shall argue—to abandoning Empiricism entirely; to giving the
Rationalist everything he could possibly want. And we should also
note that the kind of Rationalism that Mill is (implicitly, to be
sure) espousing is actually quite interesting and points in a direction that modern psychologists might well want to explore. These
points in turn.

To begin with, it's clear that Mill's proposal tacitly abandons
the demand that the logical and psychological tests for conceptual
structure should be satisfied by the same cases. On Mill's account,
psychologically simple concepts might nevertheless have semantic

entailments; indeed, they might even have *definitions* (in the sense of logically necessary and sufficient conditions). *Definability* does not guarantee *complexity* because, in point of their psychological functioning, the concepts which figure in a definition may be causal occasions—not structural constituents—of the concept they define. So, in espousing mental chemistry, Mill has given up the principle that psychological constituency explains semantic entailment. All that seems transparent enough; what may not be immediately obvious is that he has given up the Empiricist Maxim as well.

Strictly speaking, what the Empiricist Maxim says isn't, of course, that there's nothing in the mind except what's first present to the senses; Locke knew perfectly well about unicorns. Rather, the Maxim says that there is nothing in the mind except what's *either* first present to the senses *or* logically complex and constructed from sensations. Equivalently, for our purposes, it says that all *simple* ideas must be learned from their instances. Empiricist analysis in its iconoclastic mood typically used the Maxim in the disjunctive form: take a concept (GOD, SUBSTANCE, HIDDEN POWER, or whatever), show that it is neither instantiated in experience nor reducible to concepts so instantiated, and conclude that the concept is empty.

Now, one way to put my point is that if mental chemistry is endorsed, this strategy isn't going to work. On the mental chemistry view, the disjunction isn't exhaustive, since there can perfectly well be concepts which are both simple *and* not learned from their instances. Indeed, on Mill's account, that could be true of *any* simple concept; the fact that a simple concept *is* instantiated in experience is no reason at all to suppose that its instantiations play a role in the learning. Consider the concept C which, by assumption, is simple and arises by mental chemistry from (hence is *not* a construct out of) concepts A and B. (A and B may or may not be semantically related to C. The acquisition of a concept by mental chemistry—unlike its acquisition by logical construction—is neutral on the issue of logical connections between the occasioning concepts and the concept acquired.) The point is that if entertaining A and B is causally sufficient for acquiring C, then it follows that C's being simple does not require that C be learned from its instances. All that's required to learn C is *the previous acquisition of A and B.* This is to say, in effect, that some simple concepts may be triggered by other concepts, which latter may— but need not—themselves be simple. Simple concepts which arise as the effects of such triggering are, no doubt, learned *in consequence* of experience; experiences are—directly or indirectly— among their causes. But they aren't learned *from* experience, and they therefore constitute exceptions to the Empiricist Maxim.

It is, by the way, of some interest that the possibility of this sort of exception to the principles of Empiricism was noticed by, of all people, David Hume, who suggested the following example:

> Suppose . . . a person to have enjoyed his sight for thirty years, and to have become perfectly acquainted with colors of all kinds except one particular shade of blue, for instance, which it has never been his fortune to meet with. Let all the different shades of that color, except that single one, be placed before him, descending gradually from the deepest to the lightest; it is plain that he will perceive a blank, where that shade is wanting . . . now I ask, whether it is possible for him, from his own imagination to supply this deficiency, and raise up to himself the idea of that particular shade, though it had never been conveyed to him by his senses? I believe there are few but will be of the opinion that he can; and this may serve as a proof that the simple ideas are not always, in every instance, derived from the correspondent impressions; though this instance is so singular, that it is scarcely worth observing, and does not merit that for it alone we should alter our general maxim. (1963, p. 21)

Hume pretty obviously wasn't much worried about this sort of case, and I think it's clear why he wasn't. Hume took it for granted that even if not quite *all* sensory concepts are learned from experience, still all *non*-sensory are *eo ipso* complex. It's only when you put the idea that some simple concepts may not be learned from experience together with the idea that *very* non-sensory concepts (like HORSE or ELECTRON) might be simple that you get a mechanism capable, in principle, of generating devastating counterexamples to the Empiricist program.

Indeed, if you put the mental chemistry idea together with the idea that *any* (de facto lexical) concept might be simple, you get the total *abandonment* of the Empiricist program. What you're left with is an account of concept attainment that is compatible with even the more ardent Nativism—for example, with Descartes' view of concept attainment.

The Cartesian story, you'll remember, is that even logically complex (e.g. definable) concepts like TRIANGLE are typically acquired in consequence of processes of stimulus triggering. But, as we've just seen, this account can perfectly well be told couched in Mill's language of mental chemistry. I proceed to tell it so couched: "There are experiences which causally occasion the attainment of TRIANGLE. These often include (though perhaps they needn't) seeing things that are roughly triangular; they also often include (though perhaps they needn't) the prior attainment of such relatively elementary concepts as LINE, ANGLE, FIGURE, and the rest. Even, however, if the acquisition of TRIANGLE is *causally* contingent upon the prior acquisition of these elementary concepts, still the concept TRIANGLE may be *psychologically* simple. This is because, by assumption, it arises from the prior concepts by mental chemistry, not by construction. The fact that getting TRIANGLE requires previously getting LINE—if it *is* a fact; which it probably isn't—is thus a *brute* fact, and it's an *accident* that it corresponds to the *definability* of TRIANGLE in terms of LINE. For all that the Cartesian—or the mental chemistry —account requires, the brute fact might just as well have been that getting TRIANGLE is causally dependent upon first getting ELE-PHANT. If getting TRIANGLE depends on first getting LINE, that is *not* because observations of lines occur in the induction base for hypotheses about the definition of TRIANGLES; it's because the principles of mental chemistry are such that experiences of lines trigger the availability of LINE and the availability of LINE triggers the availability of TRIANGLE."

To say that it's a brute fact that TRIANGLE is ontogenetically dependent upon LINE (or, for that matter, upon ELEPHANT) is to emphasize that mental chemistry—unlike "concept learning" —requires no rational relation between a concept and its causes. It isn't, of course, to say that it's an uninteresting fact, and it certainly isn't to say that it's an inexplicable fact. What, on the mental chemistry view, explains the contingency of a concept upon its causes is, of course, the principles of mental chemistry, which is to say, the innate structure of the mind.

If this last equivalence (of the principles of mental chemistry with the innate structure of the mind) isn't obvious, that may be because we have thus far followed Mill in avoiding saying anything about *what the principles of mental chemistry are.* It's a bit curious—and it's a fact that Mill observes in the *Logic*—that while mental chemistry theorists paid quite a lot of attention to the nature of association, there's just nothing in the literature about what kinds of "fusions" of concepts mental chemistry allows. However, even the briefest consideration of what such a theory would be like suffices to show how profound the nativistic commitments of the idea actually are.

To begin with, the analogy to molecular bonding is really quite misleading; a half-hearted attempt to have it both ways. The point about molecules is that you can't (or couldn't in Mill's day) predict the properties of compounds from the properties of their elements; whereas, Mill's point about putatively complex ideas is explicitly that they don't *have* elements, that they are psychologically simple. So, then, what a theory of *mental* chemistry must do is determine the properties of concepts as a function of the properties of (not their elements but) their *causes.*

We can think of the principles of such a theory as determining a mapping from, say, concepts available onto concepts attained; in particular, we can think of the theory as enumerating the prior mental states that are causally necessary and sufficient for triggering each concept that mental chemistry gives rise to. It the theory is true, then the mind is a realization of that function. The fact that the mind is structured in the way it is explains the (brute) fact that the availability of some concepts automatically gives rise to the availability of others, just as it's the way the mind is structured which explains the brute fact that sensory stimuli trigger the sensations that they do, or that associations form on the occasions when they do. What Mill ought to say about the principles of mental chemistry is precisely what we've seen Hume did say about the associative principles: they are "original qualities of human nature."

Mill's Rationalism is historically interesting because it illuminates how short the path is from the idea that most de facto lexical concepts are simple to the idea that most de facto lexical concepts are innate. But it is also interesting because it's an interesting kind of Rationalism. I spoke of a theory of mental chemistry as a function from (triggering) concepts available onto (triggered) concepts attained. I now want to emphasize that there is nothing in the idea of mental chemistry—or, for that matter, in Mill's exposition of the idea—which constrains the *kinds* of concepts that can enter into the sorts of triggering relations that a mental chemistry specifies. In principle, mental chemistry could determine such relations among quite abstract concepts—for example, ones whose relation to experience is mediated by long chains of theory. I think this is an important idea, since *any* form of Rationalism must take into account the appearance of cumulation in the development of a conceptual repertoire, both in ontogeny and in the history of science; and the notion that some concepts trigger others may provide a means of doing so.

If you take triggering to be a relation between *stimuli* and concepts, and if you assume that practically all de facto lexical concepts are uncomplex, then you seem to be committed to saying that it's an *accident* (either of the history of the individual or of intellectual history) that we get our concepts in the order that we do. For example, you seem to have to say that, given the right distribution of impinging stimuli, children might perfectly well acquire ELECTRON before they acquire NOSE (or, indeed, before they acquire any middle-sized object concepts). Similarly, you seem to have to say that it's only an artifact of the arrangement of the triggers that we developed our geometry before our topology, or that mechanics was around before the quantum theory.

Now, of course, it *is* true that priorities in the development of the conceptual repertoire to some extent reflect arbitrary, local arrangements of the ambient stimulation. The concept SNOW is, presumably, available to children in Lapland earlier than it's available to those in Africa. And it's possible to believe that the history of astronomy would have been quite different if, on the one hand, the Earth had been the only planet in the Solar System (no data about retrograde motions) or if, on the other hand, the stars had been close enough to exhibit visible parallax. The problem is that it's hard to believe that *all* the facts about the order of development of conceptual repertoires are like these. It seems plausible that some such facts would hold over quite a wide range of possible environments because they in some sense reflect dependencies among the concepts acquired. The empiricist has a model for the existence of such dependencies, since he allows that some concepts are constructed out of others. Whether his model predicts the *right* dependencies is, no doubt, an open question: but at least it has parameters that accommodate the phenomenon in principle. If concept C is a construct out of concept A, then presumably the acquisition of C cannot precede the acquisition of A either in ontogeny or in the history of science.

But what if you're a Nativist and thus believe that definition and logical construction play a relatively small role in the specification of concepts? Can we imagine mechanisms for accounting for a "normal" order of attainment even among concepts that are viewed as primitive and hence unstructured? Or, to put the question slightly differently, can we imagine principles that determine priorities in the acquisition of a conceptual repertoire other than by appeal to the facts of semantic entailment? What follows is pure speculation.

You might think of the triggering structure of the mind as *layered,* the attainment of some primitive concepts being the effect of (hence never prior to) the attainment of others. The facts of conceptual development in ontogeny and science would thus reflect—inter alia—the orderings imposed by this triggering structure. Since, *pace* the Empiricist, it would *not* reflect the order of logical construction, it would follow that there are logically possible organisms which discover (e.g.) their set theory before their arithmetic; only that we—given the nature of our psychology —are not among them. (Nor, it seems, are our children; *vide* the apparent failure of constructivist attempts to teach these subjects in reverse natural order.)

The idea is, then, that while all primitive concepts are ipso facto triggered, there is nevertheless a hierarchy of triggers, and it is *this* hierarchy, rahter than the hierarchy of semantic entailments, which predicts the observed order of concept attainment. What's inconvenient about this idea is, of course, that we can't determine the structure of the triggering hierarchy in the way that we can determine the structure of the logical hierarchy—viz. a priori, by doing conceptual analysis. The hierarchical relations among triggers might, in principle, *go any way at all,* depending upon how the mind is put together. Whether there's any practical use to the notion of a triggering hierarchy thus depends on whether we can find anything interesting to say about the interconceptual relations that it specifies; in particular, about which concepts are at which levels.

I think that we are, in fact, in a position to make some interesting guesses. I think we are in a position to argue like this: there are two, logically independent kinds of criteria which lowest (or, anyhow, low*er*) level concepts in a triggering hierarchy ought to exhibit. If it turns out that there *is* a set of concepts which satisfy *both* these criteria (and if not all primitive concepts satisfy them), then that suggests there's something of substance to be said about the structure of the hierarchy. And if it turns out that the concepts that are basic-level by *these* criteria are not the ones that are basic-level by the criterion of logical construction, then we have the groundwork for an empirical decision between the Empiricist and Nativist accounts of concept acquisition.

The two criteria which I think it's reasonable to suppose that basic-level primitive concepts ought, in general, to satisfy are these: they should exhibit relatively *high accessibility,* both in ontogeny and in intellectual history; and they should be readily acquired by ostensive definition. I take it that the propriety of the first of these criteria is self-evident: Primitive concepts at the lower levels of a triggering hierarchy would be those whose acquisition requires relatively little mediation by *other* concepts previously attained. That is, the triggers for lower-level concepts should be largely experiential. So, given an appropriately rich environment, basic-level primitive concepts should be acquired early, and in no environment should they be acquired later than primitive concepts at higher levels.

The appropriateness of the second criterion may be less evident. I'm assuming, as a rough rule of thumb, that ostensive definability varies inversely with conceptual mediation: that the more easily a concept is ostensively introduced, the less the acquisition of that concept depends (causally) upon other concepts being acquired first. Quine has made something like this point, though in another context to be sure. He suggests that the notion *observation sentence* is to be reconstructed by appeal to the notion of ostensive definability, as follows: "the more observational a sentence is, the more nearly its use can be mastered ostensively" (1970, pp. 5-6). The idea is that the observation language is comprised of terms whose application is *not* mediated by theory; hence terms that can be learned without the mastery of the theoretical vocabulary; hence terms that can be learned by ostension.

This is a rule of thumb and should be taken with a grain of salt, for, of course, what you can learn ostensively does depend on how much *else* you know; there's a sense in which physicists can learn "Beta particle" by ostension precisely because the attainment of the concept *is* mediated by the theory they've acquired (see, for example, Hanson, 1961). Still, it's reasonable to believe that ostensively acquiring BETA PARTICLE requires a lot more laying of groundwork than, say, ostensively acquiring TABLE or NOSE or RUNS or WEEPS. I emphasize that I'm claiming this *not* on epistemological grounds, still less on the grounds that BETA PARTICLE is a construct out of concepts that subtend middle-sized objects. I'm claiming only that, in point of psychological fact, any reasonable scale of ease of ostensive definability would rank TABLE as easier than BETA PARTICLE—hence that, if ease of ostensive definability does in fact vary inversely with extent of conceptual mediation, then TABLE ought to be lower in the triggering hierarchy (more basic) than BETA PARTICLE.

The second caveat is that on the present view (as contrasted with Quine's), ostensive learning is *not* an inductive process, it's a triggering process. It is, however, easy to mistake this kind of concept triggering for induction (i.e. for "concept learning" in the technical sense), for the following reason: in concept learning, concepts are learned *from their instances,* whereas, according to the present view, in cases where basic concepts are ostensively introduced they are *triggered by their instances.* When you ostensively acquire CAT, you are acquiring a primitive concept which both subtends, and is triggered by, cats. We could, in fact, put the point like this: according to the present account of the triggering hierarchy, there ought to be a rough equivalence between: (a) the basic-level concepts, (b) concepts whose acquisition is triggered by environmental stimulation relatively uncontaminated by the triggering effects of concepts previously attained, (c) concepts that are normally ostensively acquired, and (d) concepts that are normally triggered by things that they subtend.[9]

Now then, can we find a class of concepts which exhibit relatively high ontogenetic and historical accessibility, on the one hand, and relatively high ostensive definability on the other? If we can, then it's reasonable to suppose that they are basic concepts and the notion of a triggering hierarchy is, to that extent, empirically vindicated.

It seems to me that one of the most interesting facts currently available for constraining theories of concept acquisition is that these criteria do indeed pick out the same sorts of cases. In particular, as a number of psychologists have pointed out (see especially Brown, 1958; Rosch et al (1976)), there seems to be a natural ontogenetic bias in favor of concepts at what you might describe as intermediate levels of logical abstractness. Consider, for example, such implication hierarchies as: Poodle→dog→mammal→animal→thing. If you suppose that lexical concepts are normally constructs out of their semantic entailments, then you might suppose that what children do is: they first learn THING, out of which they construct ANIMAL, out of which they construct MAMMAL, out of which they construct DOG, out of which they construct POODLE. Or, alternatively, they first learn POODLE, out of which they abstract DOG, out of which they abstract MAMMAL, out of which they abstract ANIMAL, out of which they abstract THING. The idea that concepts have internal structure can be (and has been) accommodated to either of these predicted orderings.

In fact what happens is neither. Rather, children tend to enter this hierarchy at the level of DOG and, as it were, work down to the subtended species and up to the subtending ones. Similarly, they get TABLE before they get either FURNITURE or END TABLE; they get CAR before they get either VEHICLE or VW; they get HOUSE before they get BUILDING or BUNGALOW, and so on across dozens and dozens of examples. Ontogenetic priority seems to go along, in these cases, with a cluster of other traits: the early attained concepts are often the most abstract members of their implication hierarchy which subtend objects of approximately similar shapes; they tend to be freely lexicalized; the words which express them tend to be relatively high frequency, *and,* or so it seems to me, *they tend to be especially readily acquired by ostension.* For example, I take it that you could teach "dog" ostensively to a child who had not learned "animal" or "poodle"; but I bet you'd have a beastly time trying to teach "poodle" to a child who hadn't acquired "dog", or "animal" to a child who hadn't prior mastery of some animal words at the same level of abstraction as "dog".

It bears emphasis that this coincidence, rough and ready though it doubtless is, is really quite remarkable. There's surely no *logical* reason why HOUSE should be earlier acquired and more easily ostensively defined than BUILDING or BUNGALOW. Say, if you like, that the ease of ostensive definition explains the ontogenetic priority; but notice, if you do say this, that the explanation is quite vacuous: it leaves open the question why the concepts should differ in ostensive definability. The present proposal is that both facts are consequences of the structure of the triggering hierarchy and that the structure of the triggering hierarchy is a brute fact—i.e. that it's part of the aboriginal structure of the mind.

I want to draw two morals: the first is that the range of concepts that the criteria of ontogenetic availability and ostensive definability pick out as basic does not, so far as anybody knows, parallel the order of logical abstraction, and this fact is very hard to explain on the concepts-are-logical-constructs sort of story. If you take the Empiricist account really seriously, so that lexical concepts are typically (not just constructs but) constructs out of a *sensory* base, you make a travesty of the ontogenetic data. It just isn't true that (e.g.) color and shape concepts are learned early, or that they are easily ostensively defined. Most children are still having trouble with "red" long after they have COOKIE and DADDY and DOGGIE under their belts. Nor is this simply a problem about the acquisition of vocabulary, since young children have terrible trouble learning color-based discriminations in *non-*verbal versions of the concept learning task (see, for example, Carey 1978). And, even if you give up the idea that basic concepts are epistemologically specifiable, there isn't any way that I can see of predicting the order of ontogenetic accessibility from the facts of semantic entailment. What seems to be got first, and what seems to be readily acquired from instances, is, roughly, middle-size-object/event concepts of middle-level abstractness.

The second moral is that (*pace* Quine) the ordering established by the criteria of early attainment and ready ostensive definability isn't the ordering of grades of theoreticity either. Consider such folk-psychological concepts as ANGRY, SAD, HAPPY, etc. I think there's no doubt that these are acquired early, that they must have been part of the universal prehistory of our species, and that they are easily introduced by ostension. This *isn't* to say, however, that they are relatively peripheral in any ordering of the concepts by *explanatory* centrality. If you want to say how such concepts are related to overt behavior—what role they play in folk-explanations of what organisms observably *do*—you have to tell a *very* long story; one which analytical philosophers of mind are still trying to unravel. The vocabulary of folk psychology is theory vocabulary, but it's learned early and taught ostensively for all that.

The point is that the structure of the triggering hierarchy probably isn't natural from any *philosophical* point of view, though it may be quite natural from the point of view of an ethologist. If a social organism is to survive its infancy, it better have ready access to the concepts that structure its implicit theory of the mental states of conspecific adults; the triggering constraints on such concepts had better not require the prior acquisition of a rich conceptual repertoire. There is, then, a *sense* in which basic concepts are, ipso facto, close to experience: but it's *not* the sense of "logically constructed out of concepts which subtend experiences," and it's *not* the sense of "peripheral on the scale from observation to theory." Whichever of these ways you read it, the idea that, as it were, ontogeny recapitulates epistemology, is *hopeless*. On the contrary, the only sense in which basic concepts are close to experience is this: *basic concepts are the ones that are normally triggered by encounters with their instances* (whereas the triggering of nonbasic primitive concepts is mediated by the previously attained conceptual repertoire; and, of course, complex concepts—e.g. phrasal concepts—are learned by logical construction). If, therefore, you want to know which concepts are in fact normally triggered by encounters with their instances, you can't find out by doing conceptual analysis, and you can't find out by doing epistemology. *You have to go and look.*

"Some Rationalist you are," you may now want to say. "Why, you're nothing but a closet skeptic. For isn't your view really that the facts of theory construction and of concept attainment are precisely irrational? That the history of our science and the ontogeny of our concepts, is simply the reflexive manifestation of genetic structure under the impact of environmental stimulation? What reason do you have for supposing that our concepts *apply*— that our science is *true*—if warranted inference doesn't mediate their attainment?"

I have three answers to make. The first is that the *truth* of our science doesn't depend on how we came to discover it, only on its correspondence to the facts. The origin of a concept is, no doubt, a poor predictor of its warrant; so you should establish warrant by argument to the best explanation, not by committing the genetic fallacy. A Rationalist would predict that the history of theory construction, and of the ontogeny of our concepts, might well be a matter of sudden insights and flashes of intuition; of inspiration, in short. And that seems plausible enough, given the anecdotes. What clever people tell us about how they get good ideas is that ripeness is all: you expose yourself to the play of experience, and you keep your fingers crossed. In short, what clever people tell us is that new concepts do not emerge by induction and logical construction from the repertoire of concepts perviously attained. My point is that what clever people tell us makes perfectly good ethological sense and affects the truth of our science not one whit, so long as the traditional distinction between the logic of discovery and the logic of confirmation is scrupulously observed.

Nor need a Rationalist deny that the character of the concepts we entertain depends upon the character of the world we live in. No simple concept is available unless it is triggered, and while the function from triggers onto the concepts they release is innately specified, it is the way the world is that determines which triggers we in fact encounter. Our innate endowment determines which worlds we can, in principle, understand; but only the interaction of that endowment with the stimulations we receive determines which science we actually develop.

However, I do plead guilty to this: if the trigger-concept pairings are innately specified, and if the principles of construction are too, then the space of concepts that are available-in-principle is innately closed, and we have no guarantee that the concepts required to build a true science are situated in that space. But, though I have to admit this, so too—as far as I can tell—does everybody else. For example, if you think the space of concepts is the closure of the sensory concepts under the mechanisms of association, then you must hold that only worlds which can be described by sensory concepts and constructs out of them can, in principle, be the objects of our science. Indeed, I can't make much sense of the idea that our psychology could be so arranged that we would be able to develop the right science *however the world might be.* And, even if that idea does make sense, why on earth should anyone suppose that it is true? If that is skepticism, then I am quite prepared to live with it.

Everybody's a Rationalist in the long run. Everybody accepts the requirement for a primitive conceptual basis; everybody accepts the requirement for logical construction of infinitely many phrasal concepts; everybody accepts that primitive concepts are psychologically simple; everybody accepts that simply concepts are unlearned. What distinguishes Descarte's kind of Rationalism from, say, Locke's—insofar as they differ in their views about concept attainment—is an issue over how big the primitive basis actually is. Soi-disant Empiricists are inclined, in this respect, to niggle.

I see no interesting sense in which the size of the primitive basis is an a priori question—we immediately recognize it as ethological in the case of all *other* species—except insofar as the failure of a variety of reductionist programs in philosophy indicates that the primitive basis must be a lot bigger than was once supposed. Surely all basic concepts must be primitive, just as Locke and Hume maintained. Since epistemologically grounded programs of reduction always fail, it would seem to be reasonable to accept a cluster of *non*-epistemological criteria as prima facie indices of membership in the conceptual basis: ostensive definability, early acquisition in ontogeny and in intellectual history, lexicalization, and universality and relative independence from prior concept attainment are among these indices, and, very likely, research will turn up lots of others. Current evidence suggests that there must be thousands of concepts which satisfy these criteria: inter alia, concepts which subtend middle-sized objects and events. This population of *basic* concepts represents a very conservative estimate of the population of *primitive* concepts, since the former includes only the bottom level of the triggering hierarchy, whereas the latter includes all concepts that are psychologically simple. Since all primitive concepts must ipso facto be unlearned, it looks as though the innate structure of the mind is going to be very rich indeed according to the present proposal. Our ethology promises to be quite interesting even if our developmental psychology turns out to be a little dull.

I don't expect you to be convinced. I am not convinced myself. For one thing, the evidence that nonsensory lexicalized concepts are typically unstructured would have to be *much* better than it now is before it would be rational to consider scrapping the Empiricist program in its entirety. I'll settle for this: to have convinced you that the issue about conceptual innateness is in the relevant sense empirical; to have convinced you that, in principle at least, relevant evidence can be drawn from a wide variety of research domains; to have convinced you that the question of the existence of logical and psychological structure in de facto lexical concepts is very close to the heart of the matter; and to have convinced you that, in the current state of our cognitive science, it is far from being an open-and-shut decision in favor of the concept learning model.

It seems to me that Anglo-American theorizing about concept attainment has, for several hundred years now, restricted itself to the consideration of a very small range of theoretical options. It also seems to me that the results have not been extraordinarily encouraging. Perhaps it is time to throw open our windows, kick over our traces, upset our applecarts and otherwise wantonly mix our metaphors. If we *are* going to have a cognitive science, we are going to have to learn to learn from our mistakes. When you keep putting questions to Nature and Nature keeps saying "no", it is not unreasonable to suppose that somewhere among the things you believe there is something that isn't true.

Notes

Introduction

1. Collins, in a recent (1979) paper, has called attention to the following consideration: though beliefs are causes and beliefs have truth values, still it is possible to doubt that there is anything which is both a cause and truth-valuable. The idea is that, in the sense of belief in which beliefs have effects, they are mental particulars; so that John's belief that P is numerically distinct from Jim's unless John = Jim. Whereas, in the sense in which beliefs have truth-values, they are abstract objects (e.g. propositions), so that if both John and Jim believe that it will rain, they share a belief; there is a belief that they have in common.

This distinction is both traditional and at least arguably correct, but it does very little to alter the general situation. Suppose that it is propositions that bear truth values. Then part of our theory of propositional attitudes will have to be an account of the relation that holds between me and a proposition when the proposition is one of the ones that I believe. So far as I can see, that relation will have to be mediated by a mental representation (viz. a mental particular to which causal properties are ascribed.) If that sort of treatment is correct, then the mental representation will, in turn, have the semantic property (not of being truth-valuable but) of expressing a proposition. So, on this model, there will after all be things that have both semantic properties and causal roles, and the question how anything with a causal role can have semantic properties will still have to be asked and answered. (It will have to be asked—and answered—anyhow, since token *sentences*—e.g. *this* token sentence— have both causal roles and semantic properties.) If you think this is an artifact of the model, you need some alternative way of construing the relation that holds between a proposition and someone who believes the proposition—a construal which, in particular, does not rely on the notion of mental representation. I know of none such that seems remotely plausible.

2. Dennett likes it with a "t," whereas I have generally favored the spelling "intensional" for the concept that's connected with opacity, reserving "inten-tional" for contexts connected with intent. I of course preserve the author's orthography in quotations.

3. I'm not, of course, claiming—or attributing to functionalism the claim—that *no* belief contexts are to be dispositionally construed; only that such construals don't hold in the general case. They seem, for example, to be quite beside the point in such examples as "It was John's belief that there was a fire which caused him to remark that there was a fire."

4. See Forster, (1976). There is another story (see Morton, 1969), but it's longer to tell and it leads to precisely the same philosophical moral; *all* the stories that cognitive psychologists tell lead to precisely the same philosophical moral.

5. This puzzle has, by the way, a provenance. Russell once held that to believe that P or Q is to hesitate between believing that P and believing that Q. But, as practically everyone has remarked, that won't do since you can be-lieve that P or Q because you (a) believe that P, and (b) have made the relevant inference. Nor does it work the other way around. You can be hesitating between believing P and believing Q because you are hesitating between, for example, believing P, Q or R. To get "x believes P or Q" from "x is hesitating between believing P and believing Q," you need to add "and x believes that at least one of P and Q are true." That is, you have to add "x believes that P or Q."

6. It might be suggested that the combinatorial apparatus should be de-fined over propositions, so that propositional attitudes *are* read relationally, but without postulating mental representations among the relata. This, how-ever, doesn't help because we are now going to need a theory of the relation between believing that PvQ and the proposition that PvQ, and this relation will itself have to be determined by appeal to general combintorial principles. In particular, the state of believing that PvQ is going to have to be connected with the proposition that PvQ by principles which advert to the constituents of the former; and, again, neither believing that P nor believing that Q are constituents of believing that PvQ.

I. Functionalism and Realism

1. Operationalism and Ordinary Language

1. Philosophers of Wittgensteinian persuasion have sometimes heatedly denied that the term "behaviorism" is correctly applied to the view that logical connections of the above sort exist. We do not feel that very much hangs on using the term "behaviorism" as we do, but we are prepared to give some justification for our terminology. "Behaviorism" is, in the first instance, a term applied to a school of psychologists whose interest was in placing con-straints upon the conceptual equipment that might be employed in putative psychological explanations, but who were *not* particularly interested in the analysis of the mental vocabulary of ordinary language. The application of

this label to a philosopher bent upon this latter task must therefore be, to some extent, analogical. Granted that there has been some tendency for the term "behaviorism" to be preempted, even in psychology, for the position held by such *radical* behaviorists as Watson and Skinner, who require that all psychological generalizations be defined over observables, insofar as C. L. Hull can be classified as a behaviorist there seem to be grounds for our classification. Hull's view, as we understand it, is that mental predicates are in no sense "eliminable" in favor of behavioral predicates, but that it is a condition upon their coherent employment that they be severally related to behavioral predicates and that some of these relations be logical rather than empirical—a view that is strikingly similar to the one we attribute to Wittgenstein. Cf. Hull (1943).

2. In making references to Part I of Ludwig Wittgenstein's *Philosophical Investigations* (1953), cited here as *PI*, we shall give section numbers, e.g. (PI, § 13); to Part II, we shall give page numbers, e.g. (PI, p. 220). In referring to his *The Blue and Brown Books* (1958), cited here as *BB*, we give page numbers. References to his *Remarks on the Foundations of Mathematics* (1956), cited here as *RFM*, will include both part and section numbers, e.g. (RFM, II, § 26).

3. Cf. "Let us consider what we call an 'exact' explanation in contrast with this one. Perhaps something like drawing a chalk line round an area? Here it strikes us at once that the line has breadth. So a color-edge would be more exact. But has this exactness still got a function here: isn't the engine idling? And remember too that we have not yet defined what is to count as over-stepping this exact boundary; *how, with what instrument, it is to be established*" (*PI*, § 88; italics ours). Cf. also *RFM*, I, § 5.

4. Malcolm (1958), p. 65.

5. Moore (1959), pp. 266–267.

6. Albritton (1959).

7. Note Wittgenstein's suggestion that we can "give the phrase 'unconscious pain' sense by fixing experiential criteria for the case in which a man has pain and doesn't know it" (BB, p. 55). Cf., also: "If however we do use the expression 'the thought takes place in the head,' we have given this expression its meaning by describing the experience which would justify the *hypothesis* that the thought takes place in our heads, by describing the experience which we wish to call observing thought in our brain" (*BB*, p. 8).

8. Adopted by the eleventh General International Conference on Weights and Measures in the fall of 1960.

9. *RFM*, II, § 24; III, § 29; and I, Appendix I, § 15–16. See also C. S. Chihara (1963).

10. Cf., "The person of whom we say 'he has pain' is, *by the rules of the game*, the person who cries, contorts his face, etc." (*BB*, p. 68, italics ours).

11. Shoemaker (1963), pp. 167–168.

12. Malcolm (1959), pp. 60–61.

13. Cf., "'Before I judge that two images which I have are the same, I must recognize them as the same.' . . . Only if I can express my recognition in some

other way, and if it is possible for someone else to teach me that 'same' is the correct word here" (PI, § 378).

14. Thus consider the following: "Up until the night I opened the door, I remembered my dreams. Soon after, I ceased to recall them. I still dreamed, but my waking consciousness concealed from itself what sleep revealed. If the recurrent nightmare of the iron fence awoke me, I recognized it. But if any other nightmare broke my sleep, I forgot what it was about by morning. And of all the other dreams I had during the night I remembered nothing" (Windham, 1963).

15. In *Dreaming,* Malcolm gives a number of arguments, not to be found in Wittgenstein's published writings, for the position that psychologists attempting to discover methods of measuring the duration of dreams must be using the term "dream" in a misleading and extraordinary way. For a reply to these arguments, see C. S. Chihara (1965). See also Putnam's criticism of Malcolm (1962).

16. The implausibility of this view is even more striking when Wittgenstein applies it in his philosophy of mathematics to arrive at the conclusion that every new theorem about a concept alters the concept or introduces a new concept. When the notion of conceptual change is allowed to degenerate this far, it is not easy to see that anything rides on the claim that a conceptual change has taken place. Cf. C. S. Chihara (1963).

17. P. M. Meehl and H. J. Cronbach (1956). We have followed Meehl and Cronbach's usage of the terms "reliability" and "validity" so that *reliability* is a measure of the correlation between criteria while *validity* is a measure of the correlation between a criterion and the construct whose presence it is supposed to indicate.

18. This point is susceptible of direct empirical ratification, for it can be demonstrated that in perceptual analysis, speech is analyzed into segments which correspond precisely to the segmentation assigned by a grammar.

19. Cf. Chomsky (1959).

20. Among the many psychological studies relevant to this point, the following are of special importance: Bartlett (1932); Piaget, (1928); Bruner (1958).

3. What Psychological States Are Not

1. If physicalism is the doctrine that psychological states are physical states, then we get two versions depending on whether we take "states" to refer to types or to tokens. The latter construal yields a weaker theory assuming that a token of type x may be identical to a token of type y even though x and y are distinct types. On this assumption, type physicalism clearly entails token physicalism, but not conversely.

The distinction between token identity theories and type identity theories has not been exploited in the case of behavioristic analyses. Unlike either version of physicalism, behaviorism is generally held as a semantic thesis, hence as a theory about logical relations between types. In the present paper, "physicalism" will mean *type* physicalism. When we talk about states, we will specify whether we mean types or tokens only when it is not clear from the context.

2. See Davidson (1970); Fodor (1968); Putnam (1965, 1966, 1967).

3. Not all philosophical behaviorists hold this view; philosophical behaviorism may be broadly characterized as the view that for each psychological predicate there is a behavioral predicate to which it bears a "logical relation." (See Fodor, 1968.) Thus the following view qualifies as behaviorist: all ascriptions of psychological predicates entail ascriptions of behavioral predicates, but not conversely. Though this form of behaviorism is not vulnerable to the present argument, the preceding ones are as effective against it as against biconditional forms of behaviorism.

4. See Putnam (1967, 1970).

5. See Davidson, (1963).

6. We do not intend our use of the traditional "disposition" terminology to commit us to the view that beliefs really are dispositions. (Rather, we would suggest that they are functional states in the broad sense suggested in section IV, below.)

7. The claim that organisms are probabilistic automata might be interestingly true even if *FSIT* is false—that is, even if psychological states do not correspond to machine table states. For example, it might turn out that some subset of the psychological states of an organism corresponds to a set of machine table states by which the rest of its psychology is determined. Or it might turn out that what corresponds to each machine table state is a *conjunction* of psychological states . . . , etc. Indeed, though the claim that any organism can be modeled by a probabilistic automaton is not interesting, the claim that for each organism there is a probabilistic automaton which is its *unique best* model *is* interesting. And this latter claim neither entails *FSIT* nor is it by any means obviously true.

In short, there are many ways in which it could turn out that organisms are automata in some sense *more* interesting than the sense in which everything is an automaton under some description. Our present point is that such eventualities, while they would be important, would not provide general conditions upon the type identification of psychological states in the way that *FSIT* attempts to do.

8. Very much "somehow." Obviously, believing P is not a constituent of believing PvQ in the same way that believing P is a constituent of believing P & Q. Equally obviously, there is some relation between believing P and believing PvQ, and a theory of belief will have to say what that relation is. For further discussion, see the Introduction to this volume, where this puzzle is resolved by appeal to the notion of mental representation.

4. Three Cheers for Propositional Attitudes

1. I use 'believe' as my paradigm of a verb of propositional attitude, but sometimes vary the verb to break the tedium. What I assume that all such verbs have in common (insofar as they engage the topic of this paper) is their tendency to establish opaque contexts. Opaque contexts are, for example,

those in which the substitution of coreferring expressions fails to preserve truth. That is a miserably imprecise characterization of the class of cases at issue, but no more precision is needed for the purposes at hand.

In this essay, I have followed Dennett's orthography: I use 'inten*sional*' to mean, in effect, *opaque,* and I use 'inten*tional*' to mean *opaque and psychological.* Some intensional contexts (e.g., modal ones) are thus nonintentional; but not vice versa.

2. It is worth noting (as Dennett and others have pointed out to me) that the closure of *belief* under entailment does *not* imply the transparency of such *other* propositional attitudes as, for example, remembering. Assume: *a remembers that P* and *a believes that P → a believes that Q.* It does not follow from these premises that a *remembers* that Q. Roughly, to get transparency of a propositional attitude, you need closure (under the relevant consequence relation) of *that very attitude.*

3. I am heavily indebted, in this paragraph and the next two, to some recent work of Brian Loar's. I wish to acknowledge this debt, but not to imply that Loar would agree with what I have to say here, or with the use I've made of his ideas, or, indeed, that he would wish to have anything to do with any of this.

II. Reduction and Unity of Science

5. Special Sciences

1. For expository convenience, I shall usually assume that sciences are about events in at least the sense that it is the occurrence of events that makes the laws of a science true. Nothing, however, hangs on this assumption.

2. The version of reductionism I shall be concerned with is a stronger one than many philosophers of science hold, a point worth emphasizing, since my argument will be precisely that it is too strong to get away with. Still, I think that what I shall be attacking is what many people have in mind when they refer to the unity of science, and I suspect (though I shan't try to prove it) that many of the liberalized versions of reductionism suffer from the same basic defect as what I shall take to be the classical form of the doctrine.

3. There is an implicit assumption that a science simply *is* a formulation of a set of laws. I think that this assumption is implausible, but it is usually made when the unity of science is discussed, and it is neutral so far as the main argument of this chapter is concerned.

4. I shall sometimes refer to 'the predicate which constitutes the antecedent or consequent of a law'. This is shorthand for 'the predicate such that the antecedent or consequent of a law consists of that predicate, together with its bound variables and the quantifiers which bind them'.

5. Oppenheim and Putnam (1958) argue that the social sciences probably *can* be reduced to physics assuming that the reduction proceeds via (individual) psychology. Thus, they remark, "in economics, if very weak assumptions are satisfied, it is possible to represent the way in which an individual orders his choices by means of an individual preference function. In terms of these

functions, the economist attempts to explain group phenomena, such as the market, to account for collective consumer behavior, to solve the problems of welfare economics, etc." (p. 17). They seem not to have noticed, however, that even if such explanations can be carried through, they would not yield the kind of *predicate-by-predicate* reduction of economics to psychology that Oppenheim and Putnam's own account of the unity of science requires.

Suppose that the laws of economics hold because people have the attitudes, motives, goals, needs, strategies, etc., that they do. Then the fact that economics is the way it is can be explained by reference to the fact that people are the way that they are. But it doesn't begin to follow that the typical predicates of economics can be reduced to the typical predicates of psychology. Since bridge laws entail biconditionals, P_1 reduces to P_2 only if P_1 and P_2 are at least coextensive. But while the typical predicates of economics subsume (e.g.) monetary systems, cash flows, commodities, labor pools, amounts of capital invested, etc., the typical predicates of psychology subsume stimuli, responses, and mental states. Given the proprietary sense of 'reduction' at issue, to reduce economics to psychology would therefore involve a very great deal more than showing that the economic behavior of groups is determined by the psychology of the individuals that constitute them. In particular, it would involve showing that such notions as *commodity, labor pool,* etc., can be reconstructed in the vocabulary of stimuli, responses and mental states and that, moreover, the predicates which affect the reconstruction express psychological kinds (viz., occur in the proper laws of psychology). I think it's fair to say that there is no reason at all to suppose that such reconstructions can be provided; prima facie there is every reason to think that they cannot.

6. This would be the case if higher organisms really are interestingly analogous to general purpose computers. Such machines exhibit no detailed structure-to-function correspondence over time; rather, the function subserved by a given structure may change from instant to instant depending upon the character of the program and of the computation being performed.

7. To rule out degenerate cases, we assume that n is large enough to yield correlations that are significant in the statistical sense.

8. I don't think there is any chance at all that this is true. What is more likely is that type identification for psychological states can be carried out in terms of the 'total states' of an abstract automaton which models the organism whose states they are. For discussion, see Chapter 3, above.

9. For the notion of projectability, see Goodman (1965).

6. Computation and Reduction

1. When I speak of intensionality, I shall usually have two related facts in mind. First, that psychological states (including, specifically, propositional attitudes) are typically individuated by reference to their *content;* second, that expressions that occur in linguistic contexts subordinate to verbs of propositional attitude are typically nonreferential. It is notoriously hard to say how, precisely, the first of these facts is to be construed or what, precisely,

the relation between the two facts is. Some of the discussion in this paper is tangent to those issues, but I shall dodge them whenever I can. I shall not, in particular, be attempting anything so ambitious as a general theory of intensionality.

2. Quine (1960), Davidson (1970), and Dennett (1971) are perhaps the best examples of influential physicalists to whom this charge does *not* apply.

3. The sketch of classical reductionism I have just given is very inadequate from a number of points of view. Nothing in the following discussion will exploit its inadequacies, however, and it would take considerable space to do justice to the details of the proposal.

4. I think it was a pervasive and characteristic error in positivistic thinking to infer the unity of science from the unity of the subject matter of science; viz. the epistemological thesis from the ontological one. However that may be, it is easy to find passages in the positivist literature in which the former doctrine is espoused in no uncertain terms. Thus Hempel (1949, p. 382) wrote, "The division of science into different areas rests exclusively on differences in research procedures and direction of interest; *one must not regard it as a matter of principle. On the contrary, all the branches of science are in principle of one and the same nature; they are branches of the unitary science, physics.*" (Emphasis Hempel's.) I should add that Hempel has since disavowed many of the ideas in that paper, and I do not intend to suggest that the passage I have quoted is indicative of his present views.

5. The experiences that lead to the acquisition of the rules of English are, normally, observations of utterances that formally instantiate the rules of English; there is, in that sense, a connection between the content of what is learned when one learns English and the content of the experiences that occasion the learning, and it would be a grievous error for a theory of learning to miss that connection. The equal and opposite error would be to try to parlay such connections of content into conceptual necessities, as, I think, some "ordinary language" philosophers have been inclined to do. It is not logically necessary in any useful sense of "logic" that hearing English is normally causally sufficient for speaking English; surely there are possible worlds in which it is normally causally sufficient for speaking Urdu.

6. The "prima facie" is important. For, of course, one can imagine a case in which someone knows something from which it follows (deductively or plausibly) that if small camels are brown then elephants are gray. In this case, though not only in this case, the fixation of the belief that elephants are gray by putative experiences of brown camels need not be arbitrary and might (at least to that extent) count as learning. A serious attempt to distinguish between learning and mere causal fixation of belief would, in short, need to work with a far deeper notion of "nonarbitrariness" than the examples so far might suggest. I am not, however, trying to draw such a distinction here; only to give a rough indication of the direction in which it lies. (The present case is, by the way, just a "Gettier example" transferred from "knows" to "learns"; see Gettier, 1963.)

7. I do not suppose we can generally identify the internal representation

that the subject assigns the stimulus with the representation he would (or could) supply if asked. Nor do I suppose this point needs, by now, to be argued.

8. I have used this example throughout as a paradigm of a generalization about relations between mental states that appears, prima facie, to be statable only by reference to their contents. I like this example because it is so pedestrian; it is hard to see how any psychology of learning could fail to have some such principle among its tenets. But I do not want to suggest that such examples are hard to come by. On the contrary, they are the cognitive psychologist's stock in trade. The contingencies that cognitive psychologists try to articulate are precisely those in which the contents of mental states are dependent or independent variables, or both.

9. This is to put it very roughly. We shall see what it comes to in more detail as we go along.

10. The notion that the (syntactic) objects of verbs of propositional attitudes are (semantically) fused expressions (or, what comes to pretty much the same thing, that verbs of propositional attitude must be read "non-relationally") is one that a number of philosophers have flirted with, either in the context of discussions of Leibniz's Law problems about the mind/body identity theory or in the (intimately related) context of worries about the ontological commitments of psychological ascriptions. It is not clear to me that anybody actually holds the fusion theory of propositional attitudes, but for discussions in which that option is contemplated, see Quine (1960), Nagel (1965), and Dennett (1971). The term "fusion" is borrowed from Dennett.

11. For that matter, the canonical counterpart of 'John takes himself to see a gray elephant' will have no relation (other than the reference to John) to the canonical counterpart of 'John takes himself to see an elephant,' even though (one might have thought) taking oneself to see a gray elephant *is* taking oneself to see an elephant (inter alia). If, in short, the theory wants to represent these states as connected, it will have to do so by specific stipulation; e.g., by taking some such principle as 'x takes-himself-to-see-a-gray-elephant $\rightarrow$ x takes-himself-to-see-an-elephant' as a nonlogical axiom. Fused representations are, to put it mildly, semantically imperspicuous.

12. By contrast, seeing a gray elephant is not being related to a formula, it is being related to an elephant. The present proposal concerns the construal of psychological verbs whose (syntactic) object is read opaquely. I have nothing at all to say about the notoriously difficult question of how to construe such verbs when their objects are read transparently.

13. In fact, it shows less, since it would do, for these purposes, if every organism had a language and the languages were intertranslatable insofar as the mental states of organisms overlap. It is no news, of course, that issues of translation and issues of the proper treatment of propositional attitudes tend to merge.

14. I discover, very belatedly, that an account in some respects quite like this one was once proposed by Sellars (1956). Sellars's work seems remarkably

prescient in light of (what I take to be) the methodological presuppositions of contemporary cognitive psychology.

15. I want to reemphasize that I am *not* denying that the (putative) neurological sentence tokens will satisfy *some physical descriptions or other,* just as the present sentence token satisfies some physical description or other. The question is whether their *physical* descriptions will turn out to be construable as *structural* descriptions which individuate the sentence types that the tokens belong to. (The corresponding question for natural language tokens is, approximately: does a formant analysis of an utterance represent its logical syntax. To which the answer is, of course, "resoundingly, no!")

16. Of course the merely notional status of propositional attitudes does not *follow* just from the observation that mental ascriptions are not entailed by physical ascriptions. What follows from that is only that behaviorism is false and physicalism is not better than contingently true. To get the result that propositional attitudes are fictions one needs to add some such premise as that their ascription would not be justified *unless* it followed from physics. I do not know how, precisely, such a premise would be formulated or how it could be defended.

It is worth mentioning, by the way, that the logical independence of mental and physical statements goes in both directions and has supported dubious arguments both ways. It used to be claimed that tables and chairs are notional on the grounds that physical object statements are not entailed by statements about percepts. Ho hum!

17. For example, internal representations must be at least as differentiated as the contents of propositional attitudes if they are to play the role that we have cast them for in individuating the contents of propositional attitudes. This is a strong condition; one that is not satisifed, e.g., by English orthographic sequences, since the latter do not constitute an ambiguity-free notation.

III. Intensionality and Mental Representation

7. Propositional Attitudes

1. I shall have nothing at all to say about knowing, discovering, recognizing, or any other of the "factive" attitudes. The justification for this restriction is worth discussing, but not here. (see below, Chapter 9).

2. I haven't space to discuss here the idea that 'John believes' should be construed as an operator on 'it's raining'. Suffice it (a) that it's going to be hard to square that account with such observations as I-b below; and (b) that it seems quite implausible for such sentences as 'John believes what Mary said' (and what Mary said might *be* that it's raining). In general, the objects of propositional-attitude verbs exhibit the syntax of object-noun phrases, which is just what the operator account would not predict.

3. I assume that this is approximately correct: given a sentence of the syntactic form $NP_1 \ (V \ (NP_2))$, V expresses a relation iff NP_1 and NP_2 refer. So, for present purposes, the question whether 'believes' expresses a relation in 'John believes it's raining' comes down to the question whether there are

such things as objects of belief. I shan't, therefore, bother to distinguish among these various ways of putting the question in the discussion which follows.

4. Of course, it might refer in virtue of a relation between Mary and something other than a voice. 'John is taller than the average man' isn't true in virtue of a relation between John and the average man ('the average man' doesn't refer). But the sentence is relational for all that. It's for this sort of reason that such principles as the one announced in note 3 hold only to a first approximation.

5. Note that verbs of propositional attitude are transparent, in this sense, only when their objects are *complements;* one can't infer 'there is something Ponce de Leon sought' from 'Ponce de Leon sought the Fountain of Youth'. It may, however, be worth translating 'seek' to 'try to find' to save the generalization. This would give us: 'Ponce de Leon tried to find the Fountain of Youth', which does, I suppose, entail that there is something that Ponce de Leon tried (viz., tried to do; viz., to find the Fountain of Youth).

Also, to say that *EG* applies *to* the complement of verbs of PA is, of course, not to say that it applies *in* the complement of verbs of PA. 'John wants to marry Marie of Rumania' implies that there is something that John wants (viz., to marry Marie of Rumania); it notoriously does *not* imply that there is someone whom John wants to marry (see III below).

6. Fusion has been contemplated as a remedy for untransparency in several philosophical contexts; see Goodman (1968); Dennett (1969); Nagel (1965). Note: 'contemplated', not 'embraced'.

7. 3 is not a point about *EG*. On the fusion view, there's no representation of the fact that 'the belief that Sam is nice' is about Sam even when 'belief' and 'about' are both construed *opaquely.*

8. Defining 'correspondent' gets complicated where verbs of PA take *transformed* sentences as their objects, but the technicalities needn't concern us here. Suffice it that we want the correspondent of 'John wants to leave' to be 'John leaves', the correspondent of 'John objects to Mary and Bill being elected' to be 'Mary and Bill are elected', etc.

9. I am assuming that two sentences with correspondents of *different* logico-syntactic form cannot assign the same (opaque) belief, and someone might wish to challenge this; consider 'John believes that Mary bit Bill' and 'John believes that Bill was bitten by Mary'. This sort of objection is serious and will be accommodated later on.

10. In speaking of Carnap's theory, I don't wish to imply that Carnap would endorse the uses to which I'm putting it; quite the contrary, I should imagine.

11. Where *F* might be thought of as a function from (e.g., English) sentences onto internal formulae.

12. Assuming as we may, but now needn't, do that all beliefs are expressible in English. It is, of course, a consequence of the present view that all the beliefs we can entertain are expressible in the internal code.

13. The notion that the apprehension of propositions is mediated by

linguistic objects is not entirely foreign even to the Platonistic tradition. Church says: ". . . the preference of (say) seeing over *understanding* as a method of observation seems to me capricious. For just as an opaque body may be seen, so a concept may be understood or grasped . . . In both cases the observation is not direct but through intermediaries . . . linguistic expressions in the case of the concept" (1951a). See also the discussion in Dummett (1973, pp. 156–57).

14. All of the following helped: Professors Ned Block, Noam Chomsky, Dan Dennett, Hartrey Field, Janet Dean Fodor, Keith Lehrer and Brian Loar. Many thanks.

8. *Tom Swift and His Procedural Grandmother*

1. By 'classical semantics' I'll refer to the tradition of Frege, Tarski, Carnap, and contemporary model theory. What this picks out is at best a loose consensus, but it will do for the purposes at hand.

2. Compiling doesn't, normally, take you *directly* into ML; normally there are inter-levels of representation between the language in which you talk to the machine and the language in which the machine computes. This doesn't matter for our purposes, however, since compiling won't be semantic interpretation unless each of the representations in the series from the input language to ML translates the one immediately previous; and translation is a *transitive* relation. That is: if we can represent English in a high-level language (like PLANNER, say) and if we can represent PLANNER in ML, then we can represent English in ML. Conversely, if our procedural representation of an English sentence eventuates in ML (as it must do if the machine is to operate upon the representation), then we gain nothing in point of semantic interpretation by virtue of having passed through the intermediate representations; though, of course, we may have gained much in point of convenience to the programmer.

3. Well, of course, there has to be *something* in common; the two programs have to be congruent in *some* sense; else why should they go over into the same ML representation? But what is common surely isn't the intended interpretation of the sentences qua sentences of English. It isn't what they *mean*.

4. I have left Winograd's citation conventions as I found them.

5. In what sense is ML 'strictly interpreted.? It's not just that there exists (as it were Platonically) a consistent assignment of its formulae to machine states, processes, operations, etc., but that the machine is *so constructed as to respect that assignment*. So, for example, there is a consistent interpretation of ML under which the formula 'move the tape' is associated with the compliance condition *moving the tape;* and, moreover, it is a fact about the way that the machine is engineered that it does indeed move the tape when it encounters that formula. This parallelism between the causal structure of the machine and the semantics of ML under its intended interpretation is what makes it possible to 'read' the machine's changes of physical state as *computations.* Looked at the other way round, it's what chooses the *intended*

interpretations of ML from among the merely *consistent* interpretations of ML.

6. Classical verificationism claimed only that, for a sentence to be meaningful, there must *be* (Platonically) a method of verification. This is, of course, much weaker than the present claim that to understand a sentence is to know what the method of verification is.

7. Of course, not every case of determining that something is a chair by reference to its sensory properties counts as perceiving it; consider the case where somebody tells you what its sensory properties are and you infer from the description that it's a chair. A serious discussion would have to beef up the condition, perhaps by adding that the determination of the sensory properties must involve an appropriate kind of causal excitation of the transducers by *a*. I'm not, however, attempting to construct an account of perception here; just to indicate how the PS theory arises naturally from the PS treatment of language.

8. I say that no *new* arguments have been forthcoming; but there's an *old* argument (in fact, Locke's) which is very much in the air, viz., if percepts aren't reducible to sensations, how could concepts be *learned?* A more extensive treatment than this one might have fun tracing the dire consequences of anti-nativism in both classical and PS versions of the Empiricist program (and in much of current cognitive psychology, for that matter; see below, Chapter 10).

9. See the discussion of Hume's handling of the Empiricist principle in Flew (1964).

10. For a development of this theme, see Fodor and Pylyshyn (forthcoming).

11. I am distinguishing between (a) a 'theory of reference' (and, more generally, a classical semantic theory) which consists of a function from the expressions of a language onto the objects which interpret them; and (b) a theory of the mechanism which realizes the semantics, viz. the kind of psychological theory which answers the question: 'what about a given language, or about the way that a given organism uses it, makes one or another semantic interpretation the right one for that language?' (a) and (b) *both* differ from (c) theories that operate in the area that I've called psychologized logical syntax.

Theories of type (a) are familiar from work in classical semantics. Theories of type (c) are what people generally have in mind when they talk about "internal" ("canonical", "mental") representation (hence all varieties of PS, properly construed, belong to type (c) as does practically all of modern linguistics and cognitive psychology). There are, to the best of my knowledge, no *plausible* theories of type (b), though there are plenty of *im*plausible ones. For example, Skinnerian theory is best considered as an attempt to answer the question 'What about the relation between an organism, an utterance form, and an object makes the use of the second by the first constitute a reference to the third?', the proposal being that the utterance form refers to the object when and only when the object is a discriminative stimulus for which the utterance is a discriminated response.

Perhaps it goes without saying that the desirable situation is the one where the formal semantics (type a), the account of the logical syntax of the vehicles of representation (type c), and the psychology of reference (type b) all fit together.

12. I wish to thank the many members of the AI community who read the manuscript and offered good advice (like "My God, you can't publish *that!*"). I'm especially indebted to Steven Isard, Philip Johnson-Laird, and Zenon Pylyshyn for illuminating comments on an earlier draft.

9. Methodological Solipsism

1. I shall speak of "type identity" (distinctness) of mental states to pick out the sense of "same mental state" in which, for example, John and Mary are in the same mental state if both believe that water flows. Correspondingly, I shall use the notion of "token identity" (distinctness) of mental state to pick out the sense of "same mental state" in which it's necessary that if x and y are in the same mental state, then $x = y$.

2. For extensive discussion, see Fodor (1975; and Chapter 7).

3. This is *not*, notice, the same as saying "formal operations are the ones that apply mechanically"; in this latter sense, *formality* means something like *explicitness*. There's no particular reason for using "formal" to mean both "syntactic" and "explicit," though the ambiguity abounds in the literature.

4. Some fairly deep methodological issues in Artificial Intelligence are involved here. See Chapter 8 where this surface is lightly scratched.

5. I'm told by some of my friends that this paragraph could be read as suggesting that there are *two kinds* of beliefs: opaque ones and transparent ones. That is not, of course, the way that it is intended to be read. The idea is rather that there are two kinds of conditions that we can place on determinations that a pair of belief tokens count as tokens of the same belief type. According to one set of conditions (corresponding to transparent taxonomy) a belief that the Morning Star is such and such counts as the same belief as a belief that the Evening Star is such and such; whereas, according to the other set of conditions (corresponding to opaque taxonomy), it does not.

6. I'm leaving it open that it may be to say still less than this (e.g., because of problems about reference under false descriptions). For purposes of the present discussion, I don't need to run a line of the truth conditions for transparent propositional attitude ascriptions. Thank Heaven, since I do not have one.

7. It's worth emphasizing that the sense of "behavior" *is* proprietary, and that that's pretty much what you would expect. Not every true description of an act can be such that a theory of the mental causation of behavior will explain the act under that description. (In being rude to Darcy, Elizabeth is insulting the man whom she will eventually marry. A theory of the mental causation of her behavior might have access to the former description, but not, surely, to the latter.)

Many philosophers—especially since Wittgenstein—have emphasized the ways in which the description of behavior may depend upon its context, and it is a frequent charge against modern versions of Rational psychology that they typically ignore such characterizations. So they do, but so what? You can't have explanations of everything under every description, and it's a question for empirical determination which descriptions of behavior reveal its systematicity vis-à-vis its causes. The Rational psychologist is prepared to bet that—to put it *very* approximately—behavior will prove to be systematic under some of the descriptions under which it is intentional.

At a minimum, the present claim goes like this: there is a way of taxonomizing behaviors and a way of taxonomizing mental states such that, given these taxonomies, theories of the mental causation of behavior will be forthcoming. And that way of taxonomizing mental states construes them nontransparently.

8. One might try saying: what counts for opaque type individuation is what's *in* your head, not just what's running through it. So, for example, though Alfred and Misha are both thinking "he feels faint," nevertheless different counterfactuals are true of them: Misha would cash his pronoun as: "he, Sam" whereas Alfred would cash *his* pronoun as: "he, Misha." The problem would then be to decide *which* such counterfactuals are relevant since, if we count all of them, it's going to turn out that there are few, if any, cases of distinct organisms having type-identical thoughts.

I won't, in any event, pursue this proposal since it seems clear that it won't, in principle, cope with all the relevant cases. Two people would be having different thoughts when each is thinking "I'm ill" even if *everything* in their heads were the same.

9. I'm assuming, for convenience that all the Ps are such that either they or their denials are believed. This saves having to relativize to time (e.g., having (b) and (c) read ". . . you believe or come to believe . . .").

10. I blush to admit that I had missed some of these complexities until Sylvain Bromberger kindly rubbed my nose in them.

11. It may be that Putnam *does* accept this moral. For example, the upshot of the discussion around p. 153 of his article appears to be that a Greek semanticist prior to Archimedes *could* not (in practice) have given a correct account of what (the Greek equivalent of) "gold" means; viz., because the theory needed to specify the extension of the term was simply not available. Presumably *we* are in that situation vis-à-vis the objects of many of *our* thoughts and the meanings of many of our terms; and presumably, we will continue to be so into the indefinite future. But, then, what's the point of defining psychology (semantics) so that there can't be any?

IV. Nativism

10. The Present Status of the Innateness Controversy

1. A concept is an abstract entity on *anybody's* view in that concepts are types. The interesting question is whether they are types whose tokens are mental objects. Frege seems to argue—in "The Thought" (1968)—that con-

cepts are abstract, *hence not mental.* I can't imagine why he found this line persuasive.

2. Strictly speaking, what with concepts being types, one ought to say that primitive concepts arise from the transducer outputs via a process of "abstraction". I shall usually ignore this, since it complicates the exposition without much clarifying the issues. Suffice it that such *abstractive* processes are *not* to be identified with the combinatorial processes lately discussed. Combinatorial processes take simple concepts onto complex ones, whereas abstraction takes transducer outputs (what used to be called "experiences") onto concepts in the primitive basis and, more generally, *tokens onto the types* that they are tokens of.

3. According to most traditional Empiricist accounts, there are two ways in which a complex concept can be acquired *other than* from experience: by explicit (verbal) definition, and by the operation of the faculty of "imagination", which functions to produce complex concepts by freely combining primitive ones. (The concept UNICORN is often cited, but any concept that is both complex and uninstantiated would do as well.) None of this bears on our main line of inquiry, however, and I mention it largely in a spirit of comprehensiveness.

4. This way of putting it takes the relevant hypotheses to be ones that express identity conditions on a concept: the hypothesis refers to a concept and says what its analysis is (*the concept flurg* is the concept of *something which is such and such*). It's more in the spirit of some Empiricist writing (e.g. of Locke's analysis of "framing" a concept) to think of concept attainment as simply the bringing together (e.g. by association) of the constituents that belong to the analysis of the concept. So, suppose the constituents of the concept A are B, C, and D. Framing the concept A would then be a matter of forming an association between B, C, and D. The point is that the formation and confirmation of analytic hypotheses still come in, though the content of the hypotheses is relevantly different. In the present case, to frame the concept would be to confirm something like: things that satisfy B and C typically satisfy D. There are, I think, reasons why an Empiricist is well advised to set things up the way I have them in the text, but the issue is, in any event, neutral on the questions that distinguish between the Nativist and the Empiricist view. (I am indebted to Charles Marks for bringing this point to my attention.)

5. I say this is plausible, but I don't guaranty that it's true. What the claim amounts to is that, for purposes of such inductive processes as are involved in concept acquisition, the data base can be specified *solely* by atomic sentences in the primitive vocabulary. I think that it's characteristic of Empiricists to assume this tacitly, both in psychology and in confirmation theory. The issue occasionally becomes explicit, as in the discussion of "negative facts": If there *are* negative facts, then presumably some observation sentences are molecular (they have the form (*not P*)).

6. I put the point in this uncharacteristically cautious way because there have been a variety of Rationalist theorists—e.g. Plato, Descartes, Katz—who

apparently want to appeal to the internal structure of concepts as part of their account of conceptual necessity, but who nevertheless do *not* hold that complex concepts are learned by processes involving logical construction. Indeed, I think that many philosophers are convinced that concepts *must* have internal structure precisely because they are convinced that some truths are conceptually necessary. It is, however, increasingly clear that the argument that goes: "'bachelors are unmarried' is necessary, therefore UNMARRIED must be a constituent of BACHELOR" is simply a non sequitur. (See Fodor, Garrett, Walker and Parkes 1980, where this issue is discussed at length.)

7. By the way, the primary evidence that most phrasal concepts are complex is that most phrases *are* definable: "is a brown cow" =df "is brown and is a cow"; this consideration would lead us to treat phrasal concepts as typically complex even if we didn't have the productivity problem to cope with. The application of the reduction program to phrases has, in general, gone brilliantly; whereas its application to the lexicon has, in general, gone nowhere. That, too, should worry an Empiricist.

8. What this formula *doesn't* do, of course, is provide criteria for telling *whether* something is a tiger. I think that much of the argument in "The meaning of meaning" rests on an equivocation between these two senses of "determine the extension". What Putnam's arguments seem to me to show is that the internal representation of a term needn't provide criteria for its application; they are, in fact, *anti-verificationist* arguments. But what Putnam infers from his demonstration is that the internal representation of a term needn't be, as it were, coextensive with that term—e.g. that something might be a tiger (so that "tiger" is true of it) and yet be such that the concept TIGER doesn't apply to it. This latter conclusion certainly doesn't follow from merely anti-verificationist premises, nor can I think of any other arguments that would lead one to embrace it.

9. Empiricists, too, accept that the coincidence of (a–d) defines a level of the triggering hierarchy, since sensory concepts satisfy all four conditions. Viewed from this perspective, the difference between Empiricist and Rationalist accounts is that the former postulate a *degenerate* triggering hierarchy; one in which the level of basic concepts is the only level there is.

References

Adams, R. M. (1975). "Where Do Our Ideas Come from?—Descartes vs. Locke," in Stich, S. (ed.), *Innate Ideas*, Berkeley, University of California Press, pp. 71–87.

Albritton, R. (1959). "On Wittgenstein's Use of the Term 'Criterion'," *Journal of Philosophy*, 56:851–854.

Anglin, J. M. (1970). *The Growth of Word Meaning*, Cambridge, Mass., M.I.T. Press.

Armstrong, S., Gleitman, H., and Gleitman, L. (forthcoming). "On What Some Concepts Might Not Be."

Austin, J. (1966). "Three Ways of Spilling Ink," *Philosophical Review*, 75, no. 4:427–440.

Bartlett, F. C. (1932). *Remembering; A Study in Experimental and Social Psychology*, London, Cambridge University Press.

Berlin, B., and Kay, P. (1969). *Basic Color Terms*, Berkeley, University of California Press.

Block, N. (1980). "Are Absent Qualia Possible?" *Philosophical Review*, 89:257–274.

Bloomfield, L. (1933). *Language*, New York, Holt, Rinehart and Winston.

Brown, R. (1958). "How Shall A Thing Be Called?" *Psychological Review*, 65:14–21.

Brown, R. (1976). "Reference—in Memorial Tribute to Eric Lenneberg," *Cognition*, 4:125–153.

Brown, R., and Lenneberg, E. (1954). "A Study in Language and Cognition," *Journal of Abnormal and Social Psychology*, 49:454–462.

Bruner, J. S. (1957). "On Perceptual Readiness," *Psychological Review*, 64:123–152.

Carey, S. (1978). "The Child as Word Learner," in Halle, Bresnan, and Miller (eds.), *Linguistic Theory and Psychological Reality*, Cambridge Mass., M.I.T. Press.

Carnap, R. (1947). *Meaning and Necessity,* Chicago, Phoenix Books, University of Chicago Press.

Chapman, C. F., and Maloney, E. S. (1977). *Piloting Seamanship and Small Boat Handling,* 53rd edition, New York, Hearst Books.

Cherniak, C. (1977). "Beliefs and Logical Abilities", Ph.D. thesis, Berkeley, University of California.

Chihara, C. S. (1963). "Mathematical Discovery and Concept Formation," *Philosophical Review,* 72:17–34.

Chihara, C. S. (1965). "What Dreams Are Made on" *Theoria,* 31:145–158.

Chisholm, R. (1957). *Perceiving,* Ithaca, New York, Cornell University Press.

Chomsky, N. (1959). Review of Skinner's *Verbal Behavior, Language,* 35:26–58.

Chomsky, N. (1965). *Aspects of the Theory of Syntax,* Cambridge, Mass., M.I.T. Press.

Church, A. (1951). "The Need for Abstract Entities in Semantic Analysis," in *Contributions to the Analysis and Synthesis of Knowledge,* Proceedings of the American Academy of Arts and Sciences, 80:100–112.

Collins, A. W. (1979). "Could Our Beliefs Be Representations in Our Brains?" *Journal of Philosophy,* 76:225–243.

Cronbach, L. J., and Meehl, P. E. (1956). "Construct Validity in Psychological Tests," in Feigl, H., and Scriven, M. (eds.), *Minnesota Studies in the Philosophy of Science,* Minneapolis, University of Minnesota Press, 1:174–204.

Davidson, D. (1963). "Actions, Reasons and Causes," *Journal of Philosophy,* 60:685–700.

Davidson, D. (1965). "Theories of Meaning and Learnable Languages," in Bar-Hillel, Y. (ed.), *Logic, Methodology and Philosophy of Science,* Amsterdam, Proceedings of the 1964 International Congress, pp. 383–394.

Davidson, D. (1970). "Mental Events," in Foster, L., and Swanson, J. W. (eds.), *Experience and Theory,* Amherst, Mass., University of Massachusetts Press, pp. 79–101.

Dennett, D. (1969). *Content and Consciousness,* New York and London, Routledge and Kegan Paul.

Dennett, D. (1971). "Intentional Systems," *Journal of Philosophy,* 68:87–106. Reprinted in Dennett, D. (1975).

Dennett, D. C. (1978). *Brainstorms: Philosophical Essays on Mind and Psychology,* Montgomery, Vermont, Bradford Books, Publishers.

Dennett, D. C. (1978). "Skinner Skinned," in Dennett, D. C. *Brainstorms,* pp. 53–70.

Descartes, R. (1964). *Philosophical Essays,* introduction and notes by La Fleur, L. J., Indianapolis, Bobbs Merrill.

Dummett, M. (1973). *Frege,* London, Duckworth and Company.

Field, H. (1972). "Tarski's Theory of Truth," *Journal of Philosophy,* 69:347–375.

Flew, A. (1964). "Hume," in O'Connor, D. J. (ed.), *A Critical History of*

Western Philosophy, New York and Glencoe, Ill., Free Press of Glencoe, pp. 253–279.

Fodor, J. A. (1968). *Psychological Explanation,* New York, Random House.

Fodor, J. A. (1975). *The Language of Thought,* New York; Thomas Y. Crowell, Company, paperback version, Harvard University Press, 1979.

Fodor, J., Garrett, M., Walker, E., and Parkes, C. (1980). "Against definitions", *Cognition,* 8:1–105.

Fodor, J., and Pylyshyn, (forthcoming). "How Direct Is Visual Perception? An Examination of Gibson's 'Ecological Approach'," *Cognition.*

Forster, K. (1976). "Accessing the Mental Lexicon," in Wales, R. J., and Walker, E. C. T. (eds.), *New Approaches to Language Mechanisms,* Amsterdam, North Holland Press, pp. 257–287.

Frege, G. (1968). "The Thought: A Logical Inquiry," in Klemke, E. D. (ed.), *Essays on Frege,* Urbana, Ill., University of Illinois Press, pp. 507–535.

Geach, P. (1957). *Mental Acts,* London, Routledge and Kegan Paul.

Gettier, E. (1963). "Is Justified True Belief Knowledge?" *Analysis,* 23:121–123.

Goodman, N. (1965). *Fact, Fiction and Forecast,* Indianapolis, Bobbs-Merrill.

Goodman, N. (1968). *Languages of Art,* New York, Bobbs-Merrill.

Goodman, N. (1978). *Ways of World Making,* Indianapolis, Hackett Publishing Company.

Grice, H. P. (1975). "Method in Philosophical Psychology," *Proceedings and Addresses of the American Philosophical Association,* 48:23–53.

Hanson, N. R. (1961). *Patterns of Discovery,* London, Cambridge University Press.

Hartley, D. (1966). *Observations on Man,* Huguelet, T. L. (ed.), Scholar's Facsimilies and Reprints, Gainsville, Florida.

Heider, E. (1972). "Universals in Color Naming and Memory," *Journal of Experimental Psychology,* 93:10–20.

Hempel, C. G. (1949). "Logical Analysis of Psychology," in Fiegl, H., and Sellars, W. (eds.), *Readings in Philosophical Analysis,* New York, Appleton-Century Crofts.

Hull, C. L. (1943). *Principles of Behavior,* New York, Appleton-Century-Crofts.

Hume, D. (1874). *A Treatise of Human Nature,* Vol. 1, Green, T. H. and Grose, T. H. (eds.), London, Longmans, Green, and Company.

Hume, D. (1963). *Enquiries Concerning the Human Understanding and Concerning the Principles of Morals,* Selby-Bigge, L. A. (ed.), Oxford, Clarendon Press.

James, W. (1890). *Principles of Psychology,* New York, Dover Publications.

Johnson-Laird, P. (1977). "Procedural Semantics" *Cognition,* 5, no. 3:189–214.

Locke, J. (1975). *An Essay Concerning Human Understanding,* Nidditch, P. H. (ed.), Oxford, Clarendon Press.

Malcolm, N. C. (1958). *Ludwig Wittgenstein: A Memoir,* Oxford, Oxford University Press.

Malcom, N. (1959). *Dreaming,* London, Humanities Press.

Meyer, D., and Schvaneveldt, R. (1971). "Facilitation in Recognizing Pairs of Words: Evidence of a Dependence between Retrieval Operations," *Journal of Experimental Psychology,* 90, no. 2:227–234.

Mill, J. S. (1967). *Collected Works of J. S. Mill,* Robinson, J. M. (ed.), Toronto, University of Toronto Press.

Miller, G. A. (1978). "Semantic Relations among Words," in Halle, M., Bresnan, J., and Miller, G. (eds.), *Linguistic Theory and Psychological Reality,* Cambridge, Mass., M.I.T. Press.

Miller, G., and Johnson-Laird, P. (1976). *Language and Perception,* Cambridge, Mass., Harvard University Press.

Moore, G. E. (1959). *Philosophical Papers,* London, George Allen and Unwin.

Morton, J. (1969). "Interaction of Information in Word Recognition," *Psychological Review,* 76, no. 2:165–178.

Nagel, T. (1965). "Physicalism," *Philosophical Review,* 74:339–356.

Oppenheim, P., and Putnam, H. (1958). "Unity of Science as a Working Hypothesis," in Feigl, H., Scriven, M., and Maxwell, G. (eds.), *Minnesota Studies in the Philosophy of Science,* Minneapolis, University of Minnesota Press, 2:3–36.

Osherson, D., and Smith, E. (in press). "A Note on Prototype Theory," *Cognition.*

Piaget, J. (1929). *The Child's Conception of the World,* London, Routledge and Kegan Paul.

Place, U. T. (1956). "Is Consciousness a Brain Process?" *British Journal of Psychology,* 47:44–50.

Putnam, H. (1960). "Minds and machines," in Hook, S. (ed.), *Dimensions of Mind,* New York, New York University Press, pp. 138–164.

Putnam, H. (1962). "Dreaming and Depth Grammar" in Butler, R. J. (ed.), *Analytical Philosophy,* Oxford, Oxford University Press, 1:211–235.

Putnam, H. (1965). "Brains and Behavior" in Butler, R. J. (ed.), *Analytical Philosophy,* 2:211–235.

Putnam, H. (1967). "The Mental Life of Some Machines," in Casteneda, H. (ed.), *Intentionality, Mind and Perception,* Detroit, Wayne State University Press.

Putnam, H. (1967). "Psychological Predicates," in Capitan, W. H., and Merrill, D. D. (eds.), *Art, Mind and Religion,* Pittsburgh, University of Pittsburgh Press.

Putnam, H. (1970). "On Properties" in Rescher, N., et al. (eds.), *Essays in Honor of Carl G. Hempel,* Dordrecht, Holland, D. Reidel, pp. 235–254.

Putnam, H. (1975). "The Meaning of 'Meaning'," in Gunderson, K. (ed.), *Minnesota Studies in the Philosophy of Science,* Minneapolis, University of Minnesota Press, 7:131–193.

Putnam, H. (1978). *Meaning and the Moral Sciences,* London, Routledge and Kegan Paul.

Pylyshyn, Z. (1980). "Computation and Cognition: Issues in the Foundations of Cognitive Science," in *The Behavioral and Brain Sciences,* 3:111–132.

Quine, W. V. (1960). *Word and Object,* Cambridge, Mass., M.I.T. Press.

Quine, W. V. (1970). "Grades of Theoreticity" in Foster, L., and Swanson, J. W. (eds.), *Experience and Theory,* Amherst, Mass., University of Massachusetts Press, pp. 1–17.

Rosch, E., and Mervis, C. B. (1975). "Family Resemblances: Studies in the Internal Structure of Categories," *Cognitive Psychology,* 7:573–605.

Rosch, E., Mervis, C. B., Gray, W. D., Johnson, D. M., and Boyes-Braem, P. (1976). "Basic Objects in Natural Categories" *Cognitive Psychology,* 8:382–439.

Ryle, G. (1949). *The Concept of Mind,* New York, Barnes and Noble.

Savin, H. (1973). "Meaning and Concept, a Review of Jerrold J. Katz' *Semantic Theory,*" *Cognition,* 2, no. 2:213–228.

Sellars, W. (1956). "Empiricism and the Philosophy of Mind," in Feigl, H., and Scriven, M. (eds.), *Minnesota Studies in the Philosophy of Science,* Minneapolis, University of Minnesota Press, Vol. 1.

Shoemaker, S. (1963). *Self-Knowledge and Self-Identity,* Ithaca, N.Y., Cornell University Press.

Shoemaker, S. (1972). "Functionalism and Qualia" *Philosophical Review,* 81:159–181.

Smart, J. J. C. (1959). "Sensations and Brain Processes," *Philosophical Review,* 68:141–156.

Stich, S. (1980). "Paying the Price for Methodological Solipsism"—Commentary on Fodor, J. A. (1980) *The Behavioral and Brain Sciences,* 3:97–98.

Tuchman, B. (1978). *A Distant Mirror: The Calamitous 14th Century,* New York, Knopf.

Vendler, Z. (1972). *Res Cogitans,* Ithaca, N.Y., Cornell University Press.

Wanner, E. (1979). "If Some Prime Numbers Are Better than Others, What Happens to Rosch?" Paper presented to 4th annual session of Society for Philosophy and Psychology.

Warren, H. C. (1967). *A History of the Association Psychology,* Johnson Reprint Corp., originally published by Charles Scribner's Sons, New York, 1921.

Wason, P. C., and Johnson-Laird, P. N. (1972). *Psychology of Reasoning: Structure and Content,* London, B. T. Batsford.

Windham, D. (1963). "Myopia," *The New Yorker,* 39, July 13, pp. 25–29.

Winograd, T. (1971). *Procedures as a Representation for Data in a Computer Program for Understanding Natural Language,* Cambridge, Mass., M.I.T. Project MAC.

Wittgenstein, L. (1953). *Philosophical Investigations,* New York, Macmillan.

Wittgenstein, L. (1956). *Remarks on the Foundations of Mathematics,* New York, Macmillan.

Wittgenstein, L. (1958). *The Blue and the Brown Books,* New York, Harper and Brothers.

Woods, W. (1975). "What's in a Link?" in Bobrow, D. G., and Collins, A. (eds.), *Representation and Understanding,* New York, Academic Press, pp. 35–82.

Index

Adams, R., 279
Albritton, R., 42, 319
Anglin, J., 293
Aquinas, 238
Aristotle, 182, 186, 188, 221
Armstrong, S., 295
Austin, J., 177, 213, 284

Bartlett, F., 320
Berlin, B., 193
Block, N., 17, 79
Bloomfield, L., 248–250
Boyd, R., 79
Brown, R., 189, 193, 311
Bruner, J., 320

Carey, S., 312
Carnap, R., 187–195, 197, 327, 328
Chapman, C., 284
Cherniak, C., 117
Chihara, C., 35, 319, 320
Chisholm, R., 213
Chomsky, N., 119, 120, 247, 252, 258, 280, 320
Church, A., 328
Collins, A., 317

Cronbach, L., 67, 320

Darwin, C., 80, 257
Davidson, D., 79, 83, 111, 134, 180, 321, 324
Dennett, D., 20, 100–123, 156, 179, 318, 322, 324, 325, 327
Descartes, R., 2, 26, 228, 230–232, 273, 274, 280, 305, 315, 332
Dewey, J., 177, 229
Dummett, M., 328

Field, H., 250
Flew, A., 329
Fodor, J., 26, 109, 152, 167, 177, 184, 257, 277, 288, 321, 329, 330, 333
Frege, G., 181–182, 185, 188, 202, 221, 260, 328, 331
Freud, S., 247

Garrett, M., 257, 333
Geach, P., 238
Gettier, E., 324
Gibson, J., 222, 229, 254
Goodman, N., 242, 323, 327
Grice, H., 184

Hanson, N., 310
Harmon, G., 285
Harnish, M., 79
Hartley, D., 300–301
Heider, E., 193
Hempel, C., 324
Hull, C., 259, 319
Hume, D., 205, 217, 225, 229, 259, 276, 278, 282, 291, 300, 304, 306, 315, 329

Jagger, R., 243
James, W., 229–230, 276
Johnson-Laird, P., 109, 205, 209, 214–215, 282

Kant, I., 247
Katz, J., 332
Kay, P., 193
Kripke, S., 294

Lashley, K., 80, 135
Lenneberg, E., 189
Loar, B., 322
Locke, J., 26, 205, 214, 217, 247, 276, 282, 283, 303, 315, 329, 332

Malcolm, N., 47, 51, 52, 53, 319, 320
Maloney, E., 284
Marks, C., 257
Meehl, P., 67, 320
Meyer, D., 288
Mill, J. S., 300–307
Miller, G., 209, 214–215, 282, 285–288
Moore, G., 319

Nagel, T., 325, 327
Newell, A., 136

Oppenheim, P., 322, 323
Osherson, D., 297

Parkes, 257, 333
Piaget, J., 320
Pierce, C., 229
Place, U., 147, 257
Plato, 201, 332
Putnam, H., 13, 24, 79, 80, 84–86, 94, 136, 231, 244–248, 292, 294, 320, 321, 322, 323, 331, 333
Pylyshyn, Z., 14, 329

Quine, W., 111, 219, 229, 309–310, 312, 324, 325

Rosch, E., 293, 311
Russell, B., 221
Ryle, G., 3, 16, 67, 71–73, 100, 177, 228

Sapir, E., 198
Savin, H., 299
Schaneveldt, R., 288
Sellars, W., 325
Shaw, J., 136
Shoemaker, S., 17, 46, 319
Simon, H., 136
Skinner, B., 20, 21, 252, 319, 329
Smart, J., 147
Smith, E., 297
Spencer, H., 229
Stich, S., 24

Tarski, A., 328
Tuchman, B., 118

Vendler, Z., 181, 188

Walker, E., 257, 333
Wanner, E., 295
Warren, H., 300–301
Wason, P., 109
Watson, J., 319
Whorf, B., 198
Wilson, C., 54, 55, 319

Windham, D., 320

Winograd, T., 205, 209, 218–219, 231–232, 252, 328

Wittgenstein, L., 35–62, 177, 229, 319, 320, 330

Woods, W., 215–216

Zipf, G., 281

Library of Congress Cataloging in Publication Data

Fodor, Jerry A
    Representations: philosophical essays on the foundations
of cognitive science.

    Bibliography: p.
    Includes index.
    1. Cognition—Philosophy. 2. Psychology—Philos-
ophy. 3. Functionalism (Psychology) 4. Reductionism.
I. Title.
BF311.F562   153   81-24313
MIT ISBN 0-262-06079-5